THE PURSUIT OF JUSTICE

THE PURSUIT OF JUSTICE
LAW AND ECONOMICS OF LEGAL INSTITUTIONS

Edited by
Edward J. López

Foreword by
Robert D. Tollison

Published in cooperation with The Independent Institute

Cover image: © Kelly Redinger/Design Pics/Corbis.
Front cover design by Christopher Chambers.

First published in 2010 by
PALGRAVE MACMILLAN®
in the United States—a division of St. Martin's Press LLC,
175 Fifth Avenue, New York, NY 10010.

Where this book is distributed in the UK, Europe and the rest of the world,
this is by Palgrave Macmillan, a division of Macmillan Publishers Limited,
registered in England, company number 785998, of Houndmills,
Basingstoke, Hampshire RG21 6XS.

Palgrave Macmillan is the global academic imprint of the above companies
and has companies and representatives throughout the world.

Palgrave® and Macmillan® are registered trademarks in the United States,
the United Kingdom, Europe and other countries.

ISBN: 978–0–230–10245–3

Library of Congress Cataloging-in-Publication Data is available from the
Library of Congress.

A catalogue record of the book is available from the British Library.

Design by Newgen Imaging Systems (P) Ltd., Chennai, India.

First edition: June 2010

10 9 8 7 6 5 4 3 2 1

Printed in the United States of America.

Contents

ILLUSTRATIONS

TABLES

FIGURE

FOREWORD

Robert D. Tollison

Public choice and law and economics were distinct revolutions in economic thought, expanding the economic method of *homo economicus* into areas traditionally reserved for other disciplines. Both developments took place at approximately the same time (the 1950s and 1960s), and many of the same scholars participated in laying the theoretical foundations in both public choice and law and economics. A partial listing in no particular order would include Ronald Coase, James Buchanan, Gordon Tullock, Gary Becker, Richard Posner, George Stigler, Henry Manne, Armen Alchian, Harold Demsetz, and still others. Over time, as these new subdisciplines found acceptance as "normal science," the two areas of research evolved into courses and research programs that were and largely remain independent of one another. Recognizing that I am painting with a broad brush, the law and economics subdiscipline grew into a largely normative enterprise of evaluating legal rules and institutions relative to some normative standard such as economic efficiency. One branch of public choice produced what sometimes seemed like never-ending and highly complicated analyses of voting rules and other political institutions. But a second tradition of positive public choice also emerged, in which economic methods were applied to politics and political decision-making in order to understand how government worked as opposed to how it "ought" to work. In the positive economic approach, government is not decried as being "inefficient" in some sense, but rather is seen as a purposeful enterprise organized, staffed, and run by the children of Adam Smith and Bernard Mandeville.

The maintained hypothesis here is that law and economics shied away from the positive economic analysis of law and its attendant actors and institutions. This is not to say that there have been zero contributions in this vein. The point is simply that there is more than ample room for development here, which brings me to this volume.

Edward López and his co-authors have produced an original book that contributes significantly to the positive economics of law and economics. This to me is a valuable and useful undertaking, and it will hopefully stimulate additional work along these lines. Rather than, for example, looking at law and economics as a critique of legal decision making vis-à-vis an economic efficiency standard, these authors seek to model and explain/predict judicial behavior with the standard tools of economics and econometrics. Not only do these papers model and derive testable implications in a wide variety of legal settings, they offer tests of the models, often with extensive and unique data sets. Many different legal actors are analyzed—judges, lawyers, regulators, district attorneys, plaintiff attorneys, juries, and so on.

Some of the chapters (chapters 7 and 9) follow the format of critiquing legal decisions and processes from a normative perspective, and this is unobjectionable. The bulk of the chapters, however, are new and interesting studies of legal issues in the tradition of positive economics. Even if one is interested in reform, the law of unintended consequences has a corollary—you cannot fix something if you do not know how it works. The chapters in this volume are ultimately the type of research that will provide key guidance to those who seek to improve our legal system. I say "our" because the chapters are basically about legal processes in the United States with the exception of an interesting historical chapter about the evolution of the British legal system (chapter 2).

The Pursuit of Justice, as the title suggests, will also be of value to reformers because it shows how reform requires a finely tuned awareness of the incentives and constraints that shape our legal institutions. Unfortunately, as this book shows, the U.S. legal system is not immune to the problem of government failure. Moreover, when the legal system fails the result is not just inefficiency but also injustice.

As the original generation of public choice and law and economics scholars fade into the history of economic thought, a new generation steps up to carry on, defend, and extend the hard-earned intellectual gains. That is why reading *The Pursuit of Justice* is such a refreshing intellectual experience. There is still much to do and miles to go, but the work demonstrates conclusively that there is a group of young scholars who are on the case and that there are interesting and engaging issues to examine as far as the eye can see. As my old professor and colleague, James M. Buchanan, always says, you have to keep the counters interesting. *The Pursuit of Justice* passes this test by bringing positive economic methods to bear on issues in law and economics not previously addressed from this perspective.

ACKNOWLEDGMENTS

This pursuit has been a rigorous and rewarding experience throughout, and I am grateful to many individuals and institutions who gave me their support. I thank the Earhart Foundation and Liberty Fund, Inc., for generously supporting my efforts in this project in its critical early stages. The Independent Institute provided generous financial and staff support to see this book through to its completion. In particular, I want to thank David J. Theroux, Martin Buerger, Roy M. Carlisle, Gail Saari, and especially Alexander Tabarrok, who read every word and improved every chapter. Many individual and collective thanks are due to authors of each chapter for contributing the substance of the book and for their promptness and patience during various stages of the process. For valuable comments and discussion on various parts of the book, I would like to acknowledge Benjamin Powell, Noel Campbell, Edward Stringham, Joshua Hall, Wayne Leighton, and Daniel Green. I thank Jim Buchanan and Gordon Tullock for inspiration. And most of all I thank Jamie and Lorenzo for keeping me grounded in what is truly important.

Edward J. López
San Jose, California
March 2010

CHAPTER 1

AN INTRODUCTION TO
THE PURSUIT OF JUSTICE

Edward J. López

The romance is gone, perhaps never to be regained. The socialist paradise is lost. Politicians and bureaucrats are seen as ordinary persons much like the rest of us, and "politics" is viewed as a set of arrangements, a game if you will, in which many players with quite disparate objectives interact so as to generate a set of outcomes that may not be either internally consistent or efficient by any standards.

James M. Buchanan (1979 [1999], 57)

INTRODUCTION

This book presents new research in the study of legal systems as they perform in practice. All the chapters in this volume recognize that judges, lawyers, juries, police, and forensic and other experts, all respond to incentives. In short, the players of the legal game are "ordinary persons much like the rest of us." Thus if we want to understand why the legal system sometimes fails to perform up to our ideals and expectations we must analyze the incentives available to actors in the legal arena and the institutions that set the "rules of the game." Of course, if we want to reform the legal system, we must change the rules of the game so that the individual incentives of judges, lawyers, juries, and other legal actors motivate them to act in the larger social interest. The eleven chapters that follow apply this framework to wrongful convictions, frivolous lawsuits, government corruption, takings, criminal sentencing, regulation of the legal services market, and many other issues.

The Pursuit of Justice takes its scholarly inspiration from applying to the law the methods of public choice theory, which emerged in the 1960s when scholars like James M. Buchanan, Gordon Tullock, and Mancur Olson applied the tools of economic theory to areas of collective action, namely politics and government. The new economics of collective action posed a challenge to the implicit tendency of mid-century scholars to assume that government was both willing and able to correct market failures and generate efficient outcomes (i.e., Pareto improvements). To penetrate that black box, public choice scholars developed a framework to study how political institutions create incentives for political actors—voters, interest groups, politicians, and bureaucrats. This scholarship showed that government policies do not generally lead to efficiency improvements of markets, however imperfect the latter may be. Thus, the field of public choice has become well known for the argument that the possibility of government failure must be scrutinized in comparison with market failure. This comparative framework naturally lends itself to the study of legal institutions. *The Pursuit of Justice* applies individual rationality to key decision-makers in the law, just as public choice does to political actors and, in turn, just as economics does to consumers, firms, and entrepreneurs.

The modern law and economics movement also emerged in the 1960s when scholars like Ronald Coase, Richard Posner, and Gordon Tullock began to treat legal rules as having economic causes and consequences. Law and economics showed, for example, that legal sanctions act like implicit prices on people's behavior. Economic models were developed to explain decisions such as whether a plaintiff files a suit, whether a person commits a crime, and whether bargaining between private parties can resolve a dispute better than regulation or litigation. When transaction costs exceed levels that allow such bargaining, the process of governance becomes a collective action problem and public choice theory kicks in. Law without romance predicts that key decision-makers in the law will resolve collective action problems in favor of groups that have lower costs of influencing the legal process. The chapters in this volume lend much evidentiary and argumentative support to this claim.

In summary, what does public choice offer to the economics of legal institutions? First, when the unit of analysis is an agent in the legal system—lawyers, judges, juries, and so on—each is analyzed through its rational choice facets. Incentives matter to key decision-makers in the law. Second, public choice provides a framework for analyzing legal institutions as collective action problems. Third, public choice emphasizes comparative institutional analysis, which lends itself nicely to reform considerations. The public choice revolution brought new analysis to the study of public law, wealth redistribution, and political institutions that control politicians. By comparison, the modern law and economics movement brought new analysis to common law, dispute resolution, and legal institutions that control citizens. In this book, the approach is to maintain the toolkit for analysis while shifting the locus of inquiry: How can the common law be used to redistribute wealth; how effectively do legal institutions control key decision-makers in the law? How do judges respond to the political institutions surrounding their offices? What types of reforms would be potentially beneficial? These are the kinds of questions that are considered in the chapters that follow. To lend specific context to this new locus of inquiry, I next lay some necessary groundwork and then discuss recent trends in the law. I then preview the contents of *The Pursuit of Justice* in detail.

Public Choice and Law and Economics: One View of the Cathedral

> One of the most famous essays in law and economics bears the subtitle, "One View of the Cathedral." The metaphor depicts economic analysis as one view for looking at a large, ancient, complex, beautiful, mysterious, sacred object.
>
> Cooter and Uhlen (2004, 4)

By convention, public choice has been viewed as a school of thought separate from the modern law and economics movement. Partly this is due to academic tradition, which draws boundaries around disciplines by subject matter. Yet these two schools of thought share strong historical, methodological, and ideological foundations. So it can be argued that the two traditions provide a single view of the law. By the economic approach taken in this book, it becomes apparent that public choice and law and economics are not distinct ways of viewing legal institutions but in many respects one and the same.

Mueller's classic textbook *Public Choice II* in the field defines public choice as "the economic study of nonmarket decision-making, or simply the application of economics to political science" (Mueller 1989, 1). This migratory description has gradually lost meaning as public choice got intertwined with disciplines such as philosophy (Pincione and Tesón 2006), history (Hummell 1996), finance (Mulherin 2005), psychology (Caplan 2007, Cowen 2005), development (Boettke et al. 2007), linguistics (Reksulak, Shughart, and Tollison 2004), and other fields. Thus, co-founder James Buchanan recently characterized public choice as an approach to social science rather than a part of economics: "Public choice should be understood as a research program rather than a discipline or even a subdiscipline of economics" (Buchanan 2003, 1). One could apply the argument to other schools of thought that have emerged over the past half century. It is confining to say that public choice is about politics, in a similar sense as saying institutional economics is about organizational structure, or neoclassical economics is about the firm, or behavioral economics is about experiments. Each of these fields can be viewed as broad frameworks for understanding interactions of social systems, including business, law, legislation, and constitutional design. Thus, one can view each of these disciplines as an approach to social science.

As a social science, public choice emphasizes certain principles or tools of analysis. First, people evaluate nonpecuniary costs and benefits in the same way in which they respond to economic profit and loss. In other words, political calculations act as shadow prices on rational (or purposive) behavior. Acting as political pressure groups, business firms, for example, use the market and government systems as complementary means to maximize profit. Policymakers respond to rent seeking pressure, subject to their own ideologies and a host of political constraints, by redistributing wealth toward groups that most effectively organize their collective members into unified action. Under these conditions, the benefits of policy tend to fall in concentrated areas while the costs are diffused among dispersed interests. This wreaks havoc on viewing politics as noble deliberation and highlights its resemblance to everyday transfers of wealth.

Second, legal rules and policies can be evaluated in terms of their economic and political efficiency. A policy that results in a net loss of wealth in the economy is economically inefficient. In contrast, a policy is politically efficient if it achieves a given transfer of wealth at least cost to the affected parties.[1] Thus, public choice provides a framework for explaining how policies that create net losses for society still get passed. For example, import tariffs and antitrust enforcement can be viewed as alternative instruments for restricting the competition of well-organized business groups. The instrument that imposes less lobbying, enactment, and enforcement costs is politically efficient, even though restricting competition by either means is economically inefficient.

Third, public choice emphasizes institutional structure—rather than, say, policymaker ability or intent—to understand the origins of policies. For example, since the U.S. political system is geographically based on single-representative districts, each legislator has a strong incentive to advance budget items that impart benefits to their home district while imposing the costs on the general tax fund. In this system, logrolling and omnibus bills enable policies that would otherwise fail if voted on individually. The institutional structure, not the bad politician, is the root cause of economically inefficient policies such as pork barrel spending. Thus, in order to achieve fewer bad policies, public choice analysis would suggest institutional change—divorcing representation from geography, for example (Shughart and Tollison 2005).

As suggested by its traditional moniker, law and economics is a dyadic intellectual enterprise. Economic theory provides a framework for analyzing the law, and in turn, the law provides fertile ground for testing and thereby further advances economic theory. The framework provided by economic theory essentially consists of three broad concepts and their application to legal problems.[2] First, law and economics treats subjects of the law as rational agents, which are best illustrated by the following startling example.

> [Suppose you] live in a state where the most severe criminal punishment is life imprisonment. Someone proposes that since armed robbery is a very serious crime, armed robbers should get a life sentence. A constitutional lawyer asks whether that is consistent with the prohibition on cruel and unusual punishment. A legal philosopher asks whether it is just. An economist points out that if the punishments for armed robbery and for armed robbery plus murder are the same, the additional punishment for murder is zero—and asks whether you really want to make it in the interest of robbers to murder their victims. (Friedman 2000, 8)

In approaching criminals as rational agents, law and economics examines crimes by applying cost-benefit analysis to the prospective criminal. If a change of legal rule decreases the marginal cost of murder over armed robbery, we should expect to see more armed robberies escalate to murders. More generally stated, people respond to the law as they respond to other incentives. In other words, legal rules act as shadow prices on rational (or purposive) behavior. This in turn can help support the preference for one rule over another.

Second, economics provides a framework for evaluating the societal impacts of legal rules—that is, economic efficiency. In many ways, the law shapes incentives such that individual decisions promote socially beneficial outcomes. Suppose, for example, you sell your car and accept a personal check as payment, without realizing that the buyer is intentionally defrauding you with a forged check. Suppose further that the buyer immediately disappears after reselling the car, which then changes hands several times. Eventually the police locate the car in the hands of the last owner, who has just purchased the car—*your car!*—from a used dealer nearby. Can you recover the car by suing the last owner? The law says no. In the precedent for such a case, the court reasoned that "while the...rule may seem harsh, it is in line with the purposes of the [law], to promote commerce and business..."[3] The rule supports exchange by promoting within buyers a level of trust that they can acquire good title from reputable sellers. Such a rule helps resources to flow to higher-valued uses, and offers strong incentives for sellers to guard against fraudulent mediums of exchange. Economic efficiency helps understand the basis for and social value of such legal rules.

Third, law and economics also analyzes distributional issues, for example by applying the concept of incidence that is familiar from tax burden analysis. Suppose there is a proposal to shift the punishment of white-collar crime from imprisonment to monetary fines. Furthermore, the proposal recommends spending little on enforcement while imposing severe fines on the convicted offenders. Assume that the decrease in enforcement efforts is matched by a proportionate increase in fines so that the number of crimes remains constant. Enforcement is costly to taxpayers and fines are less costly to them than prison terms, and so under these circumstances, the proposal will be an efficiency improvement. However, fewer criminals will be convicted. Thus, the total punishment costs are redistributed to the fewer individuals who get convicted and away from individuals who escape because of relaxed enforcement.[4] Economic analysis helps clarify such distributional issues in the law as well.[5]

There is little fundamental difference between public choice and the modern law and economics movement in their methodological approach. It seems quite natural, therefore, to assess government versus market failure within the legal system—that is, *legal failure*—as this book aims to do.

Where public choice and law and economics may differ is in the character of reforms they recommend. Both traditions emphasize efficient design of broad institutions and legal rules. But public choice favors constraining lawmakers to minimize their inefficiency, whereas law and economics implies freeing up markets to maximize their efficiency. For example, public choice suggests fundamental changes to constitutions—that is, rules of the game for policymakers—such as a move from majority rule to supermajority rule for legislative bodies on salient issues (Buchanan 2005). Normative law and economics suggests arranging institutions to minimize transaction costs in markets (Cooter and Uhlen 2004). Due to its broader reform emphasis, applying public choice to the law should help support broad market-based reform. One trend in recent legal reform is a focus on narrow, issue-specific changes such as asbestos at the federal level and venue, joint/several liability, hedonic damages, and other narrow points at the state level.[6] In contrast, recent broad-based legal reform (the Class Action Fairness Act) seems more positioned on public choice theory than on insights from law and economics. This suggests not only a role for public choice in analyzing the law, but also a need for doing so in order to gird future broad-based, efficiency-enhancing reform efforts.

RECENT TRENDS AND REFORMS

Recent trends in the legal system clamor for the kind of scholarly attention that the approach taken here provides. In criminal law, scores of federal judges have been grappling with new federal sentencing guidelines, which, under the January 2005 Supreme Court decision in *U.S. v. Booker*, are deemed advisory rather than mandatory.[7] Meanwhile, federal, state, and local agencies continue to lock horns over medicinal marijuana under the controversial June 2005 *Gonzales v. Reich* decision, which expands commerce clause applicability. In response to *Reich*, California's attorney general issued a statement that "Today's ruling does not overturn California law permitting the use of medical marijuana," and nine other state attorneys general followed suit.[8] These kinds of rulings and similar issues suggest a new federalism in which it is debatable how such intergovernmental tensions will be resolved. In property, the *Kelo v. New London* (June 2005) decision has markedly changed the incentives facing local policymakers; on the one hand, they were initially emboldened to more readily threaten and use eminent domain, but on the other hand, they have been constrained by a wave of new state legislation. In tort, despite the Class Action Fairness Act (CAFA), large settlements and damage awards continue to rally the cries of venue shopping, frivolous claims, and abuse. Meanwhile asbestos, tobacco, health care, and pharmaceuticals remain broad areas of waste through litigation.[9]

Recent reforms of the legal system also invite further study. At the federal level, Congress passed laws limiting the liability of firearm manufacturers and makers of certain pharmaceuticals, and judicial procedures were rewritten to instill greater consistency between state and federal courts in class action lawsuits. At the state level, voters and legislators responding to the *Kelo* backlash have enacted numerous legislative restrictions on eminent domain.[10] These actions and other reforms offer the chance to assess their effects at a scholarly level and outline the trade-offs associated with future reform.

Through a cascade of ideas put into action, public choice analysis of the law has been successful at promoting efficiency-based reforms: from theoretical to empirical research, to broad dissemination, to policymaker absorption, to reform. The CAFA became law in February 2005. This law alters plaintiffs' and their attorneys' incentives by restricting certain forms of attorney compensation and closing loopholes in interstate diversity rules for determining jurisdiction. As a general rule of thumb, plaintiffs prefer state to federal court because in nearly half the states, judges are elected and thus more sensitive to opportunities to transfer wealth from out-of-state defendants to in-state plaintiffs. Prior to the enactment of CAFA, plaintiffs could easily avoid federal courts, in favor of plaintiff-friendly state courts, by finding a single nondiverse class member, or by limiting the claim amount of one member, and so on. CAFA also installed congressional oversight, requiring the Judicial Conference of the United States to report to the House and Senate Judiciary Committees.

CAFA is a public choice reform. Public choice research illuminated the poor incentive structure that prevailed in the pre-CAFA era. Theoretical work in public choice provided the necessary context for understanding civil law partly as a mechanism for transferring wealth in a manner close, if not identical, to rent seeking in politics (Farmer and Pecorino 1999, Rubin et al. 2001, Osborne 2002). In turn, rigorous empirical evidence demonstrated that real-world patterns in tort awards were consistent with theoretical rent-seeking predictions. For example, states with elected judges featured greater award amounts against out-of-state defendants (Tabarrok and Helland 1999). Other evidence showed that the tort system was being used as a mechanism for social justice, for example, the grant of higher awards to states with greater poverty and racial minorities (Helland and Tabarrok 2003). This type of argument was conveyed to a broader audience in the successful book *The Rule of Lawyers* (Olson 2003), and ultimately through policy papers to the personnel who rewrote the rules of civil procedure and codification of the CAFA reform. Public choice ideas have consequences for the legal system.

PLAN OF THE BOOK

> It seems to be nothing more than simple and obvious wisdom to compare social institutions as they might be expected actually to operate rather than to compare romantic models of how such institutions might be hoped to operate.
>
> Buchanan (1979 [1999], 47)

Observing how the law evolves is a useful method for investigating which interests can effectively influence the law in their favor. Beginning with chapter 2 by economists Nicholas Curott and Edward Stringham, for example, we see legal institutions evolving as a result of fiscal expedience to kings.

Curott and Stringham present an economic history of the gradual centralization of English law. Starting from its pre-Norman origins, the law was polycentric and customary with voluntary participation enforced largely by the threat of outlawry made credible by social norms. Incrementally, the law was centralized over time into coerced statutory law. The motivations were largely fiscal demands of kings. Curott and Stringham are thus in the tradition of Bruce Benson (1990) and other economic histories of the rule of law.[11] Chapter 2 provides a new contribution in further informing these ideas with an extensive analysis of noneconomic histories that point generally to the same interpretations. One implication of this body of work involves the viability of voluntary institutions to enforce contract and property— essentially private law—an issue that has received sustained scholarly treatment for decades (e.g., Greif 2008, Dixit 2004, Ellickson 1991, Ostrom 1990, Benson 1990). A common presumption among many theorists is that the formation of a state generates public benefits—a "commodious" life— that would not otherwise be attained. As the body of private law scholarship continues to grow, the effect may be to broaden scholarly views on the relevant trade-offs in analyzing the law of the state. The law of the Hobbesian jungle may not be the singular, necessary alternative. Rather, it is an empirical question whether and in which circumstances law is a pure public good, versus circumstances when private, voluntary enforcement can produce cooperation in basic modes of social interaction.

To be sure, efficiency is but one of several criteria on which to judge the law. In fact, many areas of the law are non-efficient by design. For example, the high burden of proof in criminal procedure is for reasons of justice intentionally biased in favor of protecting the rights of the accused. Traditional purposes for doing so are (a) to protect citizens from the potential of overzealous prosecutors; (b) to counter the imbalance of resources that usually exists between prosecutors and defendants; and, most importantly, (c) to be more hawkish about wrongful convictions (Type II errors) than wrongful acquittals (Type I error).[12] The law intentionally elevates these other values—especially the avoidance of wrongful convictions—above the value of efficiency. However, certain aspects of legal institutions can give decision-makers bad incentives— self-interested reasons to distort the social ordering of values and instead create biases that generate bad outcomes, such as *more* wrongful convictions. Chapters 3 and 4 address these points and similar issues.

In chapter 3, economists Russell Sobel, Joshua Hall, and Matt Ryan scrutinize the effects of different types of selection methods for prosecutors and judges. Across the American states, three different selection methods are used: appointment by governor and/or legislature (29 states); nonpartisan elections (13 states); and partisan elections (8 states). The authors present survey-based data on the perceived quality of each state's overall legal system and estimate the influence of selection type on quality (controlling for populace education, judges' salaries, lawyers per capita, and voter ideology). They find that states with elected judges fare systematically worse on the quality survey, and that almost all of this effect is driven by partisan election states.

We have more to say about judicial selection mechanisms in later chapters. Sobel, Hall, and Ryan also examine the electoral effects on prosecutors. They examine data on district attorneys (DAs) in the state of New York, where DAs are elected every odd fourth year. The authors also present time series data on wrongful murder convictions and conduct a string of statistical tests to see whether wrongful convictions are sensitive to election periods. Succinctly put, the authors find that wrongful murder convictions spike upward in the period just prior to elections, then spike back down in the period that directly follows. This discussion provides some of the first evidence to explore electoral cycles in wrongful convictions, and goes a long way in demonstrating the adverse consequences that can result when legal institutions become too vulnerable to politicized incentives. This chapter calls into question the exact role of electoral incentives in judicial and prosecutorial decisions, and its chain of influence on key judicial outcomes such as wrongful convictions. This contribution seems sure to spark further empirical research on the topic.

Like political institutions and electoral incentives, the industrial organization of the legal system can also be the source of the bad incentives that bias decision-makers toward undesirable outcomes. Chapter 4, by economist Roger Koppl, inspires us to innovate cost-effective changes to make such undesirable outcomes easily preventable. Professor Koppl examines wrongful convictions from the perspective of forensic science administration and its systematic links to error rates in fingerprinting standards.[13] Koppl estimates that "false positives" (Type II errors) in fingerprinting are to blame for up to 4,762 wrongful felony convictions per year.[14] Current best practices allow for duplicate fingerprinting examinations, but even so, the incidence of wrongful convictions is high. Our forensics procedures lack genuine independence among fingerprint experts, the police, and prosecutors. Koppl's empirical work presents a cost-benefit analysis that, under conservative assumptions, shows that adopting a system of independent triplicate testing would save tens of millions of dollars per year. As the chapter states, "Triplicate fingerprint examinations in felony cases in the US would cost about $9 million annually. By eliminating over 98 percent of the false felony convictions resulting from errors in fingerprint examinations, however, the redundant examinations would save more than $61 million per year in direct expenditures on incarceration." This is the most conservative of plausible estimates: it assumes the lowest error rate of 0.8 percent and does not include the recovered nonpecuniary costs and productivity losses of false imprisonment. Koppl makes a strong case for a conceptually simple institutional reform that would improve the value of the legal system to society.

Chapters 5 and 6 feature empirical treatments of the effects that political institutions have on incentives in the judiciary. Consider first the institutions that are used to achieve judicial independence. Legislative review has the advantages of placing principled constraints on democratic majorities—to essentially increase the costs to the state of violating individual rights or becoming too corrupt. Using data from the American states and up to

165 countries, chapter 5 by economist Adriana Cordis empirically investigates the relationship between measures of judicial independence and observed or perceived government corruption rates. The judicial independence measures are judge's pay, judicial selection method, and term length. The chapter also provides results that indicate significant effects of *constitutional rigidity* (measured as less frequent amendment) on corruption. Cordis generally finds that greater independence and rigidity are related to lower corruption among government officials. That suggests some support for the argument that the judiciary can and does act as a check on the other branches of government. As with other good things enjoyed in moderation, a balance must be struck between a judiciary that is independent enough to exercise principled judicial review and a powerful court that becomes susceptible to mischief and difficult to remove.

Chapter 6 by economists Aleksandar Tomic and Jahn Hakes sheds further empirical light on how the behavior of judges responds to the formal institutions chosen for the judiciary. Tomic and Hakes model U.S. county-level incarceration and sentencing decisions as a function of judicial selection mechanisms. They use a rich data set of over 70,000 cases in 54 large-population counties between 1990 and 1998. The empirical tests are motivated by a novel argument that develops one of two channels through which fiscal politics can influence judges' decisions. In elected jurisdictions, judges have *higher* incarceration rates but they issue *shorter* sentences compared to judges appointed by statewide officials. The reason, argue Tomic and Hakes, is that the principals of elected judges (local county voters) enjoy the benefits of "tough on crime" judges locally, but share overall costs of the corrections system in a statewide fiscal commons. Appointed judges, answering to statewide politicians, are more sensitive to budget pressures because they are competing with other state expenditures (highways, education, etc.). Longer sentences help spread the average cost per conviction onto future administrations. These are powerful results demonstrating the incentive effects that different institutions have on key decision-makers in the legal system.

Common law decisions also establish many of the rules of the game for the society, as in the case of a fraudulently purchased car discussed earlier. Some of the most important rules set by judges are the limits placed on governments against infringing on individual rights. Chapters 7 and 8 take up these problems within the context of the generally expanding powers of eminent domain. The most familiar form of taking is when the government acquires title to real property for public use such as common carriage rights of way (roads, rail, power lines). The doctrine for these types of takings is evident in early U.S. jurisprudence, which institutionalized the principle that the government's chief function is to protect private property.[15] Thus, the government's takings power was limited in several key respects. Most importantly, the Supreme Court of the nineteenth century prohibited takings that transferred property from one private owner to another and upheld the fundamental fairness doctrine that no individual property owner should bear too much of the burden in supplying public uses. Takings restrictions were gradually eroded beginning in the Progressive Era and accelerating in the New Deal, as the Supreme Court increasingly deferred to legislative bodies and an ever-expanding notion of public use. By the middle of the twentieth century, the stage was set to green-light takings for such "public uses" as urban renewal (*Berman v. Parker*, 1954), divestiture of oligopoly power in real estate (*Hawaii Housing v. Midkiff*, 1984), expansion of the tax base (*Kelo v. New London*, 2005), and other types of economic development takings. By the final decade of the twentieth century, one prominent legal scholar described the public use clause as being of "nearly complete insignificance" (Rubenfeld 1993, 1078).

While it may be true that the public use clause has become "of nearly complete insignificance," at least two administrative checks do remain in federal law on the takings power. First, governments are required to pay "just compensation." Second, under *Berman* and *Kelo*, governments must demonstrate adherence to pluralistic democratic deliberation when defining public use. The *Berman* and *Kelo* opinions repeatedly refer to government's responsibility to design "a carefully considered development plan," and also to the Court's long-standing position of deference to such plans. Writing for the *Kelo* majority, Justice John Paul Stevens points out:

> Given the comprehensive character of the plan, the thorough deliberation that preceded its adoption, and the limited scope of our review, it is appropriate for us, as it was in *Berman,* to resolve the challenges of the individual owners, not on a piecemeal basis, but rather in light of the entire plan. Because that plan unquestionably serves a public purpose, the takings challenged here satisfy the public use requirement of the Fifth Amendment.[16]

Beyond just compensation and democratic deliberation, federalism also checks the takings power. Every state has its own eminent domain law, and many states do effectively constrain against takings for economic development (López, Jewell, and Campbell 2009).

Against this backdrop, chapters 7 and 8 make critical assessments of the institutional arrangements supporting expanded takings powers. Economist John Brätland argues that the concept of just compensation is necessarily inconsistent with a coerced transfer of property, regardless of the amount of compensation. Only by observing exchange by mutual assent can anyone be assured—on either epistemic or ethical grounds—that the amount of compensation was just. Fair market value is not just compensation for the same reason that every house is not fronted with a for-sale sign: subjective value. One of the undesirable effects of legislative deference is that the law withholds adequate recognition of the legitimacy of subjective value. This is a degree of majoritarian tyranny that the U.S. Supreme Court has deemed appropriate. Experience shows that holdout problems are not as severe as theory makes them out to be (Benson 2005). Thus, the conventional (market failure) argument for takings turns out to be weak on epistemic, ethical, and empirical grounds.

Strong takings powers also create scope for excessive government failure. Using different methods, chapter 8 by law professor Ilya Somin raises several pragmatic issues associated with allowing *Kelo*-style takings for economic development purposes. Urban renewal programs, exemplified by Michigan's historic *Poletown* decision,[17] generally fail to generate the promised economic benefits. Yet under the favored rational basis test, the economic development rationale can justify almost any taking that has potential to promote economic benefits. Governments and courts routinely ignore the economic and subjective costs of condemnation and the whole process invites rent seeking and corruption of otherwise sound government officials. By contrast, there is a rich history in the United States of developers using market incentives and strategies to assemble tracts necessary for genuine economic development. One must wonder at the current expanse of eminent domain powers when even Niccoló Machiavelli cautions against it:

> The Prince should nonetheless make himself feared in such a mode that if he does not acquire love, he escapes hatred, because being feared and not being hated can go together very well. This he will always do if he abstains from the property of his citizens and his subjects, and from their women; and if he also needs to proceed against someone's life [blood], he must do it when there is suitable justification and manifest cause for it. But above all, he must abstain from the property of others, because men forget the death of a father more quickly than the loss of a patrimony. Furthermore, causes for taking away property are never lacking, and he who begins to live by rapine always finds cause to seize others' property; and, on the contrary, causes for taking life are rarer and disappear more quickly. (Mansfield 1998, 67)

The chapter by Somin points to the many problems introduced, and the general harm imposed, by strong takings powers for economic development purposes. Yet the chapter also catalogs recent trends in the state courts suggesting a healthier skepticism toward such exercises of eminent domain. If more state courts were to follow the very recent leads of Michigan[18] and Ohio,[19] both of which have in the past few years overturned decisions allowing development takings, this would be beneficial to individual rights and long-term growth.

The book's last four chapters offer a series of perspectives on the political economy of lawyers and judges. The chapters deal with the issue raised earlier about the legal system being biased toward the enrichment of those groups who have comparative advantage in influencing the legal system. The opening sentence of chapter 9 by Benjamin Barton, a law professor who has written widely on the topic, puts it bluntly: "if there is a clear advantage or disadvantage to the legal profession in any given question of law, judges will choose the route that benefits the profession as a whole." Barton proceeds to demonstrate an array of broad areas of the law in which the lawyer-judge hypothesis appears to hold. These areas include the law profession's generally broad powers to self-regulate, to the relatively high degree of confidentiality ascribed to client privilege, to Supreme Court decisions that tilt the scales in favor of extant lawyers. This is not intended to indict either judges or lawyers. By all means, the rule of law depends on them (Baumol 2002). Rather, lawyer-judge draws attention to the incentives on offer for decision-makers in the legal system, and what potential biases may result. As Barton writes, for example, a case on advertising restrictions "evinces a patent sympathy for the plight of lawyer public image and a clear deference to the findings and desires of bar associations on these issues. It is hard to imagine that accountants or pharmacists would possibly have received the same treatment..." (Barton, 181). The incentives motivating this action at least partially involve judicial selection mechanisms. Judges selected by the merit plan, for example, have more to gain by ruling in favor of lawyer interests (Hanssen 2002). But consistent reluctance to "work with" lawyers may cause problems for these same judges at time for reappointment. Furthermore, most judges were lawyers earlier in their careers, so there is a natural tendency toward identifying with lawyer's concerns.

Circumstances under which lawyer-judge can impose significant social costs are when there is much to gain from using the law to redistribute wealth. In chapter 10, economist Jeffrey Haymond argues that certain types of class action tort cases create tempting opportunities to extract wealth. Haymond draws attention to the increasing number of states that use settlements with corporate defendants as a subsidy to general tax revenues. The biggest examples of this were the thwarted attempts at Microsoft and the "big tobacco" settlements of the late 1990s, which many states have parlayed into huge increases in cigarette taxes. As vilified as tobacco has become, such revenue-generating policies not only have larger deadweight loss than revenue-neutral alternatives, but they create adverse incentives for fiscal policymakers and undermine the separation of powers within states. They also unfairly place the burden of general revenue on a small minority (e.g., smokers). Haymond illustrates this by joining the concept of "tax farming," an ancient practice of using indirect ways to raise tax revenue,[20] with the public choice theory of rent extraction (McChesney 1987; 1997). In rent extraction, politicians make threats of harming a private interest, such as a firm, through regulation. The firm can pay or defy the politician's threat. If the firm pays, its cost is certain. However, if the firm calls the threat, its costs are probabilistic (depending on amount, duration, and probability of both). The same principle applies to class actions. Filing the legal complaint is the threat, and the settlement attempt is the payment. Rent extraction in the McChesney sense has also been applied to explain executive compensation (Bebchuk et al. 2002), but the idea has not been adequately explored in a general analysis of the legal system, or a more particular analysis such as class action claims. Haymond's chapter discusses several existing contributions and provides a sketch of an important future research agenda on this area. As Paul Rubin has commented, "if public choice scholars can help understand the sources of existing tort law and of the impetus for reform, they may be able to make important contributions to the policy debate" (Rubin 2005, 224). The chapter recommends itself particularly in this regard.

Other circumstances cause lawyer-judge problems if judges are not given clear rules to insulate them from succumbing to too much wealth redistribution. In chapter 11, law professor Charles Keckler describes how judges and plaintiff attorneys can together devise innovations to legal doctrines for their own enrichment. In certain class action awards, identifying and compensating individual class members is infeasible or prohibitively costly. In such cases, the distribution of damage awards may be determined from the bench according to the doctrine of *cy pres* ("as near as possible"). Judges ideally attempt to identify surrogate groups that represent the interests of the harmed class, but in practice, these types of awards tend go to concentrated interests within the legal profession. This chapter examines the notorious *Price v. Phillip Morris* (Madison County, Illinois), in which a $10 billion judgment was awarded to light cigarette buyers for fraudulent advertising. Identifying individual claimants and sorting their claim amounts, which requires evidence like cigarette purchase receipts, would be impossible. So after the state's share of 30 percent and the plaintiff attorneys' share of 25 percent of what remained, the court established a fund of over $5.3 billion and preannounced how it would be distributed, *cy pres*. Of this, 91 percent would be distributed to the legal profession, including the Illinois Bar Foundation, eleven law schools, legal aid, and the Illinois judiciary. The left over 9 percent would be distributed to the American Cancer Society and domestic violence programs.

The alignment of incentives between judge and plaintiff counsel (both want to avoid reversal on appeal) creates scope for judicial logrolling. Indeed, in *Price*, the judge sought advice from plaintiff counsel in determining the distribution. Moreover, preannouncing the future distribution creates a set of well-organized interests who (1) are in support of maintaining the judgment; and (2) have close ties to the decision process at appeal. This is a sort of instantaneous transitional gains trap (Tullock 1975). Indeed, the preannounced groups in the *Price* award all filed amicus briefs with the appeal court, a form of rent seeking to minimize the chance of reversal. The Keckler chapter models this innovation in legal doctrine and recommends reforms especially on the preannouncement strategies.

Finally, chapter 12 by policy analyst Adam Summers investigates some of the many ways that lawyers rationally employ the law for their own benefits. Summers recounts the intriguing history of legal services regulation. From the American founding through the Civil War, legal services were nearly completely free labor markets. In the late nineteenth century, states began gradually to enact legislation establishing minimum education requirements, mandatory admission to bar associations, unauthorized practice of law statutes, and so on. Today, all 50 states require licensure. Reciprocity is rare. Practitioners of the law must comply with a web of regulations, from attending a law school accredited by the American Bar Association (ABA), to limitations on advertising, to continuing legal education and even a "moral character" standard in some areas. These regulations have the familiar feel of somehow, at least by intention, of being in the public interest.

After all the law is complex, and uninformed consumers might innocently fall victim to shoddy or opportunistic practitioners. Licensure and other quality standards may help alleviate some of these asymmetric information problems. But those regulations also restrict the supply of lawyers, increasing their compensation and creating new scope for opportunism. Meanwhile, there is little basis in theory or practice to expect those regulations to assure quality services. There is at least a small amount of evidence that they impose significant costs on consumers. Summers works systematically through the economic arguments that suggest why quality might be inversely related to more stringent licensing requirements. The presumed public benefits of licensure regulations also promote a lack of attention to the effect of market competition in legal services at producing better quality and more consumer value. Thus, like chapter 2 by Curott and Stringham, the Summers chapter invites us to consider alternatives to constructivist rules that are intended to serve, but actually harm, the public interest while enriching organized groups that happen to achieve lower costs by influencing the law. In contrast, a system of voluntary certification would tap into market forces and give lawyers strong reputational incentives while providing consumers better information and choices of alternatives.

Conclusion

The Pursuit of Justice is a realistic yet hopeful study of legal institutions, which as a whole provides a rigorous analysis of an array of topics and argues for reform of currently socially wasteful aspects of the law. The chapters that follow are original contributions, not reprints. I have tried to organize the book so that it is of interest to a range of audiences, including economists, political scientists, legal scholars, and practitioners such as policy analysts, policymakers, and government officials. These professionals and other readers will find in the book a thoroughgoing analysis of a range of important legal rules, their associated incentive effects, and the resultant outcomes. Judges, lawyers, forensic experts, and government officials constrained by legal rules, all respond to the incentives that the legal system provides. Wherever we observe undesirable outcomes, we should aim to analyze the incentive structure and to consider alternative institutional arrangements that may offer better incentives to key decision-makers in the law.

Notes

1. As I am using these terms, economic efficiency most closely resembles allocative efficiency as determined by the Pareto and Kaldor-Hicks criteria. In practice, these standards tend to be reduced to measures of Marshallian surplus (Friedman 2000, Posner 1998). In contrast, political efficiency as used here resembles the standard of productive efficiency, or cost-benefit analysis, as applied to the government institution that effectuates the given wealth transfer.

2. Certainly other tools of the economics trade are routinely applied to the law, such as game theory, econometrics, and risk analysis. But the core elements of the economic analysis of law are as discussed in the text—rationality, efficiency, and incidence.

3. *Paschal v. Hamilton,* 363 So. 2d 1360; 1978 Miss. Cole and Grossman (2005, 93) provide further discussion.

4. The distributional analysis can be pushed further. Fines could be more or less costly than prison terms to the convicted, depending on the value of their time and wealth effects (even very high fines might not affect wealthy criminals as much as their less wealthier counterparts), so wealthier individuals may commit a greater share of crimes.

5. In his textbook, *Law's Order,* David Friedman also argues that the economic analysis of the law is a threefold intellectual enterprise: (1) predicting the effects of particular legal rules; (2) explaining rationally the origins of particular legal rules; and (3) arguing for certain legal rules over others based on their societal costs and benefits.

6. Joanne McMahon, "Year in Review: Legal Reform Momentum Continues," GE Insurance Solutions, undated.

7. A major problem is redundant resentencing, in which an appeals court vacates lower court sentences for misapplying federal guidelines, only to eventually reach the same sentence under *Booker.*

8. Available online at www.mpp.org., Accessed September 4, 2007.

9. The Class Action Fairness Act was enacted February 2005. The Council of Economic Advisors in 2002 estimated the annual "tort tax" (higher prices imposed by business sector to cover costs of litigation) at nearly $200 billion. Of the $40.7 billion that states have so far received in the $246 billion tobacco settlement, 95 percent has gone to fund public works projects or property and sales tax relief. (Howard Markel, "Burning Money," *New York Times,* 08–22-05, p. A13).

10. The so-called *Kelo* backlash has been the subject of a great number of studies since the Supreme Court decision in June 2005. The chapter in this volume by Ilya Somin is an excellent entry point into this literature. For an empirical analysis of the determinants of state legislation, see López, Jewell, and Campbell (2008).

11. See North and Weingast (1989), Pipes (1999), and Baumol (2002).

12. The traditional purposes are discussed further in Cooter and Uhlen (2004) (chapter 11).

13. This chapter is part of Koppl's overall project of scrutinizing and reforming the institutional and organizational structure of forensic science (e.g., Koppl 2005).

14. The exact number is not directly observable and depends on the rate of error in fingerprinting identification. As Koppl shows in chapter 4, that rate is somewhere between 0.8 and 2.0 percent.

15. "The country that became the United States was unique in world history in that it was founded by individuals in quest of private property.... [T]he conviction that the protection of property was the main function of government, and its corollary that a government that did not fulfill this obligation forfeited its mandate, acquired the status of a self-evident truth in the minds of the American colonists." Pipes (1999, p. 240).

16. Stevens, J., *Kelo v. City of New London, Conn.,* 545 U.S. 469 (2005), at 13.

17. *Poletown Neighborhood Council v. Detroit,* 410 Mich. 616, 304 N.W. 2d 455 (1981).

18. *County of Wayne v. Hathcock,* Mich. 684 N.W. 2d 765 (2004).
19. *City of Norwood v. Horney,* 161 Ohio App3d 316, 2005-Ohio-2448.
20. As Richard E. Wagner explains, "the central idea of tax farming...was...a ruler wanted to extract revenue from his subjects, and hired someone to do the extraction...It would seem as though a form of tax farming has erupted recently in the United States. It takes the form of lawyers filing class action suits, where the results of those suits replace what otherwise would have required legislation to accomplish." (Wagner 2004, p.378).

CHAPTER 2

THE RISE OF GOVERNMENT LAW ENFORCEMENT IN ENGLAND

Nicholas A. Curott and Edward P. Stringham

INTRODUCTION

Public choice economics is often referred to as the study of "politics without the romance" (Buchanan 1999). Instead of simply assuming that government agents are benevolent pursuers of the public good, public choice models them as real-life individuals who have desires and concerns of their own. From this perspective, it becomes natural to consider the possibility that any given government policy may have been created to satisfy private special interests rather than the interest of the general public (Buchanan and Tullock 1962). With its insistence on rigorous analytical tools and realistic methodology, the ascendance of public choice has simultaneously modernized research on the political process as well as engendered a healthy dose of skepticism regarding the desirability of previously accepted government functions. Curiously, the romantic, public interest notion of government retains a lingering influence in the scholarship on law. The romantic view of the law can even be found in the writings of the founders of public choice.[1]

The general premise of the public interest approach is that government courts and police exist because it is impossible to adequately provide these services in any other way, and therefore the government is merely acting beneficently to fulfill demands of the polity that would otherwise not be met. Theorists argue that only government can create the rules that reduce conflict, facilitate exchange, and bring order to society. Without government law enforcement, conflicting claims to scarce resources would lead to violence, and society would degenerate into the Hobbesian "nasty, brutish and short" outcome. According to this view, government law is necessary so that individuals can coordinate their actions to undertake the complicated arrangements that enable a modern division of labor in society and the wealth it engenders.

This sort of reasoning is evident in the writings of early public choice economists, particularly James Buchanan, Winston Bush, Gordon Tullock, and others at the Center for the Study of Public Choice in the early 1970s who sought to develop a theory of the origins of government (Tullock 1972, 1974, Buchanan 1975). In the absence of government-created rules, society is a prisoners' dilemma with a Nash equilibrium in which individuals do not respect property rights. The resulting distribution of property is suboptimal because each person must devote time and effort toward plunder or defense against predation. In Buchanan's (1975, 67) view, all individuals would agree to form government to secure property rights and prevent predation.

> They agree to appoint a referee or an umpire, inform him about the specific rules under which they choose to play, and ask that he enforce adherence to these designated rules. This is precisely the functional role assigned to the state and its law enforcement task. The state becomes the institutionalized embodiment of the referee or umpire, and its only role is that of insuring that contractual terms are honored.

The foregoing story is not too dissimilar from the one told in most high school civics textbooks. Since the 1970s, however, many public choice scholars have questioned this public interest story altogether (Benson 1990, 1994, de Jasay 1989, Ekelund and Dorton 2003). The first economist to develop a self-identified "public choice approach" to analyze the rise of the government provision of law enforcement was Bruce Benson (1990, 85). If self-interest explains how individuals behave within the legal system, it should equally explain how they interact with one other to establish the legal system itself. Benson (1990, 1994) and more recently Ekelund and Dorton (2003) examine the history of law enforcement in England through a rational choice perspective and find a completely different story from that in high school civics textbooks. Centralized police and courts were created to bring revenue to the state.

Nearly one thousand years ago, before the existence of centralized government police and courts in England, disputes were settled in a decentralized and in many ways voluntary manner.[2] When disputes occurred, private groups would ask the wrongdoer to pay restitution to the victim, and if the wrongdoer refused, he would be viewed as an outlaw. Decisions that were successful at resolving conflict became embedded in the customary practices of the community. In this way, rules of law emerged outside of the government to foster social order and provide strong incentives for individuals to interact peacefully with one another (Hasnas 2008).[3]

Over time, however, kings saw the court system as a potential source of revenue. Rather than having the full restitution go to the victim, they declared that fines must be paid to them for more and more offenses because they violated the King's Peace. After the Norman Conquest of England in AD 1066, restitution was completely replaced by a system of fines and punishments. Under this new arrangement, individuals no longer had sufficient incentive to voluntarily participate in the maintenance of law and order. The effectiveness of the old institutions gradually broke down, and the central government created new institutions to fill the void. In this version of the story of government-provided law, public policing emerged due to the alteration of property rights that occurred when government precluded restitution.

According to the accounts of Benson, Ekelund, and Dorton, the idea that government police and courts were created to address a market failure is simply a post hoc justification of what government currently does. The recognition that government did not always provide law opens the door for further scientific examinations of alternative possible institutional arrangements for providing law enforcement, including the relative desirability of private versus public methods of provision. Rules governing conduct can come into being in two different ways. One is by investing a single agency with a monopoly power to create and enforce rules that everyone in society must obey, but a second, often overlooked method is to allow individuals to follow rules that emerge over time through human interaction. The latter collections of rules are frequently enforced by an array of people. If law is defined according to noted legal philosopher Lon L. Fuller's (1964, 106) classification as "the enterprise of subjecting human conduct to the governance of rules," then the provenance of law does not lie solely in government.[4]

Law developing outside a coercive monopoly of power, whether it is customary or private, is commonly called "polycentric."[5] Examples of polycentric legal order are abundant. Historically, a large number of societies were essentially stateless, yet managed to enforce commercial contracts and develop rules for protecting individuals and their property. To take but a few examples, consider the Massims of the East Papuo-Melansian region (Leeson 2006), the Ifugao of the Philippines, various Native American tribes such as Yuroks of Northern California (Benson 1991), or precolonial African tribes such as the Tiv or Nuer (Leeson and Stringham 2005), all of which were stateless social orders or nearly so. Furthermore, large areas of the modern world operate in the absence of governments strong enough to provide effective third party enforcement of contracts or even basic protection of private property.[6]

This fertile field of study has given rise to a large and growing body of scholarly research documenting how institutional mechanisms have evolved in many situations, both modern and historical, to create incentives for individuals to cooperate in the provision of law enforcement in the absence of a government monopoly.[7] The customary law of ancient and primitive societies, which arose before state law, furnishes an ample source of case studies on how polycentric law functions in practice. These societies exhibit surprisingly complex legal systems that recognize freedom of contract, individual autonomy, and private property rights, as well as sophisticated ways of enforcing legal rules. The institutions enabling social order within this context have a wide variety. They have been based on kinship or religion, as with the Kapauku Papuans of West New Guinea (Popisil 1974); on surety, as developed by the *brehons* in Celtic Ireland (Peden 1977); and on contractual agreement, such as between the *godi* and *thingmen* in medieval Iceland (Friedman 1979, Solvason 1992, 1993).[8]

The widespread efficacy of polycentric law is also evident in an examination of the history of commerce. Greif (1989) examines how the Maghribi traders of the eleventh century Mediterranean were able to enforce contracts in extragovernmental institutions even using asymmetric information. Landa (1981) more generally describes how intermediaries can provide an institutional alternative to contract law when formal government enforcement is weak or nonexistent. Of particular note is the *Lex Mercatoria,* or Law Merchant, a sophisticated and extensive system of polycentric commercial law that emerged to meet the needs of international commerce in medieval Europe. The very system of legal rules that governed trade between merchants and provided the impetus for the Commercial Revolution was established, arbitrated, and enforced privately (Benson 1989, Milgrom et al. 1990). Even today no state-made supranational authority enforces commercial contracts between traders of different nations (Plantey 1993). Polycentric legal order is a ubiquitous feature of human interaction. Legal institutions operate so uniformly in the absence of government provision that scholars such as de Jasay (1989), Friedman (1989), and Holcombe (1997) have questioned the public goods justification of government law altogether.

The widely held belief that only government can provide law and order is perhaps due to a facet of human psychology, often conspicuous in former communist countries, in which after the government provides something for a long time it becomes difficult for the populace to imagine any alternative. As an attempt to remove the status quo bias, this chapter reexamines the story of the evolution of government law enforcement in England, as previously examined by Benson, Ekelund, Dorton, and others. Relying on books written by historians and legal scholars who have studied this area, but not necessarily from an economic point of view, we provide additional details about how the polycentric system functioned and what happened after the state monopolized it. Monopolization of law did not occur because government wanted to address a market failure. It occurred because it was a way to enhance revenue for the state. The idea that government law enforcement was chosen by individuals in need of a referee is a myth.

The chapter proceeds as follows. The next section discusses the polycentric system of law enforcement in pre-Norman England, followed by a section that provides details about the rise of government law as kings wished to find ways to enhance revenue and consolidate their power. Conclusions are given in the final section.

BEFORE MONOPOLIZATION: THE POLYCENTRIC HISTORY OF ANGLO-SAXON LAW

Imagine a time when the population of England was less than one-fiftieth of what it is now and less than 10 percent of residents lived in towns. A thousand years ago, England was quite rural and undeveloped compared to modern society, with most people being what moderns would describe as peasants. Nevertheless, compared to other countries at the time, England was relatively rich, and "the staple trade of London was already in such commonplace goods as timber, fish, wine, dairy produce, eggs and hens, wool and cloth" (Sawyer 1965, 161–163). People used oxen with a wheeled and iron-bladed plough to farm the earth (Lacey and Danziger 1999). As they said at the time, "The ploughman gives us bread and drink" (quoted in Alexander 2002, 241). Englishmen had a relatively good diet and were also about as tall as most people are today (Lacey and Danziger 1999). More important, for the purposes of this chapter, the English people began developing many important legal concepts that influence our law today (Zywicki 2004).

The origins of Anglo-Saxon law can be traced back to earlier Germanic customary law. The Anglo-Saxons descended from a group of Germanic tribes that invaded England in the middle of the fifth century AD. These invaders brought with them an elaborate and developed legal system. Legal rights and obligations were based on customary practices and enforced by kinship groups (Lyon 1980, 59). Germanic tribes were divided into *pagi*, each of which consisted of a hundred men or households. Each *pagus* was further divided into kinship groups called *vici*, which were responsible for policing. The men who made up the *vici* were bound by custom and the ties of kinship to protect each other and to pursue and capture criminals after an offense was committed. Such reciprocities formed the basis of a voluntary system for ensuring the rights and protecting the property of individuals in the community. When the *vici* successfully captured and convicted an offender, custom governed that he makes restitution according to a well-defined system of payments. To ensure compliance, offenders who did not pay restitution were outlawed. This was a large private cost, as outlaws could not seek restitution or protection from the legal system, and they might be killed with impunity. This Germanic system formed the foundation for Anglo-Saxon law (Lyon 1980, 11–18). The conversion of the Anglo-Saxons to Christianity resulted in many modifications, particularly in family law, but the basic underlying Germanic legal structure remained largely unchanged until the Norman Conquest in 1066 AD (Whitelock 1952, 134).

The Anglo-Saxons, like their Germanic ancestors, did not have a standing body of professional law enforcers similar to modern police. It was the victim's duty to seek justice after a crime was committed against him. However, a number of institutions, including the *borh* system and the *hundred*, evolved to effectively provide law and order and to ensure the protection of individuals and their property.[9] These institutions came into existence privately and relied primarily on mechanisms outside of the government.

Anglo-Saxon law rested on a foundation of a surety system known as *borh* (Morris 1910, Cam 1930, Plucknett 1956, 628–632). The *borh* system was essentially law employed among neighbors (Morris 1910, Liggio 1977, 273– 274). Neighbors formed into groups of 10 or 12 through a process of decentralized and more or less spontaneous association. Each individual was responsible for the overall good behavior of the group and agreed to pay the fines of any member who was convicted of violating the law. Every free man thus stood in pledge or surety (*borh*) to his fellow men (Stenton 1950, 251). Members of the pledge associations thus had a powerful financial incentive to monitor and police the behavior of everyone in the group and to exclude individuals with a poor reputation. In this way, each man enjoyed some measure of protection for his own life, person and property, and he also had a reciprocal duty to protect the life, person, and property of others.

Furthermore, surety associations formed a strong basis for ensuring social order, as individuals of bad character could be excluded from participating in trade and exchange. As Liggio (1977, 273) explains, "Every person either had sureties and pledge associates or one would not be able to function beyond one's own land, as no one would deal with one who had no bond or who could not get anyone to pledge their surety with him." Since the choice to pledge on behalf of another was voluntary, individuals had a strong incentive to maintain good reputations and abide by the law. Furthermore, since it was impossible to capture the benefits of social interaction without belonging to a surety, it was in the individual's own self-interest to join the association. As Benson (1990, 23) puts it, "... anyone who wanted to participate in and benefit from the social order was bonded." Mechanisms of reputation and exclusion were therefore sufficient to ensure a measure of security, order, and respect for the law through purely voluntary means.

In addition to the *borh* system, by the tenth century a legal institution called the *hundred* had come into existence; this became the primary means for dealing with theft and personal injury. The hundreds were largely concerned with violent offenses and theft, particularly the theft of cattle, and with dispensing justice (Pollock and Maitland 1899, vol. 1, 556–560). In effect, these largely voluntary associations of free men provided the police system for all of Anglo-Saxon England (Stephen 1883, 66).

The origins of the hundred are somewhat obscure, but there is little doubt that the institution has roots dating back even before the tenth century (Blair 2003, 236). The earliest description of the hundred appears in an anonymous royal decree compiled between AD 945 and 961, which enjoined that a meeting be held every four weeks and that "every man do justice to another" (232). The royal nature of the decree may give the impression that the hundred was a governmental body brought into existence by the central law-making authority to function as an organ of the state. However, this interpretation would mistake the essence of the hundred. As Loyn (1984, 146) explains: "It had full official support and sanction, but has to be read in a context of voluntary self-help, of rural peace guilds brought into being to protect property and life." It is only reasonable to infer that a formal meeting had been established in custom long before it was enshrined by the mid-tenth-century ordinance (Blair 2003, 235–236). Thus, the hundred came into being as a local organization for taking action against theft and dispensing justice, largely with nongovernment enforcement, as detailed below.

To carry out policing duties, the hundreds were composed of 10 *tithings* of 10 men each. One of the 10 men in each tithing, called a *tithingman,* would be effectively in charge. Similarly, a *hundredman* stood in charge of the hundred. The 10 tithingmen, the hundredman, and a clerk met every four weeks, mostly for administrative purposes. However, they also formed what might be considered the principal law enforcement body. The hundred-man, for example, was responsible for preventing cattle theft. He was to be informed when a theft occurred, and he would charge one or two men from each tithing to pursue the thieves and bring them to justice. To ensure that individuals performed their duties for the hundred, a system of increasing fines punished shirking (Blair 2003, 232–233).

In addition to providing law enforcement, the hundred also held a court, called a *moot,* for settling local judicial matters (Whitelock 1952, 139; Pollock and Maitland 1899, vol. 1, 42). The judicial function at that time was divided between the hundred court and a higher shire court. The shire court was one of the principal tools used by kings to raise money and exert the neces- sary influence to defend against foreign conquest. At first an ealdorman, and then later a shire reeve or "sheriff"—the king's main representative in the shire at different points—presided over the shire court. As Warren (1988, 43) emphasizes, however, although the hundred and shire courts "met at the behest of royal authority and were answerable to the king for defaults of jus- tice, they cannot in any meaningful sense be described as 'royal' courts. They did not administer a body of royal law under the direction of judges appointed by the crown: they operated by customary procedures in applying customary law."

The shire court met only twice per year and was primarily concerned with administrative tasks. In addition, the shire court would hear a few lawsuits, including some that the hundred court passed up, presumably when it was unable to reach a verdict or when the dispute ranged across the jurisdictions of two different hundreds. The hundred court, however, was the primary court for settling day-to-day disputes, "the judicial unit, so to speak, for ordinary affairs" (Pollock and Maitland 1899, vol. 1, 42).

Interestingly, the customary legal system enforced by the hundred court shared many of the characteristic features of archaic law as well as advanced customary legal systems, such as the ones developed in medieval Iceland and Ireland.[10] Law is recognized in customary legal systems because individuals have a private incentive to bind their actions in accordance with predeter- mined rules. Each individual realizes that there are benefits to be had from restricting his behavior so that it conforms with others' expectations, as long as they behave as he expects, as well. Thus, as Benson (1990, 12) has put it, "reciprocities are the basic source both of the recognition of duty to obey law and of law enforcement in a customary law system."

Since Anglo-Saxon law was largely based on a voluntary recognition of mutual benefit, instead of being coercively imposed from above, the hundred was primarily concerned, in essence, if not in all of its aspects, with the protection of individual rights and private property (Benson 1990, 20). Infractions of the rules, which included provisions for many offenses that we now define as crimes, were treated as torts. Although some public offenses did exist in Anglo-Saxon society at this time, the law was primarily concerned with righting private wrongs. The laws treated homicide, rape, theft, and all manner of wounding in great detail, and since participation and enforcement relied upon voluntary cooperation, punishment of offenses was geared toward providing restitution to the victim.

The court itself served primarily as a place for obtaining good witnesses. The court was presided over by tithing representatives called thegns. Four men from each tithing acted as *suitors* of the court. A representative body of twelve suitors formed a judicial committee, which arbitrated disputes between members in its jurisdiction (Stephen 1883, 68). This service was a duty incumbent upon the office holders, for which the king gave patronage in return. However, neither the king nor his thegns forced individuals to use the hundred court (Pollock and Maitland 1899, vol. 1, 43). Executive power was too weak at this time to compel individuals to do so, even if it had wanted to. Instead, the hundred had to rely mainly on positive incentives to incite cooperation (Benson 1994, 253). Compensation for the victim, in particular, provided a strong incentive to use the legal system, although the hundred system also provided several other private benefits, such as the return of lost or stolen cattle.

The procedure for lawsuits was stringent, and the slightest misstep at any stage could result in the loss of the case (Pollock and Maitland 1899, vol. 1, 38; Whitelock 1952, 139–142). Trials of evidence in the modern sense were virtually unknown. Instead, guilt or innocence was determined by a system of oath giving. Lawsuits began when a party who thought he had been wronged came to the hundred court and made a charge against someone in the form of an oath. If the court decided the case was valid and worthy of hearing, they would set a date of appointment and summon the defendant to appear.

On the day of the hearing, the plaintiff began with what was called a fore oath, and then he would make his accusation in front of witnesses and the accused party. Usually, the defendant would then be allowed to establish his innocence by swearing an oath. To clear himself, the defendant required corroboration, which varied according to the nature and severity of the accusation, from a prescribed number of compurgators or "oath-helpers."

Neither the defendant nor his compurgators were required to present any evidence to the court. For obvious reasons, therefore, accusations carried less weight than denials, which was established in custom as a basic principle of the law (Whitelock 1952, 140). A defendant who was able to muster the requisite number of oath-helpers was declared innocent and absolved of any wrongdoing. In a few cases, however, the defendant was not deemed worthy of making a valid oath. This would happen if, for example, he had been the subject of previous infractions or frequent accusations, or if he was caught in the act. In such cases, it was sufficient for the plaintiff to produce witnesses who would swear an oath that they were present at the scene of the crime and had observed the act with their own eyes.

The system of oath giving may appear unsophisticated and open to exploitation, but it could actually serve as a reasonable method for tapping localized knowledge. The hundred was responsible for relatively few individuals, and members of its jurisdiction had continual interaction with one another and were bonded together by mutual pledges and duties. Reputation effects were significant. Oath-helpers knew the character of the person they were helping and were likely to know the facts of the case, or at least were in a position to know them better than anyone else. Furthermore, perjury was subject to stiff penalties. Anyone found to be a perjurer was no longer considered "oath-worthy", and thereafter could only be tried by ordeal or pay a heavy fine (Whitelock 1952, 141). For all these reasons, a guilty person would have difficulty obtaining sufficient oath-helpers.

Defendants who failed in making a successful oath, either because they were unable to procure the requisite number of oath-helpers or because they were not deemed oath-worthy, were given the option of proving their innocence by way of ordeal. The trial by ordeal was intended to elicit the judgment of God, who acted as an arbitrator and, who it was thought, revealed the innocence or guilt of accused parties. The ordeal should not be viewed simply as a torment imposed on unwilling defendants, as it also provided a new opportunity to clear oneself of accusations. Notably, the mass-priest administered the ordeal after three days of fasting, during which time the defendant could change his mind and confess (Whitelock 1952, 142).[11]

To modern sympathies, the ordeal system appears primitive and even inhumane. Considered within the context of its own time, however, it may have been an effective mechanism for facilitating the peaceful resolution of disputes (Benson 1998, 199). Since existing technology made it difficult to gather evidence and definitively establish guilt or innocence, violent conflict could easily break out between disputing groups. However, under the ordeal system, individuals had a strong incentive to confess transgressions and make restitution. Belief in God was prevalent, so most lawbreakers would have feared that the ordeal would expose their guilt. In addition, the prospect of having to face an ordeal may have been an effective deterrent for potential lawbreakers. So, although it was an unsound method of determining innocence, the ordeal may have been an effective solution for some unique problems confronting dispute resolution in medieval times.

All of the procedures mentioned thus far existed simply to establish a judgment. If a defendant was found guilty, the court would order him to make monetary restitution to the victim or his family, called *bot* (Pollock and Maitland 1899, vol. 2, 451). The amount of compensation required for various offenses evolved through custom and then became formally enshrined in codes of law, which kings issued at regular intervals. A first time offender could make restitution for any crime except for a few, including arson, open theft, and concealed murder, called "bootless"; the punishment for these crimes was death and forfeiture of property (Pollock and Maitland 1899, vol. 2, 457–458). Each man in Anglo-Saxon England was ranked according to his *wergeld,* or the fixed price that was required to make restitution for killing him.[12] In a homicide case, the transgressor could make amends by paying the price of the victim's *wer* to his family. Similarly, compensation or *bot* was prescribed for other crimes as well. Often this was a fixed amount. For example, the economic compensation required for inflicting different kinds of wounds was preestablished and treated in great detail. So much would have to be given for the loss of an eye, so much for the loss of a particular finger, so much for a toe, and so on. In the case of theft, the offender would often have to pay the market price of the stolen goods.

Anglo-Saxons did not have jails for the regular incarceration of criminals. Unlike today, the legal system then was tailored to represent the interests of the victim. Indeed, to an Anglo-Saxon, incarceration would have seemed like a particularly unsuitable means of making amends for a crime, as it does nothing to make the victim whole again (Berman 1983, 55). Nevertheless, institutions developed to prevent violence even when an individual could not pay his debt. In some cases involving large payments, a reprieve would be granted to the offender, and he would be given up to a year to come up with the money (Pollock and Maitland 1899, vol. 2, 451). A form of indentured servitude, or temporary slavery, was another means of ensuring payment (449). The term would be set for a given period, usually a long one, after which the criminal was cleared.

A particularly interesting feature of Anglo-Saxon law enforcement is that courts had no power to coerce compliance with their decisions. As Pollock and Maitland (1899, vol. 1, 37) explain, "An Anglo-Saxon court, whether of public or private justice, was not surrounded with such visible majesty of the law as in our own time, nor furnished with an obvious means of compelling obedience." Instead, refusal to comply with judicial decisions put an individual outside the protection of the law. Outlaws could be killed with impunity, and heavy penalties could be assessed to anyone caught aiding them. Outlawry added the necessary weight to the decisions of the hundred court to ensure regular compliance. Individuals who did not pay restitution were outlawed (Stephen 1883, 62). Likewise, seeking personal vengeance instead of accepting restitution would also result in outlawry (Pollock and Maitland 1899, vol. 1, 47–48). Thus, individuals on both sides of a dispute had a strong incentive to accept a peaceful settlement. Refusal to submit to the decision of the hundred court also carried the potential for a blood feud, which was only lawful when a convicted offender defaulted on his payment of *wergeld* (Polack and Maitland 1899, vol. 2, 451).

Outlawry was usually a sufficiently stiff penalty to ensure compliance with the law. Sometimes, however, a wronged party had to face the opposition of a strong lord who would be tempted to shelter himself or his men from the justice of the law. In such cases, the wronged individual could go to a more powerful lord, such as an ealdorman or even the king, who would then ensure that the case was brought before the court. The king, however, did not have the sovereign power to compel obedience and did not enforce rulings. As Pollock and Maitland (1899, vol. 1, 48) explain, "His [i.e., the king's] business is not to see justice done in his name in any ordinary course, but to exercise a special and reserved power which a man must not invoke unless he has failed to get his cause heard in the jurisdiction of his own hundred." When it was necessary for the wronged party to ask for assistance, the offender was required to make an extra payment to the facilitating king or ealdorman, called *wite*, in addition to the proscribed restitution of *wer* to the victim or his kin.

The legal system of the Anglo-Saxons had many appealing features. In the early nineteenth century, the economist Edwin Chadwick wrote, "It must be acknowledged that the early state of the general police of this country possessed a degree of efficiency" (quoted in Ekelund and Dorton 2003, 275). The legal system was oriented at least fundamentally, if not in many of its aspects, toward the protection of individuals and their private property. The punishment for harming an individual or stealing his property was monetary restitution, which provided at least a measure of compensation for the victim. Moreover, while the actual process by which law is enforced under a system of outlawry should not be romanticized, it created, along with the ancillary institutions of the ordeal and the blood feud, a set of incentives that ensured at least a tolerable level of compliance. In essence, it was a system built upon the interests and preferences of the individual participants.

Government Monopolization of Law: Kings Seeing Courts as a Source of Revenue for the State

Anglo-Saxon society was highly decentralized. Government existed, but there was no nation-state. Communities were largely left to govern themselves, and its various functions and duties were typically carried out at the lowest levels. This condition particularly applied to the activities of governance that were concerned with the application of justice. Social norms and customs, as well as economic and religious factors, regulated society more than mandates of the rulers did. Local institutions, which consisted mainly of private inputs supplied by neighboring individuals, provided for the bulk of the courts and law enforcement. The incentive of self-interest ensured the effective operation of this system since participation provided private benefits. Overall, the influence of the royal authority on governance was slight. As Warren (1987, 52) explains, "...there was no central direction of the shires themselves, no system of supervision by visitation, no central office for controlling the king's officers in the shires. This was not decentralized government; it was merely uncentralized." The king's agents appealed to the sovereign's power on occasion to ensure the sanction of force, but they did not dictate the substance of the law, provide police, or administer local communities.

Royal prerogative insinuated itself into everyday affairs to the extent necessary for maintaining the preservation of the realm, but the office of kingship did not evolve for the specific purpose of providing internal law and security. Instead, kingship emerged as an outcome of competition for power and in response to constant threats of external conquest (Blair 1956, 196–198; Benson 1990, 26–30). During the Anglo-Saxon period, however, royal institutions gradually played an increasingly larger role in the administration of law.

From the beginning, the crown was involved in some pleas, called the "king's pleas" (Warren 1987, 43). These included both cases in which the king was the wronged party as well as certain serious offenses that were reserved by royal decree to be the king's prerogative. King's pleas were tried in the same courts as regular cases, but they required the presence of an authorized representative of the king. A guilty ruling did not require compensation, but instead involved punishments such as fines, forfeiture of property, and sometimes mutilation or death. The proceeds went directly into the king's treasury. Anglo-Saxon kings thus began to view law enforcement as a potential source of revenue.

As monarchical power grew stronger and more secure, so did the king's effective ability to wring profit from the legal system.[13] The first step in this process was the incorporation of *wite* as a regular feature of the legal process. At first, an ealdorman or the king received *wite* only if his services were called upon to ensure that a victim could get his case heard in court. Very early during the Anglo-Saxon period, a payment of *wite* to the king became institutionalized and was required in addition to the regular compensation of *bot* to the victim.

More substantially, kings found an opportunity to raise funds by declaring various acts to be violations of the "king's peace"; these required making a payment of *wite* to the king instead of compensation to the victim. Embedded in Anglo-Saxon law was the idea that every free man's house was protected by a peace, called *mundbyrd,* that entitled him to special compensation from intruders or anyone who burst into violent behavior on his property. This compensation was scaled according to each individual's rank, with the highest sum protecting the king's residence. Thus, originally, the king's peace merely referred to the peace of the king's own household, in the sense that he was afforded the same sort of rights as anyone else. But as royal power expanded, so did the king's peace. First it was extended to the king's lodgings as he traveled. Then gradually it began to apply to places where he wasn't even present, such as highways and bridges, to churches and monasteries, and even to markets and towns. By the eleventh century, royal officials had the power to assert that the king's peace extended over wherever it was expedient (Lyon 1980, 42).

The overall profits from justice became one of the three main sources of royal revenue, along with profits from the king's estates and from his vassals' feudal obligations. Revenue from the king's jurisdictional rights in justice comprised a small part of the king's income at first, but it became increasingly significant. Furthermore, as Benson (1994, 255) has pointed out, funds obtained in this way were expedient because they were more liquid and easy to modify than income generated from other sources. Land was the largest source of royal revenue, but until the eleventh century, payment consisted of agricultural produce and payments in kind by tenants (Lyon 1980, 44). Taxation was liquid, but relatively light. Moreover, incremental increases and adjustments in the amount collected through justice could be made relatively easily by increasing *wite* or expanding the king's peace.

Even more importantly, rights to the proceeds from pleas and forfeitures became something that the king could hand out to his supporters (Pollock and Maitland 1899, vol. 2, 453–454, Benson 1994, 255). The ability to exchange these rights played a pivotal role in the kings' expansion of power. Ealdormen received profits from justice in return for providing support in war and representing the king's interests in shire courts. Ealdormen consolidated their influence, and, becoming known as earls, began to lord over multiple shires. The office of sheriff evolved such that he became the chief representative of the king within each shire. The sheriff received land from the king but also a share of the profit generated by judicial proceedings.

The process of royal involvement in the justice system begun by Anglo-Saxon kings accelerated after the Norman Conquest of England in 1066 AD. Nominally, William I retained and ratified the legal system that he found, and most of the offenses under the Anglo-Saxon customary law were retained. However, Norman rule brought about a radical shift in the nature of legal governance.

The invaders scrapped the restitution-based system of *wergeld,* which served as the foundation of all of Anglo-Saxon law, in favor of the Norman system of fines and punishments. The range of violations treated as breaches of the king's peace was consequently greatly expanded. Indeed, cases that the general procedure of the hundred court had customarily decided could be transferred to a hearing in a royal court if the victim simply decided to add to his charge that he had suffered the wrong "against the king's peace" (Warren 1987, 135). At this time the Normans also introduced into England the concept of felonies, and acts of betrayal or treachery against one's lord. The sum of these changes altered the character of the king's relation to the law. As Lyon (1980, 190) describes it, "the fortuitous yet conscious combination of the royal prerogative with the concepts of the king's peace and felony gave royal justice a flexibility that enabled the royal court to spread its jurisdiction over all sorts of places and men and over almost any type of offense." A plausible motivation for implementing these legal changes was the Norman kings' desire to increase their income as much as possible.

The elimination of restitution also removed the most important private benefit accruing from voluntary cooperation in the legal system. Consequently, individuals no longer had a strong enough incentive to perform their duties for the hundred and tithings. The Anglo-Saxon *borh* and tithing gave way to the Anglo-Norman system of frankpledge (Morris 1910). Under this new organization, the surety and policing functions were merged and made compulsory. The lack of sufficient positive incentives induced Norman kings to resort to fining nonparticipation to ensure that criminals were pursued and members of the court did not shirk their duties.

Frankpledge was introduced to deal with many of the same problems as the *borh,* but it differed from the earlier institution in several important respects. First of all, royal fiat seems to have supplied the impetus for the adoption of frankpledge. Furthermore, whereas before a pledge group could refuse to admit an individual who was untrustworthy in the same way that a modern insurance company may refuse to cover an individual whom it considers a bad risk, the frankpledge system removed this element of choice (Warren 1987, 41). The displacement of voluntary association based on positive incentives by indiscriminate and coercive grouping undermined the ability to apply social sanction, which was essential to the *borh's* effectiveness as an assurance agency for keeping peace and social order.

The centralization of law continued under the Angevin kings, particularly during the reign of Henry II, which included a great deal of legal innovation. This period saw the culmination of the complete transformation of the legal system. As Warren (1987, xiv) describes, under the Anglo-Saxons "There was no hierarchy of royal officials and there were no formally constituted offices of state. . . . In contrast, by the middle of the thirteenth century royal authority was constantly exercised through an elaborate, bureaucratic, administrative system which reached out regularly into local communities and could deal directly with individuals." Subsequent extensions of the king's pleas provided a major avenue for the expansion of royal government into communities, and the royal court grew into a hierarchy of three separate tribunals due to the vast increase in the scope and number of cases tried in the king's name (Warren 1987, 133).

The principal cause of the centralization of law was that visiting royal justices, called *eyres,* replaced local officials as supervisors of the king's pleas. The role of itinerant justices had been waning, but Henry II vigorously revived them organizing them into circuits and sending them off on regular visitations of the shires. The king's justices adjudicated royal pleas, including new categories specifically created by legislation called "the king's assizes" (Warren 1987, 133). They also served as an administrative intermediary, and in so doing created a new relationship between the Crown and its subjects. The justices were responsible for fining tithings of frankpledge groups that they found lax in their policing, and they fined communities in which everyone was not a member of a tithing (Lyon 1980, 284). The fining function was particularly important, as it was becoming quite common for tithing members to fail their duties. For example, they might fail to call attention to a dead body or to put in surety those who were about to stand trial. In such cases those responsible would be put "in mercy," and amerced an arbitrary sum decided by the eyres (Warren 1987, 139).

The increasing need to rely on such fines is explained by the dwindling benefits of voluntary participation. The elimination of restitution was significant in this regard, but additional factors were also involved. For example, unsuccessful suits resulted in the amercement of the plaintiff for false accusation (Lyon 1980, 295). Furthermore, to ensure use of their courts, and thus to get their profits, kings found it necessary to impose penalties for attempting to circumvent the system. For example, they made it a crime for a victim to accept restitution from his injurer in lieu of taking him to a hearing before the justice of the king, or to accept the return of stolen goods (Laster 1970, 76).

The end result of the Angevin legal reformation was the complete subjugation of local custom and procedure to royal authority. The shires were no longer independent and self-contained units, as they had been on the eve of the Norman invasion. The hundred courts continued to play a central role in legal affairs, but they were completely subsumed and integrated into royal governance (Warren 1987, 199).

The local shires also continued to provide policing, in which they played an important role until the establishment of publicly funded police forces in the nineteenth century. However, coercive inducements to ensure victim and community participation were not adequate. The dissatisfaction among the populace and rising crime rates induced the creation of the public office of Justice of the Peace in 1326. Benson (1994, 258–260, 1998, 212–213) describes how public policing came to dominate law enforcement over the next several centuries. The course of this trajectory was inevitably set by the breakdown in efficiency due to the institutional shift that removed the incentives for victims and local communities to produce order.

CONCLUSION

The history of medieval England demonstrates, contrary to common belief, that law and order can be provided in a decentralized manner. It also demonstrates that government law enforcement in England was not created for public interest, but for public choice. Law should not be categorized as necessarily requiring government provision, nor should it be assumed that government provides law to advance solely or even primarily the public interest.

From a positive analysis perspective, legal history casts doubt on the public interest view that government created law enforcement to address a market failure. From a normative perspective, history also undermines the public interest view that ascribes legitimacy to government law enforcement because the public voluntarily chose it. Many of the early contributors to the field of public choice granted special legitimacy to government law enforcement because they believed that it is necessary for order (Gunning, 1972). However, these assumptions may not be true, as history shows. In James Buchanan's more recent work, he seems to recognize that government law enforcement is not necessarily the only source of order. Buchanan (2004, 268) writes that the 1970s public choice scholars' Hobbesian assumptions "led us to neglect at the time any effort to work out what the alternative of ordered anarchy would look like. What would be the results if persons should behave so as to internalize all of the relevant externalities in their dealings among themselves?"

The history of policing in England provides a partial answer to this question. It certainly was not perfect, but the polycentric system of one thousand years ago shows that order is possible without the government monopoly that we have today. Government control of law enforcement may simply be a means to enhance revenue and consolidate power for the state.

Of course, the foregoing history does not itself settle whether private provision is superior to that of the government. However, just as when Coase (1974) famously pointed out that lighthouses were originally private, it does cast doubt on whether the public aspect of the good is enough to justify government provision. An advocate of government could argue that government lighthouses and government courts are superior to private lighthouses and private courts, but these are separate arguments. The legal-economic history presented here suggests shifting the debate to these separate arguments. This area of political economy is deserving of further careful theoretical and empirical study. The idea that government law enforcement was created for the benefit of the public is a myth.

NOTES

We are grateful to Bruce Benson, John Hasnas, and Leonard Liggio for informing us of the existence of the history described in this chapter. We thank Edward López, Alex Tabarrok, Eduardo Helguera, and an anonymous referee for helpful comments and suggestions. All remaining errors and misinterpretations are our own.

1. See the Center for the Study of Public Choice monograph *Explorations in the Theory of Anarchy* (Tullock, 1972) and the follow-up *Further Explorations in the Theory of Anarchy* (Tullock, 1974). For a discussion of these works, see the edited volume *Anarchy, State, and Public Choice* (Stringham, 2005).
2. The system was decentralized and had many voluntary elements, but it definitely not a voluntaryist utopia. We will refer to it as polycentric to mean law was provided by more than one center, but we do not want to imply that all of the relationships were voluntary. Lords asserted coercive power over peasants who were not free in any modern libertarian sense. The relevant comparison, however, would not be how much liberty the typical person had then compared to the typical American today. The relevant comparison would be how much liberty the typical person had during those times compared to the typical person in other regions during those times or to the typical person in that region throughout the first half of the second millennium.
3. As Hasnas explains, "It is true that, beginning in the late twelfth century, the common law developed in the royal courts, but this does not imply that either the king or his judges made the law. On the contrary, for most of its history, the common law was entirely procedural in nature. Almost all of the issues of concern to the lawyers and judges of the king's courts related to matters of jurisdiction or pleading; that is, whether the matter was properly before the court, and if it was, whether the issues to be submitted to the jury were properly specified. The rules that were applied were supplied by the customary law."
4. Fuller (1964, 123) himself noted that "A possible objection [to his definition of law]...is that it permits the existence of more than one legal system governing the same population. The answer, of course, is that such multiple systems do exist and have in the history been more common than unitary systems."

5. The term "polycentric" is generally attributed to Michael Polanyi (1951), and was brought into the study of law by F. A. Hayek and Lon Fuller. See Barnett (1998, 257–297) for a detailed exposition of polycentric legal order.

6. According to the 2007 Failed State Index, 32 countries have governments on the verge of collapsing. Somalia has intermittently lacked any central government at all since 1991 (Little 2003).

7. For an overview of this literature, see the edited volumes Stringham (2005) and Stringham (2007).

8. Further examples of polycentric legal order include the self-enforcing institutions created by seventeenth- and eighteenth-century pirates (Leeson 2007a) and the *Leges Marchiarum* of the Anglo-Scottish borderlands in the sixteenth century (Leeson 2007b). From more recent history, Anderson and Hill (1979) describe how property rights were formed and protected in the early American West under voluntary associations, including private protection agencies, vigilantes, wagon trains, and mining camps. Similarly, Umbeck (1981) describes how secure property rights were established spontaneously during the California gold rush in the absence of formal legal authority. From the present day, Ellickson (1991) explains how ranchers and farmers in Shasta County, California manage to settle disputes outside of the formal legal system. Sobel and Osoba (forthcoming) discuss how youth gangs act essentially as protection agencies by enforcing rules in the face of government failure to protect young people from violence.

9. A well-known application of the "folk theorem" is that individuals have an incentive to cooperate in reciprocal provision even without external enforcement when they are sufficiently patient and expect to interact repeatedly (Axelrod, 1984, Sugden, 1986).In addition, many economists have argued that reputation mechanisms may be sufficient to ensure cooperation in interactions between all individuals, even those who are not involved in repeated dealings, because cheaters can be excluded from all forms of social interaction with the members of groups with whom they do have ongoing relationships (Williamson 1983, Goldin 1988; Brubaker 1988, Schmidtz 1991, Ellickson 1991). The history of Anglo-Saxon England illustrates how folk theorem-type institutional arrangements were sufficient for establishing law and order under moderately complex conditions characterized by a relatively small number of individuals.

10. See Benson (1990, 11–41) for an in-depth discussion of customary legal systems with voluntary enforcement. Friedman (1979) discusses in detail the private creation and enforcement of law in Iceland, and Peden (1977) similarly describes Celtic Irish law.

11. Anglo-Saxons, unlike other Germanic tribes, did not have an ordeal of trial by combat (Pollock and Maitland 1899, vol. 1, 39). Instead, the main forms of ordeal were fire or water (Berman 1983, 57, Whitelock 1952, 142). In the case of fire, the accused party was required to carry a red-hot iron bar nine feet. After this his hand would be enveloped, and after three days the envelope would be removed and the wound inspected to see if it was clean or festering. Those with a clean wound were presumed to have been preserved by God, indicating their innocence, and were absolved of all wrongdoing. The ordeal of water could involve hot water or cold water. In the hot water ordeal, the defendant was required to plunge his hand into a boiling hot cauldron of water and take out a stone, and he was declared innocent if his wounds were not festering after three

days. In the case of cold water, the defendant would be thrown into a river, and if he sank he would be found innocent.

12. See Seebohm (1902) for a detailed description and account of the wergeld system in Anglo-Saxon England.

13. It should be noted that while there is direct evidence that the king received significant and increasing revenue from the legal system, no systematic accounting record of its cost exists, so the exact amount of profit thereby obtained is indeterminate.

CHAPTER 3

ELECTORAL PRESSURES AND THE LEGAL SYSTEM: FRIENDS OR FOES?

Russell S. Sobel, Matt E. Ryan, and Joshua C. Hall

INTRODUCTION: POLITICS, ELECTIONS, AND THE EFFICIENCY OF GOVERNMENT ACTION

Decisions made within the legal system are typically viewed as being impartial informed only by the testimony and evidence presented and legal precedent. For this reason, many scholars treat legal decisions as exogenous events, that is, that they are independent of preexisting conditions (see, for example, Baicker and Gordon 2006). However, political scientists and legal analysts have long understood that in many cases factors outside what is presented in the courtroom affect the outcomes of legal cases.[1] The race, gender, and political affiliation of individuals involved in the legal process have all been found to play a role in determining legal outcomes.[2]

For example, at the federal level, the ideology of justices (typically inferred from the political party of the person who appointed the justice) has been found to be important in both opinion structure and outcome in administrative law cases (Cross and Tiller 1998). In addition, Republican appointees have been found to rule against the Environmental Protection Agency in environmental law cases more often than Democratic appointees (Smith and Tiller 2002). Schanzenbach (2005, 59–60) aptly categorizes the research on the effect of judicial characteristics when he states that "the literature has consistently established that when judges have discretion, they indulge personal policy preferences."[3]

Politics plays a role in influencing legal outcomes at other points in the legal process as well. District attorneys (DAs) are elected officials with considerable influence over case outcomes. Not only do DAs decide when there exists enough evidence to charge a defendant, they also decide the level of resources to devote to prosecuting the case. The legal system gives considerable leeway to district attorneys to exercise personal judgment, from the decision to prosecute to the decision to offer a plea bargain.

Simon (1991) details how pressure from district attorneys increases the man-hours devoted to finding a suspect in high-profile homicide cases. Despite the clear pressure that elections place on DAs, little empirical work has been done on this issue, with the exception of Dyke (forthcoming), who finds the probability that a defendant will be prosecuted increases in an election year. His work suggests that DAs are more likely to prosecute cases in election years that they otherwise might dismiss in nonelection years.

Elections are commonly viewed as the primary means through which voters can hold public officials accountable for their actions. According to authors such as Donald Wittman (and others from the "Chicago School"), elections are effective in this role (Wittman 1995). When elections are contestable, and competition within the political process is strong, this school holds that elections promote outcomes that are efficient and consistent with voter preferences. In contrast, authors from the "Virginia School" tradition hold a much more critical view, in which voter ignorance, interest groups, and barriers to entry result in democratic failures—inefficient outcomes that may not mirror voter preferences. However, even in the limited cases where electoral outcomes are driven by voter preferences, the question whether these majority preferences are truly accurate or rational in the first place remains (Caplan 2007).

Empirical research has consistently shown that the incentives of elected officials are distorted around election time. Garrett and Sobel (2003), for example, find that presidential decisions regarding disaster declarations to release Federal Emergency Management Agency FEMA funding to states are influenced by whether the president is currently seeking reelection. In addition, Kubik and Moran (2003) find a gubernatorial election cycle in state executions in which states are significantly more likely to conduct executions in gubernatorial election years. These are just two examples in which the empirical literature has found distorted incentives around the time of elections in areas of government policy that would, at first glance, seemingly be the least susceptible to these influences. In this chapter, we explore whether elections in the legal system tend to be efficiency-enhancing or instead result in democratic failures that compromise the quality of the legal system. In particular, we explore how electoral pressures faced by judges and district attorneys impact legal outcomes in the United States.

JUDICIAL SELECTION: THE EFFECT OF SELECTION PROCEDURE ON OUTCOMES[4]

The question of how judges should be selected has been an important one throughout the history of the Unites States. During the 1787 Constitutional Convention in Philadelphia, an ardent debate focused on who would select members of the judiciary (Farber and Sherry 1990). More recently, the last several decades have seen many states change their method of selecting judges, primarily moving away from electing their justices to some form of appointment system. From 1940 to 1990, for example, 15 states switched to a merit form of judicial selection (Hanssen 2004) in their highest appellate courts. Today, the governor or legislature appoints state supreme court justices in 29 states and popular elections are used in the remaining 21 states. In states that elect their supreme court justices, 8 use partisan elections in which candidates run on political platforms as Democrats or Republicans, and 13 use nonpartisan elections in which candidates run on their name and reputation alone (American Judicature Society 2007).[5]

An enduring question in legal scholarship is the importance of judicial selection method to judicial outcomes, with the primary focus being on the difference between appointing and electing judges. Among the many arguments put forth by those in favor of appointing judges instead of electing them is the hypothesis that judicial elections undermine public confidence in the judiciary and thus are incompatible with a strong and independent judiciary.[6] While numerous studies have found significant differences in legal outcomes between appointed and elected judiciary systems, the differential between partisan and nonpartisan elections is generally ignored in the empirical literature.[7]

Partisan elections, in particular, have a reputation for producing ideologically biased judges. West Virginia's 2004 supreme court election—the most expensive judicial election in the nation that year—is but one recent example. The incumbent and the challenger combined spent nearly $1 million and independent political action organizations spent approximately $3.5 million in total. Interest groups lined up on opposite sides of the judicial race, with organized labor supporting the Democratic incumbent and business associations supporting the Republican challenger. Both the incumbent and the challenger explicitly ran on political platforms reflecting their party's ideology, with the incumbent stressing his reputation for being a friend of labor and the challenger touting his business-friendly judicial philosophy.

Partisan elections where candidates receive public support from organized interest groups and run on political party platforms thus appear to run contrary to the notion of an unbiased and fair judiciary. Do states with partisan elections have lower judicial quality than states using nonpartisan elections? If so, are the previously found differentials between states using judicial appointment and elections really due only to the poor legal systems in the handful of states with partisan elections?

To examine this question we employ a new survey-based ranking of state legal liability systems conducted by the U.S. Chamber of Commerce. This index scores state judicial quality on a scale of zero to 100 based on a nationwide survey of lawyers.[8] Table 3.1 provides the average state ranking and the average score by state for the year 2004, stratified by method of judicial selection.

The data thus seem to confirm the commonly held belief that appointing justices leads to superior outcomes compared to judicial election. Appointive states have an average ranking of 21.1 out of the 50 states measured with an

Table 3.1 Average Judicial Quality Ranking by Selection Process, 2004

Type of System	Average Ranking	Average Score
Appointed	21.1	61.0
Elected	31.5	53.5
Partisan	39.9	47.9
Nonpartisan	26.4	56.9

Source: U.S. Chamber of Commerce, *State Liability Rankings Study: 2004.*

average score of 61.0 out of 100. States electing their judges have much lower scores, with an average state ranking of 31.5 and overall judicial quality score of 53.5. Looking at the breakdown between partisan and nonpartisan elective states, however, clarifies that the really significant decline in legal quality occurs in states that select judges using partisan elections. Partisan election states have an average ranking that would place them 40th out of the 50 states, with an average legal quality score nearly 15 points below the average appointive states. While nonpartisan election states are still below appointive states, the difference is small compared to the decline in legal quality observed for partisan elective states. Consistent with the previous literature, elections lower judicial quality compared to appointment, and partisan elections considerably lower judicial quality compared to appointive systems. What is clear is that the majority of the differential between appointed and elected systems is due to the significantly worse legal quality in the states with partisan elections.

To ensure other factors that differ across states are not driving the results in table 3.1, we now turn to regression methodology. The dependent variable is the state's liability system ranking. As control variables, we use the number of lawyers per capita, percent voting for the Democratic nominee in the 2000 presidential election, the percentage of state residents over 25 with a college degree, and judicial salary level.[9] We begin by first simply including a dummy variable for whether the state employs elections (of either type) to select judges. The results of this basic regression analysis are presented in column 1 of table 3.2. The sign on Elective is negative and statistically significant, with the interpretation of the coefficient being fairly straightforward. A state changing from judicial elections to judicial appointments would be expected to have a 4.5 point increase in legal quality, or about the difference between the 9th ranked state and the 26th ranked state.

Columns 2 and 3 include two additional explanatory variables to the basic model. In column 2, we add a measure of racial diversity commonly employed in the developmental economics literature. A number of studies have found that ethnic, linguistic, and racial diversity can lead to poor economic, legal, and social institutions (see Alesina et al. 2003 for an excellent overview of this research). According to this literature, different

Table 3.2 Determinants of State Legal Liability Rankings

Variables	OLS Estimates		
	1	2	3
Constant	43.64***	42.77***	145.81***
	(4.05)	(4.26)	(3.71)
Elective	−4.52*	−5.32**	−4.40**
	(1.92)	(2.54)	(2.07)
Education	1.06***	1.00***	1.21***
	(3.65)	(3.29)	(4.05)
Salary	0.00003	0.00011	0.00013
	(0.26)	(1.098)	(1.38)
Democrat	−0.17	−0.16	−0.07
	(1.05)	(1.11)	(0.49)
Lawyers	−2.45*	−2.35	−1.29
	(1.84)	(1.65)	(0.93)
Racial Diversity		−0.00204***	−0.00039
		(2.83)	(0.42)
Income Inequality			−22.17**
			(2.60)
R^2 Adjusted	0.26	0.36	0.40
Observations	50	50	50

Note: * indicates significance at the 10% level, ** at the 5% level, and *** at the 1% level. Absolute value of heteroskedasticity corrected t-statistics in parentheses.

ethnic, linguistic, or racial backgrounds in a society can generate disagreement over the provision of publicly provided goods such as courts and schools.

The racial diversity variable is calculated using population by race from the Census Bureau and constructed according to the following formula:

$$\text{Racial Diversity} = 10,000 - \sum_i (\text{Race}_i)^2$$

where Race_i is the percentage of a state's population belonging to a particular race. A racially homogenous state would receive a score of zero and as racial diversity increased, so would its score. Thus the expected relationship between the measure of racial diversity and legal system quality is expected to be negative, which is what we find in the regression reported in column 2 of table 3.2. More racially diverse states are associated with lower legal quality, other things being equal. More importantly, inclusion of racial diversity in the empirical model does not weaken the finding of a negative relationship between judicial elections and the quality of a state's legal system.

Finally, in column 3, we include a measure of how "extreme" the income distribution is within a state. Measured as the natural log of the product of the percentage of families earning less than $25,000 and the percentage of families earning above $100,000, this variable measures how large the upper and lower tails of the income distribution are within a state. States where the tails of the income distribution are larger might have lower judicial quality if income polarization leads to subversion of the judicial system. For example, the poor could subvert the legal system by using the courts to engage in redistribution.[10] Or alternatively, the rich can use their wealth to influence the courts, leading to corruption instead of justice. Glaeser, Scheinkman, and Shleifer (2003) present cross-country evidence consistent with inequality leading to poor legal institutions. As can be seen in column 3, the inclusion of income inequality in the regression does not change the finding that elections lower the quality of a state's legal system. The inclusion of income inequality does make the measure of racial diversity statistically insignificant, suggesting that the statistically significant finding in column 2 was the result of omitted variable bias and that it is income inequality that exerts a negative influence on judicial quality and not racial diversity.

In table 3.3, we estimate all three specifications from table 3.2, this time breaking up Elective into Partisan and Nonpartisan to see if the difference in judicial quality is the result of the difference between elective and appointive states or between partisan and nonpartisan. The results presented in table 3.3 suggest that the partisan nature of judicial elections is what matters for legal quality. While a negative and significant difference exists between partisan elections and judicial quality, the relationship between nonpartisan elections and judicial quality is not significant. The difference between elective and

Table 3.3 Comparison of Partisan vs. Nonpartisan Election States

Variables	OLS Estimates		
	1	2	3
Constant	42.37***	41.43***	121.46***
	(4.12)	(4.38)	(3.38)
Partisan	−9.36**	−10.38***	−8.79**
	(2.45)	(2.87)	(2.36)
Nonpartisan	−2.09	−2.80	−2.53
	(0.82)	(1.19)	(1.06)
Education	0.93***	0.87***	1.05***
	(3.53)	(3.37)	(3.85)
Salary	0.00005	0.00014	0.00015
	(0.57)	(1.45)	(1.62)
Democrat	−0.15	−0.15	−0.08
	(1.07)	(1.18)	(0.64)
Lawyers	−2.07*	−1.96	−1.20
	(1.76)	(1.56)	(0.96)
Racial Diversity		−0.00209***	−0.00080
		(2.79)	(1.12)
Income Inequality			−17.17**
			(2.19)
R^2	0.30	0.41	0.43
Observations	50	50	50

Note: * indicates significance at the 10% level, ** at the 5% level, and *** at the 1% level. Absolute value of heteroskedasticity corrected *t*-statistics in parentheses.

appointive states appears to be driven by the subset of states using partisan elections, with there being little difference between appointive and nonpartisan states. The findings of all other explanatory variables are consistent with the findings in table 3.2.

The larger question addressed in this chapter is whether electoral pressures are efficiency-enhancing or efficiency-reducing within the legal system. The results from our analysis suggest that elections indeed do impact legal outcomes, but that not all electoral systems are the same. The underlying nature of the elections (here partisan vs. nonpartisan) appears to also have an impact on whether electoral pressures matter. Partisan elections appear to lower judicial quality far more than nonpartisan elections.

The debate over the appropriate method of judicial selection has been contentious. On the one side are individuals arguing in favor of appointive systems of selecting judges. On the other side are individuals who argue that judges should be held accountable to the public for their judicial decisions, especially in an era where considerable policy change occurs through the court system instead of through the legislature. Both of these viewpoints have their merits. Our findings suggest that a compromise position would be to use nonpartisan elections as they lead to outcomes similar to appointive systems while still retaining electoral checks on the judiciary.[11] However, judicial elections marred by party politics are clearly detrimental to a state's legal system quality.

WRONGFUL CONVICTIONS AND THE ELECTION OF DISTRICT ATTORNEYS

While the previous section showed the effect of elections on state judicial quality, this section aims to analyze another aspect of the judiciary—how DAs are influenced by the prospect of an upcoming election.

As members of the judicial branch of government, DAs determine which cases they deem meritorious of prosecution. They also choose how to proceed in prosecuting any particular case. DAs, therefore, have the opportunity to manipulate their granted power of case choice and prosecutorial discretion for personal gain. District attorneys could have a number of individual goals in mind, be it an improved public image, experience-gaining for a better private-sector position or, as we posit in this section, an increased likelihood of reelection.

The incidence of wrongful convictions, while impossible to quantify with certainty, is likely to be at a nontrivial level. Over 40 years ago, Radin (1964) cited a highly respected (but unnamed) judge who estimated that wrongful convictions occur at a rate of 14,000 per year. Attributing even a small portion of these wrongful convictions to election pressures yields hundreds of innocent citizens convicted for the personal political gain of the local district attorney.

The concept of public servants such as DAs using their influence for personal gain is not new, as many popular examples exist of DAs manipulating the judicial process for personal gain. Mike Nifong, the DA presiding over the infamous Duke lacrosse scandal, did so in the midst of a heated reelection campaign.[12] Ultimately disbarred for his actions, Nifong was found by the North Carolina bar to have engaged in considerable misconduct including withholding exculpatory DNA evidence (Neff and Blythe 2007).[13] In an apology made the day after the attorney general of North Carolina dropped the case, Nifong admitted that there was no credible evidence with which to prosecute the accused students (West 2007). District attorneys citing their conviction records as basis for reelection are nearly as common as the elections themselves (see, for example, Murray 2007 and Lapinski 2001), and even cases of district attorneys aggressively prosecuting their political opponents exist (see Glaberson 2005).

We focus our empirical analysis of the electoral pressure on district attorneys on a measurable facet of judicial system error: wrongful convictions. In being able to set the judicial agenda, as well as playing a large role in many facets of the trial itself, district attorneys have many opportunities to adversely affect the process of legal justice. It is our conjecture that election pressures encourage greater prosecutorial misconduct that leads to more wrongful convictions.

In this study, we use a sample of cases found in *Innocent: Inside Wrongful Conviction Cases*, a collection of 109 wrongful convictions from the state of New York (Christianson 2004). The cases span most of the twentieth century and the vast majority of the cases concern a charge of murder. The sample of wrongful convictions spans 16 counties. In New York, DAs are elected at the county level by the public, and 63 district attorneys currently hold office. Though concerning a fundamentally different function of government—a different branch, in fact—DA elections are quite similar to elections for both the executive and legislative branches. Local media cover the candidates extensively, and the ready use of political rhetoric in public comments highlights the role of the district attorney as politician, particularly when elections approach. Finally, as in all elections, district attorney races can vary from effectively unopposed (Kings County, 2005) to tightly contested (Westchester County, 2005).

Table 3.4 presents a preliminary look at the role of DA elections on the wrongful convictions. DA elections occur every four years in New York, so the incidence of wrongful convictions in election years is easy to identify. Thirty-nine of our 109 wrongful convictions occurred during an election

Table 3.4   Election Years vs. Nonelection Years

Total wrongful convictions—Election years	39
Total wrongful convictions—All years	109
Z-statistic value (vs. Null)	2.60**
Z-statistic value (vs. Historical murder conviction rates)	2.47**

Note: * indicates significance at the 10% level, ** at the 5% level, and *** at the 1% level. The null hypothesis is that wrongful convictions occur in election years and nonelection years at the same rate.

year, or about 36 percent.[14] As a null hypothesis we might expect the cases to be uniformly and randomly distributed throughout the years. Testing against this null hypothesis of 25 percent (since one-quarter of wrongful convictions should occur every fourth year), we find, with statistical significance, that wrongful convictions occur more often during election years.[15]

However, this finding could have come as the result of more cases being tried during election years than otherwise; after all, if more cases are heard and convicted in election years than in other years, it would be logical to conclude that in election years we should observe greater number of wrongful convictions too.[16] Using data on the number of New York state murder convictions from 1975 to 2006, we can see whether there are electoral conviction cycles.[17] We find that electoral conviction cycles *do* seem to (weakly) exist. While the average number of convictions in a nonelection year is 296.3, the figure rises in an election year to 303.5; however, this increase does not constitute a statistically significant difference between election and nonelection years. Nonetheless, we can utilize this modest difference to modify our previous hypothesis of wrongful convictions by year being evenly distributed across all years regardless of whether there is an election or not. Instead of assuming a flat 25 percent, we can scale expected wrongful convictions in election years to the higher rate of convictions in election years. Since 25.5 percent of convictions occur during election years, we can test the hypothesis that more than 25.5 percent of wrongful convictions occur during election years. Table 3.4 shows that the difference in wrongful convictions between election years and nonelection years, considering the variation in overall convictions, is significant at the 5 percent level.

While wrongful convictions by year provide evidence of an election-year effect, additional evidence can be found by looking at the time of year that these wrongful convictions take place. Rows 1 and 2 in table 3.5 present the month of the wrongful convictions that occurred during an election year, along with the respective percentage that month comprises of the entire election year as a whole. Rows 3 and 4 correspond to the same breakdowns, only for the average figures for nonelection years. After including historical trends in convictions by month, we test three forms of our hypothesis that electoral pressures lead to excessive wrongful convictions.

The first test is that of the null hypothesis—that all wrongful convictions are spread evenly over the 12 months of the year. Row 6 displays these results. A significantly greater number of wrongful convictions occur in the month of May along with a statistically low number of wrongful convictions in the month of April.[18] While interesting in its own regard, our study concerns the incidence of wrongful convictions around election times.[19] Therefore, of more direct importance to our analysis is that a statistically very high number of wrongful convictions occur in the month of October, immediately prior to general elections during the first week of November—and a statistically *low* number of convictions occur during the month of November. The data show district attorneys rushing to bring cases to completion prior to the

Table 3.5 The Monthly Timing of Wrongful Convictions

Row	Description	Months											
		Jan	Feb	Mar	Apr	May	Jun	Jul	Aug	Sep	Oct	Nov	Dec
(1)	No. of wrongful convictions (election year)	3	3	3	0	5	4	2	3	4	8	1	3
(2)	Percentage of wrongful convictions (election year)	7.7%	7.7%	7.7%	0.0%	12.8%	10.3%	5.1%	7.7%	10.3%	20.5%	2.6%	7.7%
(3)	No. of wrongful convictions (avg. all other)	2	2	2.67	2	2	2.33	1.33	3.33	2.67	0.67	2.67	3.67
(4)	Percentage of wrongful convictions (%) (avg. all other)	0.1	0.1	0.1	0.1	0.1	0.1	0.0	0.1	0.1	0.0	0.1	0.1
(5)	Percentage of murder convictions by month	7.8%	7.8%	10.1%	9.8%	10.1%	10.3%	7.8%	5.2%	6.6%	7.8%	8.7%	8.0%
(6)	Z-statistic (vs. Null)	−0.24	−0.24	−0.24	**−3.15**	**1.70**	0.73	−1.21	−0.24	0.73	**4.60**	**−2.18**	−0.24
(7)	Z-statistic (vs. History of murder convictions)	−0.05	−0.03	−0.85	**−3.44**	0.94	−0.03	−1.05	1.19	1.55	**4.99**	**−2.27**	−0.12
(8)	Z-statistic (vs. all other nonelection years)	0.15	0.15	−0.73	**−2.93**	**2.21**	0.64	0.12	−1.44	0.18	**12.23**	**−2.53**	**−1.75**

Note: Bold type equals statistically significant beyond the 10% level.

polls opening in early November, creating both a surge of wrongful convictions in October and a dearth of wrongful convictions in November.

Our second hypothesis tests whether wrongful convictions are spread throughout the year in accordance to monthly trends in caseload. Whereby the first hypothesis implicitly assumed that all months see the same number of convictions (and therefore the null hypothesis that wrongful convictions are evenly spread over the year), this hypothesis adjusts for monthly variation in conviction rates. For example, if the number of people convicted in June is twice that of September, it would be natural to assume that twice the number of wrongful convictions would occur in June as well. To take into account monthly fluctuations in convictions, we calculate the percentage of murder convictions that occur on average by month over the 32 years of New York state murder convictions data. We then use this figure—found in row 5—as the null hypothesis to test whether we are observing an abnormal level of wrongful convictions in certain months. In the first hypothesis, when we assume evenly distributed wrongful convictions, we test the incidence of wrongful convictions in every month against the constant null value of 8.33 percent (1/12th). For this hypothesis, the null values range from a low of 5.2 percent (August) to a high of 10.3 percent (June). Row 7 presents the results. Once again, October is shown to exhibit a very high number of wrongful convictions, statistically significant at the 1 percent level. The November-shifting effect is also observed here as it was with our previous test, with a significantly low number of wrongful convictions in November to accompany the higher level in October.

Our third and final test now assumes that nonelection years are the norm—that is, the distribution of wrongful convictions in nonelection years should be the benchmark by which election year wrongful convictions are judged. This test differs from the previous two in that we are now generating a null value from the characteristics of wrongful convictions in nonelection year. We utilize this final hypothesis to discern whether wrongful convictions tend to aggregate around certain months both in election *and* nonelection years. Row 8 shows the results of this test. October still exhibits a statistically higher level of wrongful convictions along with the November-shifting effect—the same result we have observed in all three tests performed on the monthly data. A December-shifting effect is observed in this final hypothesis test as well.

It is now common knowledge that public servants use their positions of power for personal gain—after all, they, like all other actors in the economy, are utility-maximizing individuals. Public servants in the judicial branch are separated from those in the other branches only by the different scopes of influence that they possess. While favoritism in taxation, expenditure, and regulation allow for enhanced reelection prospects for legislators, district attorneys have no such authority. Instead, district attorneys use their discretion in selecting cases to pursue, and the process of prosecuting them, to increase their personal goals and well-being. We have shown that the incidence of wrongful convictions rises sharply immediately prior to elections. We feel that this empirical reality is strong evidence that district attorneys increase their scope of influence nearer to election times in order to be perceived as strong public servants. Unfortunately, this effort toward increasing the perception of their worth to the public comes at the cost of greater number of innocent defendants going to jail.

CONCLUSION

The results presented here confirm previous research showing that judicial quality is lower in states that utilize elections to select their judges. Utilizing a new data set measuring judicial quality across the 50 U.S. states we also find it is the partisan nature of judicial elections that is the primary reason for lower judicial quality in elective states that utilize partisan elections. Our research suggests that efforts to improve legal quality by "taking the politics" out of the judiciary are somewhat misguided because the primary force that lowers judicial quality is the partisanship. Moving to nonpartisan elections is likely to achieve much of the desired gains in judicial independence and quality while maintaining voter accountability over justices.

In addition, we show that the influence of elections on the judicial branch of government extends beyond judges to district attorneys. By having the power to determine not only which cases to prosecute but also how to prosecute them, DAs can choose a caseload that maximizes their personal well-being. As the incidence of wrongful murder convictions rises sharply prior to elections, we suggest that district attorneys take more aggressive measures to prosecute borderline cases as a means of appearing to be a more worthy public servant. This results in greater number of innocent defendants being found guilty.

Ultimately, these results point more specifically toward the exact impact that elections have on different sections of the judicial system. While the role of elections in influencing the outcomes of the executive and legislative branches of government have been heavily analyzed, the results presented here show that electoral forces also play a significant role on the outcomes of the judicial branch of government. These electoral pressures appear to be detrimental; our findings, thus, support the theories held by the "Virginia School" regarding the (in) efficiency of elections. It is time to view the judiciary in a similar light as we view the other branches of government and to consider institutional changes that might mitigate the influence of politics on the legal system.[20]

NOTES

1. In their paper on the effect of state school finance reforms on total local resources, Baicker and Gordon (2006) somewhat disturbingly note that constitutional language regarding the state's education system has little predictive power in determining the outcome of state school finance cases.

2. For a nice overview of the literature on the impact of the characteristics of judges on outcomes, see Schanzenbach (2005).

3. Other important research in this vein is Tabarrok and Helland (1999), Helland and Tabarrok (2002), and Hanssen (2000).

4. This section draws on Sobel and Hall (2006).

5. Partisan election states are Alabama, Illinois, Louisiana, Michigan, Pennsylvania, Ohio, Texas, and West Virginia. While party affiliations do not appear on the ballot in Ohio, candidates do receive party nominations to be placed on the ballot.

6. An example of this would be Link (2004).

7. One notable exception is Helland and Tabarrok (2002) who point out that judges elected in partisan elections have an incentive to redistribute wealth from out-of-state defendants (who cannot vote against them) to in-state plaintiffs (who can). An in-depth discussion of their research on the courts, together with some legal reform suggestions, can be found in Helland and Tabarrok (2006).

8. *State Liability Systems Ranking Study* (2004), U.S. Chamber of Commerce, Washington, D.C. The ranking uses a random survey of approximately 1000 lawyers throughout the United States. The lawyers were asked to name the states they were familiar with and then asked to evaluate those state's legal system on a variety of criteria pertaining to the overall quality of a state's legal system.

9. The sources of our data are as follows: the number of lawyers per capita comes from *The Lawyer Statistical Report* (2004); the percent voting Democratic and the percentage of residents over the age of 25 with a college degree were obtained from *The Statistical Abstract of the United States 2004–05* (2004); and the judicial salary level on the court of last resort in a state was obtained from *The Book of the States* (2004).

10. See Tabarrok and Helland (2003) who provide some insight into the role that poverty plays in tort awards.

11. An additional point to note in favor of non-partisan elections is that there does not appear to be any organized lobby in favor of non-partisan elections, unlike appointive systems. Hanssen (2002) finds evidence that the self-interest of lawyers explains state bar association support for appointive 'merit' plans since appointive systems introduces additional uncertainty that increases billable hours for lawyers.

12. See Grose (2007) for an excellent discussion of the role of racial politics in helping get Nifong reelected.

13. The Chairman of the State Bar Disciplinary Hearing Commission specifically pointed to election pressures as a reason for Nifong's actions (Neff and Blythe 2007).

14. Note that the dates assigned to each wrongful conviction correspond to the original date of wrongful conviction, not the date of eventual exoneration.

15. The test statistic is 2.5992, showing a 95 percent level of significance.

16. Of course, the fact that more cases would be heard during election years could also be political in nature. However, since we are focused on the incentive for *wrongful* conviction, we do not address this issue here.

17. Data obtained by direct contact from the New York State Division of Criminal Justice Services, March 15, 2007.

18. Statistically significant with 90 percent confidence.

19. What may be observed here is an effect of primary elections upon the rates of wrongful convictions.
20. A good example of research in this vein is the work of Roger Koppl. In a series of papers, Koppl looks at the role of institutional structure on the forensic science and has come up with several suggestions on how to change forensic science as an institution in order to minimize outright fraudulent forensic science (see, for example, Koppl 2005).

CHAPTER 4

ROMANCING FORENSICS: LEGAL FAILURE IN FORENSIC SCIENCE ADMINISTRATION

Roger G. Koppl

Oh, no, my dear—I'm—I'm a very good man.
I'm just a very bad Wizard.

The Wizard of Oz

INTRODUCTION

Replacing romance with realism in our picture of the law helps us to recognize problems in the legal system and design ameliorative measures. This point applies to an area of the law profoundly neglected by economists, namely, forensic science. Romanticized images of forensic science diminish our capacity to notice problems and respond to them with proposals for improvement. In the romanticized vision of television shows such as *CSI: Crime Scene Investigation*, forensic scientists are infallible wizards. Realism, however, requires us to see forensic experts as ordinary people who respond to the same incentives as people in other areas of human action, and in the same ways. Peart and Levy (2005) call such realism "analytical egalitarianism." Occasional bad apples notwithstanding, forensic scientists are good men and women who apply themselves diligently, often in spite of low pay and poor working conditions. They are good people, not good wizards. Because our legal system expects them to be infallible wizards, however, error rates greatly exceed readily attainable levels.

A properly designed system of redundant testing in forensic science would reduce both error rates *and* the direct money costs of administering the criminal justice system. It is not surprising that redundancy reduces error rates. If one forensic scientist has a 10 percent chance of erring, then the chance of two independent forensic scientists both erring is only 1 per cent. As in information theory, when communicating over a noisy channel, redundancy is necessary for error correction. While it is not surprising that redundancy reduces error rates in forensics, it is quite surprising that redundancy reduces the costs of administering the criminal justice system. In the proposal detailed below, redundancy is cost saving because wrongful convictions are cost inducing. The costs of redundant examinations are swamped by the savings they produce in the costs of incarcerating the wrongly convicted. In this sense, forensic tests are cheaper than prisons.

Below, I show that even if the relevant error rate in forensics is merely 0.8 percent, triplicate fingerprint examinations would reduce both error rates and the costs of administering the criminal justice system. Triplicate fingerprint examinations in felony cases in the United States would cost approximately $9 million annually. By eliminating over 98 percent of the false felony convictions resulting from errors in fingerprint examinations, however, the redundant examinations would save more than $61 million per year in costs of incarceration. The net savings to the criminal justice system alone exceeds $52 million annually. Larger initial error rates would imply both more errors corrected and more cost savings for the criminal justice system.

My proposal for redundant testing is similar to the "blind technical review" that Budowle et al. (2006) suggest might be made a part of "routine casework." They say, "A blind verification process will have a significant impact on resources; therefore, a study should be carried out to determine the best and most cost-effective approach to accomplish the objective." This chapter constitutes such a study and it shows that the "significant impact on resources" within forensic science would be more than offset by cost reductions in another part of the criminal justice system, namely the prison system.

The problem of error is real. Below, for example, I discuss the case of Cameron Todd Willingham, which has become cause célèbre since this chapter was accepted for publication in this volume (Grann 2009, ABC 2009, Kaye 2009). Willingham's execution seems to be clear case of wrongful conviction and execution based on discredited forensic techniques. In proficiency tests conducted from 1978 to 1991, "[f]ibers, paints (automotive and household), glass and body fluid mixtures" all had "improper comparison rates exceeding 10 percent" as did "animal and human hair" analysis (Peterson and Markham 1995b, 1028). Although the best group includes fingerprints, the rate of false positives there was 2 percent (1028). Peterson and Hickman (2005) report that in "the Nation's publicly funded forensic crime laboratories," 238,135 requests for latent print analysis were completed in 2002 (6). Thus, a 2 percent rate of false positives would have implied as many as 4,762 false convictions or guilty pleas. No magic prevents errors in DNA testing either. Josiah Sutton, for example, was falsely convicted and imprisoned for over four years because of a bogus DNA test performed in the Houston Crime Lab. DNA testing in the Houston Crime Lab was halted in 2002 when it was revealed that their DNA tests were unreliable.

I have proposed a system of "competitive self regulation" to improve forensic science (Koppl 2005). The key to this suite of reforms is redundant testing. I have often been told that my program would be too costly. One of the purposes of the calculation made in this chapter is to show that this objection is mistaken. I show that the proposed system of redundant testing would reduce the costs of criminal justice under a wide variety of assumptions about the error rate in fingerprint examinations and the costs of each redundant examination. In this sense, the calculation is robust. My calculation does not consider the social costs and benefits of my proposed system of redundant fingerprint examinations; it addresses only the direct money cost to the state from administering the criminal justice system. In this sense, it is an extremely conservative calculation. Ignoring the cost of compensating wrongly convicted persons who are later exonerated increases the conservatism of the calculation. In part, then, it is an "even if" argument: Even if you make optimistic assumptions about the likelihood of forensic error and even if you care only about the taxpayer costs of administering the criminal justice system, you should support redundant forensic examinations. The proposal, however, can be implemented relatively easily and relatively soon. I put it forward not only as an illustration of the benefits of redundancy, but as a proposal in its own right that can be implemented almost as soon as officials in a given jurisdiction choose to do so. I explain my proposal and cost calculations in relative detail after reviewing some evidence on forensic errors.

HOW BAD IS THE PROBLEM?

The NAS report, *Strengthening Forensic Science in the United States: A Path Forward* (NAS 2009), documents serious deficiencies in forensic science in the United States today. The report does not exaggerate when it says that "there is a tremendous need for the forensic science community to improve" and the "current situation" is "seriously wanting" (NAS 2009, S-9). Some facts illustrate this claim.

The case of the Houston Crime Lab may be the most spectacular recent example of forensic error. From December 2002 to July 2006, DNA testing in the DNA/Serology section of the lab was halted and Houston police began using a private lab for DNA tests (Bromwich 2005, 2, Khanna 2006, Glenn 2006). Testing was halted in the wake of a scandal revealing that DNA work in the lab was not reliable. Josiah Sutton, for example, was convicted of rape largely on DNA evidence that was later shown to be bogus. He was convicted and imprisoned at the age of 16 and released over four years later (Koppl 2005, 276–277). One remark in an important audit of the lab suggests the scope of the problem. "The audit team was informed that on one occasion the roof leaked such that items of evidence came in contact with the water" (FBI Director, 2002, 21).[1]

The main study of proficiency tests, covering the period 1978 to 1991, shows high false-positive error rates. Specifically, for "animal and human hair" analysis, "[f]ibers, paints (automotive and household), glass and body fluid mixtures" over 10 percent of test responses gave a positive conclusion that was, in fact, false and mistaken (Peterson and Markham1995b, 1028). In this period, the rate of false identifications for fingerprints was at least 2 percent.

In 2004, the FBI declared a "100 percent match" of Brandon Mayfield to a latent print lifted from the scene of the Madrid train bombing. The Spanish authorities objected to this identification. They seem to have been correct as the FBI later withdrew its identification and released Mayfield (Office of the Inspector General 2006).

Mayfield's print came under scrutiny because it was one of 20 "candidate prints" produced by an automated search of the "FBI's Criminal Master File" by the "FBI's Integrated Automated Fingerprint Identification System (IAFIS)" (OIG 2006, 11). Mayfield was a convert to Islam; his wife was Egyptian; he worshipped at a mosque where radical Islamists also worshipped; and, as an attorney, he had defended a radical Islamist in a legal action. An OIG (Office of the Inspector General) report on the case expressly denies that such facts played a role in the misidentification of Mayfield, saying, "the FBI examiners were not aware of Mayfield's religion at the time they concluded Mayfield was the source" of the latent. FBI examiners did not know "his religion, his marriage to an Egyptian immigrant, or his representation of other Muslims as an attorney" until "after the identification had been made and verified by the FBI Laboratory" (OIG 2006, 11). Only skeptics would question this conclusion.

In March 2007, Tara Williamson, a fingerprint examiner for the Seminole County Sheriff's Office in Florida, wrote a memo accusing her co-worker Donna Birks of misbehavior and incompetence (Williamson 2007). Her accusations seem to be correct. As of June 4, 2007, investigators from the Florida Department of Law Enforcement (FDLE) have discovered eight misidentifications (Seminole County 2007, 9–11, 34–36). In at least six cases, Birks made a positive identification from prints that should have been considered inconclusive. In at least one case, she identified someone who should have been excluded.[2] Such judgments, of course, assume that the FDLE fingerprint examiners have made correct analyses. Williamsons' memo says that Birks "reported numerous identifications without verification," that she "had a trainee with three weeks of experience verify latent print identifications," and that on one occasion she sought out a third, retired examiner to verify an identification after two "examiners in the office were not able to verify the print," that is to say, disagreed with her analysis. Williamson notes that these actions violated "basic ethical guidelines" governing fingerprint examination (Williamson 2007, 3). Birks had been promoted to latent print examiner in 1998. It is estimated that she "completed approximately 5,000 examinations and 1,500 identifications since 1996" (Seminole County 2007, 9). As of June 4, 2007, the Florida Department of Law Enforcement is reexamining 317 of those cases (Seminole County 2007, 9). (For newspaper coverage, see Stutzman 2007a, 2007b.)

In October 2007, a Maryland court ruled that the standard "ACE-V methodology" of fingerprint examination is not reliable enough for capital cases (State of Maryland). Judge Susan Souder's decision seems to reflect a scholarly literature challenging the validity of fingerprint evidence. For example, Haber and Haber (2008) say, "We have reviewed available scientific evidence of the validity of the ACE-V method and found none." The issue is not whether fingerprints are unique and constant over time, but whether ACE-V reliably connects smudged, distorted, and partial latents to prints carefully rolled in a police station. Judge Sounder's decision cited evidence that prominently included the Mayfield misidentification. She concluded "that ACE-V was the type of procedure" that Maryland rules of evidence "intended to banish, that is, a subjective, untested, unverifiable identification procedure that purports to be infallible" (State of Maryland).

Judge Souder's opinion was highly critical of the standard "ACE-V methodology" of fingerprint examination, according to which a fingerprint examiner who finds a match between a latent and a known print should seek "verification" of the match. "Verification is the independent examination by another qualified examiner resulting in the same conclusion" (SWGFAST 2002a, 4). Unfortunately, "independent" does not mean "blind." "*Blind verification* is the confirmation of an examiner's conclusion by another competent examiner who has no expectation or knowledge of the prior conclusion" (SWGFAST 2002b, 5). Blind verifications are "encouraged," but not required (SWGFAST 2002b, 5). Thus, it is expected that an "independent" verification may be made even though the second examiner knows the prior conclusion of the first examiner. Judge Souder noted such infirmities and pointed to a further important flaw, saying that "in the event the first verifier declines to confirm the identification, a second verifier can be selected." As we have seen, on at least one occasion, Donna Birks was able to shop her verification. When a fingerprint examiner has the opportunity to reject failed verifications and search for successful verifications, we have something similar to the situation analyzed by Feigenbaum and Levy (1996), who show that narrowly reproducible results may be almost as good as direct fraud for a biased and unscrupulous researcher who has a choice of techniques and the ability to report results selectively.

PUBLIC CHOICE CAUSES OF THE PROBLEM

Public choice theory predicts the sort of the problems I have noted above. In the United States and most common law countries, forensic laboratories are typically organized under law enforcement agencies. "The majority of forensic science laboratories [in the United States] are administered by law enforcement agencies, such as police departments, where the laboratory administrator reports to the head of the agency" (NAS 2009, 6–1). Budgets and performance reviews come from the police, the FBI, or the sheriff's office. (Presumably, an analysis such as that given here would apply in most other countries.) "Forensic scientists who sit administratively in law enforcement agencies or prosecutors' offices, or who are hired by those units, are subject to a general risk of bias" (NAS 2009, 6–2).

A law enforcement agency is a government bureau like any other and subject, therefore, to the same public choice analysis. Such analyses of law enforcement have been made by several scholars, beginning with a few passing remarks in Gordon Tullock's *The Politics of Bureaucracy* (1965, 164, 210, 224). Recent literature (Baicker and Jacobson 2007, Benson and Rasmussen 1995, Benson, Rasmussen, and Sollars 1995, Makowsky and Stratmann 2007) recognizes that law enforcement agencies have an incentive to expand their budgets in more or less the way described by Niskanen (1971). Following Breton and Wintrobe (1982, 27), Benson, Rasmussen, and Sollars (1995, 24) rightly note that several other motives such as security and status may compete with budget maximization. Like profit maximization, however, the goal of budget maximization is steady, sure, and almost always at work alongside others. Benson, Rasmussen, and Sollars (1995, 38–39) find evidence that police departments acted strategically to increase their discretionary budgets through asset forfeitures in drug cases. Makowsky and Stratmann (2007) reach a similar result using data on traffic tickets. They find, for example, that "officers will issue more frequent and larger fines when the net impact of revenue raised through speeding fines is greater and when other sources of revenue are restricted" (33).

If a crime lab's budget and performance reviews come from a budget-maximizing law enforcement agency, personnel in the lab have an incentive to serve the interests of that agency, rather than abstract and pristine truth. The point is illustrated by the first three entries from a list of "government entities" that are supposed to provide "independent external investigations into allegations of serious negligence or misconduct substantially affecting the integrity of forensic results committed by employees or contractors of any forensic laboratory system" (Title I of the *Omnibus Safe Streets and Crime Control Act of 1968*, Part BB, codified at 42 U.S.C. § 3797k(4) as cited in OIG 2008). Oversight of the Alaska Department of Public Safety, Scientific Crime Laboratory is provided by Alaska State Troopers. Oversight of the Anchorage Police Department, Forensic Crime Laboratory is provided by the Municipality of Anchorage, Internal Auditor and by the Anchorage Police Department, Internal Affairs. Oversight of the Alabama Department of Forensic Sciences is provided by the Alabama Attorney General's Office, the Alabama Bureau of Investigation, and the Alabama Department of Forensic Sciences.

Once a suspect has been identified, the police may acquire a sincere conviction that suspect is guilty. "Success" comes to mean convicting the suspect rather than revealing the truth. Material interests complement this psychological factor if the police or prosecutor's conviction rate is an important budget-influencing performance statistic. For these psychological and material reasons, the police and prosecution frequently desire confirmation from crime labs, not truth or objectivity. As we have seen, crime labs typically answer to law enforcement authorities who determine budget and performance reviews. This situation may also cause forensic scientists to psychologically identify with law enforcement (Koppl 2007). Crime lab personnel have, therefore, both a psychological bias and a material interest in supporting the police theory in any case. All forms of error from honest error to willful fraud are more likely to be made in favor of the prosecution than the defense.

This position of servitude to law enforcement may help explain why "law enforcement officials," including forensic scientists, "involved in what are later determined to be wrongful prosecutions across the nation often face few repercussions" (Possley and Armstrong 1999). Forensic scientist Pamela Fish, for example, was promoted "to oversee biochemistry testing at the Illinois State Police crime laboratory," even though it had been revealed about a year earlier that Fish had testified in a 1992 rape case that blood tests were "inconclusive" when her own laboratory notes show that the results excluded the suspect (Possley and Armstrong 1999). Later, Dr. Edward Blake and criminalist Alan Keel of Forensic Science Associates would call Fish's discredited work in a separate murder case "scientific fraud" (Mills and Possley 2001). In 2004, Youngstown State University hired forensic scientist Joseph Serowik to head its forensic science program even though Serowik had been suspended from his job as a lab technician in the Cleveland crime lab after his work had been discredited. His erroneous analysis led to the false conviction of Michael Green for rape. Serowik was recommended for the academic post by "Cuyahoga County Common Pleas Judge Timothy McGinty, the former prosecutor who sent Michael Green to prison for rape in 1988 with the help of the now discredited testimony from Serowik" (Gillispie and Mills 2004).

I do not claim or believe figures such as Serowik and Fish are representative of forensic science. They are not. Their histories illustrate the apparent fact, however, that the consequences of forensic error are low, at least when such errors tend to favor he prosecution's case. Most forensic scientists strive vigorously to produce true and objective results. Indeed, the professional culture of forensic science places great emphasis on integrity. My personal observations support the view that most forensic scientists sincerely adhere to a rigid norm of integrity. Their urgent desire for integrity makes it all the more unfortunate that the organization of forensics creates incentives and psychological biases that encourage forensic scientists to err in favor of the police theory in the cases they work on.

The law-enforcement incentives of forensic science may help to explain why some scientifically groundless techniques have become standard practice before being debunked. The leading example may be comparative bullet-lead analysis. Since 1963, the FBI claimed that analysis of trace metals in bullet lead allowed them to match a bullet fragment to a given manufacturer or even a specific box. A 2004 study issued by the National Academy of Sciences found that the FBI's claims for the technique were inaccurate. The FBI abandoned it a year later (Solomon 2007).

Scientifically unsound techniques of forensic analysis can lead to miscarriages of justice as illustrated by the case of Cameron Todd Willingham, who was executed in Texas in 2004. Charged with murdering his three small children by arson, he was convicted with forensic techniques that were current at the time of the fire in 1991, but discredited by the time of his execution in 2004. The presence of "crazed glass," for example, was thought to indicate that an accelerant had been used. It has since been shown that these intricately patterned cracks can also be caused by dowsing hot glass with water, which may happen when a house fire is put out. The *Chicago Tribune* reports, "Before Willingham died by lethal injection on Feb. 17, Texas judges and Gov. Rick Perry turned aside a report from a prominent fire scientist questioning the conviction" (Mills and Possley 2004). We are not in a position to know whether he was innocent, but Willingham's execution seems to be a clear case of wrongful conviction and wrongful execution.

As I noted above, the Willingham case has become a cause célèbre since this chapter was accepted for publication in this volume (Grann 2009, Beyler 2009, ABC 2009, Kaye 2009). Claims of Willingham's actual innocence should not be exaggerated. It seems unambiguous that the evidence was inadequate to eliminate reasonable doubt of Willingham's *guilt*. This fact alone, however, cannot put the hypothesis of his *innocence* beyond reasonable doubt. Judgments regarding Willingham's guilt or innocence will necessarily be more subjective and fallible than current scientific judgments of the scientific evidence brought against him.

The local fire chief in Corsicana, Texas (the scene of the crime), has written a spirited letter to the Commission Coordinator of the Texas Forensic Science Commission defending the hypothesis of Willingham's guilt on several grounds. These grounds include not only scientific matters, but also circumstances such as apparent inconsistencies in Willingham's statements over time (McMullan 2009). However we judge such evidence, the fire chief's letter expresses an investigative opinion, rather than a scientific opinion. An editorial in *Crime Lab Report* attempts to defend the original fire investigators in the Willingham case by saying, "It is a mistake, however, to prematurely assume that the investigators' conclusions were based entirely on physical evidence" (*Crime Lab Report* 2009). Such mixing of scientific and investigative opinions is inappropriate (OIG 1997).

REFORM PROPOSALS

Many scholars, journalists, activists, and others have recognized the need to improve forensic science. The three leading proposals for reform are probably independence, masking, and oversight.

Paul Giannelli is a leading figure who has called for independence. In an important article on forensics, he says that crime labs "should be transferred from police control to the control of medical examiner [ME] offices" (1997, 470). Admirably, Giannelli notes that although his proposal "is a substantial step in the right direction," it "is not a panacea" (478).

Krane et al. (2008) call for "sequential unmasking," which requires "sequencing the laboratory workflow such that evidentiary samples are interpreted, and the interpretation is fully documented, before reference samples are compared" (Krane et al. 2008). In other words, examiners are exposed to potentially biasing information only after making decisions that might be biased by such information. Risinger et al. (2002), who support the same general idea, appeal to a large empirical literature in psychology. The point may be best illustrated, however, by an important study of Dror and Charlton (2006), in which the authors had experienced fingerprint examiners analyze evidence from cases they had decided in the past. The subjects did not know they were looking at their own earlier cases. In one half of the cases they replaced the original case information with information suggesting a conclusion opposite to the original judgment. In the other half, no such contextual information was supplied. The examiners of their study reversed themselves in 6 of 48 cases. Two of the six reversals were from the 24 cases in which no biasing information had been given.

Peter Neufeld and Barry Scheck founded the Innocence Project, which has participated in over 200 DNA exonerations of persons wrongly convicted. They are important figures in any discussion of how to improve forensic science. Neufeld has argued, "Government oversight and the creation of independent academic centers to validate technologies and techniques, encourage best practices, and enforce appropriately cautious standards for the interpretation of data could dramatically enhance the reliability of forensic science and engender greater public confidence in the outcome" (2005, S113). Neufeld's plea for more scientific research is proper, I believe, but beyond the scope of this chapter. His call for oversight is representative of the "repeated calls" for "oversight" noted in a *Science* editorial (Kennedy 2003, 1625).

Students of public choice will recognize an important problem with "oversight." *Quis custodiet ipsos custodes?* Who will guard the guardians themselves? I have attempted to address this question by proposing "competitive self regulation," a suite of reforms that would institute checks and balances in forensic science (Koppl 2005). Some evidence (Pyrek 2007, 480–487) suggests my proposals may be gaining ground. As I noted earlier, structural redundancy is the key to my proposal. I favor greater attention to the role of social and institutional structures in influencing the reliability of forensic examinations.

REDUNDANCY IS COST REDUCING

Some general considerations suggest that a well-designed system of structural redundancy would lower the costs of forensic testing (Koppl 2005, 274–275). In the system I have proposed, redundant testing would occur in only a fraction of cases. In the current system, each lab's scale of operation is determined by the size of the jurisdiction it serves. Competitive self-regulation would exploit economies of scale and scope. Finally, the direct and indirect costs of injustice are likely to exceed any costs of redundant testing under competitive self-regulation.

Two points in this connection deserve emphasis. First, competitive self-regulation would require little or no increase in the number and size of crime labs in the system. In the current system, we have, essentially, one lab per jurisdiction.[3] Under competitive self-regulation, a given jurisdiction might be served by, say, six separate crime labs. Each of these labs, however, might serve six separate jurisdictions. Thus, given that redundant tests would occur in only a fraction of cases, we can introduce the external epistemic control of redundant testing with little or no increase in the physical plant and personnel required to perform forensic tests.

Second, privatization of competing crime labs would give suppliers an incentive to discover the cost-minimizing scale and scope of operation. Should traditional serology be provided by the same lab that performs DNA tests, or should these functions be separated? Should a DNA lab perform one test per day or 200? Such questions can be answered correctly only through the discovery process of the market.[4] Today, the scale of operations is determined by the coincidental matter of the population size and crime rate of a given jurisdiction. The boundaries of political jurisdictions were determined by many considerations having nothing to do with the optimal scale of operation for a modern crime lab. Similarly, the scope of operation of a crime lab is decided by bureaucratic and political decisions unconnected to the economics of forensic science services.

Far from *adding* to the costs of forensic science services, competitive self-regulation in forensics would *reduce* the cost of forensic science services. Further research is required to find a good set of detailed design features for competitive self- regulation. My co-authors and I have developed an experimental research program aimed at hammering out such particulars (Koppl 2006: Koppl, Kurzban, and Kobilinsky 2007).[5] In the meantime, however, it is possible to formulate a reasonable estimate of the costs and benefits of redundant fingerprint examinations. I will estimate the costs of triplicate examination of fingerprint evidence in felony cases in the United States.

WHAT I PROPOSE

For forensic science in general, I support random, independent, multiple examinations. This study examines a different proposal regarding only fingerprint evidence. I propose a regime in which we will have triplicate examination of fingerprint evidence in all felony cases going to trial in the United States. My proposal requires redundant testing only in felony cases that actually go to trial. Two features of my proposal distinguish it sharply from the current ACE-V methodology of fingerprint examination, namely, masking and the separation of preparing and comparing. I discuss them now.

The benefits of redundant examinations depend on redundant tests being truly independent. Under the current "ACE-V methodology" of fingerprint examination, verifications are not independent. As we have seen, it is expected that an "independent" verification may be performed even though the verifying examiner works with the initial examiner and knows what conclusion was previously reached. Indeed, the fact that "verification" is required only for identifications ensures that the verifying examiner knows what analysis his or her colleague prefers. Haber and Haber say that "if the first examiner has made an identification which is erroneous, the second examiner is likely to ratify the error, rather than discover it" (2004, 349). Thus, the regime I imagine requires a mechanism to ensure independent evaluations.

The mechanism I propose would separate the preparation of a print from its analysis in all cases, whether going to trial or not. To avoid an unconscious bias toward identification, rather than exclusion, it would be necessary that all comparisons, not just those for cases going to trial, be made by persons who did not prepare the materials for comparison. Information hiding, what Risinger et al. (2002) call "masking," would also be necessary. Case information would be "masked" or "hidden" from the examiners doing comparisons to avoid the creation of both conscious and unconscious bias. Examiners would not know whether they were making comparisons in anticipation of a felony trial; nor would they know how many (zero, one, or two) other examinations of the same evidence were being made.

What Does "The Error Rate" Mean?

Throughout this study, I speak of "the error rate." In reality, of course there are different sorts of errors. The examiner may declare an "individualization," an "exclusion," or that no judgment can be made. There are thus six types of errors to be made. One might declare an individualization when the truth is exclusion, an individualization when the truth is that no judgment can be made, an exclusion when the truth is individualization, and so on. For this chapter, however, we need only worry about "false positives" and "false negatives." A false positive occurs when an examiner declares an individualization when the truth is either exclusion or that no judgment can be made. A false negative occurs when an examiner declares either exclusion or that no judgment can be made when the truth is individualization.

Some Preliminary Assumptions

My estimate will use data for 2002. At the time this chapter was accepted for publication in this volume, I was not aware of and did not have access to a complete data set for later years. In particular, I rely in part on the "Census of Publicly Funded Forensic Crime Laboratories, 2002" (Peterson and Hickman 2005), which is a vital source for costing forensic science services under their current organization and seems to have been the most recent such census at the time I wrote this chapter.

I make the plausible assumption that the majority opinion prevails in each case. In other words, I assume that the trier of fact (be it judge or jury) will believe that the latent and known print come from the same source if two or three experts say so; otherwise the trier of fact will believe they come from distinct sources. This assumption seems sure to be approximately correct, and some such assumption is necessary to make numerical calculations.

Triplicate testing would reduce the costs of cases going to trial because it would sometimes quickly exonerate persons whose trials would otherwise be

62   ROGER G. KOPPL

longer. Indeed, if prosecutors were obliged to conduct two redundant fingerprint examinations (for a total of three tests overall) in each case coming to trial, then conducting the redundant tests would be an early step on the way to trial and it is likely that when such redundant tests exonerated the suspect, no trial would be held and nearly all the costs of trial would be saved. In order to construct a conservative cost estimate, however, I ignore the cost savings that would come through such a channel.

I noted earlier that my proposal requires masking and the separation of preparing and comparing. This mechanism would involve costs and benefits. The costs would seem to exist in two areas. First, there might be some increase in the time spent on clerical matters, for example, to track a longer chain of custody. Second, in some fraction of cases there may be shipping costs required to deliver prepared materials to geographically distant fingerprint examiners. On the other hand, the increased division of labor implied by masking would improve efficiency in two ways. First, by allowing specialization between those preparing and those comparing prints, masking would encourage increased skill levels in each area, thereby reducing the time required for each separate task (Smith 1981, vol. 1, 17–18). Second, this same specialization would eliminate the time spent switching from preparing to comparing and back again (Smith 1981, vol. 1, 18–19). Smith says that "the advantage which is gained by saving the time commonly lost in passing from one sort of work to another, is much greater than we should at first view be apt to imagine it." He says, "A man commonly saunters a little in turning his hand from one sort of employment to another. When he first begins the new work he is seldom very keen and hearty; his mind, as they say, does not go to it, and for some time he rather trifles than applies to good purpose" (1981, vol. 1, 18–19). Modern experiments support the view that task switching has a time cost (Rubinstein, Meyer, and Evans 2001, especially 766–769).

On net, this mechanism would probably be costless or nearly so. The work of preparing fingerprint evidence for comparison must be done. The work of comparison must be done. No cost attaches to separating them as long as there are multiple examiners. As I have indicated, there are only some minor clerical costs and occasional shipping costs. These mild costs would probably be at least fully offset by the efficiencies of an improved division of labor. For the current chapter, I set the net costs of this change at zero, which seems a conservative value.

What Is the Correct Error Rate?

The error rate in forensics is a fundamental assumption of the analysis. Cole (2005) and Haber and Haber (2004) have thoroughly reviewed the topic. As both Cole (2005, 1033) and Haber and Haber (2004, 358) note, we are not now in a position to reliably calculate an error rate for fingerprint analysis. Haber and Haber call for research on error rates in fingerprint examination, noting "that no estimate of the magnitude of the error rate can be determined" (2004, 358). Similarly, Cole says, "The existing data are inadequate to calculate a meaningful error rate for forensic fingerprint identification" (2005, 1033).

Cole (2005) reviewed the CTS tests studied by Peterson and Markham (1995a, 1995b), but for the period up to and including 2003. For this period, Cole reports, the overall rate of "false positive" identifications is 0.8 percent (2005, 1073). Cole selects this value as "only a lower bound" for the error rate in the field (2005, 1034). Each year's test is presented as evidence from one case, with prints coming both from suspects and from others who are not suspects. Cole's 0.8 percent rate is calculated as the number of false positives per comparison. It is not clear why this is a better measure than the number of examiners who make a false positive, which would measure the number of false positives per case. Cole reports that rate, the "examiner false positive rate," to be 5.5 percent.

Haber and Haber give strong reasons to infer a higher rate from the CTS proficiency exams. The tests were not blind, thus they were "taken with full knowledge that the fingerprint examiners and the lab as a whole are being tested." Haber and Haber note that when tests are not blind, "test score results are inflated" because "[t]est takers are more attentive, follow instructions better, and check and review their work more carefully" (2004, 346). They argue that if a "consensus error rate" of 2 percent emerges from the collaboration of two examiners, then the "individual error rate" would have to be 14 percent, calculated as the square root of 0.02. And if three persons collaborated on each test, then a consensus error rate of 2 percent would imply individual error rates of 27 percent. (Cole 2005, 1031 mislabels these inferred individual error rates as "The Habers' 'consensus error rate.'")

It is not clear how to evaluate claims of Haber and Haber on "consensus error rates." Elsewhere in the same article, as we saw earlier, Haber and Haber point out that the "verifications" of daily practice are flawed because errors in verification will be correlated with initial errors in identification. There is some tension, though no strict contradiction, between assuming independent errors in proficiency tests, but correlated errors in daily practice. Haber and Haber are probably right, however, to claim that the CTS error rates underestimate true error rates.

Neither Haber and Haber nor Cole had access at the times of their writing to the important study of Dror and Charlton (2006) discussed earlier. Dror and Charlton report that in 2 out of 24 cases in which they provided no particular contextual information, experienced fingerprint examiners nevertheless reversed their earlier decisions. One examiner changed from individualization to exclusion, another changed from exclusion to individualization. (Dror and Charlton correctly note that the absence of contextual information from the experimenters does not mean these cases are somehow "context free.") Thus, in 8.33 percent of the cases without contextual information, experienced fingerprint examiners nevertheless reversed earlier decisions. As far as I know, this figure is our only direct measure of an error rate in fingerprint examination in which two important conditions held: (1) the parties were being tested, but did not know it, and (2) they were not willfully misled by potentially deceptive contextual information. In one case, the examiner switched from "individualization" to "exclusion" and in the other, a different examiner switched from "exclusion" to "individualization." Thus, these data suggest that the rate of false positives and the rate of false negatives are equal. Unfortunately, the sample size is very small for the Dror and Charlton study involving only six experts. These were skilled and experienced experts who were willing to be given blind tests at some unknown point in the future. Thus, we may wonder whether their error rates are not low in comparison to the global average. Moreover, the absence of biasing contextual information for the second examination contrasts with the daily practice of fingerprint examination, in which domain-irrelevant information is regularly supplied. Nevertheless, the small sample size makes it impossible to draw from the study any precise estimate of global error rates in practice.

It is difficult to judge whether the rate of false positives in fingerprint identification is 0.8 percent, 2 percent, 8.33 percent, or something higher still. For the moment, I adopt 0.8 percent as a highly conservative benchmark. Later, I will note how different assumed error rates influence my calculations. As we shall see, even assuming Cole's highly conservative value of 0.8 percent, my proposal for redundant examinations would be cost saving.

Presumably, the caution of examiners would make false positives rarer than false negatives. In seeming confirmation of this logic, proficiency tests seem to show that false negatives are more common than false positives. Simon Cole, however, has noted a reason to doubt the significance of this reported difference in the rates of false positives and false negatives. "Test-takers who are far more concerned about false positives than false negatives can in effect, 'game' the test by reporting with extreme conservatism" (Cole 2005, 1031). Moreover, the important FBI fingerprint expert Bruce Budowle and his coauthors report, "a latent print examiner tends to approach the comparison to 'make an ident,' rather than to attempt to exclude." (Budowle et al. 2006).

The quoted statement from Budowle et al. (2006) is surprising. The authors do not seem to recognize that it may seem to express a strong and inappropriate bias. Nor was the article just one, perhaps aberrant, opinion that happened to get in print. The opening paragraph says, "In response to the misidentification of a latent print, senior management of the FBI Laboratory tasked a three-member review committee to evaluate the fundamental basis for the science of friction ridge skin impression pattern analysis and to recommend research to be considered to test, where necessary, the hypotheses that form the bases of this discipline." Thus, the statement must be viewed as authoritative. I do not know how to square the statement with that of Harmon and Budowle, who say, "There is as much incentive in obtaining a true result when it is an exclusion as there is in achieving a match" (2006, 607).

The higher the assumed rate of false negatives, the greater would be cost saving of triplicate examinations, because there would be more false exonerations created by independent triplicate fingerprint examinations. If one imagines a relatively high rate of false negatives, the implied false exonerations would seem to raise an obvious objection to my proposal. They do so, however, only if we neglect the fact that false convictions often correspond to implicit false exonerations. If we mistakenly convict Jim, John goes free. As long as the number of direct false exonerations created by independent triplicate examinations is less than the number of implicit false exonerations created by false convictions, my proposal will reduce the number of both false convictions and false exonerations.

Several other considerations suggest that false exonerations may not be a strong objection to my proposal. The cost savings identified by my calculations might be used to find the guilty parties who would otherwise go free; the exonerations would probably increase the likelihood of catching and convicting the truly guilty parties; and, in Blackstone's famous formula, "presumptive evidence of felony should be admitted cautiously: for the law holds, that it is better that ten guilty persons escape, than that one innocent suffer" (1765–1769, Book IV, chapter 27).

In the interest of making my initial calculation as financially conservative as possible, I assume that the rate of false negatives is equal to the rate of false positives at 0.8 percent. Later, I will show that my proposal improves justice (while reducing costs) even when we assume an 8 percent rate of false negatives.

What Would Each Comparison Cost?

The cost of each new comparison, using 2002 values, is $52.50. This value comes from multiplying the hourly cost of fingerprint examiners by the time required to conduct a fingerprint comparison. (In the case of fingerprint examination, unlike some other forensic disciplines, labor seems to be the only substantial variable cost.)

According to Peterson and Hickman (2005, 9), the estimated cost of hiring an additional 300 full-time fingerprint examiners in publicly funded forensic crime laboratories "exceeds $10.4 million." Dividing 10.4 million by 300 yields $34,667 per fingerprint examiner. Because the estimated cost reported "exceeds" the stated value of $10.4 million, we may round the figure up to $35,000 per examiner. If an examiner costing $35,000 per year works 2,000 hours per year, which is 40 hours per week for 50 weeks, then the examiner costs $17.50 per hour. (Peterson and Hickman 2005 report the figure of $10.4 million as the "cost," not a salary.)

California Investigation Services offers fingerprint examinations. According to their Web page, "An average case can involve approximately 3 to 4 hours of processing and/or examination time." If many cases involve 3 to 4 hours of processing *and* examination time, then it would be conservative to assume that the average time for comparison alone is three hours.

Multiplying $17.50 per hour by 3 hours, yields a cost of $52.50 per comparison.

An Estimate of the Savings from Redundancy

Durose and Langan (2004, 1) report that there were 1,114,217 felony convictions in the United States in 2002. According to the Bureau of Justice Statistics (BJS 2005, Table A9, 31) in 2002, prosecutors enjoyed a 91 percent success rate in felony cases ending in U.S. district courts. Thus, there were approximately 1,211,105 felony prosecutions in 2002, of which 1,111,217 ended in conviction.

Peterson and Markham estimate that fingerprints appear "in about 7 percent of the felony case filings" each year (1995b, 1028). Thus, there were approximately 84,778 felony prosecutions in 2002 involving fingerprint evidence, of which 77,147 resulted in conviction. Given our assumption of a 0.8 percent error rate in fingerprint identification, in 678 of these cases the fingerprint evidence is a false positive and likely to produce a false conviction.

Consider one of these 678 false positives going to trial. The prosecutor would request the fingerprint evidence be sent to two new examiners, each of whom, we have assumed, has a 0.8 percent chance of repeating the error of false identification and a 99.2 percent chance of correctly declining to declare a match. Given our assumption of independence, based on our proposed mechanism of separating comparing from preparing, the probability of two examinations failing to find a match in such a case is the square of .992, which is just over 0.98. Thus, triplicate testing will "save" over 98 per cent of the false felony convictions attributable to errors in fingerprint identification. In other words, of the 678 false convictions implied by our assumed 0.8 percent error rate, 667 would be prevented by triplicate comparison of fingerprint evidence.

To thus prevent 667 false convictions, it was necessary to perform an additional 169,556 fingerprint comparisons, 2 for each of the 84,778 felony prosecutions in 2002 involving fingerprint evidence. At $52.50 per comparison, the total cost comes to $8,901,690, which is $105 per case or almost $13,338 per "save."

According to the Bureau of Prisons (2002) "The fee to cover the average cost of incarceration for Federal inmates is $21,601." in 2002 (Bureau of Prisons 2002). According to *Federal Criminal Case Processing, 2002* (BJS 2005, 33, table A14), in 2002 the "mean number of months of imprisonment imposed" on convicted felons was 58.4, which is over four years and ten months.[6] It would be an exaggeration to count the cost of 58.4 months of incarceration as $105,124.87, because these costs are spread out over time. Employing a 5 percent annual discount rate, the present value of the costs of incarcerating one prisoner, at 2002 values, is $91,358. (I assume annual compounding, and an annual interest rate of 5 percent for the first four years. For the final 10 months and 12 days I prorate the annual fee and the annual discount rate.)

Triplicate fingerprint comparisons would produce an average savings of $91,358 for each person who escapes conviction because redundant fingerprint exams. Until now we have focused on the 667 persons saved from false conviction. To be complete in our accounting, however, we should recognize that some persons will enjoy a false exoneration from the system. Given our assumptions, a false exoneration would occur only when both of the redundant tests required for felony prosecutions produce a false negative. With our assumed 0.8 percent error rate, that would happen in 0.0064 percent of the cases. (This number follows from $0.008 \times 0.008 = 0.000064$.) This value implies five false exonerations in 2002. (There would be 84,777 cases requiring two redundant tests. In 0.8 percent of them the damning fingerprint evidence is false. Thus, in 99.2 percent or 84,099 of the cases the damning evidence is true. Multiplying these 84,099 cases by the 0.0064 percent chance of two false negatives gives us 5.38 false exonerations.) Thus, redundant fingerprint comparisons would produce savings of $61,465,498.69 *annually*. ([667.42 "saves" + 5.38 false exonerations] × $91,358 costs of incarceration = $61,465,498.69 reduction in costs of incarceration.) From this figure we must deduct the $8,901,690 required to fund triplicate fingerprint comparisons. The net savings from triplicate fingerprint examinations is thus $52,563,808.69 per year, which is $620.02 per felony prosecution and $78,757.21 per person saved from false conviction.

Recall that false convictions may often produce implicit false exonerations. The proposed system of redundant fingerprint examination would eliminate up to 667 such implicit exonerations, but create 5 new false exonerations. It seems likely that there would be a net reduction in the number of false exonerations. There will be, in fact, as long as more than 5 of the 667 false convictions avoided, that is, 0.75 percent, would result in the true criminal being convicted.

What If the Rate of False Negatives Is Higher?

My proposal improves justice (while reducing costs) even when we assume a much higher rate of false negatives. If we assume pessimistically that false negatives are 10 times more likely than the assumed 0.8 percent rate of false positives, and *no* avoided false convictions result in the true criminal being convicted, we would let 538 guilty persons escape to avoid 667 innocents suffering, thus placing us well within Blackstone's 10:1 formula. If avoided false convictions could result in the true criminal being convicted, the net reduction in the number of false exonerations could be as high as 129 per year.

Robustness of the Calculation

The precise calculations just completed are subject to error. But the conclusion that triplicate comparisons would be cost saving is robust. If the error rate in fingerprint examinations is 2 percent, for example, then the number of false felony convictions in 2002 attributable to errors of fingerprint

examinations would have been nearly 1,700. Redundant fingerprint examinations would have eliminated 96 percent of them, but created 33 false
exonerations. The money savings from reduced costs of incarceration would
be almost $152 million and the net savings in the costs of administering the
criminal justice system would have been almost $143 million. Cole's "exam-
iner false positive rate" of 5.5 percent implies 4,663 false convictions.
Redundancy would eliminate 89 percent of them for a net saving of $394
million in 2002 alone.

One way to test for robustness is to ask what cost of an additional comparison is so high as to just offset the savings from reduced incarcerations.
Call this maximal value c. This value is given by the equation

$$c = p(1 - p)\$45,800.5$$

where p is the error rate.[7] A graph of this equation is shown in figure 4.1.

For our benchmark error rate of 0.8 percent, $c = \$363$. Recall that the
estimated annual cost of a fingerprint examiner is $35,000. Peterson and
Hickman (2005) report the "median expectation" of "[c]rime laboratory
directors in 2002" was 264 examinations per examiner per year, but that the
median number of requests actually processed was 284 (9). Dividing our
benchmark salary by these values yields a cost per examination between
$122.38 and $132.58. Thus, even the redundant examinations were as costly
as the preparing and comparing of fingerprint evidence under the current
system, triplication would still lower costs in the criminal justice system.
Even when we accept Cole's extremely conservative value for the likely error
rate and imagine that additional comparisons would cost as much as comparing *and* preparing cost under the current system, we still conclude that triplication would reduce the costs of administering the criminal justice
system.

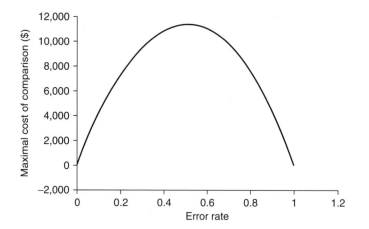

Figure 4.1   Locus of Breakeven Values.

Discussion

My proposal for redundant testing would produce a system of checks and balances in forensic science. It may seem paradoxical that a criminal justice system with built-in redundancy of forensic testing would be cheaper to run than a system lacking such structural redundancy. After all, it costs something to run redundant tests. False convictions have a cost as well, however, and in a properly designed system, this latter cost is so greatly reduced by redundant testing that the overall cost of administering the criminal justice system falls. Forensic science is a bargain for the criminal justice system, and we need more of it.

I began by noting that forensic scientists are not, in fact, infallible wizards. They are good people, I said, not good wizards. Recognizing the common sense reality of human error helps us design mechanisms that *both* reduce error rates in forensic testing *and* reduce the costs of administering the criminal justice system. Justice and economy alike are served by replacing romance with realism in our view of forensic science.

Notes

For helpful comments I thank Marina Bianchi, Sam Bostaph, Simon Cole, Chris Coyne, Randy Holcombe, Peter Leeson, Edward López, David Levy, Sandra Peart, Michael Saks, and Alexander Tabarrok.

1. In a valuable article on false convictions, Paul Craig Roberts correctly says, "DNA evidence has been especially productive of success in overturning wrongful convictions based on junk science, false testimony, and mistaken identity" (2003, 568). The debacle in Houston shows, however, that DNA is not necessarily a magic truth bullet. The proper organization of forensics is necessary for even the most scientifically grounded techniques to be reliable. The unfortunate term "junk science" may tend to divert our attention from the importance of organizational issues.

2. Birks made an "identification" of a latent related to offense report #200300010904. An FDLE analyst brought into the investigation "concluded that the latent print 'was not identified with the fingerprint standards' of the suspect" and indicated that "the print was of sufficient quality for entry into the AFIS system" (Seminole County 2007, 10). Thus, it seems to have been a useable print matched to a suspect who should have been excluded. Birks made an "identification" of a latent related to offense report #200600011738. This case might belong in the one category or the other. The FDLE analyst "compared [the latent] to that of the suspects 'without effecting an identification'" (Seminole County 2007, 10). The latent in this case was *not* declared to be "of no value." Thus, it seems reasonable to conjecture that the suspect to whom the latent was matched should have been excluded. The administrative review, however, is not clear on this point.

3. The situation here is similar to that examined by Butos and McQuade (2006), who object to government funding of science in part on the grounds that, because such funding is concentrated in a few hands, it "provides the potential for those who want to control the direction (or, in the extreme, even the content) of science to have systemic effects" (199). The monopsony position of the police with respect to forensic science services produces a similar dangerous potential for influence.

4. I agree with Bruce Benson's important remark, "turning the entrepreneurial discovery process loose on crime control may have real advantages" (1998, 341). Although Benson's path-breaking work makes a strong case for moving toward a greater reliance on competitive mechanisms, it was never meant to be an exercise in mechanism design. David Hume's warning that it "can never be the part of a wise magistrate" to "try experiments [in government] merely upon the credit of supposed argument and philosophy," suggests the value of the techniques of economic systems design as an aid to mechanism design in this as in other areas.

5. My research program in the economics of forensic science illustrates Alan Walstad's call for more work "using economic concepts to illuminate the conduct of scientific inquiry itself" (2002, p. 5). There are several parallels between Walstad's analysis and Butos and Koppl (2003), including an appreciation of the importance of invisible-hand explanations in the study of science.

6. This value is less precise than I would wish. A note to the table says, "Calculations exclude offenders given life or death sentences, and old law offenders given mixed sentences of prison plus probation. For new law offenders given prison-community split sentences, only the prison portion of the sentence is included in calculations" (BSJ 2005, p. 33). This ambiguous language also raises the prospect that the calculation does not set a value of zero to persons convicted but sentenced only to parole or otherwise not incarcerated. This seems to be the case for a later BJS publication that reports a number incarcerated equal to about 80 percent of the total of those incarcerated, on probation, and only fined (BJS 2006, 74). The 80 percent value is exaggerated because of mixed sentences involving both probation and incarceration. Even so, the 80 percent value would imply only relatively minor adjustments to my calculations. The present value of incarceration would fall by about $17,000 if the costs of administering probation were ignored. This adjustment would not alter the substance of my conclusions.

    BJS (2007) seems to suggest the correct average is only about two years. This figure would imply that my proposal would be cost saving if the error rate is above about 0.24 per cent, which is well below Cole's benchmark of 0.8 per cent.

7. The costs of redundant testing are $84{,}777 * 2 * c$, which must equal the (financial) benefits. These benefits are the product of the per person costs of incarceration, $91,601, multiplied by the number of persons correctly and incorrectly exonerated, which is $(\$91{,}601) * (84{,}777 * p * (1 - p)^2 + 84{,}777 * (1 - p) * p^2)$
    Setting them equal yields $(84{,}777 * \$91{,}601) * (p * (1 - p)^2 + (1 - p) * p^2) = 84{,}777 * 2 * c$. Thus, $\$91{,}601 * p * (1 - p) = 2 * c$, from which the given equation follows directly. Assuming different rates of false negatives and false positives would require a slightly more complicated formula.

CHAPTER 5

JUDICIAL CHECKS ON CORRUPTION

Adriana S. Cordis

INTRODUCTION

The judiciary performs a variety of functions in most systems of government. Generally, one of these functions is to ensure that the executive and legislative branches exercise their power in a manner sanctioned by law, that is, the judiciary checks executive and legislative power.[1] Hayek (1960) identifies two ways in which the judiciary provide checks and balances: judicial independence and constitutional review. Judicial independence is important because judges may not decide cases on the merits if they are under the influence of the legislative or executive branches. Constitutional review is important because legislators may enact laws and the executive branch may implement policies that benefit themselves and/or their associates. The judiciary places limits on such behavior by reviewing whether it is constitutional.

In this chapter, I investigate whether judicial independence and constitutional rigidity deter a widely studied type of abuse of power by government officials: corruption in office. Although there is extensive empirical evidence on the economic, cultural, political, and historical determinants of corruption,[2] few studies on the relation between corruption and characteristics of the judiciary are available.[3] There is, however, a general view that corruption is more likely to flourish under circumstances in which the judiciary responds to political pressure. Susan Rose-Ackerman (1999, 151) notes, for example, that "a politically dependent judiciary can facilitate high-level corruption, undermine reforms, and override legal norms." An independent judiciary may be particularly important for cases in which the government is itself a litigant or in which one of the litigants is politically connected. This line of reasoning suggests the following testable hypothesis: *states or countries in which judges are endowed with greater independence should experience lower levels of corruption*.

In a similar vein, an influential study by La Porta et al. (2004) suggests that the importance of judicial independence in guaranteeing economic and political freedom is linked to the effectiveness of constitutional review. Judges can typically declare a policy invalid if it conflicts with the legal code or with the constitution itself.[4] However, the impact of judicial review is likely to depend on the rigidity of the constitution. In the United States, for instance, there are substantial differences in constitutional rigidity from one state to another. If the legislature of a state can easily alter the state constitution as it enacts new laws, then it has much wider latitude than the legislature of a state with a rigid constitution. State constitutions are altered with a frequency that suggests that rigidity is a salient issue. From 1996 to 2005, state legislatures proposed 974 constitutional amendments, of which 78 percent were adopted. In addition, there were 156 constitutional changes proposed via popular initiatives, of which 44 percent were successful. For cases in which the judiciary exercises a reliable check on the legislative branch, the use of corrupt practices to pass a law becomes very costly. This line of reasoning suggests a second testable hypothesis: *states or countries in which constitutions are more rigid, that is, in which it is more costly to propose amendments from a legislative perspective, should experience lower levels of corruption.*

I test these hypotheses using United States and international data. First, I examine the impact of judicial independence and constitutional rigidity on corruption in the United States using state-level data on corruption convictions for the years 1996–2005. For reasons discussed below, I incorporate judicial independence by measuring judicial remuneration, method of selection, and term length. To assess constitutional rigidity, I use the legislative majority needed to propose constitutional amendments, the provision (or lack thereof) for constitutional conventions, and the provision (or lack thereof) for popular initiatives to amend the constitution.

To see whether my findings using state-level data generalize to other settings, I extend my analysis of the determinants of corruption to the country level. Since country-level data on corruption convictions are not available, I employ several survey-based measures. The first is constructed and published by Transparency International. The second is a new index put together by researchers at the World Bank (Kaufmann, Kraay, and Mastruzzi 2007). The third is constructed by the Political Risk Survey Group. My measures of judicial independence and constitutional review are drawn from a variety of sources. I obtain indices of judicial independence from the Economic Freedom of the World Report (Gwartney, Lawson, and Easterly 2007), from the Political Constraint Index Dataset, and from the La Porta et al. (2004) study discussed above. The constitutional review index is taken from La Porta et al. (2004) as well. Since this index is available only for 1995, and the availability of the other indices varies from year to year, I conduct my analysis on cross sections of between 37 to 165 countries for various years between 1995 and 2005.

EVIDENCE FROM THE UNITED STATES[5]

There is no standard methodology for measuring corruption. Researchers typically rely on either survey-based measures or on criminal convictions data. Neither approach is without drawbacks. Survey-based measures are subjective: we don't know whether the participants are biased, or whether they are sufficiently knowledgeable to express an informed opinion. On the other hand, the number of convictions for corruption is not the same as the true number of corrupt officials: only a fraction of corrupt officials are exposed, tried, and convicted. Most studies that use convictions-based measures of corruption ignore this fact. Moreover, they fail to take into account the discrete nature of the convictions data.

In a previous study (Cordis 2009), I develop an econometric methodology that recognizes the distinction between the observed number of convictions for corruption and the unobserved number of corrupt officials. I show in particular that by estimating a negative binomial regression model that includes variables that pick up differences in law enforcement effectiveness across states, it is possible to draw valid inferences about the underlying level of corruption. Although I replicate many elements of the approach here, I do not estimate negative binomial regressions. Instead, I follow most of the literature by using linear regression methods to investigate the relation between judicial checks and corruption. Specifically, I use a weighted-least-squares (WLS) approach to examine the impact of judicial independence and constitutional rigidity on corruption convictions. The analysis is conducted using data for 49 states for the years 1996–2005.[6] The dependent variable is the total number of public officials (local, state, and federal) convicted in federal court of a corruption-related crime over the 10-year sample period divided by the number of full-time state government employees.[7]

THE MODEL

To examine the effect of judicial independence and constitutional rigidity on corruption convictions, I estimate the following regression model:

(1) $\ln(Corruption\ Convictions/Full\ Time\ Government\ Employees)_i$
$= \beta_0 + \beta_1\ln(Judge\ Pay/Gross\ State\ Product\ Per\ Capita)_i$
$+ \beta_2(Merit\ Plan\ Selection)_i + \beta_3(Other\ Selection)_i + \beta_4(Term\ Length)_i$
$+ \beta_5(Legislative\ Amendments)_i + \beta_6(Legislative\ Amendments\ Squared)_i$
$+ \beta_7(Initiative)_i + \beta_8(Convention)_i + \beta_9\ln(FBI\ Agents)_i$
$+ \beta_{10}\ln(Police\ protection)_i + \beta_{11}(Racial\ Fractionalization)_i + \varepsilon_i$

I measure judicial independence using three major indicators that have been identified in the literature: remuneration of judges, method of selection, and term length.[8] Since the U.S. Constitution does not address the organization and structure of the judiciary at the state level, there is significant variation across states in these indicators. I exploit this variation in my empirical analysis.

The remuneration indicator is *Judge Pay/Gross State Product Per Capita*. It pertains to the chief justice of the court of last resort in each state. I expect this indicator to be negatively correlated with the number of corruption convictions per capita. As noted by Susan Rose-Ackerman (1999), the independence of judges is seriously threatened when they are underpaid and they work under conditions much worse than those under which lawyers and their assistants do. Higher pay relative to state norms increases the likelihood that higher quality individuals will become judges, and higher quality individuals are more likely to act independently.

The method of selecting judges is also correlated with judicial independence. In the United States, five distinct procedures are used: partisan election, nonpartisan election, legislative appointment, governor appointment, and an appointment-election hybrid named merit plan selection. There are 6 states in which judges run as members of a political party, 15 states in which the elections are nonpartisan, that is, judges do not reveal their political affiliation,[9] and 7 states in which judges are appointed by the governor or the legislature. In 21 other states judges are selected by merit plan. The methods of judicial selection were stable across states over the period 1996–2005.[10]

The consensus in the literature is that judges selected through partisan elections are the least independent, since these elections require judges to run for office in the same way as politicians. Judges may be forced to solicit campaign contributions from special interest groups, political parties, and lawyers or even possible litigants. Hence, they may feel obliged to be responsive to the wishes of those who contributed to their election. The literature suggests that judges selected through the merit plan procedure are the most independent, that is, insulated from political pressure, as merit selection[11] was proposed both as a means of separating judges from politics and as a way to call attention to professional criteria for selecting judges, such as qualifications, experience, education, training, and age. A number of previous studies, including chapter 3 of this volume, provide evidence pointing to inferior performance under selection by partisan elections.[12] As in Hanssen (2004), I create three dummy variables for *Merit Plan Selection, Other Selection* (legislative appointment, governor appointment, or nonpartisan election), and *Partisan Election Selection*. The *Partisan Election Selection* dummy is used as baseline, which means it is not included in the model. The coefficients on the two other selection variables should be negative if switching to selection procedures that endow judges with greater independence results in less corruption.

The variable *Term Length* measures the length of the initial term (in years) of the chief justice of the states' Supreme Court. Rhode Island is the only state that grants life tenure to judges. Lengthier terms shield judges from political pressure and electoral accountability, and provide the opportunity for human capital accumulation: arbitrary discretion in courts is more likely to be avoided if justices have experience and a sound knowledge of legal rules and precedents. On the basis of these arguments, I expect a negative correlation between *Term Length* and my dependent variable.

My selection of variables to measure constitutional rigidity reflects a number of considerations. There are three methods by which state constitutions are revised or amended: legislative action, popular initiatives, and constitutional conventions.[13]

Legislative action refers to constitutional amendments proposed by the legislature, including amendments proposed by a constitutional revision commission. All state legislatures can propose amendments and every state except Delaware requires that constitutional amendments proposed by the legislature be submitted to the voters for final approval or rejection. Historically, this is the principal method for initiating amendments. State legislatures proposed 974 constitutional amendments over the period 1996–2005, accounting for 85.5 percent of the proposed constitutional changes and 90.8 percent of those adopted. The variable *Legislative Amendments* represents the percentage of votes required in the state legislature to propose a constitutional amendment. In states that make it less costly to change the constitution, namely, those which require simple majority as opposed to supermajorities, legislatures are more likely to enact amendments that benefit themselves or special interest groups. I expect a negative relation between the variable *Legislative Amendments*, which is a proxy for constitutional rigidity, and corruption. However, the relation between the percentage of legislative votes required for proposing amendments and constitutional rigidity may be nonlinear since any supermajority vote, such as 60 percent or 67 percent, represents a much higher hurdle than a simple majority vote. There may be a diminishing marginal effect from requiring the approval of more than 60 percent of the legislators. Therefore I include both *Legislative Amendments* and its square in the model to capture nonlinear effects.

The variable *Initiative* is a dummy for the states that provide a constitutional initiative process (18 states in total). Like judicial review, the constitutional initiative process provides a check on the legislature by allowing citizens to overturn policies contrary to their interests. Specifically, it allows citizens to propose amendments to the constitution without the consent of their elected representatives.[14] Therefore I expect a negative sign on the *Initiative* variable.

The variable *Convention* is a dummy for the states that provide for constitutional conventions (40 states in total). The constitutional convention is a method of drafting a new constitution or revising an existing one. No convention was assembled during my sample period. The last convention convened in 1986, in Rhode Island. Since states that provide for conventions have less rigid constitutions, ceteris paribus, I expect a positive sign on this variable.

Because of the small number of observations, I am reluctant to include many control variables. One variable that the literature has consistently shown to influence corruption is *Racial Fractionalization*.[15] Following Glaeser and Saks (2004), I compute an index of racial fractionalization using the formula: $1 - \Sigma s_i^2$, where s_i is the racial share (white, black, Asian, Hispanic, other). The literature suggests that ethnic or racial heterogeneity increases corruption or reduces people's desire to oppose corruption, so I expect the sign of the coefficient on the *Racial Fractionalization* measure to be positive.

I also include two variables that are designed to capture the variation in law enforcement effectiveness across states: the number of *FBI agents* in

place and state and local government expenditures on *police protection.*
These variables control for the probability that crimes will be detected. A
larger number of FBI agents per capita or higher per capita expenditures on
police protection are expected to increase the efficiency of uncovering
criminal behavior and deterring corrupt activities; thus one might hypoth-
esize that the sign for the coefficients on both these variables should be
negative.[16]

DATA

Data on corruption convictions were obtained from the Department of
Justice's "Report to Congress on the Activities and Operations of the
Public Integrity Section." I combine the information published in the
1999–2005 reports to determine the total number of convictions by state
for a 10-year period, 1996–2005. The crimes investigated and reported by
the Public Integrity Section include vote fraud, campaign-finance violations, political shakedowns, misconduct proscribed by one of the federal
conflict of interest statutes, and obstruction of justice. Table 5.1 shows the
states with most and least corruption convictions per state government
employee over the sample period. Summary statistics for all variables are
reported in table 5.2.

The econometric analysis focuses on the existence of significant relations
between corruption and (1) the variables that measure the degree of judicial
independence or (2) the measures of constitutional rigidity. The dependent
variable is total corruption convictions divided by the number of full-time
state government employees during the same period. I use total convictions
instead of estimating a pooled regression for two reasons. First, there is

Table 5.1   States with Most and Least Convictions Per State Government Employee

Most Convictions		Fewest Convictions	
State	Convictions per 1000 Government Employees	State	Convictions per 1000 Government Employees
North Dakota	1.390	Vermont	0.327
Louisiana	1.186	South Carolina	0.323
Hawaii	1.181	Colorado	0.301
Mississippi	1.096	Utah	0.292
Florida	0.979	Minnesota	0.237
Montana	0.978	Kansas	0.232
Pennsylvania	0.968	New Hampshire	0.221
Kentucky	0.944	Iowa	0.153
Illinois	0.916	Oregon	0.107
Ohio	0.893	Nebraska	0.100

Note: Total corruption convictions over the years 1996–2005 per 1000 full-time government employee.

Table 5.2 Summary Statistics

Variable	Obs.	Mean	Std. Dev.	Min	Max	Source
Ln(Corruption convictions/ 100,000 Full-time Government Employees)	49	3.914	0.589	2.305	4.935	USDOJ & U.S. Census
Ln(Judge Pay/GSP per capita)	49	1.271	0.160	0.952	1.657	NCSC
Merit Plan Selection	49	0.428	0.500	0	1	AJS
Other Selection	49	0.448	0.502	0	1	AJS
Partisan Election Selection	49	0.122	0.331	0	1	AJS
Term Length	49	7.102	6.596	1	30	AJS & BOS
Legislative Amendment	49	0.597	0.073	0.510	0.750	BOS
Initiative	49	0.367	0.487	0	1	BOS
Convention	49	0.816	0.391	0	1	BOS
Racial Fractionalization	49	0.285	0.138	0.055	0.645	U.S. Census
Ln(Police Protection)	49	5.140	0.254	4.529	5.717	U.S. Census
Ln(FBI agents)	49	3.125	0.549	1.722	4.309	USDOJ
Population (in 100,000)	49	57.313	62.779	4.964	341.808	U.S. Census
Northeast Region Dummy	49	0.204	0.407	0	1	U.S. Census
Ln(GSP per capita)	49	10.382	0.171	10.026	10.856	U.S. Census
High School (percent)	49	83.749	4.076	76.057	90.285	U.S. Census
Urban Population (percent)	49	71.625	15.051	38.179	94.443	U.S. Census
Percent 65 or older	49	12.641	1.888	5.283	17.703	U.S. Census
Unemployment Rate	49	4.691	0.868	2.91	7.02	U.S. Census

Note: Except for the dependent variable, data are averaged for the years 1996–2005. USDOJ, United States Department of Justice; NCSC: National Center of State Courts; AJS: American Judicature Society; BOS. The Book of the States.

little time series variation in the variables used to measure judicial independence and constitutional rigidity. Second, my previous study using a negative binomial specification suggests using the logarithm of convictions as the dependent variable (Cordis 2009). Since there are instances in which a state has zero corruption convictions for at least one year in the sample, it is not possible to apply a logarithmic transformation to the annual convictions data.

Since the corruption data cover four regions of the United States (Northeast, Midwest, South, and West) that differ in many important aspects, and especially on the basis of population density, it is possible that the variance of the regression errors differs across regions. Hence, to obtain estimates that are more efficient than those produced by OLS, I estimate WLS regressions using the reciprocals of the estimated standard deviations of the OLS residuals by region as weights. The results confirm that the Northeast region has a substantially lower variance than the other regions (the coefficients for the other regions are not statistically significant in the auxiliary regression used to compute the weights).

ESTIMATION RESULTS

First, consider the estimation results for the judicial independence measures presented in table 5.3. The estimated coefficients for *Merit Selection* and *Other Selection* have the predicted negative signs and are statistically different from zero at the 1 percent significance level. The coefficients on the variables *Judge Pay* and *Term Length* are not significant at standard levels. For the variables that are statistically significant, the marginal effects are substantial. The estimates indicate that replacing the partisan election method of selecting judges with the merit plan method would decrease the convictions rate by roughly 63 percent on average over a 10-year period. Similarly, a change from

Table 5.3   The Effect of Judicial Independence and Constitutional Rigidity on Corruption in the United States

Variables	Dependent Variable Ln(Corruption Convictions/Full-Time Govt. Employees)
	WLS estimates
	Coeff. (z)
Ln(Judge Pay/GSP per capita)	0.296
	(1.06)
Merit Plan Selection	−0.455***
	(−3.40)
Other Selection Procedure	−0.355***
	(−2.68)
Term Length	0.004
	(0.97)
Legislative Amendment	−22.712**
	(−2.46)
Legislative Amendment Squared	18.731**
	(2.45)
Initiative	−0.020
	(−0.25)
Convention	−0.164*
	(−1.90)
Ln(FBI Agents)	0.254***
	(3.26)
Ln(Police Protection)	0.016
	(0.09)
Racial Fractionalization	1.622***
	(4.41)
Constant	9.440***
	(3.23)
Goodness-of-fit chi^2 (37)	110.16
Prob. > chi^2	0.000
Number of Observations	49

Notes: The table presents the results of weighted least squares regression. The model uses as weights the reciprocal of the estimated standard deviations of the OLS residuals, by region. The numbers in parenthesis are the estimated z-statistics. {***, **, *} indicates significant at 1, 5, and 10 percent level, respectively.

a partisan election selection method to nonpartisan election, gubernatorial or legislative appointment, would decrease the convictions rate by approximately 70 percent over a 10-year period, ceteris paribus.

Now consider the results on the constitutional rigidity measures. The coefficients for the variable *Legislative Amendments* and its square are both significant at the 5 percent level. *Legislative Amendment* has a negative sign and its square has a positive sign. To interpret this finding I need to look at the combined effect of these variables on corruption levels. The combined effect implies that changing the required percentage of votes for approval of amendments from a simple majority to a supermajority reduces corruption. On average, the number of corruption convictions is 16 percent lower in states that require a supermajority of 60 percent, and 10 percent lower in states that require a supermajority of 67 percent.

The coefficient on the dummy variable for *Initiative* has the anticipated sign but is not significant at standard levels. The coefficient on the dummy variable for *Convention* is significant at the 10 percent level. Its sign is not as predicted, however. According to my hypothesis, a more rigid constitution should reduce corruption, which would suggest a positive sign on the *Convention* variable. The negative sign may indicate that the provision for constitutional convention actually acts as a check on the power of the legislature. In 14 of the 40 states that allow conventions, voters can reject a convention call; therefore, to issue a successful convention call, the amendments to the constitution must benefit the majority of voters.

The results with respect to the controls for law enforcement effectiveness are mixed.

The coefficient on the variable measuring state and local expenditures on police protection per capita has a positive sign and it is not statistically significant. The coefficient on the variable *FBI agents* is positive and significant at the 1 percent level. There are at least two possible reasons why we would observe a higher number of per capita FBI agents in one state versus another. The first is that the state with a high number of FBI agents per capita places an emphasis on law enforcement; the second is that the higher number of FBI agents per capita represents a response to a higher level of criminal activity. Unfortunately, this reasoning applies to most of the variables that could be used to control for differences in law enforcement effectiveness across states.[17] The coefficient for the control variable *Racial Fractionalization* has the sign expected based on the results of previous studies and is statistically significant at the 1 percent level.

One potential shortcoming of this model is that it does not take into account the discrete nature of the corruption convictions data. In a previous study that investigates the relation between judicial independence, constitutional rigidity, and corruption, using methods appropriate for count data, I develop an econometric approach that explicitly recognizes the difference between the unobserved number of corrupt officials and the observed number of convictions for corruption (Cordis 2009).[18] The results from this specification indicate even stronger support for the hypotheses that both judicial independence and constitutional rigidity are associated with lower corruption levels. In addition to selection methods, higher relative pay for judges also turns out to be a significant factor in curbing corruption. Moreover, among the variables that measure the rigidity of the constitution, in addition to the percentage of votes required in the legislature to propose amendments to the constitution, the availability of the popular initiatives is shown to be negatively related to the number of corruption convictions.

Robustness

One potential concern is that corruption, judicial independence, and constitutional rigidity are correlated because they are jointly determined by factors omitted from the model. Notice that I use law enforcement variables and a variable measuring the racial heterogeneity as controls in my model. To assess the impact of including additional controls, I ran the regression again with variables added to account for the levels of income, education, and unemployment by state, as well as for the percentage of state residents who live in an urban area and are 65 years or older. Earlier studies, such as those by Glaeser and Saks (2004), Meier and Holbrook (1992), have found these variables to have significant effects on corruption levels across states. The inclusion of these control variables does not affect the significance of my results regarding the effect of judicial independence on corruption.

My findings regarding the relation between judicial independence and corruption could potentially be indicative of a more general relation between judicial independence and crime. To rule this out, I estimated linear regressions with crime rate per capita as the dependent variable and the same independent variables that entered the WLS regression.[19] The results of this analysis provide little evidence of a statistically significant relation between crime rates and any of the judicial independence or constitutional rigidity measures. The one variable that is consistently significant is *racial fractionalization*.

Of course, I cannot rule out the possibility that other unobserved factors account for the relation between corruption and the judicial independence and constitutional rigidity measures. The measures might be correlated with policies that reduce corruption or they might reflect endogenous selection of public officials into different states. If so, then increasing judicial independence and constitutional rigidity will not necessarily reduce corruption. Nonetheless, my results suggest that trying to deter corruption by promoting judicial independence would be a worthwhile policy experiment.

Cross-Country Evidence

Researchers do not have many options when deciding how to measure corruption at the country level. No international database of convictions for corruption by country is currently available. As a result, the literature relies on survey-based measures. There are, however, several different sources of corruption indicators. Transparency International, the World Bank, and the Political Risk Service Group are the three main sources of country-level corruption data. Each organization publishes an index that provides a rank ordering of countries from least to most corrupt. The exact methodology used to construct the index varies from one organization to another. I provide the details after discussing the empirical specifications.

The main corruption indicator used in my analysis comes from Transparency International. As a robustness check, I replicate this analysis using corruption indicators from the World Bank and the Political Risk Service Group. Like most of the literature, I use linear regression methods to investigate differences in corruption across countries. Since data availability varies across indices, I conduct my analysis on cross sections of between 37 to 165 countries for various years between 1995 and 2005. I then extend my analysis to panels of data with cross-sectional and time-series observations for 1998 to 2005. My basic approach, which directly follows La Porta et al. (2004), is to examine the effects of judicial independence and constitutional rigidity in separate models. Unlike the judicial independence measures, the constitutional rigidity measure is not available on an annual basis. Thus, using two separate models provides a more complete picture of the evidence on the relation between judicial independence and corruption in a cross-country setting.

JUDICIAL INDEPENDENCE MODELS

To examine the effect of judicial independence on corruption in a cross-section of countries, I estimate the following regression models:

(2) $Corruption_i = \beta_0 + \beta_1(Judicial\ independence)_i + \beta_2 \ln(GDP\ per\ capita)_i + \beta_3(Education\ Index)_i + \beta_4(Percent\ Protestant)_i + \beta_5(Ethnic\ Fractionalization)_i + \varepsilon_i$

(3) $Corruption_i = \beta_0 + \beta_1(Judicial\ independence)_i + \beta_2 \ln(GDP\ per\ capita)_i + \beta_3(Education\ Index)_i + \beta_4(Percent\ Protestant)_i + \beta_5(Ethnic\ Fractionalization)_i + \beta_6 \ln(Government\ Size)_i + \beta_7(Common\ Law)_i + \beta_8(Developing\ Country)_i + \varepsilon_i$

To address concerns about the sensitivity of my results to the way judicial independence is assessed, I consider three measures of judicial independence: two survey-based indices, derived from Gwartney, Lawson, and Easterly (2007) and from the Political Constraint Index Dataset, and an index based on the legal foundations as found in the legal documents of a country, constructed by La Porta et al. (2004).

My choice of control variables is based on the determinants of corruption available in the previous literature. Even though there is no commonly agreed upon empirical model to explain corruption, previous studies, such as those of La Porta et al. (1999), Treisman (2000), Adserà et al. (2000), Lederman et al. (2001), La Porta et al. (2004), and Waisman (2005), almost always include economic, cultural, and sociodemographic variables in their analysis.

I follow the literature and account for the robustness of my estimation by controlling for a number of country characteristics.

The first three controls measure the impact of economic development: the log of the gross domestic product per capita, an education index, and a dummy variable for developing countries. In general, previous studies (Treisman 2000, Waisman 2005) argue that developing countries are more affected by corruption than developed ones, and that richer and more educated societies have lower levels of corruption as more educated and richer voters are more willing and able to monitor and expose public officials when they violate the law.

The fourth control measures the percentage of the country's population that follows a Protestant religious tradition. Previous studies suggest that a country's religious tradition might influence the costs of corrupt activities. According to La Porta (1999), Protestant countries, as opposed to Catholic or Muslim countries, are less interventionist and should display better government performance because of higher ethical standards of politicians in office.

The fifth control is a measure of ethnic divisions within a country. The literature suggests that ethnic heterogeneity increases corruption or reduces people's desire to oppose corruption. In ethnically heterogeneous societies, there are more opportunities for redistribution within the group that comes to power, which is often interested in adopting policies to restrict the freedom of those outside the ruling group, and to limit the production of public goods (La Porta et al. 1999).

The sixth control is a measure of government size. Government size has an ambiguous effect on corruption. On the one hand, larger governments may imply (1) lesser bureaucratic delay, thus less rent seeking and (2) higher wages for public officials, thus lower incentives to accept bribes. On the other hand, larger governments suggest more inefficiencies and opportunities for rent seeking.

The seventh control is a dummy variable for countries with a common law legal system. The idea is that the effectiveness of a country's legal system affects the probability of getting caught and convicted of corruption. La Porta et al. (1999) suggest that common law systems, as opposed to civil law systems, offer a greater protection of property rights and are more effective owing to the willingness of judges to follow procedures, which increases the chances of exposing corruption.

To further check the robustness of my results, I include three other control variables in the panel data specifications: the log of investment as share of the gross domestic product, an index of freedom of the press, and a dummy variable for countries with a federal structure.

Higher investment leads to economic development and thus less corruption. Press freedom is important as it results in better informed voters and improved transparency, thus increasing the accountability of public officials. The effect of the federal structure on corruption could go in either direction. Some argue that competition between jurisdictions leads to more honest and efficient government (Weingast 1995), while others suggest that there are greater opportunities for corruption in a decentralized political system because one needs to influence only one segment of the government or because of an increased interaction between private individuals and public officials (Banfield, 1979).

CONSTITUTIONAL REVIEW MODELS

To examine the effect of constitutional review on corruption, I replace the judicial independence measure with an index of constitutional review. Finally, I consider a specification that includes both judicial independence and constitutional review indices. This yields the following regression models:

(4) $Corruption_i = \beta_0 + \beta_1(Constitutional\ Review)_i + \beta_2\ln(GDP\ per\ capita)_i$
    $+ \beta_3(Education\ Index)_i + \beta_4(Percent\ Protestant)_i + \beta_5(Ethnic$
    $Fractionalization)_i + \varepsilon_i$

(5) $Corruption_i = \beta_0 + \beta_1(Constitutional\ Review)_i + \beta_2\ln(GDP\ per\ capita)_i$
    $+ \beta_3(Education\ Index)_i + \beta_4(Percent\ Protestant)_i$
    $+ \beta_5(Ethnic\ Fractionalization)_i + \beta_6\ln(Government\ Size)_i$
    $+ \beta_7(Developing\ Country)_i + \varepsilon_i$

(6) $Corruption_i = \beta_0 + \beta_1(Judicial\ Independence)_i + \beta_2(Constitutional$
    $Review)_i + \beta_3\ln(GDP\ per\ capita)_i + \beta_4(Education\ Index)_i + \beta_5(Ethnic$
    $Fractionalization)_i + \varepsilon_i$

My measure of constitutional review is an index created by La Porta et al. (2004). The set of control variables used in the preceding models relating judicial independence to corruption is used here as well.

DATA

As noted earlier, the literature on corruption at the country level relies on indices of "perceived" corruption, which are almost always criticized for being subjective. However, as Treisman (2000) points out, the various organizations that administer surveys to construct cross-country ratings of corruption use very different methodologies and, still, the indices derived are highly correlated, suggesting that they do measure something very similar. Table 5.4 presents the correlations between the three corruption indicators used in my analysis: the Corruption Perceptions Index compiled by Transparency International (*Corruption TI*), the Control of Corruption Index compiled by researchers at the World Bank (Kaufman et al. 2007) (*Corruption World*

Table 5.4 Correlation Coefficients between Corruption Indicators

	Corruption TI	Corruption World Bank	Corruption PRS
Corruption TI	1.000	—	—
Corruption World Bank	0.965	1.000	—
Corruption PRS	0.824	0.822	1.000

Bank), and the International Country Risk Guide (ICRG) Corruption Index compiled by the Political Risk Survey Group (*Corruption PRS*).

The main corruption indicator, *Corruption TI*, provides data on extensive perceptions of corruption within countries. It is a composite index, computed as the average of surveys from up to 14 sources originating from 12 independent institutions. These surveys are based on the views of business people, risk analysts, journalists, and the general public; they contain questions about the "spread and amount of corruption in public and private business, the likeliness to demand special and illegal payments in high and low levels of government, the degree of misuse of public power for private benefits, the frequency of cases of corruption for politicians, public officials, policemen, and judges, or improper practices, such as bribing or corruption, in the public sphere," and so forth.[20] This index ranges from zero (highly corrupt) to 10 (highly clean). I inverted the scale to range from zero (highly clean) to 10 (highly corrupt). Table 5.5 ranks the 10 most corrupt and the 10 least corrupt countries based on this index. According to *Corruption TI*, the least corrupt country in my sample is Denmark, with an average score of 0.38, and the most corrupt is Bangladesh, with a score of 8.52. The United States has an average score of 2.41.

To measure the level of judicial independence across countries I use three types of indicators. I report the correlations between these indicators in table 5.6.

Table 5.5 Countries with Highest and Lowest Corruption Scores According to *Corruption TI* Index

Most Corrupt		Least Corrupt	
Country	Score	Country	Score
Bangladesh	8.52	Denmark	0.38
Nigeria	8.47	Finland	0.40
Myanmar	8.25	New Zealand	0.53
Haiti	8.24	Iceland	0.60
Chad	8.20	Sweden	0.77
Angola	8.10	Singapore	0.83
Paraguay	8.09	Canada	1.12
Azerbaijan	8.06	Netherlands	1.16
Cameroon	8.00	Norway	1.18
Congo Democratic Republic	7.97	Switzerland	1.21

Table 5.6 Correlation Coefficients between Judicial Independence Indicators

	Judicial Independence (I)	Judicial Independence (II)	Judicial Independence (III)
Judicial Independence (I)	1.000	—	—
Judicial Independence (II)	0.573	1.000	—
Judicial Independence (III)	0.396	0.408	1.000

The main judicial independence variable, *Judicial Independence (I)*, was compiled by the World Economic Forum Organization, and published in the Economic Freedom of the World Report by the Fraser Institute. This measure is based on the World Economic Forum's annual Executive Opinion Survey, which interviews a large number of senior business leaders. To provide the basis for a comparative assessment on a global basis, this survey ensures that the sample in each country is not biased in favor of any particular business group. Moreover, comparisons of the survey responses to hard data show that the quantitative sources and the survey results are positively correlated. The *Judicial Independence (I)* index is based on the following question: "Is the judiciary in your country independent from political influences of members of government, citizens, or firms? (1 = no − heavily influenced, 7 = yes − entirely independent)." The index has been rescaled to range from zero (heavily influenced judiciary) to 10 (entirely independent judiciary). Table 5.7 reports the countries with the highest and lowest levels of judicial independence, respectively. According to *Judicial Independence (I)*, in my sample, the country with the most independent judiciary is Finland, with an average score of 9.1, while the country with the least independent judiciary is Haiti, with an average score of 0.2. The United States has an average score of 7.6.

The next judicial independence measure, *Judicial Independence (II)*, comes from the Political Constraint Index Dataset[21] (POLCON). POLCON defines the existence of an independent judiciary by the joint existence of a POLITY score on executive constraints (XCONST) of at least three, that is, slight to moderate limitations on the executive authority, and an ICRG score on Law and Order of at least four, that is, a relatively strong law and order tradition. As noted in the POLCON Codebook (Henisz, 2005), the variable XCONST refers to "the extent of institutionalized constraints on the decision-making powers of chief executives. Such limitations may be imposed by any accountability groups [...]. The concern is therefore with the checks and balances

Table 5.7 Countries with Most and Least Independent Judiciaries According to Judicial Independence (I) Index

Most Independent		Least Independent	
Country	Score	Country	Score
Finland	9.1	Haiti	0.2
Denmark	9.0	Nicaragua	0.8
Netherlands	9.0	Venezuela	1.0
Germany	9.0	Paraguay	1.1
Australia	8.9	Burundi	1.3
New Zealand	8.9	Chad	1.4
United Kingdom	8.7	Ecuador	1.4
Switzerland	8.5	Kyrgyzstan	1.5
Norway	8.5	Bolivia	1.8
Israel	8.5	Peru	1.9

between the various parts of the decision-making process." Slight to moderate limitations on the executive authority (or an XCONST score of 3) implies that there are some real but limited restraints on the executive.

According to the International Country Risk Guide, the Law and Order index reflects the "degree to which the citizens of a country are willing to accept the established institutions to make and implement laws and adjudicate disputes." This index ranges from zero to six, with high scores indicating "sound political institutions, a strong court system, and provision for an orderly succession of power," and low scores indicating "a tradition of depending on physical force or illegal means to settle claims (Political Risk Service Group)." The *Judicial Independence (II)* measure is binary, with zero indicating a dependent judiciary and one indicates an independent judiciary.

The third measure of judicial independence, *Judicial Independence (III)*, comes from La Porta et al. (2004). Unlike the previous survey-based measures, the authors use information that originates from a country's legal documents to create this index. The index was computed as the normalized sum of (1) the tenure of Supreme Court judges, (2) the tenure of administrative court judges, and (3) a case law variable. According to *Judicial Independence (III)*, countries such as Finland, Germany, Australia, United Kingdom, United States, Norway, Israel, and the like, have a highly independent judiciary, each with a score of 1 while Algeria, Vietnam, Cuba, and Iraq have a highly dependent judiciary, each with a score of zero.

The measure of constitutional review comes from La Porta et al. (2004) and is based on information from Maddex (1995). The authors computed this index as the normalized sum of (1) a judiciary review index and (2) a rigidity of the constitution index. The judiciary review index measures the extent to which judges at the Supreme or Constitutional Court have the power to review the constitutionality of laws in a given country, and takes three values: 2, if there is full review of the constitutionality of laws, 1 if there is limited review, and zero if there is no review of the constitutionality of laws. According to the judiciary review index, countries such as Iran, Iraq, Libya, and New Zealand have a score of zero, that is, no review of the constitutionality of laws, while countries such as United States, Norway, India, and Iceland have a score of 2, which means, full review. The rigidity of the constitution index measures, on a scale of one to four, how hard it is to change the constitution in a given country. According to this measure, countries such as Japan, Iceland, Nigeria, Netherlands, and Thailand have a relatively rigid constitution, while countries such as Iran, Iraq, Israel, and United Kingdom have a relatively less rigid constitution. United States has a score of 3.

Descriptive statistics for all variables are reported in table 5.8. Most of the variables used as controls are self-explanatory, but the following need additional clarification. *Ethnic Fractionalization* is a measure of the diversity of ethnic groups within a country. To construct this measure, I used data from the CIA World Fact book and followed Glaeser and Saks (2004). The formula used to compute the index is $1 - \Sigma s_i^2$, where s_i are the ethnic shares within a country. The *Freedom of the Press* index is produced by the Freedom

Table 5.8 Descriptive Statistics of Cross-Country Data

Variable	Description	Obs.	Mean	Std. Dev.	Min	Max	Source
Corruption TI	Corruption Perception Index	1209	5.451	2.364	0.000	9.600	TI
Judicial Independence (I)	Index of judicial independence	812	5.280	2.398	0.200	9.800	WEFO
Judicial Independence (II)	Binary measure of judicial independence: 0 indicates a dependent judiciary and 1 indicates an independent judiciary	1634	0.411	0.492	0.000	1.000	POLCON
Judicial Independence (III)	Index of judicial independence	69	0.748	0.315	0.000	1.000	LaPorta et al. (2004)
Constitutional Review	Index of constitutional review	71	0.564	0.275	0.000	1.000	LaPorta et al. (2004)
Ln(Real GDP Per Capita)	Real GDP per capita (base year: 2000)	2044	8.508	1.177	5.139	10.834	PWT 6.2
Education Index	Education index based on the adult literacy rate and the combined primary, secondary, and tertiary gross enrollment ratio	2088	0.787	0.182	0.255	0.993	Human Development Indicators, UN
Ethnic Fractionalization	Ethnic heterogeneity measure	2124	0.331	0.261	0.000	0.923	CIA World Factbook
Percent Protestant	% of population with a Protestant religious tradition	2208	12.810	21.231	0.000	97.800	LaPorta et al. (1999)
Ln(Government Size)	General government spending as percentage of total consumption	2044	3.039	0.474	0.727	4.364	PWT 6.2
Common Law	Dummy = 1 for a country with a common law legal system as opposed to a civil law legal system	1176	0.326	0.469	0.000	1.000	La Porta et al. (1999)

Continued

Table 5.8 Continued

Variable	Description	Obs.	Mean	Std. Dev.	Min	Max	Source
Developing Country	Dummy = 1 for a developing country as reported by the World Bank Global Development Network Growth Database	2256	0.787	0.409	0.000	1.000	World Bank
ln(Investment)	Investment share of GDP	2040	2.454	0.640	0.000	3.991	PWT 6.2
Freedom of the Press Index	Freedom of the Press Index reported by the Freedom House	2184	46.570	24.694	0.000	100.000	Freedom House
Federal	Dummy = 1 for countries with a federal structure	1176	0.173	0.378	0.000	1.000	Treisman (2000)
Democratic	Dummy = 1 if the country has a democratic regime	540	0.259	0.439	0.000	1.000	Treisman (2000)

TI: Transparency International
PRS-ICRG: Political Risk Services-Intl Country Risk Guide, Table 3B:The Political Risk Components, 2006.
Fraser Institute: J. Gwartney, R. Lawson, and W. Easterly: Economic Freedom of the World, 2007 Annual Report.
WEFO: World Economic Forum Organization.
POLCON: Political Constraint Index Dataset.
PWT 6.2: Allan Heston, Robert Summers and Bettina Aten, Penn World Table 6.2, Center for International Comparisons of Production, Income and Prices at the university of Pennsylvania, September 2006.

House and uses the Article 19 of the Universal Declaration of Human Rights[22] as criterion. The index ranges from zero (best) to 100 (worst) and draws on surveys from a variety of sources, such as correspondents overseas, staff and consultant travel, the findings of human rights and press freedom organizations, specialists in geographic and geopolitical areas, and domestic and international news media.

RESULTS

The main focus of the econometric specifications is on the existence of significant relations between corruption and judicial independence or constitutional review. Along with the *Corruption TI* index, Transparency International reports the standard deviations of the corruption ratings: the greater the standard deviation, the greater the differences of perceptions of a country among the sources. Hence, I estimate WLS regressions using the reciprocals of the standard deviations of the *Corruption TI* index as weights.[23] As Treisman (2000) points out, this weighting places an emphasis on those scores where the respondents in the surveys gave more similar ratings than on those where the ratings were more divergent.

Tables 5.9 through 5.11 present the results of year-by-year regressions of the judicial independence measures (I), (II), and (III) on *corruption TI*, respectively, and table 5.12 shows the effect of constitutional review on *corruption TI*. In presenting the results, I always consider three distinct specifications. The first equation contains only the main variables, the second specification adds four control variables: (1) ln(GDP per capita), (2) education index, (3) ethnic fractionalization, and (4) percent protestant, and the third specification includes further controls, (5) ln(government size), (6) developing country, and (7) common law.

In presenting the results, I do not include the coefficients on the control variables. The results with respect to controls vary among regressions. However, I generally find that corruption is lower in richer countries and in countries that have a higher percent of population of Protestant religious tradition. Moreover, consistent with the previous literature, I find that corruption is lower in countries with common law legal systems and is higher in developing countries. Surprisingly, the coefficient on the education index variable and the one on the ethnic fractionalization are significant and have the correct sign only in about 60 percent of the regressions, while the coefficient on the variable measuring the government size is not significant in most regressions.

Next, consider the estimation results for judicial independence. The empirical results are consistent with my hypothesis that countries that have a relatively more independent judiciary experience lower corruption levels, ceteris paribus. Table 5.9 shows the results of year by year regressions of judicial independence (I) on *Corruption TI*. I report the results of WLS and OLS regressions for the years 1995 and 2000 to 2003, and the results of OLS regressions for 2004 and 2005. The number of observations varies considerably

Table 5.9 The Effect of Judicial Independence (I) on *Corruption TI*

	1995		2000		2001		2002		2003		2004	2005
	WLS[1]	OLS[2]	WLS[1]	OLS[2]	WLS[1]	OLS[2]	WLS[1]	OLS[2]	WLS[1]	OLS[2]	OLS[1]	OLS[1]
	Coeff. (z)	Coeff. (t)	Coeff. (z)	Coeff. (t)	Coeff. (z)	Coeff. (t)	Coeff. (z)	Coeff. (t)	Coeff. (z)	Coeff. (t)	Coeff. (t)	Coeff. (t)
							A. No Controls					
Judicial Ind. (I)	-1.178***	-0.917***	-0.906***	-0.901***	-0.783***	-0.799***	-0.981***	-0.821***	-1.145***	-0.861***	-0.836***	-0.824***
	(-35.80)	(-15.28)	(-22.90)	(-11.45)	(-30.25)	(-14.83)	(-54.15)	(-14.66)	(-63.70)	(-16.47)	(-16.00)	(-15.85)
Constant	11.524***	10.711***	10.10***	10.15***	8.937***	9.147***	9.771***	9.401***	10.53	9.747***	9.371***	9.517***
	(42.75)	(21.02)	(38.44)	(19.52)	(54.47)	(30.09)	(89.45)	(33.82)	(94.45)	(37.02)	(42.22)	(42.08)
Observations	40	40	61	61	77	77	91	91	100	100	108	118
R^2	—	0.72	—	0.68	—	0.68	—	0.68	—	0.72	0.69	0.69
							B. With Controls—1					
Judicial Ind. (I)	-0.637***	-0.616***	-0.464***	-0.465***	-0.362***	-0.344***	-0.403***	-0.389***	-0.597***	-0.458***	-0.442***	-0.410***
	(-8.25)	(-4.91)	(-7.26)	(-6.11)	(-9.20)	(-6.57)	(-11.64)	(-8.27)	(-15.62)	(-8.95)	(-8.78)	(-7.09)

Dependent Variable: Corruption TI

	(1)	(2)	(3)	(4)	(5)	(6)	(7)	(8)	(9)	(10)	(11)	(12)
Constant	22.646***	22.167**	18.03***	19.90***	22.34***	21.16***	23.12***	18.92***	23.63***	18.22***	17.30***	16.49***
	(9.76)	(8.93)	(18.87)	(10.7)	(21.49)	(13.51)	(36.79)	(20.62)	(35.82)	(19.49)	(19.20)	(17.20)
Observations	39	39	60	60	75	75	89	89	97	97	105	112
R^2	—	0.82	—	0.86	—	0.87	—	0.87	—	0.87	0.85	0.84

C. With Controls—2

	(1)	(2)	(3)	(4)	(5)	(6)	(7)	(8)	(9)	(10)	(11)	(12)
Judicial Ind. (I)	−0.276**	−0.572**	−0.306***	−0.357***	−0.259***	−0.288***	−0.262***	−0.287***	−0.216***	−0.351***	−0.394***	−0.353***
	(−2.32)	(−2.51)	(−3.85)	(−3.17)	(−4.91)	(−4.26)	(−6.12)	(−5.08)	(−4.30)	(−5.40)	(−5.92)	(−5.73)
Constant	16.968***	20.968***	10.90***	13.87	17.95***	16.91***	13.90***	14.67***	16.54***	14.02***	13.49***	12.50***
	(4.42)	(3.63)	(5.53)	(5.36)	(10.01)	(7.28)	(10.25)	(9.29)	(12.20)	(10.02)	(8.97)	(8.23)
Observations	39	39	60	60	73	73	86	86	87	87	88	87
R^2	—	0.84	—	0.88	—	0.89	—	0.9	—	0.91	0.89	0.89

Notes: The table presents the results of WLS and OLS regressions. The WLS regressions use as weights the reciprocals of the standard deviations of the *Corruption TI* index (not available for 2004 and 2005). The OLS regressions results are based on robust standard errors. In panel A the independent variable is judicial independence (I). In panel B the independent variables are (I) judicial independence (I), (2) ln(GDP per capita), (3) education index, (4) ethnic fractionalization, and (5) percent protestant. In panel C, the independent variables are (I) judicial independence (I), (2) ln(GDP per capita), (3) education index, (4) ethnic fractionalization, (5) percent protestant, (6) ln(government size), (7) developing country, and (8) common law. All variables are defined in Table 5.8. The numbers in parenthesis are the estimated z−statistics and t−statistics, respectively. {***,**,*} indicates significant at 1, 5, and 10 percent level, respectively.

over time, from 40 observations in 1995 to 112 observations in 2005. With no controls, the estimated coefficients are all significant at the 1 percent level of significance, suggesting that, on average, judicial independence is associated with lower corruption scores. For example, for the year 2002, an increase of one point in the judicial independence index (e.g., from Ghana, with a score of 5.2, to Greece, with a score of 6.2) reduces corruption by 0.9 points (approximately to Hungary or Costa Rica levels), ceteris paribus. When I add the first set of control variables to these regressions, the coefficient estimates decrease in magnitude by approximately 40 percent but they remain statistically different from zero at the 1 percent significance level. Adding the second set of control variables further shrinks the parameter estimates, but the coefficients remain statistically significant at the 1 percent level.

Table 5.10 shows the results of WLS and OLS cross-section regressions of judicial independence (II) on *Corruption TI* for the years 1998 to 2004. Once again, the estimated parameters are statistically significant at the 1 percent significance level. For example, without controls, for the year 2002, an independent judiciary reduces corruption by 4.2 points, on average. Adding the controls in Panel B does not change the significance of my results, but decreases the coefficients on the judicial independence variable. Again, for the year 2002, countries with an independent judiciary (the United States) have, on average, a corruption score that is 1.18 points lower than countries with a dependent or influenced judiciary (Albania). These results are, in general, robust to the inclusion of more controls in Panel C. The coefficients on the judicial independence variable have the expected sign and are significant at the 1 percent level for the years 2002 to 2004. For the years 1998, 2000, and 2001, the parameter estimates have the anticipated sign, but are not statistically significant, and for 1999, the coefficient has the predicted sign and is significant at the 5 percent level.

Tables 5.11 and 5.12 illustrate the effect of judicial independence (III) and of constitutional review on corruption. As discussed earlier, these measures come from La Porta et al. (2004). Data are only available for one year, 1995, which restricts the number of observations to 37, especially given that 1995 was the first year when the *Corruption TI* was released. Nonetheless, the findings regarding judicial independence support my hypothesis. In Table 5.11, the coefficient estimates are significant at the 1 percent level regardless of the specification used and suggest that an increase in judicial independence from zero (China) to 1 (the United States) reduces the corruption index by 2.52 (roughly to Spain) (Panel B).

The results on constitutional review are presented in table 5.12. With no controls, the effect of constitutional review on corruption is negative as predicted by my hypothesis and statistical significant at the 1 percent level. However, adding the controls to the estimation changes the sign of the coefficient on constitutional review, which becomes positive and maintains its significance. The specification in Panel C of table 5.12 contains both judicial independence and constitutional review measures. While the coefficient on the judicial independence index remains negative, as expected, and significant

Table 5.10 The Effect of Judicial Independence (II) on *Corruption TI*

	1998		1999		2000		2001		2002		2003		2004
	WLS[1]	OLS[2]	WLS[1]	OLS[2]	WLS[1]	OLS[2]	WLS[1]	OLS[2]	WLS[1]	OLS[2]	WLS[1]	OLS[2]	OLS[1]
	Coeff. (z)	Coeff. (t)	Coeff. (z)	Coeff. (t)	Coeff. (z)	Coeff. (t)	Coeff. (z)	Coeff. (t)	Coeff. (z)	Coeff. (t)	Coeff. (z)	Coeff. (t)	Coeff. (t)
A. No Controls													
Jud. Ind. (II)	−3.182***	−2.408***	−3.480***	−2.630***	−2.836***	−2.624***	−3.274***	−2.647***	−4.218***	−2.790***	−4.570***	−2.706***	−2.741***
	(−18.25)	(−6.32)	(−23.53)	(−7.22)	(−20.85)	(−6.98)	(−25.99)	(−7.06)	(−44.27)	(−7.80)	(−58.28)	(−7.47)	(−8.19)
Constant	6.953***	6.837***	7.237***	6.944***	7.178***	6.875***	7.009**	6.920***	7.415***	6.997***	6.710***	6.937***	7.041***
	(49.17)	(33.29)	(70.42)	(39.13)	(73.07)	(36.50)	(71.69)	(35.36)	(100.68)	(46.95)	(129.94)	(50.12)	(57.21)
Obs.	83	83	95	95	88	88	90	90	101	101	129	129	138
R^2	—	0.20	—	0.30	—	0.28	—	0.29	—	0.35	—	0.34	0.36
B. With Controls—1													
Jud. Ind. (II)	−0.890***	−0.738**	−1.259***	−0.881***	−0.861***	−0.762***	−0.779***	−0.708***	−1.186***	−0.937***	−2.587***	−0.981***	−1.119***
	(−4.09)	(−2.62)	(−6.49)	(−3.66)	(−4.83)	(−3.28)	(−4.94)	(−2.99)	(−9.90)	(−4.19)	(−25.57)	(−4.39)	(−5.14)
Constant	21.106***	19.882***	19.381***	18.841***	18.798***	19.575***	22.242***	20.822***	25.241***	20.101***	20.221***	18.430***	17.214***

Continued

Table 5.10 Continued

	Dependent Variable												
	Corruption TI												
	1998		1999		2000		2001		2002		2003		2004
	WLS[1]	OLS[2]	WLS[1]	OLS[2]	WLS[1]	OLS[2]	WLS[1]	OLS[2]	WLS[1]	OLS[2]	WLS[1]	OLS[2]	OLS[1]
	Coeff. (z)	Coeff. (t)	Coeff. (z)	Coeff. (t)	Coeff. (z)	Coeff. (t)	Coeff. (z)	Coeff. (t)	Coeff. (z)	Coeff. (t)	Coeff. (z)	Coeff. (t)	Coeff. (t)
	(24.68)	(13.39)	(25.72)	(14.86)	(29.63)	(16.73)	(33.36)	(17.19)	(47.48)	(17.87)	(56.68)	(19.68)	(18.73)
Obs.	82	82	93	93	85	85	88	88	99	99	121	121	129
R^2	—	0.77	—	0.79	—	0.82	—	0.83	—	0.83	—	0.78	0.76
C. With Controls—2													
Jud. Ind. (II)	-0.322	-0.218	-0.604**	-0.466*	-0.143	-0.312	-0.192	-0.286	-0.594***	-0.463*	-0.748***	-0.607**	-0.748***
	(-1.40)	(-0.83)	(-2.54)	(-1.91)	(-0.59)	(-1.21)	(-1.02)	(-0.99)	(-3.79)	(-1.88)	(-4.13)	(-2.49)	(-2.90)
Constant	13.972***	14.200***	13.280***	14.170***	13.251***	14.625***	17.749***	16.706***	15.700***	16.104***	16.992***	14.889***	13.653***
	(9.71)	(8.33)	(8.51)	(8.02)	(8.40)	(7.52)	(12.01)	(9.48)	(12.45)	(10.56)	(12.87)	(10.47)	(9.37)
Obs.	81	81	82	82	75	75	82	82	89	89	92	92	93
R^2	—	0.85	—	0.86	—	0.87	—	0.87	—	0.88	—	0.88	—

Notes: The table presents the results of WLS and OLS regressions. The WLS regressions use as weights the reciprocals of the standard deviations of the *Corruption TI* index (not available for 2004). The OLS regressions results are based on robust standard errors. In panel A the independent variable is judicial independence (II), i.e., JI (II). In panel B the independent variables are (1) JI (II), (2) ln(GDP per capita), (3) education index, (4) ethnic fractionalization, and (5) percent protestant. In panel C the independent variables are (1) JI (II), (2) ln(GDP per capita), (3) education index, (4) ethnic fractionalization, (5) percent protestant, (6) ln(government size), (7) developing country, and (8) common law. All variables are defined in Table 5.8. The numbers in parenthesis are the estimated z and t-statistics, respectively. {***,**,*} indicates significant at 1, 5 and 10 percent level, respectively.

Table 5.11 The Effect of Judicial Independence (III) on *Corruption TI*

	Dependent Variable	
	Corruption TI	
	WLS[1]	OLS[2]
	A. No Controls	
Jud. Ind. (III)	−7.307***	−4.041***
	(−31.38)	(−3.25)
Constant	8.471***	7.303***
	(39.92)	(7.86)
Observations	38	38
R^2	−	0.16
	B. With Controls—1	
Jud. Ind. (III)	−2.524***	−2.027*
	(−4.46)	(−1.87)
Constant	28.064***	27.157***
	(11.34)	(7.23)
Observations	37	37
R^2	−	0.76
	C. With Controls—2	
Jud. Ind. (III)	−1.681***	−2.037***
	(−2.79)	(−2.04)
Constant	12.809**	24.818***
	(2.51)	(3.15)
Observations	37	37
R^2	−	0.77

Notes: The table presents the results of WLS and OLS regressions. The WLS regressions use as weights the reciprocals of the standard deviations of the *Corruption TI* index. The OLS regressions results are based on robust standard errors. In panel A the independent variable is judicial independence (III). In panel B the independent variables are (1) judicial independence (III), (2) ln(GDP per capita), (3) education index, (4) ethnic fractionalization, and (5) percent protestant. In panel C the independent variables are those in Panel B plus (6) ln(government size), and (7) developing country. All variables are defined in table 5.8. The numbers in parenthesis are the estimated z- and t-stats, respectively. {***,**,*} indicates significant at 1, 5, and 10 percent level, respectively.

at the 1 percent level, the coefficient on the constitutional review index has the opposite sign from the one predicted by my hypothesis.

In their study, La Porta et al. (2004) find that constitutional review is a guarantee of political freedom, measured by indices of democracy, human rights and political rights. However, the authors do *not* find any statistically significant evidence of a relationship between constitutional review and economic freedom, measured by (1) an index of property rights based on a country's degree of legal protection of private property, (2) number of procedures, namely, the number of different steps that a start-up has to comply with in order to obtain legal status, (3) an employment laws index based on a country's level of worker protection through labor and employment laws,

Table 5.12 The Effect of Constitutional Review on *Corruption TI*

	Dependent Variable	
	Corruption TI	
	WLS[1]	OLS[2]
	A. No Controls	
Const. Review	−1.308***	1.645
	(−6.01)	(0.81)
Constant	2.959***	3.110***
	(19.952)	(2.39)
Observations	38	38
R^2	—	0.02
	B. With Controls—1	
Const. Review	1.869***	1.515*
	(6.54)	(1.88)
Constant	31.62***	21.172***
	(17.25)	(8.29)
Observations	37	37
R^2	—	0.75
	C. With Controls—2	
Jud. Ind. (III)	−3.066***	−2.978***
	(−6.33)	(−3.14)
Const. Review	1.200***	1.889**
	(4.43)	(2.39)
Constant	26.021***	28.373***
	(10.47)	(7.76)
Observations	37	37
R^2	—	0.75

Notes: The WLS regressions use as weights the reciprocals of the standard deviations of the *Corruption TI* index. The OLS regressions results are based on robust standard errors. In panel A the independent variable is const. review. In panel B the independent variables are (1) const. review, (2) ln(GDP/capita), (3) education index, (4) ethnic fract., and (5) percent protestant. In panel C the independent variables are (1) jud. ind. (III), (2) const. review, (3) ln(GDP/capita), (4) education index, and (5) ethnic fract. Variables are defined in table 5.8. The estimated z and t-stats are in parentheses. {***,**,*} indicates significant at 1, 5 and 10percent level, respectively.

and (4) government ownership of banks in 1995, that is, the share of assets of the top 10 banks in a given country owned by the government of that country in 1995. This suggests that it may be possible to reconcile the findings from the cross-country analysis with the evidence for the United States by gaining a better understanding of the relationship between political freedom and economic freedom.

Overall, it appears that the relation between judicial independence and corruption is robust to the way judicial independence is assessed, to the estimation technique, and, in general, to the inclusion of various control variables.

Robustness Checks

To check the sensitivity of my results to the way corruption is measured, I replicate the above analysis of the effect of judicial independence measures (I) and (II) on two other corruption indicators, *Corruption World Bank* and *Corruption PRS*, respectively.[24] Once more, the results are consistent with my hypothesis and similar with those reported in tables 5.9 and 5.10.[25]

As a further robustness check, I extend my analysis of the effect of judicial independence on corruption to panels of data with cross-sectional and time series observations for 1998 to 2005. Table 5.13 reports the results of pooled OLS, WLS, and panel data regressions using *Corruption TI* as dependent variable, and judicial independence (I), (II), and controls as independent variables.[26] One of the key issues when considering panel data regressions is the choice of estimator. I believe that the "between" estimator would best fit my models, since this estimator captures the cross-country information in the data. Moreover, my independent variables of interest, as well as many of the controls, exhibit very little variation over time. As a result, the information content of the data is provided mostly by the cross-country variation in the data.

For completeness I also report the results of "random effects" and "fixed effects" estimations. The presence of time- invariant independent variables in the specification makes it difficult to use a "fixed effects" model. To facilitate this, I decompose every time-variant variable in the model into two variables: *average(s)* and *delta(s)*. *Average* is just the mean of each variable over the sample period, by country, while *delta* is the difference from the mean. I then fit a random effects model on all *averages* and *deltas* along with the variables that do not vary over time. The coefficients I obtain should equal the coefficients that would be estimated separately by the "between" estimator and the "fixed-effects" estimator, respectively. Table 5.13 reports the results of panel regressions of judicial independence measures on *Corruption TI* for the years 2000–2005 and 1998–2004, respectively. With or without controls, the coefficient estimates are significant at the 1 percent level and have the predicted sign. These additional robustness checks provide further evidence in support of my hypothesis that judicial independence is associated with lower corruption levels.

Conclusion

The availability of convictions-based data on corruption for the United States, along with the development of several country-level survey-based corruption indices in the 1990s, makes it possible to study the causes and consequences of corruption, and numerous authors have done so over the last 15 years. Previous empirical studies focused less on the legal environment, and more on aspects related to the political, economic, cultural, and socio-demographic environment of each country. This chapter addresses the importance of judicial checks and balances in limiting the abuse of power by the executive and legislative branches of government. I investigate the relation

Table 5.13 The Effect of Judicial Independence on *Corruption TI*: Pooled OLS, WLS, and Panel Estimations

Independent Variable	Dependent Variable							
	Corruption TI							
	Judicial Independence (I)					Judicial Independence (II)		
	2000—2005					1998—2004		
	OLS[1]	WLS[2]	BE[3]	FE[4]	RE[5]	OLS[1]	WLS[2]	BE[3]
	A. With Controls—1							
Judicial Independence	−0.400***	−0.452***	−0.447***	−0.053**	−0.123***	−1.077***	−1.637***	−1.375***
	(−18.23)	(−23.03)	(−8.34)	(−2.57)	(−6.16)	(−11.58)	(−24.40)	(−5.37)
Constant	17.996***	23.967***	16.498***	16.496***	17.849***	19.148***	22.567***	16.954***
	(31.04)	(54.26)	(20.26)	(20.68)	(24.93)	(36.38)	(70.91)	(16.01)
Observations	473	289	538	538	538	582	480	582
R^2	0.87	—	0.87	0.02	0.82	0.81	—	0.81
	B. With Controls—2							
Judicial Independence	−0.315***	−0.249***	−0.388***	−0.063***	−0.097***	−0.587***	−0.659***	−0.753***
	(−12.25)	(−10.26)	(−5.87)	(−3.02)	(−4.80)	(−5.80)	(−8.33)	(−2.91)
Constant	14.576***	15.172***	13.332***	13.403***	13.756***	15.752***	14.781***	16.304***
	(17.98)	(16.89)	(8.27)	(8.29)	(10.35)	(19.94)	(21.34)	(8.03)

Observations	445	284	481	481	481	481	540	457	540
R^2	0.90	—	0.90	0.03	0.87	0.87	0.87	—	0.89

C. With Controls—3

Judicial Independence	−0.317***	−0.284***	−0.377***	−0.063***	−0.096***	−0.597***	−0.727***	−0.753***
	(−12.58)	(−11.72)	(−5.56)	(−2.98)	(−4.65)	(−5.82)	(−9.06)	(−2.82)
Constant	15.324***	17.524***	13.112***	13.028***	14.110***	15.997***	15.612***	16.249***
	(16.82)	(19.23)	(7.19)	(6.94)	(10.21)	(17.20)	(20.84)	(6.97)
Observations	442	321	478	478	478	540	457	540
R^2	0.90	—	0.90	0.05	0.87	0.87	—	0.89

Notes: The table presents the results of ordinary least squares, weighted least squares, and panel regressions. The OLS regressions results are based on robust standard errors. The WLS regressions use as weights the standard errors of the perceived corruption levels. The panel regressions use the between estimation method. In panel A the independent variables are (1) judicial independence, (2) ln(GDP per capita), (3) education index, (4) ethnic fractionalization, and (5) percent protestant. In panel B the independent variables are those included in panel A plus (6) ln(government size), (7) developing country, and (8) common law. In panel C the independent variables are those included in panel B plus (9) ln(investment), (10) federal, and (11) freedom of the press index. All variables are defined in Table 5.8. The numbers in parenthesis are the estimated t-statistics and z-statistics, respectively. [***,**,*] indicates significant at 1, 5, and 10 percent level, respectively.

between two distinct components of the checks-and-balances function—judicial independence and constitutional review—and a specific type of abuse of power by government officials: corruption in public office. I carry out my analysis using measures of corruption derived from criminal convictions data and measures of corruption derived from survey data.

The findings from my analysis of United States data suggest that differences in judicial independence and constitutional rigidity at the state level explain a substantial portion of the observed variation in the number of corruption convictions across states. First, in states where judges have a greater degree of independence (merit plan selection), there is less corruption. Second, in states that have more rigid constitutions (larger legislative majorities required to propose constitutional amendments), there is less corruption. The findings from my analysis of cross-country data regarding the effect of constitutional review on corruption are less compelling. Nonetheless, it is clear that higher judicial independence is associated with lower corruption levels, ceteris paribus. To address concerns that survey-based indicators do not accurately measure the variables of interest, I conduct the empirical analysis using three distinct sets of corruption and judicial independence indicators. In general, the estimation results are not sensitive to the way corruption is measured.

These findings have potentially important policy implications. Research using country-level data suggests that high levels of corruption limit investment, retard economic growth, lead to ineffective government, and create economic inefficiencies and inequalities. I find evidence that judicial reforms could help reduce the prevalence of corruption in developing economies around the world. This conclusion is tentative, however, because of endogeneity concerns, which is to say, that there may be unobserved country characteristics that affect both institutional design and corruption outcomes. Further work and estimations with good instrumental variables is needed before firm policy implications can be drawn regarding the effect of judicial independence or constitutional review on corruption. Nonetheless, it is encouraging that the results are generally consistent with economic hypotheses concerning the relation between corruption and characteristics of the legal system.

NOTES

I thank Chris Kirby, Robert Tollison, Michael Maloney, William Dougan, Todd Kendall, Cotton Lindsay, and John Warner for helpful comments on this chapter.

1. This chapter appeals to the theory of political agency as formulated by Barro (1973), Ferejohn (1986), Persson, Roland, and Tabellini (1997), and Maskin and Tirole (2004). According to this theory, separation of powers, and particularly the institution of checks and balances, limits abuse of power by creating conflicts of interest between the legislative and the executive branches, or by requiring agreement of both branches in the law-making process.
2. See Svensson (2004) for a survey of this literature.
3. Alt and Lassen (2008) argue that various forms of checks and balances are precautionary devices against government corruption. They test this hypothesis

using Boylan and Long's (2003) survey of State House reporters' perceptions of public corruption along with data on the presence of divided government and on judicial selection, and find that states in which (1) the executive and the legislative branches of government are controlled by different political parties, and (2) judges are elected rather than appointed experience lower levels of corruption. This latter result contradicts the long-standing belief that appointed judges are more independent (Hall 1987, Hall 2001, Feld and Voigt 2003, Besley and Payne 2003, Hanssen 2004, Sobel and Hall 2007). More broadly, La Porta et al. (2004) examine data for 71 countries and find that both judicial independence and constitutional review act as important guarantees of economic and political freedom.

4. The foundation for exercising judicial review in the United States is *Marbury v. Madison* 5 U.S. 137 (1803), a decision pronounced by Chief Justice John Marshall.

5. This section draws on Cordis (2009).

6. I exclude the state of New Mexico from my analysis because data on the number of corruption convictions were not available for the years 1996 to 2005.

7. Previous studies normalize the number of corruption convictions by the general state population rather than by the number of government employees. I use the number of government employees because this should be a better indicator of the number of individuals who could potentially engage in corrupt acts.

8. Feld and Voigt (2003) include these three variables in constructing an index of de jure judicial independence across 71 countries around the world.

9. A Supreme Court decision, *Republican Party of Minnesota v. White 536 U.S. 765(2002)* ruled that the requirement of judges not to discuss political issues is unconstitutional, thus providing judges with the right to tell voters about their positions on specific political and legal issues that might come before them.

10. Arkansas adopted Amendment 80 in 2000, which changed the judicial selection method from partisan to nonpartisan elections. North Carolina passed the Judicial Campaign Reform Act in 2002, which established nonpartisan elections for Supreme Court judges effective 2004. These changes do not affect the significance of the results.

11. The American Bar Association endorsed the merit selection in 1937.

12. See also Hall (1987), Hall (2001), Tabarrok and Helland (1999), Hanssen (2002), Besley and Payne (2003), and Sobel and Hall (2007). Criticism of judicial election dates back to 1835, when Alexis de Tocqueville (1954, 289) wrote: "Some other state constitutions make the members of the judiciary elective, and they are even subjected to frequent reelections. We venture to predict that these innovations will sooner or later be attended with fatal consequences; and that it will be found out at some future period that by thus lessening the independence of the judiciary they have attacked not only the judicial power, but the democratic republic itself."

13. My analysis does not include constitutional commissions. Constitutional commissions are advisory bodies established to assist the governor, the legislature or a convention on constitutional matters. The Utah Revision Commission is the only commission established on a permanent basis since 1977. Other commissions that were created and operated over the 1996–2005 period were Alabama Citizens' Constitution Commission (2003), Florida Constitution Revision Commission (1998–2000), California, Nebraska, and New Mexico Constitution Revision Commission (1996–1998) (*Source: The Book of the States*, various years).

14. The importance of the initiatives process in the United States has been documented in studies by Romer and Rosenthal (1979), Kalt and Zupan (1990), Matsusaka (1992), Matsusaka (1995), and Matsusaka (2004).

15. See Mauro (1995), Easterly and Levine (1997), La Porta et al. (1999), Treisman (2000), Glaeser and Saks (2004).

16. A higher number of FBI agents per capita in one state versus another could indicate that the state places an emphasis on law enforcement or it could reflect a response to a higher level of criminal activity. See Lopez, Jewell, and Campbell (2009) for a similar argument in the context of corruption and the states' choice of eminent domain restrictions.

17. Endogeneity and reverse causality are often an issue in corruption studies. In general, researchers have had little success in identifying suitable instrumental variables. See, for example, Alt and Lassen (2003) and Glaeser and Saks (2004).

18. The number of officials convicted for corruption is an unknown fraction of the total number of corrupt officials. In my previous study, I assume that each corrupt official faces some risk of being revealed as corrupt, and that this risk does not vary across individuals *within* a state. I further assume that the number of officials convicted of corruption in each state can be expressed as the outcome of n_i independent Bernoulli trials where n_i is the unobserved number of corrupt officials in state i. To obtain an empirical specification, I model n_i as a negative binomial process whose mean depends on a vector of explanatory variables. See Cordis (2009) for complete details.

19. The data on crime rates are taken from the Statistical Abstract of the United States, which provides the number of crimes reported to law enforcement agencies in each state. The variable used in the regression is the average number of crimes (violent and nonviolent) per 100,000 population by state over the sample period.

20. A detailed description of the methodology for the Corruption Perceptions Index is available at: http://www.transparency.org/policy_research/surveys_indices/cpi, last accessed on April 30, 2008.

21. The POLCON Dataset is available at http://www-management.wharton.upenn.edu/henisz, last accessed on April 30, 2008.

22. Article 19 of the Universal Declaration of Human Rights states: "Everyone has the right to freedom of opinion and expression; this right includes freedom to hold opinions without interference and to seek, receive, and impart information and ideas through any media regardless of frontiers."

23. Transparency International does not report the standard errors of the *Corruption TI* index for the years 2004, 2005, and 2006.

24. Since I do not have data on these corruption indices for the year 1995, I cannot estimate models using the measures of judicial independence and constitutional review from La Porta et al. (2004).

25. Tables of results for the year by year WLS and OLS estimations of the effect of judicial independence measures (I) and (II) on the *corruption World Bank* and *corruption PRS* indicators are available upon request.

26. Tables of results for the pooled OLS, WLS, and panel data regressions using *corruption World Bank* and *corruption PRS*, respectively, as dependent variables, and judicial independence (I), (II), and controls, as independent variables are available upon request. All estimates are consistent with the findings reported in table 5.14.

CHAPTER 6

EFFECTS OF JUDICIAL SELECTION ON CRIMINAL SENTENCING

Aleksandar Tomic and Jahn K. Hakes

INTRODUCTION

Hardly an election goes by without politicians appealing to voters by saying they are tough on crime. Legislators and government executives most commonly make these claims of intolerance to crime. However, in some states the judges are also chosen by popular elections. In other states, the governor or the state legislature appoints judges. This variation in methods of judicial selection can help reveal whether political pressures lead to systematic differences in incarceration and sentencing choices between elected and appointed judges. Although judges are supposed to be impartial interpreters of the law, as rational agents they are subject to political pressure from either their constituents or the appointing body, be it the governor or the state legislature. If the voters demand a tough stance on crime, then elected judges should pass strict sentences to maintain voter support. Appointed judges are selected for office by elected politicians, and thus are not too far removed from the same pressure to pass harsher sentences. State-level funding of prisons makes state officials accountable for prison overcrowding. Thus, judges appointed by state legislatures and governors will have relatively more incentive to find punishments other than incarceration for minor felons.

We analyze a dataset of over 70,000 cases representing criminal trials between 1990 through 1998 from 54 of the 75 most populous counties of the United States. The dataset identifies characteristics of the defendant, the crime, the county, and the mechanism of judicial selection. Therefore, our analysis focuses on general jurisdiction and county-level judges. Our regression analysis finds that elected judges are more likely to incarcerate a defendant. Furthermore, after correcting for selection effects, we find that appointed judges tend to pass longer sentences.

PREVIOUS STUDIES ON SELECTION AND SENTENCING

The ultimate cause for discrepancies in sentencing and incarceration decisions due to judicial selection method lies in how judges of each type respond differently to voters' desires for toughness on crime. Thus, our interest falls within the subset of principal–agent studies that more generally investigates the differing motives and behavior of elected and appointed agents. These differences have been studied in many contexts, perhaps most thoroughly via the study of appointed versus elected regulators, as in public utility commissioners. The theoretical models presented trace back to Peltzman (1976), as adapted by Crain and McCormick (1984). Besley and Case (2003) summarize the existing literature. Besley and Coate (2000a, 2000b) develop more complex models that address the bundling of policies that occurs when regulators are appointed, and the unbundling of policies that occurs through elections and citizens' initiatives. Our explanation of the differing sentencing motives by elected and appointed judges, presented in the section "Theoretical Differences in the Costs and Benefits of Appointed and Elected Judges," is based on differences in accountability and in responsibility for differing bundles of policies, particularly the financing of prisons.

While the literature on regulators offers some useful insights, Posner (1994) more directly addresses the topic by specifically analyzing the comparative effects of election versus appointment on judicial behavior. He develops a model showing that judges, much like everyone else, act rationally and respond to incentives.

Subsequent studies attempting to provide empirical support for the influence of judicial selection processes have tended to focus on the outcomes of civil law suits. While we are instead interested in the effects of the mode of judge appointments in the criminal justice system, the findings of these studies broadly confirm the existence of agency problems within the courts more generally. Helland and Tabarrok (1999, 2000, and 2002) found that elected judges tend to impose larger judgments on out-of-state defendants in civil lawsuits than do appointed judges. Hanssen (1999) found that appointed judges are indeed more independent than elected ones, as measured by higher uncertainty in regard to the decisions of courts run by appointed judges than in courts run by elected ones. These empirical findings are consistent with Posner's (1994) theoretical model. Turning from the civil courts to the criminal justice process, there is abundant evidence that the legislative and executive branches of state governments respond to political pressure from voters to be "tough on crime." DiIulio (1996) reports that all 30 Republican gubernatorial candidates who were elected or reelected in 1994 promised to get tough on crime. Between 1993 and 1997, 25 states enacted "three strikes and you are out" legislation, many of which were passed by referenda (Wright, 1998). Levitt (1997) finds that mayors and governors increase the size of the police forces in election year, which suggests pandering to the voters' desire to see their leaders are "tough on crime."

Nearly all previous studies of how different judges themselves react to political pressure for toughness on crime have focused upon sentencing discrepancies, and furthermore have concentrated their interest upon either specific institutions, such as the U.S. Supreme Court and state supreme courts, or on specific kinds of cases, such as death penalty cases.[1] Canon and

Jaros (1970) examine the dissent among the state supreme court justices. They find that socioeconomic and political influences affect the dissent indices, but the effect is strongly conditioned on the presence of the intermediate appellate courts. Where there are fewer intermediate appellate courts, external variables exert more influence than when there are more intermediate appellate courts. Furthermore, Canon and Jaros (1970) find that selection system and tenure do not affect courts' sensitivity to socioeconomic and political considerations, but they "are related to dissenting behavior in unknown ways" (Canon and Jaros, 1970). Later, Brace and Hall (1990) expanded the study to dissent rates in state supreme courts and found lower dissent rates in states with appointed supreme court justices.

In subsequent studies, Brace and Hall (1993) revisit the issue of judicial dissent in the specific context of the death penalty. They find that justices in states with a partisan election system are more likely to dissent in favor of death penalty. In addition, Brace and Hall (1995), Hall and Brace (1996), and Hall (1995) address individual behavior of the state supreme court justices in death penalty cases. More importantly, Brace and Hall try to discern what influences other than case characteristics affect the decision whether to uphold the death penalty. Their papers vary in modeling and estimation techniques but reach the same conclusion: elected justices are more likely to uphold a death penalty, especially when they are more vulnerable to electoral pressure as they approach reelection.

Although the papers above vary in specific interest—judicial behavior in civil trials, candidate platforms on crime prior to executive or legislative elections, judicial dissent on criminal sentencing—what they share is their support of the theoretical positions of Peltzman (1976) and Posner (1994) that political agents, and judges more specifically, react to political pressure. One large remaining hole in the literature, however, is whether political pressure can affect criminal sentencing conditions on a more systematic basis. Aside from highly publicized death penalty cases and those cases being tried in higher courts, to date no study has sought to identify systematic differences in sentencing among lesser crimes where the actors within the criminal justice system are less likely to be observed on a case-by-case basis.

It is arguable that the stakes are highest at the point of sentencing, both for the defendant and for the criminal justice and corrections system, as an incarceration decision by a judge will have an effect not only on crime prevention and deterrence in the community, but also on the defendant, as a (first) prison term will place a stigma that will remain with the defendant for the rest of his or her life. When the resulting biases in sentencing decisions are aggregated over thousands of defendants, there are significant potential consequences for communities, as they attempt to finance the prison system and cope with differing proportions of convicted felons residing among them.

Nearly all of the previous contributions in the study of incarceration and sentencing have used data from a single state or the federal court system and have employed a variety of empirical methods. Bushway and Piehl's (2001) summary of the research on empirical modeling of sentencing decisions is quite helpful. They conclude that the most sound method is a two-stage model in which the first question estimated the decision whether to incarcerate and the second equation models the sentence length conditional on incarceration.

By using a multistate, individual-defendant dataset that includes all felonies tried in the general jurisdiction courts, we are able to take a look at the day-to-day decisions of judges, relating not only to highly politicized and publicized cases, such as death penalty ones, but also more "mundane" felonies like thefts, assaults, and so forth. The dataset details many characteristics of the case and the defendant, allowing us to better control for case context and isolate the effect of the judges' political considerations on their decisions. We show that political considerations and incentives built into the selection system play a significant role in sentencing decisions throughout the caseload of the criminal justice system.

JUDICIAL SELECTION METHODS

We limit our investigation to methods used to select judges for general jurisdiction state courts, which are the first courts that adjudicate newly filed criminal cases. Judicial selection methods can be divided into two broad categories: one featuring appointment by a governor or a legislative body of the state and the other through direct elections. Within these categories, however, there is a great deal of variety with respect to constraints upon power of appointment, term lengths, and processes for incumbents to receive subsequent terms.[2] Examples of many of these various methods of selection can be found among the counties in our data. Using the data provided by the American Judicature Society, we summarize in table 6.1 the methods of judicial selection in each state with counties that are in our sample.

While the variety of judicial selection methods and term lengths is astounding, we believe it is not only acceptable but preferable to group selection methods into the two broad categories of locally elected judges and appointed judges.

The core of our model (as developed further in the following section) is that the difference in incentives that elected and appointed judges face stems from the difference in the constituencies to whom they are accountable. Regardless of whether judges are elected in partisan or nonpartisan elections, they are elected at the county, not the state level, and appointed judges are appointed by a statewide body, whether they go through a nominating commission or not. The difference in objectives of the county population and state officials when it comes to incarceration and sentence length decisions, we believe, drives judicial behavior. This is best tested by clearly differentiating between elected and appointed judges, rather than becoming distracted by details that do not as significantly affect sentencing motives.

Our court cases come from the 75 most populous counties in the United States, which are spread across 23 states. In our sample, judges are elected in

Table 6.1 Judicial Selection Mechanisms

State		Initial Selection Method	Initial Term	Method of Retention	Length of Additional Terms
Alabama		Partisan election	6 years	Re-election	6 years
Arizona		Merit selection through nominating commission	2 years	Retention election	4 years
California	Higher court	Gubernatorial appointment without nominating commission	12 years	Retention election	12 years
	Lower court	Nonpartisan election	6 years	Non-Partisan Election	6 years
District of Columbia		Merit selection through nominating commission	15 years	Reappointment by judicial tenure commission	
Florida	Higher court	Merit selection through nominating commission	1 year	Retention Election	6 years
	Lower court	Nonpartisan election	6 years	Retention election	6 years
Georgia		Nonpartisan election	4 years / 6 years (higher court)	Re-election	4 years / 6 years (higher court)
Hawaii		Merit selection through nominating commission	10 years	Reappointment by Judicial Selection Commission	10 years
Illinois		Partisan election	6 years	Retention Election	6 years
Indiana		Partisan election	6 years	Re-election	6 years
Kentucky		Nonpartisan election	8 years	Re-election	8 years
Massachusetts		Merit selection through nominating commission	to age 70		
Maryland	Higher court	Merit selection through nominating commission	See note 1.	Retention Election	10 years
	Lower court	Merit selection through nominating commission	See note 1.	Non-Partisan Election	15 years
Michigan		Non-Partisan Election	6 years	Re-election	6 years

Continued

Table 6.1 Continued

State		Initial Selection Method	Initial Term	Method of Retention	Length of Additional Terms
Missouri		Merit selection through nominating commission	1 year	Retention election	6 years / 12 years (higher court)
New Jersey		Gubernatorial appointment without nominating commission	7 years	See note 2.	to age 70
New York	Higher court	Merit selection through nominating commission	14 years	See note 3.	5 years
	Lower court	Partisan election	14 years	Re-election	14 years
Ohio		Partisan election	6 years	Re-election	6 years
Pennsylvania		Partisan election	10 years	Retention Election	10 years
Tennessee		Partisan election	8 years	Re-Election	8 years
Texas		Partisan election	4 years / 6 years (higher court)	Re-Election	4 years / 6 years (higher court)
Utah		Merit selection through nominating commission	First general election > 3 years after appointment	Retention Election	6 years
Virginia		Legislative appointment without nominating commission	8 years	Reappointment by legislature	8 years
Washington		Nonpartisan election	4 years / 6 years (higher court)	Re-election	4 years / 6 years (higher court)
Wisconsin		Nonpartisan election	6 years	Re-election	6 years

Notes
1. Until the first general election following the expiration of one year from the date of the occurrence of the vacancy.
2. Reappointment by the governor with advice and consent of the Senate.
3. Incumbent reapplies to nominating commission and competes with other applicants for nomination to the governor. The governor may reappoint the incumbent or another nominee. The senate confirms the appointment.

Source: Table derived from: American Judicature Society. Judicial Selection in the States: Appellate and General Jurisdiction Courts. http://www.ajs.org/selection/Jud%20Sel%20Chart-Oct%202002.pdf

Alabama, California, Florida, Georgia, Illinois, Indiana, Kentucky, Michigan, New York, Ohio, Pennsylvania, Tennessee, Texas, Washington, and Wisconsin. Judges are appointed in Arizona, California (higher court), District of Columbia, Florida (higher court), Hawaii, Massachusetts, Maryland, Missouri, New Jersey, New York (higher court), Utah, and Virginia.

From the latter category of states with appointed judges, however, one group of states does not fit comfortably. Judges initially appointed by the statewide bodies in Arizona, California, Florida, Maryland, Missouri, and Utah are subject to retention election within the county. As judges in these states are initially appointed, they are indebted to the state-level appointing body, yet they must please local voters in order to remain on the bench. To make certain that we are not misrepresenting judicial incentives in these states, and to statistically test whether sentencing decisions in these states align more closely with decisions made by elected judges or by career appointees, we fit specifications assigning this group of states alternatively to either camp. A comparison of the two sets of results yields insight as to the strength of the incentives created by local accountability, and supports our central hypothesis.

THEORETICAL DIFFERENCES IN THE COSTS AND BENEFITS OF APPOINTED AND ELECTED JUDGES

Because of the ways in which prisons are funded, voters in local judicial elections have different objectives from those of governors or other elected state-level officials. The negative effects of individual crimes, and of high crime rates, are mostly felt locally. Dangerous and safe neighborhoods are often separated by a few miles, or sometimes just a few blocks. The benefits of keeping felons off the streets are felt directly at the local level, and it is for this reason that police and sheriff's departments and criminal courts are often established at the local or county level. As prisons are generally state-funded, however, when a judge sends a defendant to prison, the whole state contributes to the cost of incarceration. Therefore, citizens benefit at local levels from incarcerating criminals, but they share the costs of incarceration with the rest of the state. Consequently, when pressuring judges to be tough on crime, local voters may be less sensitive than statewide officials to the costs of the prison system. The resulting overcrowding of prisons and higher incarceration costs might not please the rest of the state, but they are not the judge's constituents.

It would be rational then for elected judges, responding primarily to citizen voters at the county level, to send relatively more convicted felons to prison. However, if the judges making the incarceration decisions are state-level appointees—whether appointed by the governor or the state legislature—the costs of incarceration are not a fiscal commons. The state budget is required to immediately provide housing for all incarcerated criminals, if not through their own prison system, then at least by financing the housing of the criminal at another penal institution elsewhere. As the incarceration costs are at the state level, they are internalized by the decision-maker (i.e., the person or group of people who appoint state judges), and their appointees will internalize the costs as well. The result is a balancing of marginal costs of incarceration and marginal benefits of keeping criminals off the streets.

To more specifically distinguish the sentencing objectives between elected and appointed judges, our model treats judges as rational public officials, loosely following the tradition of Stigler (1971) and Peltzman (1976). As judges in this context are agents, their utility is a function of their own material welfare, and their ability to maintain the favor of their patrons (either voters or the appointing body). That level of favor, in turn, depends upon their judicial record (in which their incarceration and sentencing decisions figure prominently) and upon the ability of patrons to monitor the judge and hold the judge accountable for deviations from their preferences.

An elected judge's objective function, then, will be to optimize

$$\gamma = f(U_e; V_1(I, S, Z, M_e)), \tag{6.1}$$

where

U_e is the judge's utility from serving on the bench (and leisure away from it), and

V_1 is a function of preferences of voters in local judicial elections, which contains

I, the fraction of convicted felons that get incarcerated,

S, the average sentence length imposed,

Z, a vector of other relevant judicial qualifications and characteristics, and

M_e represents the ability of the electorate to monitor the judge's decisions.

Partial derivatives γ_I and γ_S depend on cost of crime relative to cost of keeping a prisoner incarcerated as filtered through voter preferences.[3] As the cost of crime rises relative to cost of incarceration, the median voter will prefer higher incarceration rates and longer sentences. As mentioned previously, the practice of funding prisons through the state budget externalizes some of the voters' marginal costs of incarcerating local criminals and in equilibrium can be expected to tilt preferences on the margin toward stricter sentencing. It is possible that these derivatives could also be affected by asymmetric information. As the potential victim of crime, the voter is aware of the cost of crime, but might not be fully informed about the cost of incarceration and sentence (e.g., the average citizen of a death penalty state might not know the cost of administering an execution). This is one possible reason for difference in behavior between the two types of judges. If the voter underestimates the cost of incarceration, or does not have to bear the full cost of incarceration, then he is inclined to desire more incarceration. The model predicts higher incarceration rates for elected judges, however, even without an assumption of asymmetric information.

Appointed judges have a similarly structured objective function, except that their continued tenure depends upon reappointment by state-level officials who face election. While appointees do not have to cater directly to voters, the appointing body (either the state legislature and/or the governor) communicates voter preferences to them through their own decisions. From the appointee's perspective the objective function is

$$\alpha = g\left(U_a;\ A(M_a;\ V_s(I,\ S,\ Z,\ W))\right) \tag{6.2}$$

where I, S, and Z are as in equation (6.1),

U_a is the judge's utility of labor and leisure,[4]

A is the objective function of the appointing body, which includes

M_a, the ability of the appointing body to monitor the appointee's decisions, and

W, a vector of all other policies managed by the appointing body.

Since the appointing body is itself elected, voter preferences for S, I, and Z still enter the judge's objective function, although indirectly and as expressions of statewide rather than local voter preferences. Because of the differences in jurisdiction and authority, elections for state-level officials will additionally indicate preferences across a larger bundle of issues and policies, such as welfare programs, education, taxation, and so on.[5] As incarceration costs of convicted felons are not externalized at the state level as they are for local judges, V_I and V_S are likely to be relatively more receptive, on the margin, to punishments that result in less prison overcrowding.

When faced with the costs of prison overcrowding, the available options include (1) reducing incarceration rates, (2) offer shorter sentences or earlier paroles, (3) use nonincarceration forms of punishment, such as fines or suspended sentences, for lesser offenses, (4) diverting funds from other government services into the prisons budget, or (5) raising tax revenues to pay for the additional expenditures. Options (1), (2), and (3) would disappoint voters in high-crime areas and voters who highly prioritize "toughness" on crime, whereas option (4) would alienate proponents of the program targeted for the budget cut and option (5) has empirically been shown to please few voters.

On this margin, state government officials will prefer lower incarceration rates and appoint judges who will deliver such rates. However, if voters have a taste for "tough on crime" stances, as evidence suggests they do, then a possible way to compromise is to pass longer sentences to the defendants who receive incarceration. By contrast, an elected judge, not having to worry about providing funding for extra inmates, is free to incarcerate more offenders. This is accentuated by the fact that local voters are beneficiaries of such behavior, but the whole state has to foot the bill, thus allowing the voters to pass the cost of crime prevention to the rest of the state. If voters can better monitor the incarceration rate than the average length of sentence however, then elected judges have no incentive to issue longer sentences. Appointed judges are more likely to be under pressure to reduce the number of short-term incarcerations. But the appointing body can ask for longer sentences in order to keep the "tough on crime" appeal to voters, resulting in appointed judges passing longer sentences, conditional on the incarceration decision.[6]

The wider range of issues for which state-level officials are responsible allows the appointing body an opportunity to offset the political damage of being potentially seen as "weak" on crime. Whereas a locally elected judge who fails to incarcerate convicted felons or who imposes shorter sentences is countering voters' wishes on issues that are central and defining to the judge's platform, the appointing body can truthfully claim that their relative leniency allows them to successfully champion other issues, such as keeping taxes low or defending the funding of other vital programs. For example, voters might be truly disappointed by low incarceration rate of convicted felons, but may still elect the governor based on her achievements in improving education funding.

If state-level voter preferences, controlling for other issues, motivate a reduction in the prison population, the lowest (political) cost means of doing so is likely to be to lower the rate of short-term incarceration. There are three reasons for this. First, the cost of crime relative to cost of incarceration is lower in crimes that call for short-term incarceration. Therefore, the substitute punishment of a suspended sentence or a large fine (as with driving under influence [DUI] offenses) is considered more appropriate here than for, say, violent crimes. Second, as more minor felonies also tend to be low-profile cases, they are easier to conceal from voters, so that the partial derivatives α_I and α_S will be of lower magnitude. Moreover, faced with a marginal choice between higher overall incarceration rates and long sentences for violent felons (a trade-off forced by prison capacity constraints), state-level voters may prefer longer sentences and less incarceration of more minor felons owing to the administrative costs of churning: processing new inmates and paroling more current inmates within the penal system. Finally, some (if not most) of the cost of long-term incarceration can be passed to a future administration. This makes long-term incarceration relatively cheaper to the current office holder by externalizing the costs in much the same way that occurs at the local jurisdictional level. This holds to the extent that closely contested election races result in discounting of future outcomes that occur after the next election, and may be especially true in the presence of term limits on state offices. If a judge is appointed, the objective function makes clear that pleasing the appointing body is more important to the judge than pleasing the voters. The body will reappoint the judges who have cooperated with the administration, even if that entails helping to free up budget funds by not overcrowding the prisons.

Elected judges do not have the luxury of issue-bundling. Their records are open for review by voters and, more likely, for criticism by their opponents. Since judges are not held liable by voters for other policies, they are free to pass the cost of incarceration and sentences to the other office holders in the state. In other words, the local judge probably has little authority over education provision or tax policy, and is unlikely to be seen as the most responsible contributor to state budget problems. This frees the judge to pass some of the cost of incarceration and sentencing to other parts of government. It is up to the governor and the legislature to make ends meet.[7] Thus, on the margin, elected judges should be more likely to send convicted felons to prison.

Seeing the differing incentives faced by elected and appointed judges, and how elected judges are able to exploit the rest of the state for the benefit of their constituents, one might easily wonder why the state legislatures do not change the selection process in favor of state appointment, especially as that change would give them more authority to control the judiciary. Hanssen (2001) points out that the judicial selection process can, indeed, be endogenous. However, his model applies more to the higher courts than to general jurisdiction courts. The main motivation of politicians to alter the judicial selection process arises from the ability of higher court judges to strike down pieces of legislation. The cost of political capital required to change an established system of elected judges for state general jurisdictional level criminal courts, possibly through state constitutional amendment, can easily be anticipated to be higher than the cost savings of reducing prison overcrowding and the loss of being able to credibly blame prison overcrowding problems upon the local judges (read "someone else"). For this reason, it is not surprising that, according to information available at the American Judicature Society's web site, there has not been a switch from election to appointment, or vice versa in any state in the sample during the eight-year data-sampling period of this study.[8,9] Thus, endogeneity of judicial selection mechanism is not a problem in this chapter.

DATA AND ESTIMATION

Criminal and County Characteristics

The United States Bureau of Justice Statistics produces a series of data releases that contain case characteristics, defendant characteristics, judicial selection system, and basic demographics. These data allow us to control for felony case contexts closely enough to allow examination of the effects of judicial selection on sentencing and racial disparities.

The data series, obtained from the Third Inter-University Consortium for Political and Social Research (ICPSR), is titled "State Court Processing Statistics: Felony Defendants in Large Urban Counties." By combining the 1990, 1992, 1994, 1996, and 1998 releases, we obtain a dataset of 72,602 observations on felony defendants in 54 of the nation's 75 most populous counties. These counties account for around a third of U.S. population and about a half of all crime in the United States. The Bureau of Justice Statistics (BJS) divided the 75 counties into four strata according to the number of filings, and from them, 54 counties were chosen for data collection. All of the most active counties (first stratum) were chosen, and other counties were sampled so that each stratum of activity had successively lower representation in the sample. In other words, the authors engaged in stratum sampling to accommodate the different county sizes, and the data are weighted accordingly. The filings represent all filings for the month of May of the sampling year. The data include adjudication information and case information to make it possible to estimate the desired models. One advantage of the file is that it provides multiple years of data, both before and after the wave of "three strikes and you are out" laws, so it is possible to test whether the judges responded to this revelation of voter preference for stiffer punishments.

The data on judicial selection come from the American Judicature Society's publication titled, "Judicial Selection in the States: Appellate and General Jurisdiction Courts." The courts in the dataset are all general jurisdiction courts.

Information on dates of adoption of three-strike laws comes from Wright (1998), and the estimates of jail overcrowding are derived from the data in Bureau of Justice Statistics' *Annual Survey of Jails: Jurisdiction-Level Data* series for the appropriate year. The summary statistics for each of our variables of interest are presented in table 6.2. Most of the variable names are self-explanatory. *Pro se* defense denotes a defendant who is representing himself at the trial. As the summary statistics show, the largest racial category of defendants is black (47 percent), while only 28 percent are white. The

Table 6.2 Summary Statistics

Variable	Mean	Std. Dev.
Incarcerated	0.392	0.488
Sentence Length (Months)	29.505	92.389
Elected Judge Presiding	0.488	0.500
Number of Prior Felony Convictions	0.953	2.119
No Prior Felony Convictions	0.652	0.476
Number of Charges	2.294	1.857
Female Defendant	0.192	0.632
White	0.281	0.450
Black	0.473	0.499
Asian	0.015	0.123
Hispanic	0.196	0.397
Other	0.004	0.063
In Custody at Time of Arrest	0.011	0.105
Dismissed	0.297	0.435
Convicted	0.690	0.462
Acquitted	0.011	0.106
Guilty Plea	0.550	0.498
Jail Overcrowding	1.056	0.222

Notes: The maximum sentence length recorded was 1440 months. The maximum numbers of charges and prior felony convictions are 69 and 91, respectively. Levels of jail overcrowding range from 0.501 to 1.746. The raw data set contains 72,602 observations, and 58,336 observations after removing cases with missing values for control variables.

adjudication outcome is not reported for 10,576 cases, but for those that are reported, 69 percent resulted in conviction, of which roughly 80 percent were pleaded. Only 1 percent of cases ended in acquittal, while 29.7 percent of the cases were dismissed. Roughly 39 percent of defendants are incarcerated (about half of those convicted), and the average sentence is around 30 months. Roughly 65 percent of the defendants are first-time felons. About half of the cases are decided by elected judges. Jails are on average slightly overcrowded—on average, they are at 105 percent of their rated capacity—but this figure varies from jails that are half full to those running at 175 percent of their rated capacity.

Table 6.3 reports the incarceration rates and conditional mean sentence lengths of defendants by the nature of conviction charges and by judicial selection method. Elected judges generally convict fewer defendants in all categories of crime. At the 10 percent significance level, elected judges incarcerate more of the defendants with convictions in assault, theft, weapon, other violent, other property, and other drug felonies. Elected judges also pass longer sentences (at 10 percent significance) in cases involving robbery, burglary,

Table 6.3 Rates of Incarceration and Mean Sentence Lengths, by Conviction Charge and Judicial Selection System

	Elected			Appointed		
	Number of cases	Percentage incarcerated	Mean sentence length[a]	Number of cases	Percentage incarcerated	Mean sentence length[a]
Conviction Charge						
Murder	72	97.1	389.2	109	97.1	374.1
Rape	175	84.4	118.3	198	79.3	113.9
Robbery	726	89.7	85.1***	1291	87.4	65.0***
Assault	677	75.9***	43.5	1649	68.7***	36.0
Other violent	525	76.4*	31.0	711	71.9*	40.4
Burglary	1229	75.7	42.9***	2058	77.8	33.2***
Theft	1711	70.8***	24.8***	2527	64.1***	20.3***
Other property	1705	59.8*	22.4***	1925	56.7*	21.2***
Drug trafficking	2208	76.7	37.1***	4501	78.2	29.1***
Other drug	2766	68.8***	20.7	3292	64.2***	20.8
Weapon	551	68.7*	17.89**	811	64.2*	30.7**
Driving	431	81	10.81	660	77.9	12.6
Other Public	443	69.3	12.2***	470	64.8	21.03***
Unknown felony	51	56.3**	17.0	146	74.8**	22.1

Notes: * Significant at 10 percent; ** significant at 5 percent; *** significant at 1 percent (two-tailed *t*-test for difference in the means).
[a] Means are conditional upon incarceration.

theft, other property, and drug trafficking, while appointed judges pass longer sentences in cases involving weapon and other public felony charges.

Empirical Model and Estimates

We analyze the incarceration decision and the length of imposed sentence decisions in a two-step procedure, following Heckman (1976), noting that only convicted defendants are incarcerated and only those who receive incarceration are sentenced to any time in jail or prison. To successfully estimate a two-stage selection model we have to find factors that influence the incarceration decision, but not the length of sentence. Jail overcrowding, whether the defendant is on parole, probation, or is a fugitive at the time of trial, and whether the defendant has been rearrested before the trial are factors that will influence the incarceration decision, but not the sentence length, and these variables can serve as instruments that allow us to properly identify the model.

The incarceration decision is estimated first using a Probit model. The indicator variable for incarceration is regressed on the set of explanatory variables listed in table 6.4 for the sample of all 58,336 observations in which there was a conviction, and for which we have data on all the control variables. Table 6.4 summarizes the predicted effects of each of our variables of interest upon judges' incarceration decisions, and upon the length of imposed sentences conditional upon a decision to incarcerate. The resulting first-stage model is:

$$P_{incarc} = F(\beta_0 + X_{1i}\beta_{1i} + X_{2i}\beta_{2i} + X_{3i}\beta_{3i}) \quad\quad (6.3)$$

Table 6.4 Predicted Effects of Variables Upon Incarceration and (Conditional) Sentence Length

Variable	Incarceration	Sentence length (Conditional)
Elected judge presiding	+	+/−
Number of prior felony convictions	+	+
No prior felony convictions	−	−
Number of charges	+	+
Female defendant	−	−
Guilty plea	+	−
Race	?	?
In custody at the time of arrest	+	+
Overcrowded jail	−	
Three strikes	+	
On probation at the time of arrest	+	
On parole at the time of arrest	+	
Rearrested prior to trial	+	
Fugitive	+	

where X_1 is a vector of case characteristics (such as conviction charge),
X_2 is a vector of defendant characteristics (such as the defendant's age), and
X_3 is a vector of jurisdiction characteristics (such as whether an elected judge is presiding.

The second-stage regression estimates the length of sentences. The model controls for selection effects by including the inverse Mills ratio of the predicted probability of being incarcerated, as computed from the first-stage Probit regression. Besides the inverse Mills ratio, the factors that determine the length of the sentence include many variables that predict the likelihood of incarceration. The model is:

$$\text{Timemax1}_i = \beta_0 + Z_{1i}\beta_{1i} + Z_{2i}\beta_{2i} + Z_{3i}\beta_{3i} + \varepsilon_i, \qquad (6.4)$$

where Z_1, Z_2, and Z_3 represent the same three categories of variables as in equation (6.3), and ε_i is the error term.

The marginal effects from the first-stage Probit are reported in the first column of table 6.5, while the results of the second-stage equation are reported in the second column of the same table. Generally, repeat offenders, those who commit multiple crimes or those who commit "harder" crimes, pose a higher crime risk if not put in prison and can expect a stiffer sentence. Thus, we expect the number of total charges, number of previous felony convictions, and the seriousness of the crime to have a positive impact on both the likelihood of incarceration and the length of sentence. Indeed, each previous felony offense increases the likelihood of incarceration by 1.4 percent and the expected sentence length by 2.04 months.[10] Similarly, first-time felons are 16.4 percent less likely to be incarcerated and receive sentences that are 3.18 months shorter, conditional upon incarceration. Each additional charge increases likelihood of incarceration and sentence length by 1.6 percent and 1.88 months respectively.

Our models control for the severity of the conviction charge, although we do not report the coefficients in tables 6.5 and 6.6. The conviction charge is the most serious charge for which the defendant was convicted. The coefficients are in line with expectations, as defendants committing more serious crimes are more likely to be incarcerated and receive longer sentences. Judges are more lenient on females both in likelihood of incarceration and sentence length. Female defendants are 5.2 percent less likely to be incarcerated, and receive sentences that are 2.72 months shorter on average. Defendants can also enter into plea bargains and, as the summary statistics in table 6.2 show, the vast majority do. Depending on the structure of the plea bargain population, it is possible that those who plea bargain are more likely to be incarcerated, as the terms of the plea bargain typically involve accepting a sentence, albeit a shorter one. These effects are apparent in the results, as those who enter into a plea bargain are much more likely to be incarcerated (50.6 percent), but with sentences that are, on average, nearly five years shorter, given incarceration.

Consistent with Mustard's (2001) findings, we expect that minorities are more likely to receive incarceration and receive longer sentences. We find

Table 6.5 Incarceration and Sentence Length Models (Judges Grouped by Initial Selection Method)

	Incarceration[†]	Sentence Length[††]
Elected judge presiding	0.036	−6.74
	(4.20)**	(5.48)**
Number of prior felony convictions	0.014	2.039
	(6.50)**	(6.10)**
No prior felony convictions	−0.164	−3.175
	(19.99)**	(2.42)*
Number of charges	0.016	1.879
	(8.16)**	(3.87)**
Female defendant	−0.052	−2.723
	(7.73)**	(3.43)**
Guilty plea	0.506	−55.877
	(72.73)**	(10.53)**
Black	0.042	0.252
	(6.73)**	(0.19)
Hispanic	0.066	−1.172
	(8.58)**	(0.76)
Asian	0.02	−8.583
	(0.82)	(3.17)**
Other	0.007	3.421
	(0.18)	(1.26)
In custody at the time of arrest	0.183	9.473
	(7.09)**	(1.62)
Overcrowded jail	−0.002	
	(0.12)	
Three strikes	0.062	
	(3.75)**	
On probation at the time of arrest	0.076	
	(9.77)**	
On parole at the time of arrest	0.129	
	(11.05)**	
Rearrested prior to trial	0.047	
	(4.81)**	
Fugitive	0.094	
	(5.41)**	
Observations	58,336	56,381

Robust z-statistics in parentheses

* Significant at 10 percent; ** significant at 5 percent; *** significant at 1 percent.

[†] Dependent variable is a binary variable equal to 1 if defendant is incarcerated, 0 otherwise. Also included are: dummy variables for conviction offense, state fixed effect dummies, year dummies, legal representation dummies (public defender omitted), age of the defendant, age square, dummy variable for defendants under 18 years of age. Marginal effects (result of dprobit command in Stata) are reported.

[††] Dependent variable is the sentence length in months, truncated at 1440 months. Also included are: dummy variables for conviction offense, state fixed effect dummies, year dummies, legal representation dummies (public defender omitted), age of the defendant, age square, dummy variable for defendants under 18 years of age. Second-stage coefficients (result of Heckman command in Stata) are reported.

that blacks are 4.2 percent more likely to be incarcerated than white defendants and Hispanics 6.6 percent more, while the likelihood of incarceration for Asians and other races is not significantly different from that for whites. However, after controlling for the likelihood of incarceration, minorities do

Table 6.6 Incarceration and Sentence Length Models, Re-Classifying as Elected Judges Those Appointed Judges Who Are Subject to Retention Elections

	Incarceration[†]	Sentence Length[††]
Elected judge presiding	0.116	−27.957
	(8.76)**	(7.99)**
Number of prior felony convictions	0.015	2.039
	(6.58)**	(6.10)**
No prior felony convictions	−0.162	−3.536
	(19.71)**	(2.71)**
Number of charges	0.016	1.942
	(8.03)**	(3.98)**
Female defendant	−0.052	−2.837
	(7.71)**	(3.57)**
Guilty plea	0.507	−55.812
	(72.90)**	(10.48)**
Black	0.043	0.401
	(6.83)**	(−0.30)
Hispanic	0.065	−0.91
	(8.51)**	(−0.59)
Asian	0.02	−8.113
	(−0.79)	(3.01)**
Other	0.01	2.319
	(−0.26)	(−0.87)
In custody at the time of arrest	0.184	9.115
	(7.11)**	(−1.55)
Overcrowded jail	0	
	(−0.03)	
Three strikes	0.062	
	(3.73)**	
On probation at the time of arrest	0.077	
	(9.84)**	
On parole at the time of arrest	0.128	
	(10.97)**	
Rearrested prior to trial	0.046	
	(4.78)**	
Fugitive	0.091	
	(5.36)**	
Observations	58,336	56,381

Robust z-statistics in parentheses.
* Significant at 10 percent; ** significant at 5 percent; *** significant at 1 percent.
[†] Dependent variable is a binary variable equal to 1 if defendant is incarcerated, 0 otherwise. Also included are: dummy variables for conviction offense, state fixed effect dummies, year dummies, legal representation dummies (public defender omitted), age of the defendant, age square, dummy variable for defendants under 18 years of age. Marginal effects (result of dprobit command in Stata) are reported.
[††] Dependent variable is the sentence length in months, truncated at 1440 months. Also included are: dummy variables for conviction offense, state fixed effect dummies, year dummies, legal representation dummies (public defender omitted), age of the defendant, age square, dummy variable for defendants under 18 years of age. Second-stage coefficients (result of Heckman command in Stata) are reported.

not receive significantly sentences different from whites receive, except for Asians, who receive sentences that are on average eight months shorter than those for whites. Finally, defendants in custody are more likely to receive incarceration, as this typically just represents an extension of their current sentence, with the model estimating a 9.47-month average increase in sentence length.

Now turning to examine the variables that appear only in the first-stage model, we expect overcrowding of jails to decrease the probability of a defendant being incarcerated, but the estimation shows the magnitude of the effect to be statistically insignificant. Since three-strikes laws provide for mandatory incarceration of repeat felons, the sign on the three-strikes dummy should be positive. The data support this hypothesis, as being subject to three-strikes legislation increases a felon's likelihood of incarceration by 6.2 percent. Similarly, as defendants who were on parole or probation at the time of arrest, those who were fugitives at the time of trial, and those rearrested prior to the trial, all show higher propensities to commit further crimes if released, we expect that they should be more likely to be incarcerated. This is indeed the case. The likelihood of incarceration is increased for each factor, with estimates of 7.6, 12.9, 4.7, and 9.4 percent for the indicator variables for being on probation, being on parole, being rearrested prior to trial, and being a fugitive, respectively. As controls in both stages, in addition to the indicators for conviction charges mentioned previously, we added the age of the defendant, age squared, and indicator variables for a defendant under age 18, and type of legal representation. We also use indicators to control for unobservable state-specific effects, particularly differences in state laws, and for the year, to control for year-specific effects across states. This is consistent with methodology reported in Besley and Case (2003) and Shepherd (2002).

Finally, we look at the elected versus appointed judges. Following the logic of the model we developed earlier, the coefficient on the dummy variable representing an elected judge should be positive in the first-stage models, as elected judges should be more likely to incarcerate the defendant. In the second stage, the coefficient could be either positive or negative, although the net effect of the influences mentioned in the section "Theoretical Differences in the Costs and Benefits of Appointed and Elected Judges" is likely to favor shorter sentences. We find that elected judges are 3.6 percent more likely to incarcerate the defendant, yet elected judges pass sentences (conditional on incarceration) that are 6.74 months shorter than those passed by appointed judges.

As a sensitivity test of our central hypothesis, we also estimated the results in a model that groups elected judge counties together with counties that have appointed judges facing retention elections. The results, as seen in table 6.6, further support our central hypothesis, as the trade-off between incarceration and sentence length is exacerbated. As seen in table 6.6, the elected judge variable, which here indicates both elected judges and appointees facing retention elections, shows that elected judges are almost 12 percent more likely to incarcerate convicted defendants, while appointed judges hand down sentences that are more than two years longer on average.

Conclusion

The model that we develop in this chapter suggests that when controlling for case characteristics, time effects, and state effects, elected judges make sentencing decisions that lead to higher incarceration rates, but with shorter sentences than those issued by appointed judges. This is consistent with the trade-off that the appointing bodies face, where the desire to appear to be tough on crime conflicts with the need to provide funds to house prisoners. State-level appointing bodies, more accountable for violations of budgetary constraints than are local judges, can pressure appointed judges to decrease the number of short-term incarcerations. This reduces prison population pressures, and has the side effect of yielding higher average sentences. This behavior allows the appointing body to allocate funds to different pending issues while still appearing to be "tough on crime." In effect, the current appointing body is able to pass some costs of appearing "tough on crime" to future generations of politicians.

Elected judges also act in accordance with incentives provided by voters. By incarcerating more defendants elected judges are able to pass the cost of crime deterrence in their county to the rest of the state, which should be in line with local voters' preferences. Furthermore, even (initially) appointed judges cater to local voters in those counties where retention elections determine whether the judge continues beyond the initial appointment.

Despite the idealistic call for judges to be purely "independent interpreters of the law," our results demonstrate that judges respond to the political incentives created by their jurisdiction's method of judicial selection. Knowing that judges do indeed act as do other rational agents in the political system, communities, citizens, and reformers are well advised to explicitly consider the rational self-interest of judges as well as those of opposing advocates when crafting regulations or designing new institutions.

Notes

1. Brace and Hall (1990, 1993, 1995), Canon and Jaros (1970), Hall (1995), and Hall and Brace (1996), all of which we discuss below.
2. Table 6.1 details these subtleties. For instance, some of the states where judges are appointed use merit selection through a nominating commission, while others do not. Some states select judges through partisan elections, while other states have nonpartisan elections. The reappointment rules vary widely as well, as some states where judges are elected prescribe retention elections (an up-or-down referendum upon the incumbent) at the end of the term (as do some states where judges are initially appointed), while other states require reelection campaigns against a possible field of challengers. Yet other states use a mix of election and appointment methods, depending on the court level, and in Arizona, reappointment rules vary according to the population size of a county. Furthermore, both initial terms and term length after retention vary across states in a manner that does not suggest a systematic pattern. Initial terms vary

from one year in Florida, to the appointment until the age of 70 in Massachusetts.

3. The former cost includes defensive expenditures (e.g., installing antiburglar alarms), which are a direct cost of preventing crime.

4. We here present no theoretical reason to expect the job satisfaction of appointed judges to systematically differ from that of elected judges, after controlling for other jurisdictional variables in the model. We differentiate the utilities only to establish that this is a parameter open for future conjecture.

5. Besley and Coate (2000) develop a model of how the bundling of policies influences the behavior of appointed and elected regulators.

6. We do not claim that elected judges are necessarily more lenient on the defendants, but simply that appointed judges issue, on average, longer sentences as a consequence of the incarceration/sentence length trade-off.

7. Of course, the judge cannot completely indulge in this behavior because of two factors: first, the existence of higher courts that can overturn the judgment (especially in those states with an elected general jurisdiction judiciary combined with appointment of higher court judges), and second, the regulators can withdraw their party's support for the judge if he or she "crosses the line," which can be especially effective in states with partisan election systems.

8. http://www.ajs.org

9. There have been, however, adjustments in details of selection (e.g., eligibility requirements, adjustment to procedure, and so on). Although quantifying these and analyzing their impact would be an interesting topic, it is outside the scope of this chapter. Most of the adjustments were to procedures for selection of higher court judges.

10. Throughout this subsection, we use phrases such as "percent more likely" and "percent less likely" to describe what are actually percentage point changes in the expected probability of incarceration, $\hat{P}_{incarc}$.

CHAPTER 7

ECONOMIC DEVELOPMENT TAKINGS AS GOVERNMENT FAILURE

Ilya Somin

INTRODUCTION

In *The Wealth of Nations,* Adam Smith famously argued that decentralized market transactions generate wealth "by an invisible hand" (Smith 1976) and that they usually achieve this end better than direct governmental efforts to control the allocation of resources. Takings for "economic development" are based on the exact opposite assumption: that resources will often fail to generate as much wealth as they should unless their allocation is controlled by the visible hand of the state. Unfortunately, the visible hand of eminent domain often destroys as much wealth as it creates and too easily becomes a grasping hand serving the interests of the politically powerful at the expense of the targeted weak.

As a general rule, economic development takings represent a failure of the political process, not a useful tool for promoting economic growth. Far from curing market failure, as advocates claim, economic development takings represent an almost textbook example of government failure in the legal system, under which organized interest groups use the power of government to benefit themselves at the expense of a poorly organized and often "rationally ignorant" public.[1]

The Supreme Court's recent decision in *Kelo v. City of New London,* which upheld development condemnations in a close 5–4 vote, has focused national attention on the issue of economic development takings (545 U.S. 469 [2005]). *Kelo* and recent state court decisions have rekindled the debate over whether government can condemn private property and transfer it to new private owners for the purpose of promoting "economic development." Both the Fifth Amendment to the federal Constitution and all state constitutions contain a "public use clause" that prohibits government from taking private property except for a "public use."[2] In the nineteenth century, these provisions were often interpreted in such a way as to forbid most takings that transfer condemned private property to other private parties.[3] However, over the last 50 years, the U.S. Supreme Court and many state courts allowed that restriction on the condemnation power to atrophy.

In the leading 1984 case of *Hawaii Housing Authority v. Midkiff*, the Supreme Court held that condemnations and private-to-private transfers are acceptable under the public use provision of the Takings Clause, so long as they are "rationally related to a conceivable public purpose" (467 U.S. 229, [1984], at 241). As a result of *Midkiff* and similar decisions in many state courts, local governments have been able to undertake so-called economic development takings—transfers from one owner to another simply because the new owner is expected to make a greater contribution to the local economy. A 2002 treatise concludes that "nearly all courts have settled on a broader understanding [of public use] that requires only that the taking yield some public benefit or advantage" (Dana and Merrill 2002).[4] This statement was not entirely accurate even at the time it was written,[5] but it did reflect the dominant view of the late twentieth century.

More recently, however, the public use issue has been dramatically reopened. In *Kelo v. New London*, the U.S. Supreme Court upheld the economic development rationale in a surprisingly narrow 5–4 decision (545 U.S. 469 [2005]). *Kelo* followed closely after *County of Wayne v. Hathcock* (684 N.W.2d 765 [Mich. 2004]), in which the Michigan Supreme Court overruled *Poletown Neighborhood Council v. City of Detroit* (304 N.W.2d 455 [Mich. 1981]), the most famous earlier decision justifying economic development takings.[6] While it was not the first decision upholding so-called economic development takings,[7] *Poletown* was by far the most widely publicized. The notoriety stemmed from the massive scale of Detroit's use of eminent domain: destroying an entire neighborhood and condemning the homes of 4,200 people, as well as numerous businesses, churches, and schools, so that the land could be transferred to General Motors for the construction of a new factory (Somin 2004a).

In addition to the highly publicized cases of *Hathcock* and *Kelo*, the supreme courts of Illinois, Oklahoma, Ohio, and South Carolina have recently invalidated or significantly restricted the economic development rationale for takings.[8] Eleven state supreme courts now categorically forbid virtually all economic development takings,[9] and several others, at the very least, restrict them.[10] In the wake of *Kelo*, a massive political backlash against economic development takings has emerged, resulting in new legislation restricting eminent domain authority in 43 states.[11] Similar measures have been enacted by Congress and in an executive order by President George W. Bush (Somin 2009, 2149–53).

Legal rules permitting economic development takings allow politically powerful interest groups to "capture" the condemnation process for the purpose of enriching themselves at the expense of the poor and politically weak. While such takings are not the only type of condemnation subject to this kind of abuse, they are especially vulnerable to it because "economic development" can justify almost any condemnation that transfers property to a commercial enterprise. Several other aspects of economic development takings also exacerbate the danger, including the failure to require the new owners of condemned property to actually provide the economic benefits that supposedly justify condemnation in the first place, and the refusal of courts to consider the social costs of condemnation as well as the claimed benefits.

ECONOMIC DEVELOPMENT TAKINGS AND THE POLITICAL PROCESS

The Economic Development Rationale Can Justify Almost Any Taking That Benefits a Commercial Enterprise

The main danger posed by "economic development" takings is the possibility that this rationale can be used to condemn virtually any property for transfer to a private commercial enterprise. As the Michigan Supreme Court explained in *Hathcock:*

> [The] "economic benefit" rationale would validate practically *any* exercise of the power of eminent domain on behalf of a private entity. After all, if one's ownership of private property is forever subject to the government's determination that another private party would put one's land to better use, then the ownership of real property is perpetually threatened by the expansion of plans of any large discount retailer, "megastore," or the like. (*Hathcock*, at 786, emphasis in original)

Courts in at least two of the other states that forbid economic development takings have reached the same conclusion. In 2002, the Supreme Court of Illinois refused to allow a "contribu[tion] to economic growth in the region" to justify a taking because such a standard could justify virtually any condemnation that benefited private industry since "every lawful business" contributes to economic growth to some degree.[12] Similarly, the Supreme Court of Kentucky banned the economic development rationale in 1979 largely because "[w]hen the door is once opened to it, there is no limit that can be drawn" (*Owensboro v. McCormick*, 581 S.W.2d 3 [Ky. 1979] at 8).[13] The U.S. Supreme Court dissenters in *Kelo* have also focused on this threat, warning that "nearly all real property is susceptible to condemnation on the Court's theory" that the economic development rationale is a sufficient justification (*Kelo*, at 504 [O'Connor, J., dissenting]).

Those decisions and dissents may slightly overstate the case, but their main point is sound. Economic development can rationalize virtually any taking that benefits a private business because any such entity can claim that its success might "bolster the economy." It is perhaps possible to try to limit the scope of the development rationale by requiring that the economic benefit gained exceed some preset minimum size. This, indeed, is what the *Poletown* court tried to do when it held that the benefit must be "clear and significant" (*Poletown*, at 458). Yet this amounts simply to saying that any taking benefiting a sufficiently large business enterprise can qualify. Moreover, this rationale actually creates perverse incentives to increase the amount of property condemned for any given project (Somin 2004a).

Even some of the defenders of the economic development rationale admit that it is extraordinarily broad. At the *Kelo* oral argument, Justice Sandra Day O'Connor asked New London's counsel Wesley Horton whether the economic development rationale would allow condemnation of "a Motel 6 [if] a city thinks 'if we had a Ritz-Carlton, we'd get higher taxes.'" Horton answered that that would be "OK." (*Kelo*, U.S. Supreme Court Oral Argument Transcript, 2005 WL 529436 at 20–21). In response to Justice Antonin Scalia's question asking whether "[y]ou can take from A and give it to B, if B pays more in taxes," Horton answered "[y]es, if it's a significant amount" (at 21).

Almost any condemnation that benefits a large business at the expense of a smaller competitor, a residential owner, or a nonprofit organization, could be rationalized on the grounds that there would be a "significant" increase in tax revenue. Residential owners and especially nonprofit organizations (which generally do not pay taxes on their property) are especially vulnerable.[14] While the economic development rationale may not be literally limitless, it is certainly close to it.

The Absence of Binding Obligations on New Owners of Condemned Property

The danger of abuse created by the economic development rationale has been exacerbated by courts' failure to require new owners of condemned property to actually provide the economic benefits that justified condemnation in the first place. The imposition of such obligations probably would not eliminate all the harm created by economic development takings. But their absence is likely to exacerbate it.

The lack of a binding obligation creates incentives for public officials to rely on exaggerated claims of economic benefit that neither they nor the new owners have any obligation to live up to. Courts in a number of jurisdictions have held that property cannot be condemned without assurances that it will be employed only for public uses that are precisely specified in advance.[15] Unfortunately, decisions permitting economic development takings depart from this principle.

1. *Poletown's* failure to impose binding legal obligations on the new owners of condemned property

The *Poletown* court upheld the massive condemnations in Detroit primarily, if not solely, because of the "clear and significant" economic benefits that the GM factory was expected to provide for the city. Indeed, the majority suggested that if the expected benefits were not so great, "we would hesitate to sanction approval of the project" (*Poletown*, at 459). This fact renders all the more dubious the court's failure to require either the city or GM to ensure that the expected benefits would actually materialize.

Yet, as Justice Ryan emphasized in his dissenting opinion, the court failed to impose even minimal requirements of this kind.[16] *City of Detroit v. Vavro*, a 1989 Michigan Court of Appeals decision interpreting *Poletown*, confirmed Ryan's view, holding that "a careful reading of the *Poletown* decision reveals that... a binding commitment [to provide the economic benefits used to justify condemnation] is unnecessary in order to allow the city to make use of eminent domain" (442 N.W.2d 730 [Mich. Ct. App. 1989], at 731–732.) Indeed, the *Vavro* court went on to conclude that *Poletown* did not even require the new owner to proceed with the project that was initially used to justify the condemnation, much less proceed with it in a way that provided some predetermined level of economic benefit to the public.[17]

2. Inflated claims of economic benefit in *Poletown*

The *Poletown* condemnations dramatically illustrate the danger of taking inflated estimates of economic benefit at face value. The City of Detroit and GM claimed that the construction of a new plant on the expropriated property would create some 6,150 jobs (*Poletown*, at 467 [Ryan, J., dissenting]). The estimate of "at least 6,000 jobs" was formally endorsed by both Detroit mayor Coleman Young and GM chairman Thomas Murphy.[18] Yet neither the city nor GM had any legal obligation to actually provide the 6,000 jobs or the other economic benefits they had promised.

The danger inherent in this arrangement was apparent even at the time. As Justice Ryan warned in dissent, "there are no guarantees from General Motors about employment levels at the new assembly plant...[O]nce [the condemned property] is sold to General Motors, there will be no public control whatsoever over the management, operation, or conduct of the plant to be built there" (*Poletown*, at 480). "[O]ne thing is certain," Ryan emphasized, "[t]he level of employment at the new GM plant will be determined by private corporate managers primarily with reference, not to the rate of regional unemployment, but to profit" (*Poletown*, at 480). Justice Ryan's warning was prescient. The GM plant opened two years late; and by 1988—seven years after the *Poletown* condemnations—it employed "no more than 2,500 workers" (Michael 2001, 300). Even in 1998, at the height of the 1990s economic boom, the plant "still employed only 3,600" workers, less than 60 percent of the promised 6,150 (Michael 2001, 325).

3. Inability to impose binding obligations as a systematic weakness of the economic development rationale for condemnation

The failure to impose any binding obligations on the new owners of property is not an idiosyncrasy limited to any one state. The same problem is evident in every state that permits economic development takings.

The *Kelo* case itself was remarkably similar to *Poletown* in this respect. As the dissenting opinion in Connecticut supreme court in *Kelo* pointed out, "[t]here are no assurances of a public use in the development plan [under which the owners' property was condemned]; there was no signed development agreement at the time of the takings; and all of the evidence suggests that the economic climate will not support the project so that the public benefits can be realized" (*Kelo*, at 602 [Zarella, J., dissenting]). Years after the condemnations were upheld by the U.S. Supreme Court, the New London development plan, used to justify the *Kelo* condemnations, had little prospect of success. The plan's poor outlook is the result of "contract disputes and financial uncertainty" and the unwillingness of investors to commit to a flawed project, not just the adverse publicity resulting from the public backlash against the Supreme Court's decision (*Kelo*, at 602).

Like Connecticut, other states that allow economic development condemnations also fail to require either the government or the new owners to actually provide the promised public benefits.[19] Thus, *Poletown* and *Kelo* highlight a systematic shortcoming of the economic development rationale generally. It is not an idiosyncratic problem confined to Connecticut and pre-*Hathcock* Michigan.

Why would such a systematic legal failure arise? I suggest two tentative explanations. First, requiring a binding commitment to the creation of specific economic benefits for the community might severely constrain the discretion of the new owners, thereby possibly leading to inefficient business practices. For example, if GM had been required to ensure that at least 6,000 workers were employed at the Poletown plant, it might have been forced to forgo efficient labor-saving technology. Courts may well be reluctant to intrude so severely on the new owners' business judgment. While this is a serious problem with requiring binding commitments, it also provides a strong argument against permitting economic development takings in the first place. If there is no effective way to ensure that the promised economic benefits of condemnation are actually provided, this circumstance supports the *Hathcock* court's conclusion that economic development projects are best left to the private sector (*Hathcock*, at 783–784). Moreover, mandating the employment of a particular minimum number of workers might only exacerbate the market distortion caused by the use of eminent domain to artificially reduce the cost of land for the firm in question. Both factors will tend to cause overinvestment in the project in question.

A second possible explanation is that some judges may have an unjustified faith in the efficacy of the political process and thus may be willing to allow the executive and legislative branches of government to control oversight of development projects. For example, the *Poletown* majority emphasized that courts should defer to legislative judgments of "public purpose" (Poletown, at 458–459). Whatever the general merits of such confidence in the political process, it is seriously misplaced in situations in which politically powerful interest groups can employ the powers of government at the expense of the relatively weak.[20]

4. Lack of binding obligations increases the danger of interest group capture

In the absence of any binding obligations to deliver on the promised economic benefits, nothing prevents municipalities and private interests from using inflated estimates of economic benefits to justify condemnations and then failing to monitor or provide any such benefits once courts approve the takings and the properties are transferred to their new owners.

Localities and businesses can sometimes circumvent the public use requirement simply by overestimating the likely economic benefits of a condemnation. Municipalities may overestimate intentionally, or they may simply take a private business' inflated estimates at face value. Both business interests and political leaders dependent on their support have tremendous incentives to overestimate the economic benefits of projects furthered by condemnation. Courts are in a poor position to second-guess seemingly plausible financial and employment estimates provided by officials. Even if governments and businesses do not engage in deliberate deception, there is a natural tendency to overestimate the public benefits and the likelihood of success of projects that advance one's own private interests.[21] For example, government officials and major league sports owners repeatedly claim that public financing for sports stadiums will create major economic benefits for cities, despite overwhelming evidence to the contrary.[22] Whether corporate and government leaders deliberately lie or honestly believe that "what is good for General Motors is good for America," the outcome is likely to be the same.

Ignoring the Costs of Condemnation

An especially striking aspect of the *Poletown* decision was the majority's failure to even mention the costs imposed by condemnation on the people of Poletown or the city of Detroit as a whole. Unfortunately, this problem is not confined to Michigan's *Poletown*-era jurisprudence; it also arises in other states that permit economic development takings.

1. The economic costs of *Poletown*

The *Poletown* case dramatically illustrates how the promised economic benefits of condemnations often fail to materialize and are outweighed by the massive costs. Not only did the new GM plant create far fewer jobs than promised,[23] but the limited economic benefits the plant did create were probably outweighed by the economic harm the project caused the city.

According to estimates prepared at the time, the "public cost of preparing a site agreeable to... General Motors [was] over $200 million," yet GM paid the city only $8 million to acquire the property (*Poletown*, at 470 [Ryan, J., dissenting]). Eventually, the costs of the condemnation rose to some $250 million (Somin 2004a, 1018). In addition, we must add to the costs borne by the city's taxpayers, the economic damage inflicted by the destruction of some 600 businesses and 1,400 residential properties (Michael 2001).[24] Although we have no reliable statistics on the number of people employed by the businesses destroyed as a result of the *Poletown* condemnation,[25] it is quite possible that more workers lost than gained jobs as a result of the decision. If we conservatively assume that the 600 eliminated businesses employed an average of slightly more than four workers, the total lost work force turns out to be equal to or greater than the 2,500 jobs created at the GM plant by 1988.[26] And this calculation does not consider the jobs and other economic benefits lost as a result of the destruction of numerous non-profit institutions such as churches, schools, and hospitals. Overall, even if we consider the *Poletown* condemnation's impact in narrowly economic terms, it is likely that it did the people of Detroit more harm than good.

The failure of the *Poletown* takings to produce any clear net economic benefit for the city has significance beyond the case itself. In *Poletown*, the magnitude of the economic crisis facing Detroit and the detailed public scrutiny given to the city's condemnation decision led the court to conclude that the economic benefit of the taking was particularly "clear and signifi-cant." The court even went so far as to say that, "[i]f the public benefit was not so clear and significant, we would hesitate to sanction approval of such a project" (Poletown, at 459). If the claimed "public benefit" of even so "clear" a case as *Poletown* ultimately turned out to be a mirage, it seems unlikely that courts will do any better in weighing claims of economic benefit in more typical cases where the evidence is less extensive and less closely scrutinized.

2. Ignoring costs in other states

Other states that continue to permit economic development takings also give little or no consideration to the harm they cause. In *Kelo*, the Connecticut supreme court conceded that the plaintiff property owners in the case would suffer serious harm if forced out of their homes and businesses.[27] In addi-tion, some $80 million in taxpayer money had been allocated to the develop-ment project, without any realistic prospect of a return that rises above a tiny fraction of that amount (Kelo, 843 A.2d 500 [Conn. 2004] [Zarella, J., dis-senting], at 596–600). Yet the court refused to consider the significance of those massive costs, claiming "the balancing of the benefits and social costs of a particular project is uniquely a legislative function" (Kelo [Conn. 2004], at 541, note 58). The U.S. Supreme Court agreed, emphasizing that "we decline to second-guess the City's considered judgments about the efficacy of its development plan" (*Kelo*, at 488). Contrary to the Connecticut court, the political process often cannot be depended on to give due consideration to the "social costs" of economic development takings; such condemnations generally benefit the politically powerful, while the costs tend to fall on the poor and politically disadvantaged. Yet the approach adopted in *Poletown* and *Kelo* is similar to that followed in other states that permit economic development condemnations.[28] To this day, there is not a single state that permits economic development takings, yet requires the government to pro-vide proof that the economic benefits of condemnation will exceed the costs.

The same problem recurs with "blight" condemnations, takings justified by the allegedly dilapidated or unsafe state of the property in question. For example, the Supreme Court's landmark 1954 decision in *Berman v. Parker* (348 U.S. 26 [1954]), which held that blight condemnations are permissible under the Takings Clause, simply ignored the costs inflicted on the over 5,000 lower-income African American residents who were expelled from the area condemned.[29]

3. Nonmonetary costs of economic development takings

In addition to the economic costs to communities and homeowners, economic development takings also inflict major nonpecuniary costs on their victims by destroying communities and forcing residents to relocate to less desired locations. As Jane Jacobs (1961, 5) explained in her classic 1961 study,

[P]eople who get marked with the planners' hex signs are pushed about, expropriated, and uprooted much as if they were the subjects of a conquering power. Thousands upon thousands of small businesses are destroyed. . . . Whole communities are torn apart and sown to the winds, with a reaping of cynicism, resentment and despair that must be seen to be believed.

While "fair market value" may compensate homeowners and businesses for part of the financial losses they incur, it does not compensate them for the destruction of community ties, disruption of plans, and psychological harm they suffer.[30] These kinds of costs are known in the literature as losses of the owners' "subjective value."[31] Scholars from a wide range of ideological perspectives have reinforced Jacobs' early conclusion that development condemnations inflict enormous social costs that go beyond their "economic" impact, narrowly defined.[32] The existence of such large uncompensated costs exacerbates the danger posed by government failure in the decision to undertake economic development condemnations.

Economic Development Takings and Interest Group "Capture" and Rent Seeking

Obviously, economic development takings are not the only exercises of the eminent domain power vulnerable to rent seeking and capture by interest groups seeking to use the powers of government for their own benefit. Indeed, interest group capture of government agencies and rent seeking are serious dangers for a wide range of government activities.[33] However, there are three major reasons why economic development takings are especially vulnerable to this threat: the nearly limitless applicability of the economic development rationale; severe limits on electoral accountability caused by low transparency; and time horizon problems.

1. Nearly limitless scope

As we have seen, the economic development rationale for takings can potentially justify almost any condemnation that benefits a commercial enterprise.[34] Such a protean rationale for the use of eminent domain exacerbates the danger of interest group capture by greatly increasing the range of interest groups that can potentially use it. By the same token, it also increases the range of projects that those interest groups can hope to build on condemned land that is transferred to them; presumably, any project that might increase development or produce tax revenue would be acceptable. Both factors tend to increase the attractiveness of eminent domain condemnations as a means of making political payoffs to powerful interest groups.

2. Severely constrained electoral accountability

Interest group manipulation of economic development takings could be curtailed if public officials responsible for condemnations faced credible threats of punishment at the polls after they approved condemnations that reward rent seeking. Unfortunately, such punishment is highly unlikely for three important reasons. First, the calculation of the costs and benefits of most development projects is extremely complex, and it is difficult for ordinary voters to understand whether a particular project is cost-effective or not. Studies have repeatedly shown that most voters have very little knowledge of politics and public policy.[35] Most are often ignorant even of basic facts about the political system (Somin 1998, 416–419). Such ignorance is not an accident or a consequence of "stupidity." It is in fact a rational response to the insignificance of any one vote to electoral outcomes; if a voter's only reason to become informed is to ensure that she votes for the "best" candidate in order to ensure that individual's election to office, this turns out to be almost no incentive at all because the likelihood that any one vote will be decisive is infinitesimally small.[36] Ignorance is likely to be an even more serious problem in a complex and nontransparent field such as the evaluation of economic development takings.

While the same danger may exist with some traditional takings, these usually at least produce readily observable benefits such as a road or a bridge—public assets that can be seen and used by the average voter. Moreover, these benefits usually become apparent as soon as the project in question is completed. By contrast, the alleged public benefit of economic development takings is a generalized contribution to the local economy that the average citizen often will not notice, much less be able to measure.

Second, even if voters were much better informed, democratic accountability for economic development takings may often be inadequate. Unlike with most conventional takings, the success or failure of a project made possible by economic development condemnations is usually apparent only years after the condemnation takes place. In the *Poletown* case, the GM factory did not even open until 1985, four years after the 1981 condemnations and two years behind schedule (Wylie 1989). Moreover, not until the late 1980s did it become clear that the plant would produce far less than the expected 6,000 jobs (Wylie 1989, 214–215, Michael 2001).

By that time, of course, public attention had moved on to other issues, and in any event, many of the politicians who had approved the 1981 condemnations might no longer be in office. Given such limited time horizons, a rational, self-interested Detroit political leader might well have been willing to support the *Poletown* condemnations even if he anticipated that the expected benefits would eventually fail to materialize. By the time this became evident to the public, he could be out of office in any event. In the meantime, he could benefit from an immediate increase in political support from General Motors and other private interests benefiting from the taking.

Finally, the danger of government failure in this field is greatly exacerbated by the fact that the targets of economic development takings are usually poor and politically weak. Since World War II, some 3 to 4 million Americans have been displaced by economic development and "urban renewal" takings, most of them poor and minorities (Somin 2007a, 269–270). In the 1960s, urban renewal takings were sometimes referred to as "negro removal," because so many of them targeted poor African Americans (Pritchett 2003, 47). A 2007 survey suggests that most recent economic development takings also target the poor (Carpenter and Ross 2007).

Targeting the poor makes it less likely that the victims of economic development takings will be able to effectively resist in the political process, even in cases where the taking in question causes more economic harm than it creates benefits. The poor suffer from a variety of disadvantages in the political system. They are less likely to vote (see, e.g., Teixeira 1992, Wolfinger and Rosenstone 1980), less likely to engage in other forms of political activity, and of course less likely to make financial contributions to political campaigns.[37] In addition, the poor also have lower levels of political knowledge than more affluent citizens (see, e.g., Caplan 2007, Carpini and Keeter 1996, Somin 2004c). Low political knowledge makes it more difficult for poor voters to determine what policies government officials are pursuing and whether or not they serve the voters' interests.[38] Moreover, owing in part to their low average levels of education, the poor are less likely than the affluent to be able to make effective use of the information they do know, and more likely to be misled by faulty reasoning or deception.[39]

It could still be argued that abusive condemnations will be constrained by the power of property owners over local governments. Because property owners are the dominant interest in many localities,[40] they may be able to use their political power to prevent inefficient economic development condemnations. However valid this argument is with respect to other functions of local government, it is flawed when applied to economic development takings. Because of their nontransparent nature and the general problem of widespread ignorance, property owners are unlikely to be able to determine which development condemnations serve their interests and which do not. Moreover, even in situations where voters do understand the trade-offs involved, the relevant variable is not the political power of property owners generally, but the power of those who are targeted for condemnation. The targeting of the poor also reduces the likelihood of effective resistance. Even if property owners are politically powerful as a group, this fact will not prevent eminent domain abuse if such abuses usually target subsets of owners who are politically weak.

HOLDOUT PROBLEMS

The danger of government failure posed by economic development condemnations might be tolerable if they were needed to achieve their ostensible objective: allowing socially beneficial development projects to go forward without being blocked by "holdouts." Large-scale development projects can and do succeed without recourse to the power of eminent domain. Private developers have effective ways to prevent and deal with potential holdouts.

Preventing Holdouts without Condemnation

The most common argument for economic development takings is that they are necessary to facilitate economic development in situations where large-scale projects require assembling a large number of lots owned by numerous individuals. If the coercive mechanisms of eminent domain cannot be employed, the argument asserts, a small number of "holdout" owners could either block an important development project or extract a prohibitively high price for acquiescence.[41]

For example, let us assume that a group of 50 contiguous properties with separate owners are each worth $100 when in their current uses ($5000 in all), but would be worth a total of $50,000 (an average of $1000 each) if combined into a single large development project in order to build a factory. There would thus be a net social gain of $45,000 ($50,000–$5000) from combining the properties into a single tract. However, if the owners of the separate properties know that a developer is trying to buy them all up in order to build the factory worth $45,000 more than the current use of their lands, any one of them could try to hold out and refuse to sell unless the developer gives them, say, $5000. And it would be rational for the developer to accede to this demand if it were made by only one owner; in such an eventuality the developer still makes a net gain of about $40,100 ($50,000–$5000 [paid to the holdout]-$4900 [paid to the other 49 owners who, by assumption, sell at the market price of $100]). However, if all 50 current owners (or even just 10 of them) resort to the same strategic gambit, the project will be blocked. In this scenario, payments to the owners will equal or exceed the project's expected profit. In theory, then, holdouts could block many socially valuable assembly projects.

In analyzing holdouts, it is important to distinguish between "strategic holdouts"—those who refuse to sell because they hope to obtain a higher price and are holdouts in economic sense of the term—and "sincere dissenters" who genuinely value their land more than the would-be developer does. The former are attempting to take advantage of the developers' assembly problem in order to raise the price, as the above example illustrates. The latter, by contrast, are not attempting to get a better price but are instead unwilling to sell because they genuinely place a high enough value on their property that they prefer to keep it rather than accept any payment that the buyer is willing to offer. For example, the property owners in *Kelo* and

Poletown refused offers of increased compensation and repeatedly indicated that their objective was to keep their homes rather than to obtain a higher price from the condemning authority.[42] As New London's lawyer noted at the *Kelo* oral argument, "there are some plaintiffs who are not going to sell at any price. They want to stay there" (*Kelo*, U.S. Supreme Court Oral Argument Transcript, 2005 WL 529436 at 27).

In a situation where there are sincere dissenters, transferring their property to a developer would actually lower the overall social value of the land because, by definition, the dissenters value it more than the developer does. An ideally efficient policy would, therefore, enable developers to prevent strategic holdouts but not allow them to override the wishes of sincere dissenters.

As is suggested by the existence of numerous large development projects that did not rely on eminent domain, private developers have tools for dealing with holdout problems without recourse to government coercion. For reasons well summarized by Lloyd Cohen, holding out is not a simple strategy: "The successful holdout requires accurate information and a high degree of negotiating, bargaining, and bluffing skills" (Cohen 1991, 359). The would-be strategic holdout needs to first know that there is an assembly project going on and then be able to bargain effectively with those undertaking the project. Developers seeking to prevent holdout problems must therefore either deprive potential holdouts of the "accurate information they need" or take away their ability to "negotiate, bargain, and bluff" (Cohen 1991, 359).

Fortunately, there are at least two common strategies that can help achieve these objectives. The first—operating in secret—stymies potential holdouts by depriving them of information. The second—precommitment—undercuts the would-be holdout's ability to bargain. In both cases, developers are able to prevent strategic holdouts, but cannot victimize sincere dissenters.

1. Assembling property in secret

In many cases, developers can negotiate with individual owners in secret or use specialized "straw man" agents to assemble the properties they need without alerting potential holdouts to the possibility of making a windfall profit by holding the project hostage.[43] Secret assembly prevents holdouts by denying them knowledge of the existence of a large assembly project.

The major drawback of secret assembly is the possibility of detection. As soon as potential holdouts learn that the land in the area is being bought up as part of a large assembly project, they have the information that they need to engage in strategic bargaining. However, empirical evidence suggests that this is not as serious a problem as might be thought.

Even high-profile property owners undertaking major projects have routinely used secret assembly successfully. For example, the Disney Corporation resorted to it to assemble the land needed to build Disney World in Orlando, Florida in the 1960s (Wheeler 2000a, 3–4). Disney has also made effective use of the same strategy to acquire land for a major new theme park in Virginia.[44] Others who have successfully used the same strategy include Harvard University, which has repeatedly used it to acquire property for major projects in the Boston area, and locally prominent developers in Las Vegas, Providence, and West Palm Beach, among others (Kelly 2006, 29–30). If even high-profile developers such as Disney and Harvard can successfully utilize secrecy without their plans being discovered in time for holdouts to take advantage of the information, then lesser-known developers—who are less apt to be closely watched by the public and the press—should be able to use the same approach with at least equal prospects of success.

As Daniel Kelly points out in an important recent article, the use of secrecy to prevent holdouts has a major advantage over eminent domain. Condemnation "may force a transfer where the existing owners actually value the land more than the private assembler." By contrast, secrecy "eliminates the risk of erroneous condemnations" because it relies on "voluntary transactions, which ensure that every transfer is mutually beneficial and thus socially desirable" (Kelly 2006, 29). In the terminology used here, secret assembly allows developers to prevent strategic holdouts but does not allow them to ignore the wishes of sincere dissenters.

The availability of the secret assembly strategy helps explain why eminent domain should in at least some cases be available for traditional public uses such as government-owned facilities and private common carriers, even though it should not be used to transfer land to private developers. Unlike a private developer, government often cannot operate in secrecy because of the need for open deliberation and transparency in public administration (Kelly 2006, 31–33).[45] Moreover, secrecy in government, even if feasible, might pose a heightened risk of corruption (Kelly 2006, 32–33, Merrill 1986, 81). These points are vital to emphasize because many commentators have long assumed that the "holdout rationale applies equally to both takings for the government and takings for private parties" (Kelly 2006, 13).

A slightly different rationale can be used to justify the use of eminent domain for private common carriers such as railroads and public utilities. In order to build a railroad or power line that connects Point A to Point B, the developer must acquire properties that connect with each other in a narrow, relatively straight line between A and B. Moreover, he or she cannot leave out even a small stretch of the distance, lest there be a break in the resulting railway or power line, rendering the whole useless. Other things being equal, it is reasonable to assume that it is much more difficult to conceal the true purposes of such an unusual pattern of acquisition than those of the acquisitions for projects such as Disney's or Harvard's. The logic is very similar to that which justifies the use of eminent domain to acquire land to build publicly owned roads (see Fischel 1995, 68–70).[46] Furthermore, because of the highly regulated nature of public utilities, their acquisition processes may often require public openness for some of the same reasons as those of government. Therefore, common carriers and public utilities may need to utilize eminent domain, while ordinary developers probably will not.

Even in the case of roads and other infrastructure facilities that require the acquisition of rights of way along a predetermined route, it is possible that private developers can effectively use secret assembly and other noncoercive means to overcome assembly problems in at least some cases, as economist Bruce Benson shows in a recent article (Benson 2005, 170–171). Even in this classic scenario, which is particularly conducive to potential holdouts, the need for condemnation may be overstated. If so, this fact strengthens the case for secret assembly as a superior alternative to condemnation in situations where private parties seek to acquire property for economic development.

2. Precommitment strategies

A second mechanism by which developers can prevent holdout problems without recourse to eminent domain is by means of "precommitment" strategies or "most favored nation" contract clauses. The developers can sign contracts with all the owners in an area where they hope to build, under which they commit themselves to paying the same price to all, with, perhaps, variations stemming from differences in the size or market value of particular properties. By this means, the developer successfully "ties his hands" in a way that precludes him from paying inordinately high prices to the last few holdouts.[47] Precommitment strategies work because they prevent the would-be holdout from being able to "negotiate, bargain, and bluff" (Cohen 1991, 359). Any such attempt at bargaining or bluffing can be met with the response that the buyer is unable to accept the holdout's terms because doing so would render the entire project unprofitable by requiring an equally hefty payout to all the other sellers.

In some respects, a precommitment approach is even better than secrecy, because it can potentially be utilized even by assemblers such as government agencies and public utilities, which must operate openly. At the same time, precommitment may be a more difficult strategy to implement effectively because it requires that the buyer predetermine a set price for each lot to be purchased in advance of beginning the assembly process. This increases the likelihood of making a mistake (such as offering too low a price as a result of underestimating a seller's "subjective value") that might lead to the failure of the assembly effort. Furthermore, empirical evidence on the use of precommitment strategies is much sparser than that for secrecy; the literature on the former has not—so far—revealed real-world examples of successful use of this strategy for major development projects comparable to the use of secrecy by Disney, Harvard, and others.

3. Implications

Between them, secrecy and precommitment provide alternatives to eminent domain that render it largely unnecessary in the case of private economic development projects. They also help explain why private assembly projects can and should be distinguished from the assembly of land for government use or for common carriers and utilities. Nonetheless, it is impossible to categorically rule out the possibility that there might be socially beneficial economic development projects that can only succeed through the use of eminent domain. We can, however, conclude that such projects are likely to be extremely rare, in light of the fact that even major projects undertaken by prominent corporations and universities success-fully rely on secret assembly.

In theory, of course, we should still allow the use of eminent domain for those rare efficient development projects that cannot utilize secrecy or pre-commitment to prevent holdouts. Unfortunately, however, there is no way of confining the use of the economic development rationale to those rare cir-cumstances. Once the prospect of "economic development" is allowed to justify takings, it can and has been used by powerful interest groups to facil-itate projects that either fail to provide economic benefits that justify their costs or could have been undertaken without resorting to coercion or both (see section on "Economic Development Takings and the Political Process"). The political power of the beneficiaries of condemnations is likely to be a far more potent determinant of the decision to condemn than any objective economic analysis of holdout problems.

CONCLUSION

Economic development takings represent a classic form of government fail-ure, under which organized interest groups exploit shortcomings in the political process. While judicial decisions in some states have banned or cur-tailed such condemnations, it is unlikely that this trend will spread to all or most other states in the near future.

In the wake of the *Kelo* decision, a public outcry against economic devel-opment takings has led to the enactment of eminent domain reform laws purporting to curb economic development condemnations in some 43 states, as well as by the federal government (see Somin 2009, 2114–53). However, the very same problems of accountability and public ignorance that exacer-bate the costs of economic development condemnations have also helped ensure that the majority of these laws actually impose few or no constraints on eminent domain authority (Ibid.). Rationally ignorant voters often can-not tell the difference between reform laws that impose meaningful restric-tions on eminent domain and those that claim to do so but are in fact merely cosmetic.[48]

At the same time, however, the trend of judicial decisions in recent years is markedly more skeptical of economic development takings than in the preceding several decades. Even *Kelo* itself was noteworthy for the fact that four justices would have banned economic development takings outright. This was a major departure from earlier unanimous decisions that gave gov-ernment nearly unlimited discretion to condemn property for virtually any reason that might conceivably serve a "public purpose" (Somin 2007a, 224–225, 231–233). Even the majority opinion in *Kelo* gave government slightly less discretion to condemn property than was available under previ-ous Supreme Court decisions (Somin 2007a, 227–229). On the political front, the *Kelo* backlash has had very mixed results; much new legislation seems likely to be ineffective. However, some 19 states have indeed enacted legislation that bans or severely curtails economic development condemnations (see Somin 2009, 2138–48).[49]

It is unlikely that either judicial or political action will fully eliminate economic development takings any time soon. However, the *Kelo* decision and its aftermath have created an unusual opportunity to at least limit the scope of this form of government failure.

NOTES

For helpful suggestions and comments, I would like to thank Benjamin Barros, Dana Berliner, Scott Bullock, Lloyd Cohen, Steve Eagle, Jim Ely, Rick Hills, Edward López, Francesco Parisi, Sasha Volokh, Alan Weinstein, Michael Wheeler, and an anonymous reviewer. I would also like to acknowledge the contributions of Susan Courtwright-Rodriguez, Andrew Grossman, Amanda Hine, Greg Staiti and Carlos Wall, who provided valuable research assistance, and Roger Skalbeck of the George Mason University law school library, who helped with library materials. Some of the material in this chapter is adapted and updated from Somin (2007a).

1. For the standard economic theory of government failure, see Tullock (2002).
2. For example, U.S. Const., Amend. V: "...nor shall private property be taken for public use without just compensation."
3. See, for example, Claeys 2004 (detailed discussion of limited eighteenth and nineteenth century conceptions of public use that banned most private-to-private takings); Ely, Jr. (2003) [describing how nineteenth century courts generally upheld "private to private" takings only in cases where the new private owner was a common carrier such as a railroad or regulated a public utility]; Sandefur (2003) [providing detailed discussion of nineteenth century state jurisprudence constraining "public use," especially in New York and California].
4. See also Eagle (2005) (noting that "[i]n the twentieth century, the "public benefit" approach clearly predominates.").
5. See, for example, *Baycol, Inc. v. Downtown Dev. Auth.*, 315 S0.2d 451, 457 (Fla. 1975) (holding that a " 'public [economic] benefit' is not synonymous with 'public purpose' as a predicate which can justify eminent domain"); *In re Petition of Seattle*, 638 P.2d 549, 556–57 (1981) (disallowing plan to use eminent domain to build retail shopping, where purpose was not elimination of blight); *Owensboro v. McCormick*, 581 S.W.2d 3, 8 (Ky. 1979) ("No 'public use' is involved where the land of A is condemned merely to enable B to build a factory"); *Karesh v. City of Charleston*, 247 S.E.2d 342,,345 (S.C. 1978) (striking down taking justified only by economic development); *City of Little Rock v. Raines*, 411 S.W.2d 486, 495 (Ark. 1967) (private economic development project not a public use); *Hogue v. Port of Seattle*, 341 P.2d 171, 181–191 (Wash. 1959) (denying condemnation of residential property so that agency could "devote it to what it considers a higher and better economic use" [at 187]); *Opinion of the Justices*, 131 A.2d 904, 905–06 (Me. 1957) (condemnation for industrial development to enhance economy not a public use); *City of Bozeman v. Vaniman*, 898 P.2d 1208, 1214–15 (Mont. 1995) (holding that a condemnation that transfers property to a "private business" is unconstitutional unless the transfer to the business is "insignificant" and "incidental" to a public project).
6. For a detailed discussion of *Hathcock* see Somin (2004a).

7. See, for example, *Prince George's County v. Collington Crossroads*, 339 A.2d 278, 287 (Md. 1975) (1975 Maryland high court decision holding that "industrial development" qualifies as a legitimate public use).

8. See, for example, *City of Norwood v. Horney*, 853 N.E. 2d 1115. 1140–42 (Ohio 2006) (following County of *Wayne v. Hathcock* in holding that "economic development" alone does not justify condemnation); *Bd. of County Com'rs of Muskogee County v. Lowery*, 136 P.3d 639, 646–52 (Okla. 2006) (holding that "economic development" is not a "public purpose" under the Oklahoma state constitution); *Ga. Dep't of Transp. v. Jasper County*, 586 S.E.2d 853, 856 (S.C. 2003) (holding that even a "substantial...projected economic benefit" cannot justify a "condemnation"); *Southwestern Ill. Dev. Auth. v. National City Env.*, 768 N.E.2d 1, 9–11 (Ill.), *cert. denied*, 537 U.S. 880 (2002) (holding that a "contribu[tion] to economic growth in the region" is not a public use justifying condemnation).

9. The 11 states are Arkansas, Florida, Illinois, Kentucky, Michigan, Maine, Montana, Ohio, Oklahoma, South Carolina, and Washington. See Somin (2007a).

10. See, for example, *Merrill v. City of Manchester*, 499 A.2d 216, 217–18 (N.H. 1985) (economic development condemnation for industrial park not a public use where no harmful condition was being eliminated); *Opinion of the Justices*, 250 Ne.2d 547, 558 (Mass. 1969) (holding that economic benefits of a proposed stadium were not enough of a public use to justify condemnation).

11. For an analysis of these laws, many of which are likely to prove ineffective, see Somin (2009).

12. *Southwestern Ill. Dev. Auth. v. National City Env.*, 768 N.E.2d 1, 9 (Ill.), *cert. denied*, 537 U.S. 880 (2002).

13. The McCormick Court is quoting 26 Am.Jur.2d Eminent Domain § 34, at 684–85 (1966).

14. See *Kelo v. City of New London*, Amicus Br. of Becket Fund for Religious Liberty, 2004 WL 2787141 at 8–11, 8 n. 20 (explaining the special vulnerability of religious nonprofits and listing numerous examples where they have been targeted by economic development takings).

15. See, for example, *Cincinnati v. Vester*, 281 U.S. 439, 447–48 (1930) (holding that "private property could not be taken for some independent and undisclosed public use"); *County of San Francisco v. Ross*, 279 P.2d 529, 532 (Cal. 1955) (*en banc*) (invalidating agreement that lacked controls over the use of the condemned property because "[s]uch controls are designed to assure that use of the property condemned will be in the public interest"); *State ex. rel. Sharp v. 0.62033 Acres of Land*, 110 A.2d 1, 6 (Del. Super. Ct. 1954), *aff'd* 112 A.2d 857 (Del. 1955) (holding that "[t]he doctrine of reasonable time prohibits the condemnor from *speculating* as to *possible* needs at some *remote* future time") (emphasis in the original); *Alsip Park Dist. v. D & M P'shp*, 625 N.E.2d 40, 45 (Ill. App. Ct. 1993) (holding that "[I]f the facts" in a condemnation proceeding "established that...[the condemnor] had no ascertainable public need or plan, current or future for the land, defendants [property owner] should prevail"); *Mayor of the City of Vicksburg v. Thomas*, 645 S0.2d 940, 943 (Miss. 1994) (holding that property may only be condemned for transfer to "private parties subject to conditions to insure that the proposed public use will continue to be served"); *Krauter v. Lower Big Blue Nat. Res. Dist.*, 259 N.W.2d 472, 475–476 (Neb. 1977) (holding that "a condemning agency must have a present plan and

a present public purpose for the use of the property before it is authorized to commence a condemnation action.... The possibility that the condemning agency at some future time may adopt a plan to use the property for a public purpose is not sufficient"); *Casino Reinvestment Dev. Auth. v. Banin*, 727 A.2d 102, 111 (N.J. Super. Ct. 1998) (holding that when a "public agency acquires...property for the purposes of conveying it to a private developer," there must be advance "assurances that the public interest will be protected").

16. *Poletown*, at 480 (Ryan, J., dissenting) (noting that "there will be no public control" over the GM plant scheduled to be built on the Poletown site).

17. *Vavro,* at 731 (upholding a taking transferring property to the Chrysler Corporation for the construction of a new auto assembly plant despite the fact that "Chrysler...has not entered into a binding commitment with the City of Detroit to construct the [plant] following the city's use of the power of eminent domain").

18. See *Poletown*, at 467–68 (citing statement of Mayor Young and reprinting letter from Thomas A. Murphy, Chairman of the Board, General Motors, to Coleman A. Young, [October 8, 1980]).

19. See, for example, *Gen. Bldg. Contractors v. Bd. of Shawnee Cty.* Comm'rs, 66 P.3d 873, 881–883. (Kan. 2003) (upholding economic development condemnation for purpose of building industrial facility for later transfer to private owners with whom no development agreements had as yet been reached); *City of Jamestown v. Leevers Supermarkets, Inc.*, 552 N.W. 2d 365, 373–374 (N.D. 1996) (following *Poletown* approach and concluding that economic development takings will be upheld so long as the "primary object" of the taking is "economic welfare"); *City of Minneapolis v. Wurtele*, 291 N.W. 2d 386, 390 (Minn. 1980) (holding, in a case endorsing the constitutionality of economic development takings, that "a public body's decision that a [condemnation] project is in the public interest is presumed correct unless there is a showing of fraud or undue influence"); *Cf. Vitucci v. New York City Sch. Constr. Auth.*, 289 A.D. 2d 479, (N.Y. App. Div. 2001) (holding that an economic development taking passes muster despite the fact that the property was originally condemned to build a school, because "as long as the initial taking was in good faith, there appears to be little limitation on the condemnor's right to put the property to an alternate use upon the discontinuation of the original planned public purpose"). The Maryland Court of Appeals decision endorsing economic development condemnations was partly based on the fact that the government "will maintain significant control over the industrial park" that the new owner used the condemned property to build. *Prince George's County v. Collington Crossroads*, 339 A.2d 278, 283 (Md. 1975). However, the control in question involved merely the right to regulate the facility to ensure "health, safety, and welfare, control...hazards and nuisances, and guidelines for assuring a high quality physical environment"; and a guarantee that part of the project would be used as "open space." It did not create a binding obligation to produce any actual economic benefits for the community of the kind that were used to justify condemnation in the first place.

20. For a more extensive analysis of weaknesses in the political process that might justify stronger judicial review, see Somin (2004c) (showing how political ignorance undermines common "countermajoritarian difficulty" arguments against judicial review) and Somin 2004d (showing how political ignorance and interest group exploitation of the political process strengthen the case for aggressive judicial review).

21. See Pinker (1999) (explaining how deception is more effective if those who seek to deceive actually believe their own lies, as a result of which self-interested self-deception may be a common genetic tendency of humans).

22. See, for example,, Noll and Zimbalist (1997).

23. See discussion below and accompanying text.

24. The estimate of the number of businesses eliminated in the Poletown takings is in fact unclear. While Marie Michael cites a figure of 600, other sources cite much lower numbers, in the range of 140 to 160. See Somin (2004a, 1017, note 52) (providing a detailed discussion of the conflicting estimates). If the lower estimates are correct, it would be much less likely that the number of jobs lost from the businesses shut down was equal to that created by the new factory. However, it is important to remember that the lost jobs were wiped out immediately whereas the new ones did not begin to appear for four years after the 1981 condemnations and that the job losses suffered from wiping out the businesses do not include jobs eliminated by the destruction of Poletown's churches, schools, and hospitals, nor those lost as a result of the expulsion of over 4000 residents.

25. At the time, opponents of the condemnations claimed that 9000 jobs would be lost because of them. See Bukowczyk 1984. This partisan estimate, like GM's own promise that 6,000 jobs would be created, must be viewed with skepticism.

26. According to data compiled by the city, some one-third of the affected businesses closed down immediately, while two-thirds of the remainder (approximately 40–45 percent of the original total) relocated to other parts of Detroit (see Jones, Bachelor, and Wilson 1986. Even if we assume—implausibly—that those relocated businesses that stayed in Detroit continued to employ as many workers as before, the area would have suffered a net job loss if the approximately 350 businesses that either shut down or moved outside of the city employed an average of just seven workers each. And, obviously this does not even consider the job losses and other economic costs inflicted by the destruction of schools, churches, and other nonprofit institutions.

27. See *Kelo v. City of New London*, 843 A.2d 500, 511 (Conn. 2004) *aff'd* 545 U.S. 469 (2005) (noting that two of the plaintiffs' families have "lived in their homes for decades and others had put enormous amounts of time, effort, and money into their property").

28. See cases cited in note 8, all of which set highly deferential standards for evaluating economic development takings that take little or no account of social costs.

29. See *Berman*, at 30 (mentioning the number of people to be expelled, but not considering the costs to them). Ultimately, only 300 of the 5900 new homes built in the area were affordable to its former residents, most of whom were even worse off after the condemnation than they had been before. See also Gillette (1995).

30. See generally Fullilove (2004) (describing extensive social and psychological costs of forced relocation); Gans (1982) (same); Frieden and Sagalyn (1989) (same); cf. Merrill (1986) (showing how the use of eminent domain systematically imposes "uncompensated subjective losses" because most property owners value their holdings at more than their market value). But see Garnett (2006) (providing evidence that many owners whose property is condemned receive greater than market value compensation). However, this is not the same

as proving that the compensation is enough to fully offset the loss of subjective value.

31. For a helpful discussion see Merrill (1986), 82–84.

32. See, for example, Radin (1988) (making the case for limitations on the eminent domain power because of the connection between "personal property" and individuals' sense of personhood and community); Aladjem 1988 (same); Epstein (1992) (criticizing *Poletown* as a "notorious" decision that "sustained a takeover of a neighborhood by General Motors that ignored huge elements of losses to the private owners who were dispossessed" and arguing for strict judicial constraints on similar condemnations).

33. For a recent summary and analysis of the literature on rent-seeking and capture, see Mueller 2003.

34. See the section "Preventing Holdouts without Condemnation."

35. See Somin (2004c) (summarizing evidence of extensive voter ignorance); Somin (1998) (same).

36. For a more detailed discussion, see Somin (1998), 435–438.

37. For the data on political activity and donations, see Verba (1995).

38. See, for example, Somin (2004e) (explaining dangers of political ignorance).

39. See Caplan 2007 (showing how education, which is highly correlated with income, is a strong predictor of voter ability to reason effectively about economic issues).

40. See generally Fischel (2001) (providing extensive evidence of the ability of homeowners to influence local governments to adopt policies that protect their interests and maximize property value).

41. See Merrill (1986) (describing the "holdout" rationale for use of eminent domain); see also Calabresi and Melamed (1972) (classic description of the holdout problem); Cohen (1991) (rigorously distinguishing holdouts from free-riders).

42. See Wylie (1989, 83) (noting that "for the many who wanted to stay in Poletown, the primary concern was how much money they would be offered for their homes").

43. *See* Posner 1977, 43–44 (describing these methods); Munch 1976, 479 (same).

44. While the plan for the Virginia Park was eventually shelved due to local opposition, the failure was not due to land assembly problems but to the threat to Disney's public image caused by its plan to build in the vicinity of historic Civil War sites. See Wheeler (2000b) 2, 8–9, 11–12. See also Hilzenrath (1993), A1 (describing success of Disney's secret assembly strategy in Virginia).

45. See also Merrill (1986), 81–82 (arguing that government cannot operate in secrecy because of the need for openness and deliberation).

46. But see Benson (2005) (arguing that private road builders may still be able to use secret purchase effectively and also have other noncoercive means of avoiding holdout problems that prevent the acquisition of rights of way).

47. See Schelling (1960), 35–43 (classic explanation of the ways in which tying one's own hands can be an advantage in negotiations); see also Kochan (1998), 88–90 (explaining how precommitment strategies used to prevent holdouts in corporate transactions can be applied to economic development projects that might otherwise need to resort to eminent domain).

48. This point is discussed in detail in Somin (2009), 2155–70, which cites survey evidence showing that only 13 percent the public both knew whether their states

had enacted post-*Kelo* reforms, and whether those reforms were likely to be effective.

49. Unfortunately, 13 of the 20 states with the highest incidence of economic development takings have passed ineffective legislation or none at all. See Somin (2009), 2117–19.

CHAPTER 8

ON THE IMPOSSIBILITY OF "JUST COMPENSATION" WHEN PROPERTY IS TAKEN: AN ETHICAL AND EPISTEMIC INQUIRY

John Brätland

INTRODUCTION

The taking power (or eminent domain power as it is known in the United States) has evolved along with metastasizing power of democratic governments. A "taking" is an act of coerced confiscation undertaken to achieve a public use of private property.[1] This evolved taking power has been condemned; for example, George Reisman has asserted that eminent domain "appears to constitute a clear violation of the principle of individual rights and thus have no place in a capitalist society" (Reisman 1996, 422). In even more searing language, Murray Rothbard has observed: "...when government confers a privilege of eminent domain...it has virtually granted a license for theft" (Rothbard 2004, 1139). Are these statements irresponsible hyperbole? After all, the constitutions of Western democracies promise and mandate payment of what is labeled "just compensation." But in what way can compensation be made "just" if the exercise of the taking power is no more than officially sanctioned thievery? Can the act of compensating dispossessed owners be made just in a way that nullifies or negates Rothbard's charge of theft? This chapter explores the ethical and epistemic answers to these questions.[2]

In strict principle, just compensation is that level of payment for a taking of property that renders the property owner whole. But what are the principles of just property transfer that maintain wholeness of the owner relinquishing property in such an exchange? Are these same principles properly reflected in the compensation paid in the context of coercive takings? Contemporary jurisprudence deals with these questions by ignoring the underlying ethical issues and pursuing a largely pro forma view of due process with respect to just compensation. The recent history of jurisprudence regarding the taking power has given the phrase "just compensation" an oddly Orwellian connotation in that it cynically suggests something that is materially counter to evident reality (Greenhut 2004, 52).

Compensation as deemed appropriate by public authority has taken the form of paying fair market value (estimated market price) to owners of taken property (Knetsch 1983, 38). Fair market value can be briefly described as the price upon which two willing and informed parties agree to an uncoerced transfer of property (Black 1979, 537). Unfortunately, in a takings proceeding, this definition necessarily devolves into the condemning authority's decree because a voluntary transaction does not take place. Even supporters of the need for a governmental taking authority hold the view that payment of fair market value does not represent just compensation (Epstein 1985, 183, Ellickson 1973, 736–737: Knetsch and Borcherding 1979, 241, Reisman 1996, 422–423). They note that payment of fair market value means that the owner is a damaged party since owners are virtually never willing to sell their property for an estimated market price (Epstein 1985, 183).

The normative concern of making the property owner "whole" raises two questions that are largely ignored by officials when property is taken. First, is there any level of compensation that can be truly just if it is coercively imposed upon the property owner? Second, is there an epistemic basis on which the taker of the property can objectify the standard of wholeness for the property owner? To answer these two questions, one must distinguish between a taking, which is coercive, and a property transfer between two mutually assenting parties, which is voluntary. One notes that one critical distinction between voluntary transfer of property and coercive transfer of property is that assent is missing in the latter but is clearly a central element in the former. This chapter explores the ethical breach evident in the taking process and the fact that no compensation can be considered just in the absence of explicit assent.

The power accorded to governments in the taking power has the effect of exposing public officials to an "ethical hazard" in which they become inured to the ethical assault on property owners of coercive confiscation on the property owner. Put bluntly, it is a corrupting element in governmental action. The ethics of employing just compensation as a presumed means of rendering the property owner whole ceases to have relevant bearing upon their decisions with respect to the exercise of the taking power. This power provides a legally sanctioned institutional means by which officials can act as political entrepreneurs; fundamentally unethical means can be employed by officials to achieve political gain. In essence, officials have clear incentives to employ coercive power while at the same time avoiding the social and legal opprobrium that would normally accompany an extortive act.

The epistemology of just compensation is inextricably bound up with the frequently misunderstood fact that valuation can never be more than a "subjective" ranking of options made by an individual at a particular moment in time. Just compensation is any payment sufficient to induce the property owner to rank the payment above the option of retaining his property. In such circumstances, the property owner assents to the exchange. Since assent is critical, fair market value is eliminated as a legitimate standard of just compensation as is any vain attempt at use of imputed reservation prices or "efficient premiums" to make allowance for personal valuations of property not reflected in market prices. Hence, no compensation can be made just in a coercive transfer of property. No just compensation can be estimated in the absence of assent. But since all takings are coercive, the real economic cost of taken resources can never be reckoned. This epistemic barrier to transparency serves the political interests of aggressive government officials intent on exploiting the power to take private property.

ETHICS OF ASSENT IN PROPERTY TRANSFER AND ETHICAL HAZARD OF THE TAKING POWER

The ethical foundations of property and property transfer are central to an examination of just compensation. This section outlines ethical principles of ownership, property transfer and the extent to which "fair market value" represents just compensation for coercive property transfers. The discussion reveals that assent and just compensation are inextricably linked. The absence of assent means that the power to take property fosters a type of ethical hazard. The power to take property is exercised by public officials functioning as political entrepreneurs trying to earn political profit by reallocating taken resources. The ethics of property transfer cease to be a central concern for political entrepreneurs. Public officials must still obtain a type of assent in property transfer. However, this assent is not that of property owners but rather those who are in a position to affect the official's success in achieving his objective of political profit.

Ethical definition, Origins, Acquisition, and Transfer of Property

How does an ethical definition of property relate to issues of just compensation in takings under eminent domain? One's first reaction to this question may be to dismiss it. But the proper definition of property has a direct bearing on the ethics of the taking process and the possibility of just compensation. The term "property" is used prominently in everyday discourse with the implicit assumption that there is a universal understanding of its meaning. Most people have an intuitive understanding of what the concept of property means without seeing a need to examine the foundations underlying its true nature. But such a definition is useful in helping one to discern not only the legitimate foundations of property but also the ethical implications of different aspects of property transfer and how just compensation relates to such transfer.

The most thoughtful definitions of the word "property" start from its more basic synonyms such as characteristic, feature, aspect, or attribute. Each of these terms properly applies to an individual human being. For example, one's arm is clearly a vital attribute of one's being, in the sense that it is an attribute or characteristic of the person. In this sense, property is rightly understood to be a possessed feature. Another critical aspect of property is the owner's ability to control his or her property.[3] Under normal circumstances, the individual human being is able to control his arm. If one's arm is one's property, the coherent extension of this argument is that one's body, its abilities, and the benefits of its abilities are also one's property. This inference accords completely with received rational norms of natural law.[4] It rests on the idea that every person owns his or her self in an indisputable sense. This idea was given coherent expression by John Locke in his *Second Essay on Government* (Locke 1948 [1688, 14–26).[5]

Building on the ethical legitimacy of self-ownership, one can make a useful distinction between property that is intrinsic to one specific human being and property that is not intrinsic (hence extrinsic) to a particular person (Hülsmann 2004, 51). For example, ownership of the body is a type of property that intrinsically belongs to one uniquely specifiable human being. But other forms of property are clearly not originally intrinsic to a particular human being. If property is not intrinsic to a particular human being, what ethical means of acquisition by the individual assures legitimate ownership? The term "ethics," as applied in this context, is focused most particularly on the origins and integrity of legitimately acquired rights of private property. As Rothbard notes, self-ownership was the building block on which Locke was able to formulate his theory of original appropriation; the individual becomes the rightful owner of all unowned, nature-given goods, which he puts to use before anyone else does (Rothbard 2004, 92). By extension, it is clear that with the use of the property that an individual owns, he may acquire ownership by creating or manufacturing goods that have value in use or value in exchange. The individual may also become a legitimate owner of property through a voluntary gift or grant voluntarily made by another party. Finally, as Murray Rothbard explains, the individual may acquire legitimate ownership through the process of voluntary exchange with another party (Rothbard 2004, 92). Ownership implies one's right to employ these resources as one sees fit so long as one does not thereby, without invitation, change the physical integrity of another's property or delimit another's control over his property without his consent.

The above-described principles of property acquisition form a kind of chain of just holding or the chain of just transfer, meaning that the justice of each holding of property is contingent upon the justice of the preceding holding of the property (Nozick 1974, 151–153). To be a just transfer of extrinsic property, the actions necessary to effect the transfer must be uncoerced or voluntary. Logically extending the metaphor, the chain of just holding amounts to a chain of just compensation since all holdings emerge out of mutual agreement and assent. However, to the extent that coercion supplants assent as the basis for the transaction, the chain is broken. Hence with takings under eminent domain, there can be no chain of just holding nor, by implication, a chain of just compensation. In fact, attempts at such transfers by a private party would be classified as criminal under the law; specifically, such attempts would come under the heading of *extortion,* which Black's Dictionary of Law defines as:

> Obtaining property from another induced by wrongful use of actual or threatened force, violence, or fear or under the cover of official right. A person is guilty of theft by extortion if he purposely obtains property of another by threatening to inflict any harm that would not benefit the property owner. (Black 1979, 525)

The central importance of assent in the just holding and transfer of property is clear, compelling, and not open to any qualification. Any transfer of justly held property in which assent is not present involves not only an ethical breach but a act of criminality punishable as such under the law.

The Ethics of Fair Market Value as Compensation

One could plausibly argue that a principle of just transfer is upheld if governments taking property compensate owners on the basis of value to the owner (Knetsch and Borcherding 1979, 237–239).[6] The phrase "value to the owner" is only roughly synonymous with the term "reservation price" and is intended to refer to that price at which the owner would willingly relinquish his property in a transfer of property free of coercion. Since valuation cannot be more than a relative subjective ranking (Mises 2003, 177–180, Mises 1998, 204–206), a reservation price is that level of compensation that would be just sufficient to prompt the owner to rank the payment (price) above the property itself.

The reservation price or value-to-the-owner principle has shown itself to be essentially impossible to apply. In discussing the difficulties leading up to the demise of this principle, Jack Knetsch and Thomas Borcherding have observed, "[T]he intent of the value-to-the-owner criterion seemed to be the awarding of compensation that would retain or restore the original level of well-being of expropriated owners" (Knetsch and Borcherding 1979, 238). In their description of the public appropriation of private property in Canada, Knetsch and Borcherding acknowledge that jurists have fallen back on the use of fair market value of the property as a valid index of just compensation. "Other [Canadian] jurisdictions, starting with Ontario in 1970, and including the federal government, have substituted the standard of market value as the basis for compensation. This value is commonly defined as 'the amount that the land might be expected to realize if sold in the open market by a willing seller to a willing buyer.'"[7] Knetsch (1983, 38) cites four reasons for jurisdictions abandoning value-to-the-owner and the subsequent reversion to fair market value:

> The first is that although such things as emotional attachment or sentimental value may be important to individual owners of property, they are not readily and objectively measurable. A second reason is that the award would be expected to vary in each case. The third alleged drawback of the value-to-the

owner for determining compensation is that it would result in excessive claims and a consequent burden to taxpayers. The fourth argument against the value-to-the-owner approach to compensation involves the owner's duty to give up land which the community requires.

All these reasons for governmental reversion to fair market value are targets for well-deserved and severe criticism. For example, in many cases in which coercive taking is undertaken by a government, the property may be a homestead, or a residence in which the individual or family has lived often for generations. Emotional attachment and sentimental value may be compelling reasons for attachment and the dominant basis for the valuation of property on the part of the owner. The courts may ignore the basis for valuations argued in litigation, but in so doing, cast aside any pretense of a truly ethical or just compensation. The other reason given for reverting to the fair market value standard is that payment will vary between instances. In reality, valuations of a given resource vary across individuals, and each individual's valuation of a given resource may differ across time.[8] Moreover, there is no defensible rationale for limiting compensation in order to protect taxpayers from excessive burden. If transfer of the property truly serves the public interest, then the public's willingness to pay should exceed any price acceptable to the owner. Taxpayers should pay the full price of the coercive takings that their elected officials presume to undertake. If government officials take property, they should suffer the hostile opprobrium of taxpayers. There is no compelling reason why the property owner should unduly bear the pain of an involuntary property transfer.

The fourth reason that Knetsch gives for governmental resolve to pay only fair market value is premised on the awkward notion that the owner has some sort of civic duty to surrender his land to the community. This perspective is reflected in a 1949 opinion written by Justice Felix Frankfurter in which the latter states that "the value of property springs from subjective needs and attitudes; its value to the owner may differ widely from its value to the taker... In view, however, of the liability of all property to condemnation for the public good, loss to the owner of nontransferable values deriving from his unique need for the property or idiosyncratic attachment to it, loss due to the exercise of the police power,... is properly treated as part of the burden of common citizenship" (*Kimball Laundry v. United States* (338 U.S. 1[1949]) as quoted in Benson 2005, 184).[9]

The ethical breach implicit in these four rationales can be brought into sharper focus by examining the nature of fair market value and the implications of the coercion that always accompanies the taking of property. Consider the following legitimate definitions of fair market value (Black 1979, 537): (1) the price at which the property would change hands between a willing buyer and a willing seller, neither being under any compulsion to buy or sell and both having reasonable knowledge of the relevant facts; (2) by fair market value is meant the price in cash, or its equivalent, that the property would have brought at the time of the taking, considering its highest and most profitable use, if then offered for sale in the open market, in competition with other similar properties at or near the location of the property taken, with reasonable time allowed to find a purchaser; (3) the price that the asset would bring by bona fide bargaining between well-informed buyers and sellers at the date of acquisition; (4) the price at which bona fide sales have been consummated for assets of like type, quality, and quantity in a particular market at the time of acquisition; and (5) the amount of money which a purchaser is willing, but not obligated to buy, would pay an owner who is willing but not obligated to sell, taking into consideration all uses to which land is adapted and might in reason be applied.

While the definitions are clearly similar, none of the definitions support the possibility of just compensation in the event of a coercive taking. Thus, fair market value and the ethical considerations of just compensation are mutually exclusive.

Certainly each of these definitions can be used to make an ex post assessment of whether or not fair market value was received in a particular sale of property that has already occurred. But no rational or logical basis exists for applying any version of these definitions as a prescription for just compensation in transfers of property that are involuntary. Consider the following example of exchange between two private parties one of whom has the coercive power (perhaps through physical threat) to force an exchange. In this example, two parties, Anderson and Williams, are each contemplating a transaction involving land. Williams is in possession of 20 acres of land for which Anderson is prepared to pay $800,000. Williams wants $1,000,000, however. But in this case, Anderson is in a position to exert coercive power over Williams, and decides that he will pay only $800,000; moreover, Anderson has done market research on numerous recent transactions involving similar land nearby and has determined that $800,000 represents fair market value for the 20 acres. In other words, all of these transactions satisfy the conditions specified on one or more of the definitions of fair market value given above. Williams acknowledges that $800,000 is a typical price but makes clear that he does not agree to the transaction. Nonetheless, Anderson presents this price of $800,000 to Williams in the form of an ultimatum and forces the exchange. Anderson has in effect imposed a taking upon Williams. When an individual does this, it is called predation and it may be illegal. When a government does this, it is called serving the public interest.

Hence, one can see that applying any of the previously listed definitions of fair market value as a benchmark does not result in anything that could be honestly viewed as just compensation. Clearly no application of the above listed definitions of fair market value is remotely valid in assessing justice of compensation received by Enders in the exchange described above. As Ellen Frankel Paul has noted, "...given the nature of the act—that government is seizing your property, and that you have not voluntarily consented to the exchange,...no 'market' transaction could be involved" (Paul 1987, 81). All that can be said is that if the conditions specified in the definition are met or were met, just compensation is, by definition, received by both parties. The standard itself is only applicable to a particular transaction that has been voluntarily consummated and each of the parties has explicitly given assent. But as a benchmark in assessing what compensation should be in a transaction that has not taken place, application of fair market value can never be deemed ethically just.

The Ethical Implications of Overt Assent in Assessing Just Compensation

The actual nature of a voluntary exchange yields a clearer understanding of the injustice of using fair market value as benchmark in determining just compensation. The process of property exchange commences in situations in which each of the parties ranks certain property in the possession of the other party more highly than the property that each would like to relinquish in exchange. In this example, Williams contemplates the sale of 20 acres of his property to Anderson. Neither party has the power to exert coercion on the other. In this case, Anderson offers Williams $1,000,000 for the land and Williams readily agrees. Clearly this transaction was consummated because each of the two parties ranked what was offered in the exchange more highly than the property that each was prepared to relinquish in the trade. However, it may be useful to examine more closely what occurs in such an exchange. First, each of the two parties acknowledges that the other person is the legitimate and rightful owner of the property that each would like to obtain in the exchange. Anderson acknowledges that Williams is the owner of the land and Williams acknowledges that Anderson is in rightful possession of $1,000,000. Second, both Anderson and Williams wish the other party to allow them to become the owner of the property being acquired in the exchange. In other words, Anderson wishes that Williams will let Anderson become the owner of the 20 acres of land and, analogously, Williams wishes that Anderson will let Williams become the owner of the $1,000,000. Third, Anderson assents to Williams' wish on the condition that Williams assents to Anderson's wish. The transfer is characterized by mutual assent.

Mutual assent is critical to the ethical legitimacy of the exchange and the transfer of property. In this latter example, there can be no question whether compensation is just. Just compensation is determined not on the basis of the amounts exchanged in the transaction, but rather on the basis of the fact that the exchange was completed on the basis of mutual assent. The key element is mutual assent to the transfer and assent to the wishes and expressed intentions of the other party. The evidence of assent leads to the clearly valid conclusion that each party has been compensated to the extent of his reservation price.[10] What has been described in the above hypothetical transaction would satisfy each of the definitions of fair market value listed above (in the preceding section of this chapter). It also serves as a fair and legitimate indicator of just compensation. But the fairness and the justice of the compensation is contingent on the mutual assent of the particular parties to the transaction. As Murray Rothbard has observed "we must conclude, then, with modern, post medieval economic theory, that the *only* 'just price' for any transaction is the price voluntarily agreed upon by the two parties" (Rothbard 1998, 249).

Without assent, damage has been inflicted on at least one party by the transfer of property. But with some few exceptions, the jurisprudence regarding takings has failed to acknowledge the owner as a damaged party. Yet the payment by governments of compensation equivalent to fair market value does leave the owner in a damaged state that is properly recognized in other areas of law. The damage arises principally from (1) the fact that the owner in most cases feels a special attachment to the property (usually land) taken and (2) compensation in the amount of fair market value in virtually all cases will not afford the owner the means necessary to buy a comparable property yielding equivalent enjoyment. In their examination of compensation issues arising from expropriation of private property, Knetsch and Borcherding call attention to the following incongruity in the way in which property law deals with damage: "It is most interesting to note that real estate transactions are normally treated differently in the event of contractual breach. For breach of contract, courts favor an award of damages to the party suffering loss. In real property cases, specific performance is commonly ordered largely on grounds that real property usually has unique attributes for the buyer so that he or she cannot be expected to find a duplicate with a cash settlement" (Knetsch and Borcherding 1979, 242). Mark L. Pollot pursues this same line of argument by calling attention to the special place accorded protection of contracts in Article I, Section 10 of the U. S. Constitution. The contracts clause of Article I states that "No state shall . . . pass any law *impairing* the Obligations of Contract" (Pollot 1993, 105). Pollot goes on to note: "To the extent that our observation that the contracts clause and the just compensation clause [of the Fifth Amendment] embody the same values is valid, it suggests that the terms 'use' and 'take' include the concept of impairment. Impairment was defined in the eighteenth century literature as meaning 'to diminish; to injure; to make worse; to lessen in quantity, value or excellence.'" (Pollot 1993, 105 106).

In a taking, the property owner is a damaged party as surely as if he were the victim of a perpetrated tort. A tort "is a direct invasion of some legal right of the individual" (Black 1979, 1335). The parallel to tort damage is not lost on Richard Epstein who notes: "[T]he simple rule that requires full damage in tort or contract should apply with remorseless force in cases of government taking . . ." (Epstein 1995, 129). While there are several costs of displacement that are likely not to be covered by payment of fair market value, damage is made ethically evident by the absence of explicit assent—not by the extent or magnitude of compensation. In spite of the fact that the initial intent of the *eminent domain* provisions of the U.S. Constitution may have been to "keep the property owner whole," this objective cannot be ethically achieved with any prescribed and imposed payment by the government. Even though compensation in any given circumstance may be financially substantial, the damage to the property owner still exists in an ethical sense. The absence of any action expressing overt assent in the transfer is all the evidence that one needs to infer that the property owner has sustained damage. An imposed level of compensation fails as an ethically just standard of compensation. On strictly ethical grounds, coercive takings cannot render any sort of justice to the property owner regardless of the amount of compensation offered by government. The property owner is certainly not made ethically whole by the payment of a premium even if the additional payment is generous.

Ethical Hazard of the Power to Take: Looking for Assent in All the Wrong Places

The central point of the preceding discussion is that just compensation in the transfer property hinges on the explicit assent of both parties to the transfer. Without that assent of the property owner relinquishing property, no ethically legitimate basis exists by which one can view compensation as just. But the whole purpose of the taking power granted to democratic governments is to eliminate the encumbrance of obtaining the property owner's assent in the transfer. Means are provided by which public officials can function as political entrepreneurs seeking political profit. Political profit may take various forms including enhanced power, public acclaim, increased job security, or possibly prospects for achieving higher, more powerful public office. Public officials functioning as political entrepreneur must be able to influence and even control the allocation of resources in the name of the public welfare. In exercising this power, the public official may pursue collective undertakings that have been described as either productive or predatory (Holcombe 2002, 143). These distinctions are strictly academic in the context of this discussion. It suffices to note that any publicly undertaken reallocation of property that involves the coercive taking of private property is inherently predatory in that these actions are an ethical assault on the property eights of dispossessed owners. Moreover, the political profit as perceived by the public official need not be linked to any positive net benefit accruing to the affected community (Holcombe 2002, 148–149: Sutter 2002, 206).

In marshalling resources for public use, the political entrepreneur must still acquire assent, but the requisite assent is not that of the owner of the private property at issue. In a taking, the assent of the property owner would be ignored, by definition.[11] But, the assent that is critical to the political entrepreneur's success is that which must be achieved through the processes of political cooperation, compromise, logrolling, and catering to the wants or demands of democratic constituencies. This assent may involve strategies reliant on the support of constituent-voters, organized interest groups, and party leaders.

However, political entrepreneurs serving democratic constituencies face an ethical hazard in the taking of property for public use. In effect, the ethical hazard associated with the taking power arises from the fact that public officials are insulated from the opprobrium that would normally be directed toward perpetrators of coercive taking of property. Actions that would be deemed criminal behavior, if undertaken by a private party, are given legal sanction under the taking power. Moreover, to the extent that property can be coercively taken under circumstances in which only fair market value is paid as compensation, the true extent of the opportunity cost of the governmental undertaking is never fully reckoned by those with the power to make decisions (Greenhut 2004, 64–65). Political entrepreneurs have a strong incentive to not only avoid these costs but also to deflect any public scrutiny of the cost issue. The taking power affords the political entrepreneur that protection since the ethical issues of justice and just compensation do not need to be squarely addressed. Hence, ethical hazard is reflected in the fact that for the political entrepreneur, the assent of other officials and constituencies becomes a central practical concern allowing the coercive impact on the property owner to be ignored.

EPISTEMICS OF SUGGESTED OPTIONS TO RESTORE "WHOLENESS"

As noted above, various writers have acknowledged the reality that property owners are damaged when paid fair market value in takings. They have proposed various solutions. One option focuses on payment of the owner's reservation price as a just solution to the issue of compensation. Others have taken the position that the property owner should be paid a premium over fair market value to arrive at just compensation (Epstein 1985, 183, Ellickson 1973, 736–737, Knetsch and Borcherding 1979, 241, Reisman 1996, 422–423).[12] Not surprisingly, these alternatives lack epistemic means by which to impute a level of compensation to the owner that offsets damage and renders the property owner whole. In other words, both of these options face problems arising from attempts to apply an essentially empty theory of valuation (North 1992, 34). But this reality means that the true social cost of coercively transferred resources can never be estimated, imputed, or reckoned in a scientifically legitimate way. This awkward fact is seen to work in the interest of public officials eager to present proposed projects as yielding greater social benefits than are possible in reality.

Valuation and Action Epistemically Reflective of Just Compensation

By definition, compensation that results in the property owner being made "whole" is just. Wholeness implies justice and vice versa. Presumably compensation sufficient to render the property owner whole must faithfully reflect the owner's valuation of his or her property. But fundamentally, valuation is never more than a ranking of possible courses of action made by individuals when confronted with a range of options. In other words, valuation is always a subjective, one-dimensional ranking on a single unified ordinal scale that each individual establishes for himself. For one doing the valuing, valuation involves nothing quantifiable. In essence, as Mises has noted, "a judgment of value does not measure, it arranges in a scale of degrees, it grades. It is expressive of an order of preference and sequence, but is not expressive of measure and weight…The difference between the valuations of two states of affairs is entirely psychical and personal. It is not open to any projection into the external world" (Mises 1998, 97).

For the individual property owner, the relative ranking is between his property and alternative hypothetical levels of compensation. He will always rank the prospective compensation either above or below his property. In this sense, the owner simply ranks, chooses, and sets aside. This process of value is universally true for all human beings and is always the basis for all conscious action including the sale of property. This process has been described as a trilateral relationship between one human being and two things being valued (Hülsmann 2003, xxxvi–xxxvii). The valuation always involves preferring and relinquishing that which is not ranked more highly. But one should emphasize that this ranking by the property owner is not immutable and is always subject to change as the experiences and circumstances facing the property owner change.

Valuation cannot be divorced from choice and choice cannot be divorced from action. Action is always an effort to exchange one state of affairs for one that is thought by the actor to be more satisfactory. The actions of individual human beings differ because people have dissimilar objectives and differing bundles of goods over which they have legitimate claims of ownership. The ranking of goods by their respective owners may diverge and their respective goals may differ. Hence, one can readily appreciate the reality that even the owners of similar properties may rank their holdings in very different ways. But such differences in ranking foster differing expressions of assent to proposed offers of exchange. When two individuals value property owned by the other more highly than certain items that they themselves possess, a voluntary exchange is likely to occur because *all* voluntary exchanges make both parties better off (Rothbard 1998, 249). But of important note is the fact that acts of exchange reflect differences in valuation without reflecting actual valuation. Here again, the critical feature of the exchange is the overt expression of assent; the valuations themselves are never overt, measurable or quantifiable as in the utility of neoclassical welfare theory. What can be known about valuation only reveals itself in overt action reflecting the owner's preference for compensation offered over his property. As Mises notes, "One must not forget that the scale of values or wants manifests only in the reality of action. These scales have no independent existence apart from the actual behavior of individuals" (Mises 1998, 95).

The implications for the concept of reservation price are devastatingly clear. The reservation price does not exist for the unassenting owner of property and cannot be imputed, estimated, or forecast. Wholeness exists as a sense of being or a state of mind much in the manner of satisfaction. Only the property owner can be the judge of what compensation is sufficient to render him whole. In other words, "wholeness" is a totally subjective state; it can only be assessed or gauged by the individual whose wholeness is in question. For the individual property owner whose property is being taken, wholeness, much like the mythical utility of neoclassical economics, cannot be given any objective content by which some external entity has the ability to detect its presence or to prescribe measures that would assure its attainment (Buchanan 1979, 87). Nonetheless, the notion of assuring the owner compensation approximating or exceeding his reservation price has been expressed in other variations that aspire to impute an appropriate premium above fair market value. These variations are examined below.

The Mythical Inframarginal Owner and His Reservation Price

The preceding discussion noted the fact that one of the principal reasons for reversion to fair market value as compensation to the owner bore on the difficulty in measuring value to the owner. Yet implicit in the use of the word "difficulty" is the idea that somehow, with enough effort and data, valuation can somehow be imputed. Once imputed, this presumed value is to be applied as the basis for compensation with the result that the property owner is somehow rendered whole. This idea emerges out of the unfortunate fact that economists have never fully abandoned the idea that valuation is something measurable and still somehow a feature of an individual's preexisting and stable utility function. While economists were grudgingly taught long ago that interpersonal comparisons of utility have no scientific validity, economists have continued to cling on to the notion that utility still exists in some nascent form in the mind of the individual (Robbins 1932,132). But as James Buchanan notes "...we cannot, as external observers, possibly know utility functions because such functions do not, and cannot, exist independently of the action of choice" (Buchanan 1979, 87).

Nonetheless, this idea of utility also carries over into the way economists find themselves thinking about compensation in the context of takings of private property. This thinking manifests itself in the well-meaning but misguided notion that the property owner has a preexisting reservation price that somehow emerges from a utility function that is thought to preexist in the mind of the owner.[13] In the context of just compensation for the taking of property, the idea is that if ethical breach is to be avoided, justice then hinges on being able to pay the unassenting owner a level of compensation at least equal to this reservation price. In essence, the task facing the economist is to use "clever means" to discover it.

One way in which economists try to give some concreteness to the idea of reservation price is to model it in the context of supply and demand schedules. Economists are accustomed to thinking about supply and demand schedules as preexisting, empirical realities that are relatively stable through time and are, hence, amenable to some type of estimation. But there is the risk that these schedules are overused metaphors in economics. To illustrate this point, assume that there is a market for the type of land being appropriated by government, and also assume that a roughly approximated market price for similar properties emerges and that this price can be empirically discerned.[14] Of no incidental importance is the fact that any estimate of current market price yields only historical information; this is a reality that fits only with considerable awkwardness into economists' analytical framework. "All the prices we know are past prices. They are facts of economic history.... The experience of economic history never tells us more than at a definite date and a definite place two parties A and B traded a definite quantity of commodity a against a definite number of units of money p" (Mises 1998, 327).

Within this metaphorical supply and demand framework, economists label one who places his land for sale at a market price the *marginal seller*. This price is just sufficient to induce him to sell. In other words, an expressed willingness on the part of the owner to sell reveals a ranking of the prevailing market price above the retention of the property. Hence, in a theoretical sense, the successful seller can be seen as a marginal seller. Moreover, in such an instance, the price is revealed to be ethically just in that the seller has explicitly assented to a transfer at the market price. There can be no question that, at the moment at which the land is sold, the seller has received just compensation.

But, the real issues surrounding just compensation bear on those who are unwilling to relinquish their property at the fair market price. To deal with this analytical issue, economists have contrived the notion of the reservation price. Of course, in a taking, prior to any voluntary decision to sell, a reservation price, were it to exist, would be unexpressed reservation price. By what analytical means can economists deal with the notion of an unexpressed reservation price in the context of takings? In trying to make the reservation price a magnitude that can be estimated, the economist may retain the presumption of the preexisting supply schedule. Within the context of such a supply schedule, these owners are referred to as inframarginal suppliers or, in this case, as inframarginal owners. By definition, the inframarginal owner is an unwilling seller at the market price or at fair market value but would be a potential seller at a higher price. Obviously, the market price at which similar properties may be exchanged on the market has no bearing on the aspirations or planned actions of the inframarginal owner. But from the economist's perspective, this property owner has a preexisting reservation price above the market price or above the price for similar properties being purchased and sold in the market. In the context of the economist's supply and demand framework, the property owner's reservation price would place him on an upward sloping supply schedule to the right of what may be a fair market price. By attempting to employ this conceptual framework, one may be tempted to make the case that the task of awarding just compensation is only one of finding or imputing the preexisting reservation price on a preexisting supply schedule. But even if the supply schedule were to preexist in the manner presumed, what epistemic basis exists by which to place a property owner's decision to sell at one point on this schedule rather than another? There is no answer to this question.

Ludwig von Mises (1998, 330) has placed the importance of these imagined demand and supply schedules in proper perspective:

> ...it is necessary to comprehend that such pictorial or mathematical modes of representation do not affect the essence of our interpretation and that they do not add a whit to our insight. Furthermore it is important to realize that we do not have any knowledge or experience with the shape of such curves. Always what we know is only the market price—that is, not the curves but only the point which we interpret as the intersection of the two hypothetical curves.

To further amplify the point being made by Mises, one can note that an actual observable market price at which transactions have actually occurred provide only historical evidence of situations in which buyers and sellers have, in the past, made choices and acted to express mutual assent to market exchanges. But other points on these schedules are only hypothetical conjectures. These points on a hypothetical supply curve do not represent choices, nor can they be presented as prospective choices that would result in prices. The points on the supply schedule are only imaginary and represent nothing of any epistemic significance. They are simply hypothetical exchanges that may be made by hypothetical property owners who may rank a hypothetical price above the option of retaining of their property. Until such choice is manifested in the overt action of expressing assent to the exchange, it remains only a hypothetical contingency not of the real world and not amenable to any sort of imputation. Preference must be demonstrated; it cannot be imputed.[15]

Another approach to the derivation of reservation prices would be to employ survey methods to yield the desired answers. Property owners would be presented with various hypothetical contingencies to reveal preferences and "thus indirectly assess their reservation value or the amount of payment necessary to leave them as well off as they would be without the taking of their property" (Knetsch 1983, 51). One may be tempted to conclude that these proposed techniques of contingent valuation have overcome imputational barriers to deriving reservation prices. As developed by economists, these techniques of contingent valuation purport to educe information on valuations of things that are not revealed in market transactions (Mitchell and Carson 1989, 129). Murray Rothbard (1997, 217) has exposed the uselessness of such information:

> One of the most absurd procedures based on a constancy assumption has been the attempt to arrive at a consumer's preference scale not through observed real action but through quizzing him by questionnaires....no assurance can be attached to the mere questioning of people. Not only will a person's

valuations differ when talking about them than when he is actually choosing, but there is also no guarantee that he is telling the truth.

In the absence of demonstrated preferences revealed through acts of exchange, answers to questionnaires cannot be considered meaningful[16] because this method involves reliance on a procedure in which the property owner is to reveal valuation in response to hypothetical specified situations. However, until the property owner is actually confronted with legitimate offers of purchase, no epistemically valid inferences can be made.

Clearly these confused attempts at imputing the valuations placed upon property by owners will not do. They are based on a pretence of knowledge rather than on sound economic analysis. In summary, it is sufficient to note that attempts to at least conceptually apply the standard of reservation price to compensation issues have arisen because of a misunderstanding concerning the epistemic nature of value and the misguided notion that value to the owner can ever be imputed. In fact, the reservation-price standard is a thorough epistemic fallacy because there is no valid means by which a government is able to establish what compensation can restore the owner to an "original level of well-being or wholeness." Being the victim of an act of coercion and an involuntary transfer of property, it can never be clear to anyone but the owner what compensation must be forthcoming to "replicate a level of well-being."

Epistemic Emptiness of Proposals to Pay Premiums to Assure Just Compensation

While some analysts and scholars accept the nonexistence of the reservation price and the fact that the concept provides no analytical guidance in the payment of compensation, the policy of paying a premium over fair market value is held out as a realistic and desirable alternative (Knetsch and Borcherding 1979, 246–248). From the perspective of good intentions, these well-meaning proposals are superior to the payment of fair market value. But clearly they encounter the same epistemic barriers that invalidate the notion of compensation based on the owner's reservation price. The problem of imputing an efficient premium is essentially equivalent to an attempt to impute an efficient price. This epistemic barrier is aptly captured by James Buchanan: "...the issue is not simply one of information. The central issue is the critical interdependence between market choice itself and the informational content of this process which can only be revealed as the process is allowed to occur" (Buchanan 1979, 86).

The discussion here will focus on two examples offered by scholars who seem to have sharply differing perspective on the underlying epistemic issues involved. These alterative approaches can be found in the work of two economists: Jack Knetsch and George Reisman. Jack Knetsch's alternative is outlined his book, *Property Rights and Compensation*. Though he is critical of current jurisprudence on takings policy, he is nonetheless of the belief that governments should retain the power to coercively appropriate property for public use. Knetsch's frame of reference is jurisprudence in various parts of the former British Empire including Canada and Australia.

Knetsch first discusses the prospect of applying a uniform percentage premium to all properties taken. "In some jurisdictions it has been common practice in cases of compulsory purchase to offer an award somewhat in excess of market price as an informal recognition of the involuntary nature of the exchange. A five or ten percent premium is not unusual" (Knetsch 1983, 49). But he is immediately in a very vulnerable epistemic position when he asserts that "[s]uch a policy would need to depend on some consensus of average difference between reservation and market price" (Knetsch 1983, 49). While he acknowledges that preferences may vary widely between property owners, he seems to believe that reservation values can be gleaned through the employment of survey techniques. "Each presumably would receive an equal premium even though reservation values would be expected to vary widely depending on individual circumstances and the preferences of each property holder" (Knetsch 1983, 49).

Knetsch, quite understandably, is forced to reject the uniform premium in light of the fact that it fails to make adequate allowance for the individual preferences and the differing circumstances of individual property owners. But he finds himself considering empirical and quantitative techniques designed to achieve at a solution through legislative means that cannot but fail epistemically:

> A variation on the policy of paying a uniform premium could include an explicit attempt at differentiation among the payments of a premium over market prices by tailoring compensation to individual owners. That is, some owners would receive larger payments than others based on some factor or factors that might be recognized as proper cause. Discernment of such factors is not a trivial problem, of course. But perhaps it is not an impossible problem either, especially if fairly crude indices are accepted as having some relation to what can be widely regarded as reasons to vary compensation awards. *Differentials could be established quite simply, although perhaps with some degree of arbitrariness, by means of a legislative schedule of premium awards.* (Knetsch 1983, 49, emphasis added)

In discussing the differentials in valuation between owners, Knetsch critically reviews various valuation criteria that include the following: (1) the interest of the claimant in the land; 2) the length of time during which the claimant resided on the land; (3) the inconvenience likely to be caused to the claimant by reason of his removal from the acquired land; (4 the period after the acquisition of the land during which the claimant has been or will be allowed to remain in possession of the land; (5) the period during which the claimant would have been likely to continue to reside on the land; and (6) any other matter which is relevant to the circumstances of the claimant (Knetsch 1983, 51). He believes that these criteria are useful but "do not provide a complete definition for determining appropriate award in individual cases" (Knetsch 1983, 51). In referring to "appropriate award," Knetsch is making reference to reservation prices. Again, Knetsch suggests survey methods to arrive at estimate of reservation prices. "The reservation prices of a cross section of property owners (not owners involved in current compulsory taking action) might be obtained by survey methods that pose various alternative contingencies and record the owners' expressed preferences among them" (Knetsch 1983, 51). He suggests that this approach could be refined by asking questions in the surveys that ask owners to express their preferences for trading off one value for another and indirectly assessing reservation values. Not surprisingly, Knetsch's proposal is an epistemic dead end. All the admonitions spelled out above apply here with equal force. To reiterate Rothbard's point, "no assurance can be attached to the mere questioning of people. Not only will a person's valuations differ when talking about them than when he is actually choosing, but there is also no guarantee that he is telling the truth" (Rothbard 1997, 217).

In his book *Capitalism,* Reisman offers a different approach to the compensation of dispossessed property owners (Reisman 1996, 422–423). Like Knetsch, Reisman believes in cooperative (governmental) efforts requiring public uses of privately owned resources and believes that, at least for the present, governments should retain the power to take property for strictly public uses. Like many others who have examined the injustice of current abuses of eminent domain jurisprudence, Reisman is critical of recent trends in which private property is taken but not committed to uses that are public in nature. For example, he is understandably critical of practices in which property is taken for the purpose of transferring it to private developers. In taking a longer perspective, he believes that the taking power of eminent domain should be gradually phased out through an amendment to the U.S. Constitution.[17]

But as a shorter-term solution to the violation of property rights imposed by coercive transfers of property, Reisman considers a radical procedure for the awarding of premiums. Reisman considers the realities of instances in which property owners do not want to sell. This situation may well arise in circumstances in which the owner has a deep emotional attachment to the property. To deal with these situations, Reisman recommends a particular approach to compensation that includes the payments of very generous premiums. Unlike Knetsch, Reisman is apparently much more skeptical of the ability of governments to impute premiums that provide any assurance of making the property owner whole. What Reisman offers as an alternative amounts to a rather generous rule of thumb in which the property owner is paid a premium several times greater than the "ostensible" or estimated value of the property. Reisman's view is that premiums paid on this scale would remove much of the vicious force associated with current takings procedures and would actually induce owners to willingly relinquish their property for public use. He also believes that the added governmental outlays for compensation would force governments to be more restrained in the acquisition of private property.

But would Reisman's generous premiums provide epistemic assurance that compensation is just? Such assurance would only be valid if the premium represented a multiple over fair market value that would prompt all prospectively dispossessed owners to "voluntarily" relinquish their property. But obviously no such assurance could be made. One likely scenario would be that in which some owners refuse any offers of generous compensation made by the government. The owner would not willingly relinquish property for any price. But Reisman is prepared to question the motives and rationality of such recalcitrant owners. "There would still be *irrational, capricious individuals* to be sure but their number would almost certainly not be great enough to constitute a significant barrier to the accomplishment of some important cooperative venture" (Reisman 1996, 422, emphasis added). But clearly there is no epistemically legitimate reason for such an inference. His perspective is in sharp contrast with Jack Knetsch's interpretation of such behavior, "...owners are unwilling to sell their holdings,...not because they are irrational or unreasonable but simply because they place a higher value on the particular properties (Knetsch 1983, 39). Nonetheless, from an epistemic perspective, both the Reisman and the Knetsch proposals are empty dead ends. The premiums emerging from either proposal would be no more than the application of coercively imposed rules of thumb.

Assent as the Critical Epistemic Indicator of Wholeness and Hence Justice

Given the above admonitions, what compensation renders the property owner whole and is thus demonstrably just? The only legitimate answer is compensation sufficient to induce the property owner to explicitly assent to the transfer. Richard Epstein almost concurs: "In principle, the ideal solution [i.e., compensation] is to leave the individual owner in a position of indifference between the taking by the government and the retention of the property" (Epstein 1985, 182). But since indifference cannot be the basis for an action, a more appropriate wording of Epstein's criterion would be the following: just compensation is that payment just sufficient to induce the owner to rank the payment offered above retention of his property.[18] This ranking can only be revealed in an explicit act expressing assent to the exchange. This act of assent is the only epistemically legitimate means by which compensation can be proven just. The property owner would never assent to a compensation that left him in a less preferred or damaged state. Assent to the property transfer is the epistemic proof of wholeness. In this demonstrable sense, the property owner emerges from the transfer, by his own assessment, free of damage.

Without assent, no prescribed level of compensation, generous though it may be, can be just in any epistemic sense of the word. This standard holds irrespective of the property owner's actions or presumed motivations. For example, a property owner may pursue a tough bargaining strategy with the government, demonstrating the behavior of someone who would normally be labeled a "stubborn speculative hold out." To some, the label of speculative holdout may imply some antisocial motivation but no such presumption is warranted in the issue at hand. For a property owner to hold out for a higher compensation is a legitimate motivation and entirely appropriate in the face of governmental attempts to acquire property. The fact that the owner may or may not have speculative intent in holding out for a higher price is immaterial to the justice of the compensation. At this point the epistemics and the ethics of just compensation come together. The issue of just compensation in coercive takings, as promised in the Fifth Amendment to the U.S. Constitution, contains an obvious and irreconcilable contradiction. Assent cannot at the same time be reconciled with a coercive taking. Since the process of eminent domain is defined by coercive taking, compensation for the taking cannot be made just. "Justice" cannot be reconciled with the apparent ethical breach represented by coercion itself.

Epistemic Barrier to Reckoning True Social Cost As an Advantage to Government

When a taking occurs, the presumptive intent of officials is the use of the property for some public purpose. In an ideal world free of perverse incentives, no such action would be undertaken unless there was some recognizable net benefit associated with such a reallocation of resources. But the process of coercively taking property does not fit the niceties of an ideal world. As the preceding discussion makes clear, taken property is obtained at prices always below the amount that would prompt voluntary assent on the part of the property owner; that is, resources are obtained more cheaply than if the properties were obtained at prices upon which property owners agreed. This fact has two consequences that work to the advantage of public officials engaged in the taking of property. First, it allows officials to present their proposed projects in the most favorable light possible. For example, in "buying" the taken property, an artificially low burden is placed upon taxpayers in governmental acquisition of the property. In this sense, entrepreneurial public officials have an incentive to abuse the taking power and, in some cases, even take more property than may be needed for a proposed project (Benson 2005, 186). Moreover, this underpricing of the resources acquired through takings means that officials are able to represent the net benefits of public projects in a misleadingly inflated way. Lower tax burden and inflated net benefits have obvious appeal to the constituency targeted as the beneficiaries of projects employing taken resources.

Second, since assent is absent from takings transactions, the true social costs of proposed projects can never be reckoned by anyone under any circumstances since the requisite information can never come into existence (Buchanan 1969, 84; 1979, 87). This issue is one of the most pernicious aspects of takings since it works to the covert advantage of aggressive public officials in quest of political profits. Since, no voluntary transactions occur in the taking of property, the actual dollar outlays are essentially meaningless as a benchmark of the opportunity cost associated with the property transfer. Put differently, the prices actually paid do not emerge from decisions made at the margin and thus do not begin to reflect anything approximating legitimate economic costs of transferring resources. As James Buchanan notes: "...genuine opportunity costs must include the individual's evaluation of enjoyments foregone...The evaluations of individuals should be relevant in any attempt to derive normative statements..." (1969, 58, 60). The individual's evaluation of enjoyments foregone (cost) is only reckoned, but not necessarily revealed, at the margin in voluntary transactions in which property transfer is not coerced. Obviously, these costs are subjective, entirely personal and unique to the individual victims of the taking process. Since reservation prices or optimal premiums are not measurable or even imputable, the true social costs of confiscatory property transfers remain a mystery. But public officials are all the happier for this epistemic opacity. The predatory activities of governments are not only fostered by the law but are protected by the absence of information that can never come into being.

CONCLUSION

Can the concept of just compensation be reconciled with the coercive taking of private property? More specifically, can the concept of just compensation for private property be reconciled ethically or epistemologically with the coercive taking of such property by a governmental authority? From both an ethical and epistemic perspective, the answer is a clear *no*. From an ethical perspective, one can assert without risk of refutation that if the surrender of property by a property owner is not voluntary, the presumption of injustice and harm is manifest. Ethical breach is evident. But the fact that governments have the power to take property means governmental officials are open to ethical hazard in that they have an incentive to act in an unethical way while the law itself protects and even encourages such predatory behavior.

But from an epistemic perspective, the absence of assent bars any conceivable inference that compensation can be just in a transfer of property. In addition, no epistemic means are available to make any such determination. Market-based benchmarks or professional appraisals are epistemically relevant to those willing to sell at a so-called market price. However, these estimates or surveys have no relevance whatsoever in gauging just compensation for the unassenting owner. The concepts of reservation prices and efficient premium are equally devoid of meaning from an epistemic perspective.

If the means by which governments acquire property were altered so that just compensation were the dollar amount that would induce the property owner to voluntarily relinquish his property, the government would then face a fundamental check on its powers to acquire property. The individual property owner would then have the power to prevent the government from proceeding with a project if the government were unwilling to pay a mutually agreeable price. The individual property owner, through the ethical exercise of his rights, would be able to block the coercive, confiscatory appropriation of private property. Moreover, there would be ethical and epistemic assurance that so-called government projects would take into account the true social cost of the resources employed. But such transparency is counter to the interests of public officials. With coercive transfers of property, prices paid for resources are below valuations of owners but by an amount that can never be known. The consequent but inevitable ignorance of social cost serves the purpose of officials eager to present projects in the most beneficial light.

NOTES

The views expressed in this study are strictly professional perspectives held by the author and do not necessarily reflect the policy of the U.S. Department of Interior in Washington, D.C. The author thanks Jörg Guido Hülsmann, David Gordon, Roy Cunningham, Laurent Carnis, Paul Cleveland and Edward J. López for thoughtful comments on an earlier version of the chapter that was presented as a paper at the Southern Economic Association Conference, Charleston S.C., November 2006. They bear no responsibility for remaining errors.

1. The provision in the U.S. Constitution that property is to be taken only for public use was once thought to be an implicit check on the scope of takings activity by government. Unfortunately, this stipulation has been transmuted into a taking authority for the public good regardless of the extent to which "public use" is intended or not. This unfortunate change is perhaps nowhere more evident than in the 2005 *Kelo v. City of New London* decision of the U.S. Supreme Court. While *Kelo* itself is clearly destructive of private property rights, the state and local backlash across the United States has been described as a largely corrective development (López and Totah. 2007, 397–416).

2. This author is using the adjective "epistemic" as being roughly synonymous with 'epistemological.'... " a proposition is epistemic if and only if it has some implication for what, in some circumstances, is rationally worthy of belief" (Honderich 1995, 241). The noun "epistemics" will be used as being roughly synonymous with epistemology.

3. The reality of control means that the individual necessarily possesses the property, uses the property to serve his own ends, and is able to dispose of what he possesses and uses in whatever manner and for whatever purpose that best serves his ends. Implicit in possession, use, and disposition is the ability to enjoy whatever the benefits or proceeds that may accompany ownership (Hülsmann. 2004, 51).

4. Natural law has been defined "as system of principles for the guidance of human conduct, which independently of enacted law or of the systems peculiar to any one people, might be discovered by the rational intelligence of man, and would be found to grow out of, and conform to his nature, meaning by that word, his whole mental moral and physical constitution.... These express necessary and obligatory rules of human conduct which have been established through...human reason" (Black 1979, 925).

5. The concept of self-ownership has been championed in recent times by thinkers such as Murray Rothbard (1998, 31–32).

6. The phrase "chain of just transfer" is from Nozick (1974, 151).

7. Ibid. Alternative but similar definitions are examined in the following discussion.

8. Issues of valuation are addressed at greater length later in the chapter.

9. In the exercise of the police power, governments are not even obligated to pay anything for what amounts to a taking of property. The stated objectives of the police power focus on the health, safety, morals, and general welfare of the community. If these objectives had continued to define the scope within which the police power can be applied, this role of government would not have evolved into the assault on private property that one sees today. Regulatory intervention undertaken in the name of the police power results in functional takings with no compensation paid to the land owner. Zoning restrictions are perhaps the most egregious example of property being essentially taken without any compensation to owners. A second flagrant example of institutionalized injustice is the exclusion from compensation of any enhancement in the value of taken property arising from government actions. The courts in the United States have taken this position: "Government condemners should not...reward owners whose land has appreciated through an anticipation of government plans" (Paul 1987, 81). In discussing this issue, Ellen Frankel Paul references *United States v. Reynolds*, 397 U.S. 14 (1970). Under this perverse logic, the inclusion of scarcity rent in the compensation would mean that the owner would be paid an "undeserved windfall" since the prospects open to the property owner in the absence of the taking would have borne no surplus or scarcity rent. A third example of institutionalized injustice is found in the lack of compensation for goodwill lost in the process of taking property. The destruction of goodwill is a common occurrence in the taking of property by governments but compensation is generally denied. Goodwill is an intangible capital asset owned by commercial firms that emerges through actions that are essentially investments yielding a net future return as a result of a community of loyal customers, expanded sales, and expanded markets. In denying compensation in this area of takings, law has become another form of institutionalized injustice making just compensation a virtual impossibility.

10. The discussion below examines the reservation price concept more carefully. The reservation price has its own mythology bearing on the idea that it even exists in the owner's mind prior to the actual transaction.

11. The one exception to this rule arises in those instances in which the property owner has sufficient political influence to bargain for a significantly higher level of compensation (Benson 2005, 185).

12. In the *Kelo v. City of New London* case, Professor Thomas Merrill submitted an amicus brief in which he argued in that "[a]djusting compensation awards to provide more complete indemnification would be a far more effective reform of the existing system of eminent domain than increasing federal judicial review of public use determinations." Brief for the American Planning Association et al. as Amici Curiae Supporting Respondents at 28, *Kelo v. City of New London*, 125 S. Ct. 2655 (2005) (No. 04108), 2005 WL 166929; *see also*: James E. Krier and Christopher Serkin, *Public Ruses*, 2004 Michigan. ST . L. REV. 859, 867 (arguing that compensation levels should increase as the "publicness" of a project diminishes).

13. The payment of the owner's reservation price is essentially the idea that the owner should be paid a price at least equal to his valuation of his own property (Knetsch and Borcherding 1979, 247). See also Knetsch (1983, 45).

14. One of the principal and practical reasons for labeling the assumption of an equilibrium price for land as unrealistic is that such property is heterogeneous in

nature with unique features of location or resource content. While there is some degree of substitutability between land properties in different uses, the competitive forces in the land market can never produce a uniform price as one might expect to see during a trading period for a relatively uniform commodity. Moreover, real market prices fluctuate as buyer and sellers adapt to their interpretation of emerging market information.

15. Murray Rothbard observes: "Demonstrated preference...eliminates hypothetical imaginings about individual value scales. Welfare economics has until now always considered values as hypothetical valuation of hypothetical 'social states.' But demonstrated preference only treats values as revealed through chosen action" (Rothbard 1997, 240).

16. Mises observes that "one must not forget that the scale of values or wants manifests itself only in the reality of action, these scales have no independent existence apart from actual behavior of individuals" (Mises 1998, 95).

17. Reisman offers a longer-term proposal to replace the current constitutional authority of eminent domain. This proposal would be one in which the rights of way for roads, railroads, pipelines, and so on would be acquired far in advance of the time of actual construction and would be "understood to be a precondition for an area's future development." Even though private property would be held under the contingency that the government would at some point in the future exercise a long-term public claim of right-of-way, property owners would still have the right to refuse to relinquish their property in the event of such a claim (Reisman 1996, 422).

18. On the inapplicability of "indifference" to human action, see Rothbard (2004, 307, 309).

CHAPTER 9

THE LAWYER-JUDGE HYPOTHESIS

Benjamin H. Barton

Here is the lawyer-judge hypothesis in a nutshell: if there is a clear advantage or disadvantage to the legal profession in any given question of law, judges will choose the route that benefits the profession as a whole.[1] In support of this hypothesis I offer examples drawn from multiple, distinct areas of the law. In so doing I hope to establish the accuracy of the theory and its far-reaching consequences. As a bonus, I also offer a single explanation for a series of puzzling legal anomalies.

The legal issues discussed in this chapter cut across professional responsibility, evidence, constitutional law, criminal procedure, and torts. Though all of them have been explained within their own boundaries, I argue that they are better understood as examples of the lawyer-judge hypothesis in action. These are cases where judges simply found a way to treat lawyers better than other litigants. The first section lays out a theoretical basis for my hypothesis. The following four sections lay out specific legal examples of the lawyer-judge hypothesis. Finally, the last section briefly discusses (without coming to any conclusions) the ramifications of the lawyer-judge hypothesis.

THEORY

In recent years there has been an increasing focus on judicial decision-making processes and the behavior of judges. This study has, at its heart, the following summary: Judges are people too; they are driven by the same combination of incentives, experiences, and cognitive biases that drive the rest of us. Arguing in this vein, political scientists study the "attitudinal model," which argues that political ideology is the single best predictor of judicial decisions (Segal and Spaeth 1993); cognitive psychologists study judicial heuristics (Bainbridge and Gulati 2002); and economists wonder what incentives control judicial behavior (Posner 1993, Rubin 2005, Helland and Tabarrok 2006, 2002).

While some empirical studies have suggested ways these various incentives play out in practice (Bainbridge and Gulati 2002), scholars have had a hard time translating these incentives into substantive law, that is, finding areas of the law where they apply sufficiently to have a predictive value.[2] In this way the empirical studies have suffered from a "missing link" problem—they have established that judges take certain shortcuts in deciding all cases, but they have not shown a rule that predicts an outcome in any particular type of case. The lawyer-judge hypothesis bridges this gap by establishing predictable legal results from judicial attitudes and incentives.

This chapter uses aspects of each of the above areas of study, as well as the sociology of the professions and the new institutionalism, to discuss why we would expect judicial incentives and proclivities to lead to decisions that favor the legal profession. I start from the most external reasons, and then proceed to the internal and more important reasons.

Most studies of judicial incentives focus on nonmonetary incentives, such as maximizing leisure time, prestige, or opportunities for further judicial promotion rather than salary effects, on the assumption that judicial decisions have no effect on salaries (Posner 1993, 13–23). Nevertheless, the lawyer-judge hypothesis shows that at least one class of decisions, those that directly affect the legal profession, can have direct and indirect judicial salary effects.

A brief study of judges—who they are, how they are trained, what their jobs are like, and salary effects—leads to the inevitable conclusion that judges will regularly favor the interests of lawyers over other litigants. Many judges rely on lawyers to get or keep their jobs. Most state judges face some type of election (either contested or retention) (Bureau of Justice Statistics 1998) and lawyers provide most of the elected judiciary's campaign donations. In elective states—including merit selection states with retention elections—bar associations frequently endorse judicial candidates, and conduct and publish "bar polls" on the judges (Schotland 1985). Many judges were selected for their positions through "merit plans" that place substantial selection authority in state and local bar associations (Armitage 2002). Any judge who hopes to join the federal judiciary relies upon the American Bar Association (ABA) for a favorable rating. Bar associations have further massaged the judicial salary incentive by working tirelessly for higher salaries for judges (American Bar Association and Federal Bar Association 2001).

Further, the vast majority of judges were practicing attorneys before taking the bench. Most judges are members of bar associations.[3] Of course bar association membership and a career as a lawyer only begin to describe the effects of judicial "membership" in the legal profession. It is accurate to say that judges are, both temporally and emotionally, lawyers first. Most judges have spent the bulk of their careers and formative working years as lawyers. Their peer group, former colleagues, and many of their friends are all likely to be lawyers. Each of these contacts and experiences work on a conscious and subconscious level. On a conscious level, any judge will think hard about the reactions of his or her peer group and friends to a decision that will have a substantial effect on them.

Judges also work in a remarkably insulated world. Americans pride themselves on having an independent judiciary. Judges are sheltered, to the extent possible, from direct lobbying and even much contact with the nonlawyer public with the exception of litigants, witnesses, and jurors. The regular contact between judges and lawyers thus looms even larger in the judicial worldview, and makes judges an easy target for formal and informal lawyer lobbying.

A closer examination of the nuts and bolts of a judge's job also demonstrates how critical lawyers are to the work of judging. In the advocacy system, most judges rely on the lawyers to do the great bulk of the work in trying, briefing, researching, or investigating cases. When the system is working properly, the judges sit back and decide cases based on the legal and factual work of the lawyers. On a more basic level, most judges probably do not want to face regularly a courtroom of disgruntled lawyers, simply because of their ongoing working relationship.

The above factors may be considered the many conscious reasons for judges to favor lawyers. The subconscious reasons, however, are at least as important, if not more. Here the work of the new institutionalists is particularly instructive. The "new institutionalism" defines institutions broadly as "formal and informal rules that constrain individual behavior and shape human interaction; *institutional environment* varies with a person's position in society" (Eggertsson 1996; emphasis in original). Under this definition, institutions are groups joined by constraining and defining behaviors and thought patterns.

Judges, as a defined group and "institution" respond to the world, and particularly to judicial decisions, as *lawyers*. Legal thinking itself is a powerful and constraining institution. The goal of American law schools, to teach our students to "think like a lawyer" (Johnson 1991), is thus quite explicit in institutionalizing the process of legal analysis. Judges have had the transformative experiences of law school and practice, and they approach the world in a very specific way.

Most judges are also likely to be individuals who thrived under the written and unwritten rules of the legal world. Judges thus approach their work with a prescribed set of heuristics, behaviors, and notions about the world. These cognitive institutions are precisely why they succeeded as lawyers and why they are valued as judges. Nevertheless, these same factors lead judges to overempathize with lawyers. On a subconscious level, when judges face a question that will impact the legal profession, they naturally react in terms of how it will affect "us" more than "them."

Thus, as a matter of theory, the lawyer-judge hypothesis seems like a natural fit. Nevertheless, scholars of the legal system have had a long-standing blind spot when it comes to judges. We tend to believe that judges are independent adjudicators of the law who disregard their personal preferences and proclivities when they decide cases. Because of this blind spot, theorists have tended to examine at the effect of judicial incentives and heuristics around the edges of jurisprudence, looking for evidence of self-interest in judicial shortcuts, or administrative duties (Smith 1995). The lawyer-judge hypothesis, by contrast, proposes evidence of jurisprudential self-interest: areas of the law where judicial preferences and self-interest actually lead to concrete and otherwise inexplicable results.

Lawyer Regulation

The necessary starting point for consideration of the lawyer-judge hypothesis is the judicial role in creating and maintaining the American system of lawyer self-regulation, because the fruits of that self-regulation underlie many of the other examples of the lawyer-judge hypothesis. Since the publication of *The Wealth of Nations*, economists have theorized that professional self-regulation tends to benefit the profession itself (Smith 1776 [1991]). Virtually every occupational license and regulatory scheme—from barbers' to doctors'—has been dissected to show the underlying self-interest involved.

The creation and maintenance of the unique self-regulatory apparatus of the American legal profession speaks volumes about the relationship of the bench and bar. The first thing to note is that state supreme courts, and not state legislatures, govern the regulation of lawyers in all the 50 states (Barton 2003). Thus, only lawyers have the true claim to professional self-regulation: from top to bottom, they are governed by lawyers. Predictably, this control has led to "a degree of self-regulation far beyond either the reality or even the expectations of any other professional group" (Moore 1989, 14–16).

The hows and whys of this self-regulation establish well judicial support for the legal profession. It is important to note that it was not always so. Until the mid-nineteenth century, state legislatures set the general requirements for bar admission and district courts generally governed the administration of admissions. Bar associations were small or nonexistent. From the late nineteenth century onward, bar associations reformed, and state supreme court control over lawyer regulation eventually became the rule in all the 50 states (Barton 2005).

The jurisprudential basis for this move was state supreme courts' claim of an "inherent authority" to regulate the practice of law as an outgrowth of the constitutional separation of powers between the legislative and judicial branches. Using this inherent judicial authority, many state supreme courts barred state legislatures from regulating lawyers (Alpert 1983). The state supreme courts' "inherent authority" over lawyer regulation is an obscure and rarely noticed doctrine. Essentially state supreme courts hold that state constitutions' creation of a judicial branch presupposes certain uniquely "judicial" powers. State supreme courts have thus struck down any legislative act that "encroaches" upon the judiciary or "judicial" powers, allowing state supreme courts to control rulemaking authority, the regulation of lawyers, and in some cases, judicial funding (Wolfram 1986, 22–32).

It is odd that judges would not at least *share* these regulatory powers, if not take a clear back seat to legislatures, who regulate every other American profession. Nevertheless, many state supreme courts (with strong bar association support) have claimed sole authority over lawyer regulation. Moreover, because the inherent authority is claimed as a result of state constitutional law, judicial control over the legal profession can only be challenged by a change in court precedent or a constitutional amendment.

Public choice scholars can probably guess the results of this inherent authority over lawyer regulation. Courts have used their inherent authority to advantage lawyers in a variety of ways. Some of the uses have been particularly protectionist, ranging from aggressive prosecution of the unauthorized practice of law (Dowling 1935, 636–637) to the creation of mandatory fee scales (*Lathrop v. Donahue*, 102 N.W.2d 404 [Wisc. 1960], 413–414).

Nevertheless, the use of inherent authority that has most benefited lawyers is the creation of unified bars in the majority of American states. In these states a lawyer must be a member of the state bar association to practice law (McKean 1963). The bar is unified (otherwise termed integrated) in 36 states and the District of Columbia (Radke 1988). This mandatory connection between a professional license and membership in a professional organization is unique to the legal profession. Like a "closed shop" in labor law, this requirement offers these bar associations unique opportunities for funding, lobbying, and overall group power.

The history of bar unification is particularly instructive. The first states were unified by statute, but in 1939 Oklahoma became the first state supreme court to unify by court order (In re Integration of the State Bar of Oklahoma, 185 Okla. 505 [1939]). Following Oklahoma, the remaining states were unified by court action (McKean 1963). This granted the legal profession a court-created bar structure (an exceptional lobbying and financial advantage) ready, willing, and anxious to self-regulate.

Naturally, state supreme court justices have generally granted these bar associations much of the court's regulatory power. Even in states without a unified bar, state supreme courts delegate their regulatory authority to lawyers and bar associations (Barton 2003). So from the state supreme court justices down to lawyers, all are regulated solely by lawyers. As a general rule, foxes make poor custodians of henhouses, and I have argued at length elsewhere that self-regulation has led inexorably to self-interested regulations (Barton 2001). There are a number of examples from the ABA Rules, which include regulations restricting competition through stringent rules on advertising, client solicitation, client referrals, and unauthorized practice in another jurisdiction or assisting in unauthorized practice (American Bar Association 2008). These regulations are defended as a hedge against creeping commercialization, but critics see naked restraints of trade (Calfee 1997, Ippolito and Mathios 1990, Rhode 1981, Benham 1972).

My favorite example is the requirements for entry to the practice of law. Raising entry barriers has been the sine qua non of bar associations and lawyer lobbying (Sunderland 1953, 72–75). Since state supreme courts have controlled lawyer regulation, entry barriers have evolved from virtual nonexistence to the complex system of today. Lawyers, of course, have an excellent reason to favor higher entry standards: they decrease the supply of legal services and raise the price for those services. Moreover, the higher prices are a windfall for the current members of the profession lobbying for more difficult standards; they enjoy the higher prices without having to meet the new, higher standards.[4] While rising entry standards have multiple benefits to lawyers, there is little evidence that the benefit to consumers is equivalent to the higher cost of services (Barton 2001, 445–448).

It is also interesting to contrast the interests of bar associations and judges in entry barriers with more direct means of controlling errant lawyers, that is, disbarment or court sanctions. The enforcement of the Rules of Professional Conduct has been notoriously lax (Rhode 2002). Likewise, courts have been quite reticent to impose sanctions of any kind on shoddy lawyering in their courts. This reticence is puzzling, given that greater enforcement might actually improve the administration of justice and the ease of any particular judge's job. In this case, judicial sympathy for lawyers apparently trumps any individual interest in sanctions.

In sum, state supreme courts have taken a remarkably expansive view of the separation of powers and their "inherent authority" to gain control over lawyer regulation. These cases arise as a matter of state constitutional law, but are best understood as example of judicial sympathy and empathy for bar associations and the legal profession as a whole.

LAWYER-CLIENT PRIVILEGE

One of the oldest and most ingrained examples of the lawyer-judge hypothesis is the attorney-client privilege. I seek to demonstrate three things. First, the attorney-client privilege has been accorded a unique and vaunted position among all professional privileges. Second, the primacy of the attorney-client privilege—in comparison to other privileges like those accorded physicians, spouses, or clergy—cannot be justified solely jurisprudentially. Instead, the difference is most likely the inherent sympathy that judges have had for the importance of the attorney-client relationship. Third, the special treatment of the attorney-client privilege, in conjunction with rules of professional conduct requiring confidentiality, make legal services much more attractive to clients.

The attorney-client privilege is a rule of evidence that protects most attorney-client communications from compelled disclosure. The classic statement of the privilege comes from the nineteenth century common law masterpiece, *Wigmore's Evidence*. The privilege applies "(1) [w]here legal advice of any kind is sought (2) from a professional legal adviser in his capacity as such, (3) the communications relating to that purpose, (4) made in confidence (5) by the client, (6) are at his instance permanently protected (7) from disclosure by himself or by the legal adviser, (8) except the protection be waived" (Wigmore 1961, § 2292).

Courts have long treated the attorney-client privilege as the flagship evidentiary privilege.[5] Courts frequently "wax poetic" (Imwinkelried 2002, § 6.2.4) about this "most sacred of all legally recognized privileges" (In re Grand Jury Proceedings, 162 F.3d 554 [9th Cir. 1998],556–557). It holds a special position as the "oldest and most venerated of the common law privileges of confidential communications" (*U.S. v. Edwards*, 303 F.3d 606 [5th Cir. 2002], 618). It "serves a salutary and important purpose: to encourage full and frank communication between attorneys and their clients and thereby promote broader public interests in the observance of law and administration of justice" (*Southern Scrap Material Co. v. Fleming*, 2003 WL 21783318 [E.D. La. 2003]).

"Thus, it is reasonable to expect that a conversation with an attorney would be private" (*Sherbrooke v. City of Pelican Rapids*, 2006 WL 3227783 [D. Minn.2006]). It is a "strong and absolute privilege" (*Fru-Con Const. Corp. v. Sacramento Mun. Utility Dist.*, 2006 WL 2255538 [E.D.Cal. 2006]) (barring waiver and other limited exceptions), and must "receive unceasing protection" (*Lanza v. New York*, 370 U.S. 139 [1962],143–144). It "seeks to protect a relationship that is a mainstay of our system of justice" (*Gould, Larson, Bennet, Wells and McDonnell, P.C. v. Panico*, 869 A.2d 653 [D. Conn. 2005], 656).

The courts protect the attorney-client privilege by more than just rhetoric, however. A comparison of the treatment of lawyers and other professionals by the courts is quite instructive. Of the three longest standing "professions," lawyers are the only one to receive continuous common law protection, and as a result lawyers have been, and are still, in a much better position than their compatriots.

There has never been a common law physician-patient privilege in England or the United States (DeWitt 1958, 9–14). While the attorney-client privilege was originally recognized during the reign of Elizabeth I and protected as a "point of honor" for lawyers (Wigmore 1961, at § 2290), the physician-patient privilege was famously rejected in 1776. The doctor at issue refused to disclose "a confidential trust . . . consistent with [his] professional honour." Lord Mansfield replied: "If a surgeon was voluntarily to reveal these secrets, to be sure he would be guilty of a breach of honour . . . but, to give that information in a court of justice, which by the law of the land he is bound to do, will never be imputed to him as any indiscretion whatsoever" and required disclosure (Shuman 1985,671).

In fact, the protection of physician-patient communications in this country is as a result of state statutes[6] (Strong 1999, 397–399). This makes the privilege much less powerful than the attorney-client privilege for several reasons. First, there is no statutory physician-patient privilege whatsoever in approximately one-fifth of the states (Best 2004, § 2380). Second, even where the protections exist, the privilege suffers "significant variations and numerous exceptions" (Weissbrodt, Pekin, and Wilson 2006, 61). Third, the fact that the privilege was not recognized at common law means it is generally inapplicable in federal courts applying federal law (*Jaffee v. Redmond*, 518 U.S. 1 [1998], 10).

For a particularly blunt comparison between the attorney-client and physician-patient privileges, it is helpful to look where the rubber hits the road: the wisdom of trial attorneys. In a *Trial* magazine list of testimonial objections, the privileges are summarized as follows: "All states recognize the attorney-client privilege.... On the other hand, the physician-patient privilege is weak"[7] (Lipton 2005).

The clergy-penitent privilege has a similar history. Before the reformation, there was a priest-penitent privilege that protected priests from testifying (Mitchell 1987). Following the reformation, however, English courts repudiated the privilege, and American courts followed suit (Montone 1995, 267–269). Similar to the physician-patient privilege, the clergy-penitent privilege has grown primarily as a result of state statutes (Yellin 1983) Furthermore, although the clergy-penitent privilege is recognized in all the 50 states, its statutory basis differs state by state and it is subject to many more exceptions than the attorney-client privilege (Montone 1995, 283–286).

In comparison to accountants, however, doctors and clergy get off easy. There is no federal accountant-client privilege (*Couch v. United States*, 409 U.S. 322 [1973], 335). Likewise, most jurisdictions have refused to recognize an accountant-client privilege as a matter of statutory or common law (Imwinkelried 2002, § 6.2.4).

Nevertheless, comparing the justifications for these various privileges with those that historically underpin the attorney-client privilege does not offer a strong argument for the great variation in treatment.[8] Courts and commentators have generally used a utilitarian approach to defending the attorney-client privilege, arguing that the societal benefits outweigh the costs. As the Supreme Court has stated, the privilege's "purpose is to encourage full and frank communication between attorneys and their clients and thereby promote broader public interests in the observance of law and the administration of justice. The privilege recognizes that sound legal advice or advocacy serves public ends and that such advice or advocacy depends upon the lawyer being fully informed by the client" (Upjohn Co., 449 U.S. 383 [1981], 389).

Some of the best known historical formulations of this utilitarian justification are particularly telling in terms of the lawyer-judge hypothesis. *Annesley v. Earl of Anglesea* (17 How. St. Tr. 1129 [Ex. 1743]) quoted in *Wigmore's Evidence*, specifically references the business interests of lawyers in the privilege: "all people and all courts have looked upon that confidence between the party and attorney to be so great that it would be destructive to all business if attornies [sic] were to disclose the business of their clients."

Other early courts explicitly recognized the judiciary's need for a fully functioning cadre of lawyers as a justification: the privilege is necessary "out of regard to the interests of justice, which cannot be upholden, and to the administration of justice, which cannot go on without the aid of men skilled in jurisprudence, in the practice of the courts, and in those matters affecting rights and obligations which form the subject of all judicial proceedings" (*Greenough v. Gaskell*, 39 Eng. Rep. 618 [Ch. 1833], 621). Thus the utilitarian defense includes two key aspects of the lawyer-judge hypothesis, an implied concern for the welfare and business of lawyers, and concern over the ease of the administration of justice.

The relative importance placed on the attorney-client relationship, and the disrespect paid to doctors and patients and other professional relationships, is hard to defend conceptually. Assuming that it is true that candor between attorneys and clients is so critical that we should protect it in court, is candor between doctors and patients really less important? Just in terms of the societal interests involved I would think that health frequently (if not always) trumps legal advice in importance. Similarly, the relationship between a worshipper and her clergy-person seems equally worthy of societal support and care.[9]

The physician-patient privilege (among others) was scorned at common law. *Wigmore's Evidence* offers a particularly scathing rebuke. Wigmore applied a four-part test to balance the costs and benefits of all privileges[10] and found that only the three privileges that had been recognized as common law—husband-wife, priest-penitent, and attorney-client—conformed to all four factors (Wigmore 1961, § 2285). Wigmore argued vociferously against the physician-patient privilege. Interestingly, one of his main arguments was that doctors did not really need the privilege, because people would consult doctors in all candor regardless of any privilege. He called it "ludicrous" to suggest a seriously ill person would withhold vital information from a doctor out of fear of later exposure in court (Wigmore 1961, § 2380a). Moreover, Wigmore made much of the fact that states, such as New York, that had a physician-patient privilege, reported no difference in usage of doctors from nonprivilege states (Wigmore 1961, § 2380a).[11] Wigmore also carps that "[t]he real support for the privilege seems to be mainly the weight of professional medical opinion pressing upon the legislature" (Wigmore 1961, § 2380a). Last, the physician privilege has been criticized as fostering fraud. "More than a century of experience with the statutes has demonstrated that the [physician-patient] privilege in the main operates not as the shield of privacy but as the protector of fraud.... [The privilege] runs against the grain of justice, truth and fair dealing" (Cleary 1972, 228).

The same questions that presented in the doctor-patient scenario fit lawyers and clients: Would lawyer-client communication truly be crippled without the privilege? Are many clients actually fully forthcoming with their lawyers regardless of the privilege? I do not ask these questions to argue for the abolition or curtailment of the privilege, but just to note that the empirical and theoretical basis for differentiating between lawyers and doctors (or clergy or accountants) is not nearly as clear as courts have suggested. Instead, when faced with a balancing test between the importance of a professional relationship and the truth-seeking function, courts repeatedly chose the truth-seeking function except for a very narrow group of relationships headlined by the attorney-client relationship. While this choice has been defended on jurisprudential grounds, it is better explained by the lawyer-judge hypothesis.

It is also worth noting what an exceptional product the attorney-client privilege allows lawyers to sell to clients. In conjunction with extremely tight professional confidentiality rules and norms,[12] the attorney-client privilege offers clients protection for almost all disclosures. As Professor Daniel Fischel has noted, the privilege and the ethics rules offer an unbeatable combination (Fischel 1998). If you are concerned at all about later confidentiality in court and need someone to talk to, you would be well advised to choose a lawyer.

On a final note, the very structure of attorney-client disclosure/waiver hints at the privilege's true beneficiaries. Generally, any disclosure to a third person outside the confidential relationship waives the privilege.[13] These rules are particularly stringent for clients: a word about a privileged matter to a friend or relative, or even a lack of care with privileged materials can affect a waiver. Two notable exceptions have been made for law firm practice. First, the privilege is not limited only to lawyers; any agents, secretaries, or paralegals are included (*United States ex rel. Edney v. Smith*, 425 F. Supp. 1038 [E.D.N.Y. 1976], 1046). Second, in a case of inadvertent disclosure during discovery, privilege may be maintained under certain circumstances (*K.L. Group v. Case, Kay & Lynch*, 829 F.2d 909 [9th Cir. 1987]). Last, while courts carefully protect these privileges in most court actions, we shall see that disclosure is allowed to defend a malpractice action or in a fee dispute.

THREE SUI GENERIS SUPREME COURT CASES

Bar associations have played a small part in two recent revolutions in American Constitutional law: the First Amendment's protection of commercial speech and the reconsideration of the law of takings. In each of these areas, the Supreme Court signaled an aggressive new approach and followed with a series of cases that generally drift in the direction of increased constitutional protections for commercial speech and against government takings. In each of these areas, small but important exceptions to the general thrust of the law were drawn up specifically for lawyers. While the Supreme Court offers a series of justifications for these cases, taken in light of the state of the law as a whole, they are classic examples of the lawyer-judge hypothesis.

Ohralik

Bans on lawyer advertising and client solicitation are practically as old as the profession itself (Drinker 1953, 23–24). In America, lawyer regulators began to systematically bar advertising and client solicitation around the turn of the twentieth century. These bans were a key part of the bar's professionalization project, and they mirrored anticompetitive regulations in other professions. The bans were justified as a protection for the unsuspecting public against "ambulance chasers" and other unscrupulous lawyers (*Karlin v. Culkin*, 162 N.E. 487 [N.Y. 1928], 488–489). Regardless of the justifications, the results were clearly anticompetitive. Existing practitioners (who were the drafters of these rules) were able to charge inflated prices without worrying about being undercut by competing lawyers advertising or soliciting their clients.

Beginning in the 1970s, the Supreme Court began to overturn the most blatant of these anticompetitive practices.[14] The bulk of this work was accomplished by the nascent First Amendment commercial speech doctrine. Prior to 1976, commercial speech had not been protected under the First Amendment. *Virginia Board of Pharmacy* (425 U.S. 748 [1976]) began a series of Supreme Court cases applying the First Amendment to commercial speech and advertising. The Court's second major commercial speech case, *Bates v. State Bar of Arizona* (433 U.S. 350 [1977], 363–385) held that the State Bar of Arizona could not ban truthful advertising of prices for routine legal services.

Bates followed *Virginia Board of Pharmacy* by one year, and at first reading appears compelled by the reasoning of *Virginia Board,* an 8–1 decision that truthful advertising of drug prices could not be banned. Nevertheless, the opinions in *Bates* itself make clear how hard it was for the Court to apply the commercial speech doctrine to the legal profession. The Court split 5–4 on the First Amendment issue, and each of the four dissenters noted the special nature of legal services and the unwelcome and "profound changes" the decision would bring to the practice of law (*Bates,* at 386).

A year later the Court decided *Ohralik v. Ohio State Bar Association* (436 U.S. 447 [1978]) the first of our lawyer-judge hypothesis cases. In *Ohralik,* the Court held a ban on in-person client solicitation by lawyers constitutional.[15] The Court distinguished *Bates* because of the potential for client abuse from in-person solicitation.

In retrospect, *Ohralik* is an unusual commercial speech case. *Ohralik* gives great deference to the interest of the states in regulating lawyers as officers of the court, and even notes how a ban on solicitation serves the goal of "true professionalism" (*Ohralik,* at 460–461). This deference to bar association regulation has been a moving target for the Court. In the cases where the Court strikes down bar regulation it tends to reject arguments based on "professionalism" or the public image of lawyers (consider *Bates,* at 368–372) but in cases like *Ohralik* where these regulations are upheld, the Court expressly credits them.

Further, *Ohralik* is one of the very few cases where the Court upheld a blanket prohibition on commercial speech because it might sometimes tend toward "fraud, undue influence, intimidation... and other forms of vexatious conduct" (*Ohralik,* at 462). As a general rule, the Court has been clear that the government can always bar the dissemination of commercial speech that is false or deceptive (*Friedman v. Rogers,* 440 U.S. 1 [1979]), or that proposes an illegal transaction (*Pittsburgh Press Co. v. Human Relations Comm'n,* 413 U.S. 376 [1973]). Nevertheless, *Ohralik* does not ban only false speech. To the contrary, it is precisely the type of "blanket prohibition against truthful, nonmisleading speech about a lawful product" that the Court reviews with "special care" and which "rarely survive[s] constitutional review" (*44 Liquormart, Inc. v. Rhode Island,* 517 U.S. 484 [1996], 504). In fact, outside of *Ohralik* and a few cases from the 1980s that are now widely considered overruled, the Court has not sustained any other general ban on advertising under the commercial speech doctrine (Volokh 2003, 732–740).

Moreover, the reasoning of *Ohralik* has only ever been applied to the legal profession. In *Edenfield v. Fane* (507 U.S. 761 [1993]) the Court expressly refused to apply *Ohralik* to a rule that barred in-person solicitation by CPAs. The comparison between *Edenfeld* and *Ohralik* is stark and particularly telling. *Ohralik* was an 8–0 decision where the Court seemed to find it obvious that "the state interests implicated [were] particularly strong" and that in-person solicitation is dangerous and harmful to clients and the profession as a whole (*Ohralik*, at 460–463). *Ohralik* also accepted the ABA's "three broad grounds" of justification for the in-person ban with little comment (*Ohralik*, at 460–463). In short, the Court in *Ohralik* shows a particular sensitivity to the concerns of bar associations and the Court's palpable distaste for in-person solicitation by lawyers pervades the entire opinion.

By contrast, the 8–1 *Edenfield* decision was deeply skeptical of a ban on in-person solicitation for accountants. While *Edenfield* recognized the importance of protecting consumer privacy and discouraging fraudulent solicitation, the Court seemed utterly flummoxed by the assertion that a ban on in-person solicitation could possibly fit those goals (*Edenfield*, at 768–773). The Court specifically took the Florida Board of Accountancy to task for their lack of underlying evidence supporting a claim of danger to the public (*Edenfield*, at 771–773) despite accepting similarly "broad" assertions of public danger in *Ohralik* (*Ohralik*, at 460–463).

Edenfield does attempt to distinguish *Ohralik*, but in so doing basically limits *Ohralik* to lawyers: *Ohralik* is a "narrow" holding that depends "upon certain unique features of in-person solicitation by lawyers" (*Edenfield*, at 774). The main difference appears to be that a lawyer is a "professional trained in the art of persuasion" and thus much more likely to succeed in taking advantage of a potential client (*Edenfield*, at 775). It is ironic that the Court upholds an ethical rule on the assumption that lawyers are uniquely dangerous and unprofessional. Moreover, the distinction between the persuasive powers (and relative ethics) of lawyers and accountants is quite puzzling, and an example of the justices using their own impressions of the two professions to come to two totally opposed holdings on a very similar issue.[16]

Florida Bar v. Went For It, Inc.

Nevertheless, *Ohralik* can possibly be explained as an early case decided before the Court settled on the more muscular First Amendment approach of the late 1980s and 1990s. The 1995 case of *Florida Bar v. Went For It, Inc.*, however, is harder to explain, especially in light of the earlier cases *In re R.M.J.* (455 U.S. 191 [1982]) and *Shapero v. Kentucky Bar Association* (486 U.S. 466 [1988]).

In re R.M.J. dealt with, among other things, a Missouri lawyer sending out professional announcement cards that listed certain qualifications (like membership in bar of the United States Supreme Court) to a broad list of recipients. This mailing violated the Missouri bar's allowed language on qualifications, and also was mailed outside of the permissible recipients. The Court rejected the Missouri Bar's rules, and specifically held that a ban on mailings cannot be sustained (*R.M.J.*, at 193–205).

In *Shapero v. Kentucky Bar Association*, the Court more explicitly held that a state bar association could not ban truthful and nondeceptive direct mail solicitations to clients. The Court distinguished *Ohralik*, holding that a mailed solicitation implicated few of the dangers noted of in-person solicitation (*Shapero*, at 473–478).

Based on these precedents and *Bates v. Arizona*, a Federal District Court and the Eleventh Circuit struck down a Florida ban on direct mailings to accident victims within 30 days of the accident. *Florida Bar v. Went For It* (515 U.S. 618 [1995]) however, overturned these courts and upheld the bar rule.

The Court had "little trouble crediting the Bar's interest as substantial" (*Went For It*, at 625). The interests stated were protecting the privacy of accident victims, "preserv[ing] the integrity of the legal profession" and defending "the reputation of the legal profession" (*Went For It*, at 624–625). There are a couple of interesting notes about these two justifications. While it is true that *Ohralik* relied on two separate justifications (both protecting privacy and potential to mislead), later cases had generally treated *Ohralik* as a high potential for deception case and not a privacy case (*R.M.J.*, at 202). By contrast, *Went for It* includes no allegation that the advertising at issue was actually or even potentially false or misleading. Instead, the biggest problem seems to be the effect upon the public perception of lawyers.

Moreover, the harm to reputation justification is in direct conflict with the Court's resistance to the suppression of commercial speech on "paternalistic" grounds (*44 Liquormart*, at 497), and the Court's earlier holding that lawyer advertising cannot be banned on "the mere possibility that some members of the population might find [the advertising] offensive" or that "some members of the bar might find [it] beneath their dignity" (*Zauderer v. Office of Disciplinary Counsel*, 471 U.S. 626 [1985],648). Similarly, in *Bolger v. Youngs Drug Products, Corp.* (463 U.S. 60 [1983]) the Court rejected a government ban on "intrusive" and potentially "offensive" advertisements for contraceptives. The Court stated that a state interest in protecting mail recipients from offensive materials was of "little weight" because the Court has "consistently held that the fact that protected speech may be offensive to some does not justify its suppression" (*Bolger v. Youngs Drug Products Corp.*, 463 U.S. 60 [1983], 71). This is especially so in direct mail cases where the recipient can exercise the "short, though regular, journey from mail box to trash can" (*Bolger*, at 72).

The Court thus had a relatively weak factual and legal case on either privacy or consumer protection grounds. Nevertheless, a close reading of the case shows the great credit that the Court gave to bar association worries and evidence about the low public opinion of lawyers (*Went For It*, at 625–634). More than any of the other lawyer advertising cases, *Went For It* evinces a patent sympathy for the plight of lawyer public image and a clear deference to the findings and desires of bar associations on these issues. It is hard to imagine that accountants or pharmacists would possibly have received the same treatment,[17] and, just as the ban on in-person solicitation allowed by

Ohralik has been limited to lawyers, the Court has never upheld an advertising ban like Florida's for any other profession.

Ohralik and *Went For It* thus present a puzzle to students of the commercial speech doctrine. They are now both well-known and venerable precedents, yet in an area of increasing scrutiny of governmental regulation of advertising, they have basically been limited to their facts. Kathleen Sullivan has noted that *Ohralik* and *Went For It* are "difficult to square with the Court's other advertising decisions" (Sullivan 1998, at 578–579).

Brown v. Legal Foundation of Washington

There are other areas of constitutional law dealing with lawyers that have produced puzzling results. A recent Fifth Amendment takings case, *Brown v. Legal Foundation of Washington* (538 U.S. 216 [2003]) struck me as another apt example from a totally distinct area of the law.

The Fifth Amendment takings clause, like the First Amendment's commercial speech doctrine, has recently been a central concern of the Court. In relevant part, the Fifth Amendment states "nor shall private property be taken for public use, without just compensation." This simple injunction contains (at least) three distinct issues: "whether the interest asserted by the plaintiff is property, whether the government has taken that property, and whether the plaintiff has been denied just compensation for the taking" (*Phillips v. Washington Legal Foundation*, 524 U.S. 156 (1998), 172).

The Court has recently decided two takings cases concerning state IOLTA ("Interest on Lawyers Trust Accounts") programs. Every state in the Union has an IOLTA program (*Brown*, at 220).[18] IOLTA programs take advantage of the fact that lawyers are frequently called upon to handle client funds for a short period of time, or in amounts small enough that establishing a separate account would be administratively burdensome. In these situations lawyers are required (or encouraged) to place the client funds in an IOLTA account, and the interest generated from these accounts are used by state bar or supreme court authorities to pay for legal services for the poor (*Brown*, at 220–226).

I discuss the two recent IOLTA takings case below. Because takings law is very technical the discussion becomes slightly abstruse in places. The key point to remember is that IOLTA programs use the interest generated from client funds for a government program. In deciding whether these transactions are a "taking," the Court faced several difficult questions. The first was whether the interest itself was "property" under the takings clause. Because the IOLTA programs only targeted small amounts of money, or money that was held for a brief period of time the IOLTA supporters argued that the interest itself was not "property." Second, if the interest was property the Court needed to decide if it was taken. Last, assuming the government took property, the Court needed to value the loss.

As I demonstrate below, the third question has been relatively uncontroversial under takings law: if the government takes property it must pay recompense, no matter how small. Nevertheless, it is in the valuation of their loss that the IOLTA plaintiffs lost: the Court found a taking of private property, but ordered no compensation, despite the fact that state governments gain substantial sums from their IOLTA programs. In short the court held that IOLTA programs take property from private parties, and then valued that property at zero for the private parties, despite the fact that the property had a clear and easily calculable value to the government.

The first IOLTA takings case held that the interest on client funds was not "property" under the Fifth Amendment (*Washington Legal Found. v. Massachusetts Bar Found*, 993 F.2d 962 [1993], 975–976). In *Washington Legal Foundation v. Texas Equal Access to Justice Foundation* (94 F.3d 996 [5th Cir. 1996]) the U.S. Fifth Circuit of Appeals held that IOLTA interest was property subject to the Fifth Amendment Takings Clause. In *Phillips v. Washington Legal Foundation* (524 U.S. 156 [1998]), a 6–3 majority of the Supreme Court agreed. The Court held that because "interest follows principal" the interest on client IOLTA funds was the clients' property (*Phillips*, at 164–172). Interestingly, the Court did not reach the issue of whether IOLTA funds were actually " 'taken' by the State, or what amount of 'just compensation,' if any, [was] due respondents" (*Phillips*, at 172).

Phillips is thus a weird, incomplete case. On the one hand, it explicitly left open the question of whether IOLTA programs cause a Fifth Amendment taking. On the other hand, it was hard to imagine after *Phillips* that IOLTA programs did not constitute a compensable taking, because once the Court has found that the government has taken property from a private party, it is usually all over but the crying: if the government takes private property, recompense follows briskly.[19] Once the Court has found a taking, it has found governmental action unconstitutional even if the damages were minuscule or nonexistent, as in *Loretto v. Teleprompter Manhattan CATV* (458 U.S. 419 [1982]) where the Court held that even if a taking increased the value of a property it might still be compensable.

Further, the Court's decision in *Webb's Fabulous Pharmacies, Inc. v. Beckwith*, 449 U.S. 155 [1980]) seemingly foreclosed IOLTA's most promising argument: that the government was not "taking" anything, because the interest itself was government-created value that otherwise would not have existed. In *Webb's Famous*, a Florida statute allowed a county clerk to collect interest on a court interpleader fund. Without the statute and the clerk's actions, the fund would not have earned interest. Nevertheless, the Court cited the familiar maxim that interest follows principal, and explicitly rejected the argument that the Florida court "takes only what it creates." The Court found a taking and required the state to disgorge the interest earned to the recipient of the underlying interpleader funds (*Webb's*, at 453–454).

Nevertheless, the first few cases after *Phillips* were a mess, as courts struggled to answer the unsettled question of whether IOLTA constituted a taking, and what, if any, just compensation was due. The main battleground seemed to be whether to apply the per se test for physical takings, or the ad hoc *Penn Central* test for regulatory takings.[20]

The choice between the two tests in these cases was much more than academic. In takings cases, the choice of the test usually presages the case's outcome. In cases where the per se test is met the Court always finds a taking, and the only remaining question is just compensation.[21] By contrast, cases considered under the ad hoc, *Penn Central* standard frequently result in a finding of no taking at all[22] (Sagoff 1997, 849). The post-*Phillips* cases seemed to follow this logic exactly: the cases that applied the *Penn Central* test found no taking, whereas the per se cases found an unconstitutional taking and required either full repayment or suitable equitable relief.

In *Brown v. Legal Foundation of Washington* (538 U.S. 216 [2003]) however, the Supreme Court broke the mold and found a per se taking of private property for public use, but refused to require any compensation. The Court began its analysis with a glowing review of the "public use" requirement, calling IOLTA a "dramatic success" serving the "compelling interest" of providing legal services to the poor.[23] The Court then reiterated its holding in *Phillips* that IOLTA interest was the private property of the plaintiffs and held that "a per se approach is more consistent with the reasoning in our *Phillips* opinion than *Penn Central*'s ad hoc analysis." Thus, the "interest was taken for a public use when it was ultimately turned over to the foundation," leaving only the question of "just compensation" (*Brown*, at 235).

The Court held that "just compensation" is measured "by the property owner's loss rather than the government's gain" (*Brown*, at 235–236). Because the IOLTA interest is only supposed to be generated when the transaction costs of creating a separate bank account would be more than the interest earned, the Court concluded that the loss was always zero, and required no compensation at all (*Brown*, at 239–241).

It is still too early to know if *Brown* will turn out to be a sui generis case that stands outside the mainstream of takings jurisprudence the way that *Ohralik* and *Went-for-It* have in the commercial speech area. There are several telltale signs that *Brown* will be limited to its facts and will not signal a shift in takings jurisprudence. The first is the Court's finding of no compensation whatsoever, despite placing the taking in the per se category. As the Court itself has repeatedly noted, once a per se or "categorical" taking has been found it applies a "clear rule" and the government must pay damages, "no matter how small" (*Brown*, at 234). If there is any clear theme from the Court's per se takings cases, it is that once a per se taking is found the government will have to pay *something*. In short, once the Court finds a per se taking, all that remains is cutting a check for the amount of the taking. Nevertheless, in *Brown*, the Court found room within its previously relatively uncontroversial "just compensation" doctrines to deny relief.[24]

Second, *Brown* is difficult to square with *Webb's*, especially the Court's explicit rejection of the government-created value argument. *Brown* distinguishes *Webb's* by noting that in *Webb's* the state of Florida collected both a statutory interpleader fee and the interest generated, as well as noting that the IOLTA interest only exists because of the pooling of funds that would otherwise generate no interest (*Brown*, at 238 n. 10). Nevertheless, in *Webb's*

Florida's entire argument was that the state statute itself created the interest at issue and that in the absence of the statute there would be no interest to collect. The *Webb's* Court rejected that argument, noting that regardless of whether a state statute created the interest, the interest still belonged to the owner of the underlying principal. As a conceptual matter, this argument looks quite similar to an argument the Court accepted in *Brown:* that without the government-created system pooling IOLTA funds there would be no net interest. Yet in *Brown*, the Court allowed the government to keep the government-created value (*Brown*, at 235).

Finally, one way to predict that *Brown* will prove to be a sui generis holding is the difficulty of imagining another type of per se taking where the government will take something of obvious value that has absolutely no value to the plaintiff. In fact, the Court's holding that just compensation is measured by the loss to the plaintiffs is likely to prove a relative side note as the battle over regulatory and per se takings rages on. As Christopher Serkin has argued, *Brown* will not prove "one of the most important valuation cases in recent years," but will instead be treated as a "prosaic" and fact-specific treatment of fair market value (Serkin 2004, 421).

MIRANDA'S RIGHT TO SILENCE AND RIGHT TO COUNSEL

Miranda v. Arizona is another case where the Court signals a special appreciation for the legal profession. In 1966 the Supreme Court revolutionized the law of police interrogations with *Miranda v. Arizona* (384 U.S. 436 [1966]). *Miranda* required that police officers warn a suspect in custody prior to interrogation "that he has a right to remain silent, that any statement he does make may be used against him, and that he has a right to the presence of an attorney, either retained or appointed" (*Miranda*, at 444). If these warnings are not given prior to interrogations, statements taken in violation of *Miranda* generally cannot be introduced at trial.

There are two points worth noting at the outset. The first is that criminal defendants have a large number of constitutional and procedural safeguards that might be useful to know at the time of arrest, including bond rights, the right to a jury, the right to a speedy trial, and so on. Nevertheless, the Court lists only two: the right to remain silent and the right to an attorney. Second, consider the government-sponsored free advertising the Court granted the legal profession in *Miranda*. The very first thing a government official must tell a future criminal defendant strongly suggests that it would a good idea to hire a lawyer. Moreover, consider how often the *Miranda* rights have been read in movies, television shows, or books.

The *Miranda* warnings tell a suspect of two broad rights: the right to remain silent and the right to an attorney. In the *Miranda* opinion itself, neither right is favored over the other, and both are treated as critical to safeguarding a suspect's rights. In particular, if a suspect exercises either right, the interrogation must stop. "Once warnings have been given, the subsequent procedure is clear. If the individual indicates in any manner, at any time prior to questioning, that he wishes to remain silent, the interrogation must cease." Similarly, "[i]f the individual states that he wants an attorney, the interrogation must cease until an attorney is present" (*Miranda*, at 473–474).

The Court's treatments of these two rights, however, have diverged radically over time, with *Michigan v. Mosely* (423 U.S. 96 [1975]) and *Edwards v. Arizona* (451 U.S. 477 [1981]) serving as the two prime examples. In *Mosely*, the Court faced the question of how to handle a second round of questioning after a suspect had already invoked his right to remain silent. The Court cited *Miranda* for the proposition that the "right to cut off questioning" must be "scrupulously honored" (*Mosely*, at 104). Nevertheless, the Court held an interval of "more than two hours," questioning by another officer about a different crime, and a new set of *Miranda* warnings, was sufficiently scrupulous (*Mosely*, at 104). From the outset, *Mosely* was seen as a significant weakening of *Miranda*, and later cases have made clear that there is no different crime requirement and that the police can scrupulously honor a suspect's right to remain silent by pausing their interrogation for a period as short as an hour or two. (Custodial Interrogations 2006,177 n.568).

Mosely is thus notable for both its part in the long-term project of eroding *Miranda*'s protections, and its role as the first case to really differentiate between the right to remain silent and the right to counsel. As *Mosely* made clear, its holding on the malleability of a declared desire to exercise the right to remain silent had no effect on the requirements following a request to speak to a lawyer (*Mosely*, at 101 n. 7). While the results of an exercise of either right were treated quite similarly in *Miranda* itself, for the first time *Mosely* establishes that the right to remain silent is to be treated less favorably. There are no post-*Mosely* Supreme Court cases on how to treat questioning after an unambiguous request to remain silent, but the other Supreme Court cases on the treatment of silence at trial are generally unfriendly.

Edwards v. Arizona made the distinction between silence and counsel even clearer. *Edwards* was decided in 1981, and fell directly during a period of erosion for *Miranda* protections (Lunney 1999, 745–786). *Edwards* dealt with a situation analogous to that considered in *Mosely:* a suspect had asked for counsel, and before counsel had arrived, the police reinstituted their interrogation, and the defendant eventually confessed (*Edwards,* at 479–480). The Arizona Supreme Court relied on *Mosely* and held that if the confession was gained voluntarily during the second interrogation, *Miranda* was satisfied (*State v. Edwards*, 594 P.2d 72 [Ariz.1979], 77–78). The Arizona Supreme Court thus held that the right to a lawyer should be treated the same as the right to remain silent, that is, rather shabbily.

The Supreme Court reversed and held that the right to a lawyer is much better protected than the right to remain silent. *Edwards* is a strident decision and one of the few post-*Miranda* decisions to unequivocally embrace *Miranda*'s language and holding (albeit only for the right to counsel). The Court noted that it had "strongly indicated that additional safeguards are necessary when the accused asks for counsel" and held that once an accused asks for counsel she cannot be questioned until she meets with counsel or she herself "initiates further communication" (*Edwards*, at 481–485). *Edwards* also discussed *Mosley* and made explicit the differential treatment between a request to remain silent and a request for counsel.

Given that *Edwards* is surrounded by *Miranda* cases that refer to the warnings as a nonconstitutionally required, prophylactic measure (Klein 2003, 1337–1338, n.6), the stridency of the opinion is striking. The Court states "[t]he Fifth Amendment right identified in *Miranda* is the right to have counsel present at any custodial interrogation" and creates a bright line requirement that all questioning stop following a request for counsel (*Edwards*, at 485–486).

The cases that followed *Edwards* generally built upon this bright line rule.[25] The fact that the Court has followed up on *Edwards* at all is noteworthy. The Court kept the right to counsel question salient through multiple cases, strengthening its protections. By contrast, the Court's last real statement on the effect of an unequivocal request to remain silent was *Mosley*, and this has resulted in a long, slow drift in the federal courts where even the protections offered by *Mosley* have been diluted.

In *Smith v. Illinois* (469 U.S. 91 [1984]), one of the first post-*Edwards* cases, the Court reiterated that once an unequivocal request for counsel is made all questioning must stop, and later equivocal statements about wanting a lawyer were of no consequence. In *Arizona v. Roberson* (486 U.S. 675 [1988]), the Court held that when an accused has requested counsel he may not be questioned later by a new set of detectives about a totally separate crime, even if the second detectives did not know of the request for counsel. The Court recognized the factual similarities to *Mosley* (the second set of detectives investigating a second crime), but again distinguished the import of a request to remain silent (*Roberson*, at 683).

In *Minnick v. Mississippi* (498 U.S. 146 [1990]), the accused requested counsel, met with counsel, and then was questioned by the police without his lawyer present. *Minnick* has a lengthy passage discussing the efficacy of the bright line *Edwards* rule, and well encapsulates a theme that runs throughout all of these cases: what is the point of having *Miranda* rights at all if the police can question you regardless of your request for an attorney? (*Minnick*, 498 U.S. at 152–156). In this regard, the justices' experience as lawyers seems extremely relevant. Every lawyer knows and fears the possibility that their client will be talking to opposing parties outside of the lawyer's presence and say something that can never be retracted or fixed.

In sum, there is now little doubt that the right to counsel is better protected by *Miranda* and its progeny than the right to remain silent. Aside from the Court's familiarity and natural understanding of the importance of counsel, however, there is not much to support placing the right to counsel above the right to remain silent. On the contrary, the right to remain silent seems to be the more central right protected by *Miranda*.

Insofar as *Miranda* is constitutionally based, it is based squarely on the Fifth Amendment's right to avoid self-incrimination, and not the Sixth Amendment's right to counsel. *Miranda* itself referred to self-incrimination, and in *Dickerson v. U.S.*, the Court noted the many references in *Miranda* and its progeny to the Fifth Amendment in holding that the *Miranda* holding was constitutionally required (*Dickerson v. U.S.*, 530 U.S. 428 [2000], 440 n.5) The Sixth Amendment's right to counsel, by contrast, does not attach until "prosecution is commenced" not during the police investigation of a crime (*Texas v. Cobb*, 532 U.S. 162 [2001], 167–168).

Because *Miranda* is a Fifth Amendment self-incrimination case, it makes little sense to elevate the right to have counsel present during questioning above a straightforward and direct invocation of the suspect's right to remain silent, because the right to remain silent, not the right to a lawyer, is the right protected by the Fifth Amendment. This is especially so since the Court treats a request for counsel as an invocation of Fifth Amendment rights: "an accused's request for an attorney is per se an invocation of his Fifth Amendment rights, requiring that all interrogation cease" (*Fare v. Michael C.*, 442 U.S. 707 [1979], 719).

Furthermore, it is dubious to suggest that protecting the right to counsel will do more to counteract coercion or police questioning than a firm right to remain silent. As the Court has repeatedly noted, "any lawyer worth his salt will tell the suspect in no uncertain terms to make no statement to police under any circumstances" (*Moran v. Burbine*, 475 U.S. 412 [1986], 436 n. 5). In fact, the very first thing any lawyer summoned to a police station by a *Miranda* request will do is find out what the client has already said, and strongly advise the client to say nothing further. Given that the main protection presented by the lawyer is silence, shouldn't a direct request to exercise Fifth Amendment rights be treated at least as favorably as a request for the ancillary right to a lawyer during questioning? Instead, a direct request to remain silent requires only a short pause in the questioning, while a request for a lawyer requires a full stop until a lawyer is consulted, and most likely a full stop of all interrogation.[26]

As such, *Edwards* and its progeny stand out as another sui generis prolawyer decision. While the Court was busily eroding the *Miranda* protections on multiple fronts, it chose to retain quite robust protections for accused who clearly expressed a desire for a lawyer. The advantages to the legal profession are clear: Whatever else an accused should know, she should know to request a lawyer first and foremost.

RAMIFICATIONS?

As the foregoing discussion has shown, the lawyer-judge hypothesis explains a diverse subset of cases and doctrines that directly effect the legal profession. So what? It may be that while judges treat lawyers differently and better, this treatment is justified. Maybe lawyers are, in fact, special. Lawyers do play an important role in our society and legal order, but does that justify certain jurisprudential latitudes? Most would agree that it is self-evidently harmful to have the judiciary favor one group of persons over others. Further, the collection of regulatory and case law advantages listed above are hardly calibrated to further the lawyer's role as an officer of the court.

Assuming the phenomenon exists (and that it is bad), can anything realistically be done about it? First, gathering the cases, making the argument, and shedding light on the trend may be enough to shift the law in some of these areas. As the discussion (in the section "Theory") of the underlying theory noted, some or all of this effect is the result of unconscious judicial bias toward their own experiences and naturally increased empathy for litigants who share similar backgrounds and experiences. Perhaps pointing out the cumulative effects of these unconscious decisions will lead to some reforms.

Second, it may be that our system of selecting judges from the ranks of lawyers is the best possible model for our legal structure and society, and therefore the costs associated with it are bearable. Again, recognizing those costs and weighing them against the benefits is worthwhile. On the other hand, it may be that the costs of the current system outweigh the benefits. Given the general public distrust and dislike of lawyers, there may be many other objections to their dominant role in the judiciary aside from any bias toward lawyers in general.

I do not think it is obvious that all judges should be lawyers. On the contrary, it may be right that no lawyers should be judges. In many civil law countries, judges are trained and educated separately from lawyers. Perhaps that is a better model.

Moreover, the idea that only lawyers should be judges is of relatively recent vintage in the United States. In the eighteenth, nineteenth, and early twentieth centuries, many judges and justices of the peace were not lawyers (and many current justices of the peace are still nonlawyers) (Dawson 1960). Predictably, bar associations were at the forefront of the (largely successful) effort to eliminate lay judges (Provine 1986, 1–60). These efforts occurred simultaneously to the bar's overall professionalization movement that included the push for a bar examination, required legal education, and the unified bar. Given the potential benefits to the profession, and the key role that the judiciary played in the success of the professionalization movement, bar associations clearly made a wise choice.

Aside from history and international precedents, Adrian Vermeule has recently argued that there should be at least one nonlawyer justice of the U.S. Supreme Court, and possibly more (Vermeule 2007). Nonlawyer judges can also be defended on populist or egalitarian grounds. It is beyond the scope of this chapter to build a complete defense or indictment of the primacy of lawyer judges. However, I will note that this chapter does add another wrinkle to a larger ongoing debate about the structure and nature of our judiciary.

Nevertheless, the lawyer-judge hypothesis established herein proves that lawyers have enjoyed preferential treatment. The severity of the problem and what should be done about it, if anything, are ultimately issues for further contemplation and study.

Notes

Some of the material in this chapter is adapted from Barton (2007).

1. In this chapter, I use the expressed desires of bar associations as a proxy for what the profession as a whole would prefer, or at least a majority of the members of the profession who are in bar associations. If it strikes you as overreaching to refer to the "interests of the legal profession" in the article, please add the modifier "as expressed by bar associations."
2. One notable exception is the empirical work on tort awards (Helland and Tabarrok 2006).
3. In the 36 states with a unified bar, judges are licensed attorneys, and ipso facto are members of the state bar association. Twenty-seven states explicitly require their supreme court justices to be members of the state bar (The Council of State Governments 1978, 7–8).
4. Generally, current practitioners are grandfathered (or grandmothered) in under new, more stringent entry regulations. The bar exam has continued to become more difficult, and recently passage rates have declined substantially (Merritt 2001). This explains why every complaint about *current* practitioners is solved by a burden upon *future* practitioners. Consider the growing utilization of the Multistate Professional Responsibility Exam ("MPRE") as a response to claims of unethical lawyers, or the drive to establish the bar examination and legal education as a response to perceived lawyer incompetence. If the worry was over currently incompetent practitioners, raising entry barriers for future lawyers would do little to assist with the immediate problem.
5. Please forgive the upcoming "Zagat's" approach to case law. The language itself is so telling short quotes speak volumes.
6. One exception is the Supreme Court's recognition of a federal psychotherapist-patient privilege in *Jaffee v. Redmond* (518 U.S. 1 [1998]).
7. This warning is echoed in evidence texts that suggest that doctors or psychiatrists hired as experts for trial should examine their patients as part of the legal team so that the more stringent protections of the attorney-client and work product privileges attaches to their work (Imwinkelried 2005, 302).
8. The justifications for the attorney-client privilege have been divided into two broad categories: utilitarian (or instrumentalist) and nonutilitarian (or humanistic). The utilitarian approach balances the societal costs and benefits of any privilege; the nonutilitarian approach looks at fundamental values, like privacy, and decides whether the privilege is consistent with those values (Imwinkelried 2002, § 6.2.4). This chapter focuses on the utilitarian approach, because it has been dominant among courts and commentators.
9. Furthermore, clergy have a much stronger constitutional argument for a privilege than lawyers do (Colombo 1998).
10. Wigmore asked a four-part question before approving of any privilege: (1) the communications must originate in a confidence that they will not be disclosed; (2) this element of confidentiality must be essential to the full and satisfactory maintenance of the relation between the parties; (3) the relation must be one that in the opinion of the community ought to be sedulously fostered; and (4) the injury that would inure to the relation by the disclosure must be greater than the benefit thereby gained for the correct disposal of litigation (Wigmore 1961, § 2285).

11. Given the utter lack of empirical data to support Wigmore's claims concerning the attorney-client privilege, this complaint is somewhat paradoxical (Imwinkelried 2004).

12. The Rules of Professional Conduct provide extraordinary protections for lawyer's confidentiality (American Bar Association 2008).

13. "The moment confidence ceases...privilege ceases" (In re San Juan Dupont Plaza Hotel Fire Litigation, 859 F.2d 1007 [1st Cir. 1988]).

14. For example, *Goldfarb v. Virginia State Bar* (421 U.S. 773 [1975]) held that mandatory fee schedules violated federal antitrust law.

15. "In-person client solicitation" means asking a potential client for work face-to-face.

16. It is also worth noting the vote tallies on the two cases (*Ohralik* was 8–0 and *Edenfield* was 8–1), and that the Court considered each case relatively straight-forward, regardless of how incompatible they seem. A simple comparison of the vote totals for the lawyer and nonlawyer professional regulation cases is also illuminating. As noted above, *Virginia Board* was an 8–1 decision striking down an advertising ban by pharmacists. A year later, the Court split 5–4 on a similar ban in *Bates*. The main difference between the cases was the Court's impression of lawyer advertising as quite distinct from pharmacist advertising.

    Similarly, the Court split contentiously 5–4 (with no majority opinion) in *Peel v. Disciplinary Comm. of Illinois* (496 U.S. 91 [1990]) over an attorney advertisement claiming NBTA certification as a civil trial specialist. Four years later, the Court struck down an accountant rule barring an advertising using the terms "CPA and CFP" by a lawyer 7–2 in *Ibanez v. Board of Accountancy* (512 U.S. 136 [1994]). Again, the main difference in the split appeared to be the Court's greater sensitivity to concerns about lawyer advertising.

17. As discussed above, *Edenfield v. Fane* (507 U.S. 761 [1993]) makes this point abundantly clear for accountants. In *Went For It* the court upheld a ban on lawyer solicitation by mail, which is much less obtrusive than an in-person solicitation. By contrast, the *Edenfield* Court made short work of an accountant ban on in-person solicitation.

18. The origin of these programs is actually an excellent example of the unique powers of lawyer self-regulation. They were created in 45 states under the inherent authority of state supreme courts, and by statute in the other 5. In Indiana and Pennsylvania, IOLTA was originally statutory, but the Supreme Courts of those two states Supreme Court invalidated the statute and created the IOLTA program by court order (*Brown*, at 221 n.2).

19. In fact, IOLTA proponents were "surprised" by their victory in *Brown* and IOLTA opponents were "[t]asting victory" after *Phillips* (Morris 2005, 612–615).

20. For example, when *Phillips* was considered on remand to the Western District of Texas the court applied the ad hoc approach and found no taking (*Washington Legal Found. v. Texas Equal Access to Just. Found.*, 86 F.Supp.2d 624 [W.D. Tex. 2000], 643–647). On appeal to the Fifth Circuit, the court overturned that decision and applied the per se test (*Washington Legal Found. v. Texas Equal Access to Just. Found.*, 270 F.3d 180 [5th Cir. 2001], 186–189). The Ninth Circuit followed a different path. The original panel to rule on an IOLTA program post-*Phillips* applied the per se test and found an unconstitutional taking (*Wash. Legal Found. v. Legal Found. of Wash.*, 236 F.3d 1097 [9th Cir. 2001],1100–01), while a later en banc decision applied the ad hoc approach and found no taking

(*Wash. Legal Found. v. Legal Found. of Wash.*, 271 F.3d 835 [9th Cir. 2001][*en banc*], 854–857).

21. "When the government physically takes possession of an interest in property for some public purpose, it has a categorical duty to compensate the former owner…no matter how small [the compensation due]" (*Tahoe-Sierra Pres. Council, Inc. v. Tahoe Reg'l Planning Agency*, 535 U.S. 302 [2002], 322–323).

22. "Our jurisprudence involving condemnations and physical takings is as old as the Republic and, for the most part, involves the straightforward application of per se rules. Our regulatory takings jurisprudence, in contrast, is of more recent vintage and is characterized by essentially ad hoc, factual inquiries, designed to allow careful examination and weighing of all the relevant circumstances" (*Tahoe-Sierra*, at 321–322).

23. It is worth noting how closely this section hews to the bar association praise of these programs, even including the statistic that IOLTA funds provide "legal services to literally millions of needy Americans" (Brief for the ABA as Amicus Curiae in Support of Respondents, *Brown v. Washington Legal Foundation*, 538 U.S. 216 (2003) (No. 01–1325), 2002 WL 31399642, at *4–7). This section also parallels the section in *Went-For-It* where the Court uncritically credits each of the bar association factual defenses for the advertising restrictions at issue (*Went for It*, at 624–625). One other interesting parallel in these cases is the role of Justice O'Connor. She was a longtime defender of lawyer regulation of advertising, and authored *Went-For-It*. In *Phillips* she joined a 6–3 majority finding that the interest was the private property of the plaintiffs, but in *Brown* she switched sides to help create a 5–4 majority allowing IOLTA programs to continue.

24. It would be an error to call any part of takings jurisprudence wholly uncontroversial. Nevertheless, prior to *Brown* few of the Court's cases had hinged on the valuation question; the bulk of the work was done on the ins and outs of the taking itself.

25. The main exception is the series of cases that have required a clear request for counsel to trigger *Edwards*, rejecting more equivocal or unclear requests (*Davis v. U.S.*, 512 U.S. 452 [1994]).

26. One obvious difference between a request for a lawyer and a request to remain silent is that the request for a lawyer has a natural ending point (the arrival of the lawyer). Nevertheless, given that *Miranda* is focused on the Fifth Amendment, a request to remain silent should be treated at least as well as a request for a lawyer, that is, a request for silence should be honored until the suspect invites further communication or is provided with a lawyer.

CHAPTER 10

CLASS ACTION RENT EXTRACTION: THEORY AND EVIDENCE OF LEGAL EXTORTION

Jeffrey Haymond

INTRODUCTION

The tort system strikes a necessarily imperfect balance between deterrence and opportunism. Few doubt that a "jackpot" mentality underpins many of the sensational cases reported by the media. The costs of the tort system are high,[1] and the legal system may be overtaxed and unable to quickly provide justice in nonfrivolous cases. Nevertheless, while many cases appear to be frivolous, access to legal redress is an important freedom. For every critic of ambitious lawsuits, there is a defender who claims to seek only justice; for every legal action that one can criticize, there is always some public interest rationale that defenders are quick to highlight. This rationale is almost always in the form of "David vs. Goliath," in that the legal process supports plaintiffs with less power (political or economic) seeking justice against defendants with greater power.

Class action lawsuits are especially controversial. Many consumer class actions are portrayed as a way to correct small harms to large numbers of people (which, when aggregated, lead to a large loss in social welfare). Absent a class action mechanism, these harms cannot be corrected, because the costs of seeking legal redress outweigh any individual benefit. Further, without the threat of a class action, large tortfeasors may have less incentive to safeguard against imposing harms—in other words the threat of a class action restrains businesses from practices that harm the society. While businesses may modify their behavior in positive ways, there may also be unintended consequences that public interest proponents do not fully consider.[2]

As this chapter shows, both theory and evidence suggest that the current implementation of class actions results in outcomes that do not meet public interest ideals. The trial lawyers' incentive structure can lead to opportunistic behavior, as pursuit of profits may outweigh considerations of the benefit to the class as a whole.[3] As Kiement and Neeman (2004, 103–104) note:

> Most class actions are "lawyer driven" and the class attorney maintains all but
> absolute control over the lawsuit. She usually initiates the suit, selects the class
> representative, and controls the litigation process and settlement decisions.
> The class representative, while supposedly in charge of the litigation as fidu-
> ciary for all those similarly situated, is in reality only a token figurehead with
> no actual control over the lawsuit.

The trial lawyers' incentives are substantially monetary; plaintiff counsels' share of awards is nominally in the range of 25 percent to 30 percent of the total, but the effective share is often much higher. A RAND study of insurance class actions reported trial lawyer fees as a percentage of actual monetary distribution, in addition to a percentage of the common fund (RAND 2007). When calculated in this manner, the median effective fee increased from 30 percent to 47 percent, while one-fourth of the cases saw the effective fee rise to 75 percent or more, even rising above 90 percent in 5 of the 48 cases reviewed. Yet the consumers received as little as $3.50 per person, with the median benefit being $97, and in most instances only a fraction of the class members received any monetary benefit (RAND 2007, 2).

Class actions may be especially worrisome in capital markets. According to a blue ribbon study group, the Committee on Capital Markets Regulation,[4] the societal value of securities class action lawsuits deserves reconsideration. The group noted that the deterrent value of securities class action lawsuits is likely low, given that virtually all costs are borne by the company and its insurance carriers, rather than by corporate management (costs which the shareholders ultimately pay). Further, the committee recognized that securities class action lawsuits insufficiently compensate shareholder victims, since the suits capture only 2 percent to 3 percent of investor losses, with significant transactions costs (total defense and plaintiff attorney's fees in excess of 50 percent of the settlement value). They also point out the circularity of one group of shareholders paying another group. The public interest case is further tarnished by the committee's observation that current securities class action lawsuits may systematically transfer funds from "buy and hold" small investors to active institutional traders (Interim 2006, 78–79).[5]

Class action lawsuits do provide economically disadvantaged citizens a mechanism to address wrongs of wealthier opponents. Furthermore, class actions may be more effective deterrents compared to other regulatory procedures. Yet the public interest rationale has its critics from academia, government, and the media who believe that class actions are often simply instruments for trial lawyers to extort defendants with "deep pockets."[6] Anecdotes that support this belief are widely available in the media.[7] However, anecdotes are just that, and any view that suggests that class action lawsuits may be a tool for extortion must be backed by theory and empirical evidence. This chapter describes the theory of legal rent extraction, a framework for understanding class actions as legalized extortion, and documents empirical evidence for legal rent extraction. In particular, the chapter examines implications of securities class actions for capital markets. Finally, the impact of ongoing attempts at class action reform is reviewed.

Theory of Rent Extraction

Public choice theory assumes that individuals make decisions based on self-interest, whether those individuals are acting in market or nonmarket institutional settings and extends the neoclassical model of economic choice to individuals acting in legal and political contexts. Individuals maximize an objective function given their constraints, with pecuniary motivation (one argument in the agent's objective function), often one of the strongest of motivating factors. Public choice theory explains much of government behavior that is paradoxical from a public interest view. Rent seeking, a well-known subset of public choice theory, explains how agents seek to gain an economic benefit from government action without adding any value to the product. Gordon Tullock (1967) introduced the concept and detailed theoretically how extensive the cost of rent seeking can be to society.[8] George Stigler (1971) added to the body of thought with his seminal work on regulation. In his model, businesses seek government regulation to ensure protection of producer interests, because regulation offered a legal mechanism to cartelize an industry. Private attempts at cartelization were notoriously ineffective because of cheating, costs of negotiation, and possible new entrants. Out of the Tullock and Stigler approach emerged an understanding of politics as exchange. Positive political analysis examined the benefits that government and industry could provide each other, and identified the relevant transaction costs.

McChesney (1997) suggested the theories of rent creation[9] and regulation are actually part of a larger theory of rent extraction. As McChesney relates, "once the politician is seen as an independent actor in the regulatory process, his objective function cannot be treated as single-valued. He will maximize total returns to himself by equating at the margin the return from votes, contributions, bribes, power, and other sources of personal gain or utility" (1997, 22). In some cases, politicians may choose to levy demands on businesses, which must either comply or face negative sanctions. In the politician's process of maximizing returns, one would expect to see a trade-off between rent creation and rent extraction, depending on what specific circumstances allow. For McChesney, rent extraction is possible because the politician receives, in effect, a property right to extract wealth by virtue of election to office. Politicians exercise this right by threatening business with costly government regulation and, for a price, declining to implement the threatened action. The threat of costly action is targeted against privately created capital, and the more immobile or inelastic is the capital, the more effective is the threat.

If government action were undertaken for the purpose of rent extraction, we would expect to see the proposed action as reducing the value of the targeted private capital. Upon rent extraction and removal of the threat, the capital value would not be restored fully (reflecting the rents extracted). Nevertheless, government actions that reduce private wealth may also have plausible public interest rationale. If the proposed action is subsequently retracted consistent with public interest hypotheses, however, the capital value should be recovered (McChesney, 1997, 72). This can be tested empirically via event studies.[10]

A number of empirical event studies have confirmed the rent extraction hypothesis. McChesney cites Beck, Hoskins, and Connelly (1992) for their work with a sample of Canadian firms threatened with negative government action that was subsequently retracted (1997, 74). McChesney (with slightly different methodology) corroborated this scenario with his own review of the Clinton administration's failed attempt to implement price controls with its proposed health care legislation. Haymond (2001) followed this methodology in analyzing the tobacco industry's landmark Master Settlement Agreement (MSA) in 1998, which supported the rent extraction hypothesis and provided linkage to legal rent extraction, as shown below.

Tobacco Rent Extraction

While rent extraction theory suggests private capital will be targeted, the choice of a particular private capital depends on the circumstances. For instance, if a lawmaker sits on a committee that regulates pharmaceuticals, we would expect the lawmaker to extract more rent from drug companies than from other sources. Likewise, timing may enable extraction; when U.S. capital markets are embroiled in a subprime lending credit crunch, politicians may threaten additional regulation (unless sufficiently compensated). In addition, if a company or industry becomes unpopular, then politicians have little risk of public backlash by threatening punitive action.

With the tobacco settlement, many factors likely led to an opportunity for rent extraction. In the early 1990s, budget issues were driving politics; Ross Perot's candidacy for president was largely focused on balanced budget considerations. George H.W. Bush ultimately lost the 1992 election in part because he violated his campaign promise of "no new taxes." Politicians have a problem when they want more fiscal resources, if raising taxes is politically difficult and voters also want a balanced budget. Rent extraction offers one strategic solution, on the condition that a threatened industry provides enough compensation for the lawmakers to not (completely) follow through on threats of costly regulation. If industry does not pay, then implementation of the threat will still yield fiscal resources, albeit in a less attractive form for lawmakers.

For all these reasons, the tobacco industry was an ideal target for rent extraction in the early 1990s. It was widely believed to profit by addicting its clients to a product that would ultimately kill them; politicians would face little voter backlash by targeting this unpopular industry. The tobacco companies also had high free cash flows that were virtually recession proof, making it potentially quite remunerative. The congressional elections of 1994 proved to be a critical turning point; with the Democrats' loss, they needed an issue that could separate them from Republicans. Although tobacco had historically contributed to both parties, a decided shift occurred as Democrats eschewed tobacco. Common Cause reported that "tobacco industry PACs switched their giving from Democratic to Republican congressional candidates starting in 1995" (Common Cause 1997).[11] In addition, despite the Democrats' stand against the tobacco industry, the party did accept significant contributions that were funneled to state parties, where tracking was much more difficult and received less scrutiny (Common Cause 1997).

The Democrats' loss of contributions from the tobacco industry was partially offset by more money from trial lawyers (who stood to benefit greatly from state-sanctioned lawsuits against the tobacco industry). According to the American Tort Reform Foundation, the top 25 recipients of trial lawyer donations from 1997 through October 1999 were associated with the Democratic Party (Cherry 2000, 3).[12] Republicans reacted by attacking Democratic sources of wealth; trial lawyers were targeted in Republican campaigns as well as in the Contract with America. As Newt Gingrich's press secretary commented on Gingrich's position on the proposed tax settlement, "Whom does it benefit? Our children and their precious health, or a bunch of trial lawyers and their bank accounts?" (Ridenour 1997, 1). The large fees requested by trial lawyers in the state lawsuits only increased Gingrich's skepticism. In the Florida case, the proposed settlement had a 25 percent contingency fee, which allowed *each* lawyer a staggering $233 million! As Robert Levy notes, "Assuming they worked 24 hours per day, 7 days per week, for 42 months, they (the law firm) would earn $92,593 per hour—that's $7,716 per hour for each of the 12 lawyers."[13] The presiding judge stated that the magnitude of the lawyer's claims "shocks the conscience of the Court" (Levy 1999, 1).

In 1993, the EPA linked Environmental Tobacco Smoke (ETS, also called second-hand smoke) to cancer by labeling ETS a class A carcinogen[14] and energized the antismoking movement. Public opinion was also shaped by several *60 Minutes* episodes, one of which featured a high-profile "defector" from the tobacco industry, a former researcher, Dr. Jeffrey Wigand, who claimed to receive death threats for speaking out. *60 Minutes* journalist Mike Wallace said:

> What Dr. Wigand told us in that original interview was that his former colleagues, executives of Brown & Williamson Tobacco, knew all along that their tobacco products, their cigarettes and pipe tobacco, contained additives that increased the danger of disease. And further, that they had long known that the nicotine in tobacco is an addictive drug, despite their public statements to the contrary, like the testimony before Congress of Dr. Wigand's former boss, B&W's Chief Executive Officer Thomas Sandefur.[15]

Rep. Henry Waxman held congressional hearings that served to further discredit the industry, with one featuring CEOs of the leading tobacco companies denying under oath that tobacco was addictive, which Rep. Waxman called "the turning point" for tobacco.[16] The tobacco companies entered into secret negotiations with government agencies and trial lawyers in the spring of 1997 to resolve the states' lawsuits (Haymond 2001, 32). The media reported possible settlement fees as early as February 1997, with cigarette price increases identified as the funding mechanism. To make the settlement a "long-term contract," federal legislation was identified as necessary for implementation. Regulatory pressure from both the Food and Drug Administration and Federal Trade Commission increased through 1997, especially after the Liggett Group turned against the industry (2001, 32). President Clinton entered the fray in September 1997, demanding any national tobacco settlement satisfy his requirements as well. By spring of 1998, legislation working through Senator McCain's Commerce Committee featured a price tag of $500 billion, with less industry protections. The tobacco industry vigorously opposed this version of the legislation and went on a full-scale offensive to combat it. Sympathetic politicians such as Senator Ashcroft joined the battle, noting that "only in Washington would bad choices by free people become an excuse for a big tax hike ... In Washington, taxes and spending are the only things more addictive than nicotine" (Mathis 1998). The national tobacco bill officially went down to defeat on June 17, 1998, with the MSA signed with the states in November 1998, at a significantly lower amount ($206 billion over 25 years). Haymond's empirical analysis of the tobacco settlement provided strong support for rent extraction theory (2001, 34–35); the tobacco industry was threatened with punitive action that was subsequently retracted for a price. The capital value of the industry was abnormally reduced by the threat, with the retraction of the threat failing to restore the capital value (reflecting the rents that were extracted).

Legal Rent Extraction through Government-Sponsored Litigation

In an innovative use of legal pressure analogous to class action lawsuits, States' Attorneys General embarked on a new approach to regulation with the tobacco issue, bypassing the legislative branch through the use of lawsuits filed by private attorneys under a contingent fee basis. This was effectively used against the tobacco industry to accomplish goals that never could have been implemented via the legislature given the political realities (Regulation 2000, 3). In addition, government-sponsored litigation allowed for "voluntary" agreement to change business practices (such as restrictions in advertising), which could be challenged for constitutionality if mandated by law (2000, 3). While the tools used by the Attorneys General were not class action suits, their effect was much the same. According to Texas Attorney General John Cornyn (2000, 34),

> These are not suits that are made to be tried. None of these suits were brought to a conclusion. Rather than resting on established legal theories of causation and damages, these cases presented novel legal theories. These cases were based on a coercive power that is similar to that seen in private class action lawsuits: they cannot be tried because the ramifications of an adverse decision would be catastrophic. The defendants make the only decision they can—they figure out how much it will cost to buy off a lawsuit and then they purchase their peace .[17]

Additional pressure was levied on the tobacco industry by states "changing the rules in mid-game" to ensure victory in court. Florida, Maryland, and Vermont all passed legislation that specifically stripped the tobacco industry of its traditional defenses for past conduct while allowing statistical analysis to prove causation and damages (Bandow 1998, 5–8). Maryland passed their legislation only after trial lawyer Peter DeAngelos agreed to reduce his firm's fee from 25 percent to 12.5 percent, which was still reported to be $1 billion. These acts show how integral the legislature can be for legal rent extraction—it is doubtful the suits would have been settled absent legislative "fixing" of the outcome.

Former New York Attorney General Spitzer elaborated on the public interest position, "I would never enter into an agreement with the plaintiffs' bar on a contingency fee basis to give away billions of dollars. But that has nothing to do with the tobacco settlement. The tobacco settlement has to do with public health" (Regulation 2000, 7). Many of the proponents of the tobacco litigation demanded money for purposes related to smoker's health: education programs, smoking cessation programs, and the like. Many opposing the tobacco litigation suggested agents were acting in their self-interest: governments wanted an indirect way to raise taxes and initiate new spending as well as pay off favored constituents (trial lawyers).

It is revealing to analyze the actual uses of the new tobacco money on a state-by-state basis. If the public choice hypothesis is correct, the bulk of the money would go to fund activities which have nothing to do with tobacco or health. If Attorney General Spitzer's public interest view is correct, most of the expenditures would support public health initiatives. The Campaign for Tobacco-Free Kids (CTFK) has documented state expenditures since the tobacco MSA was approved. In their 2006 report, CTFK provided a detailed review of each individual state's spending of tobacco settlement money. In addition, the Centers for Disease Control (CDC) has recommended minimum spending levels necessary to finance a comprehensive tobacco control program for each state. It is therefore possible to examine and test the level of spending against the minimum necessary to assess the public interest hypothesis of the tobacco settlement. As the CDC noted, the "approximate annual costs to implement all of the recommended program components have been estimated to range from $7 to $20 per capita in smaller States (population under three million)," and slightly less per capita as the size of the states increased (CDC 1999, 1). This funding would include items such as community programs to reduce tobacco use, chronic disease programs, school programs, enforcement, statewide programs, countermarketing, cessation programs, surveillance and evaluation, and administration. Each of these areas had specific recommendations for spending by the CDC, typically between 20 percent and 25 percent of total annual tobacco settlement money. In addition, the CDC established a "minimum" standard of funding for each state, which is less than the 25 percent suggested.

If the public interest explanation of the tobacco MSA is correct, and the issue was all about improving the public health, then the states would use the settlement money to create and maintain programs that actually reduce smoking. As the CTFK notes, both the Institute for Medicine and the Surgeon General have released reports highlighting the effectiveness of the existing limited tobacco prevention programs (Show 2001, ii). The funding provided by the MSA would easily support this type of program nationwide and still leave at least 75 percent for other urgent government needs. If, however, the effect of the settlement was not to improve public health, but rather to provide politicians funds for desired spending, we should see little of the money actually spent on public health considerations.

To test the competing hypotheses, one can use a simple one-tailed t test. The null hypothesis is that the states spend 100 percent of the CDC minimum required spending (which, again, for each state is less than 25 percent of their tobacco settlement revenues).

H_0 : $\mu = 100\%$ of CDC minimum (public interest)

H_1 : $\mu < 100\%$ of CDC minimum (public choice)

with a test statistic of

$$z_0 = \frac{X - \mu}{\sigma / \sqrt{n}},$$

The null hypothesis is rejected if $z_0 < -z_\alpha$. For $\alpha = .01$, the critical z-value is -2.33. Using the data from CTFK (Appendix 10.1) for 2007, the actual z-statistic is -88.39, far below the required -2.33; therefore the null hypothesis (public interest) is strongly rejected in favor of the alternative hypothesis (public choice).

This result strongly supports that the effect of the states' pursuit of the MSA was to provide an additional source of revenue for state legislatures. As the CTFK report notes, "The tobacco settlement has resulted in an increase in the amount of money being spent at the state level on tobacco prevention and cessation, but the numbers are woefully short of what the CDC has concluded represents the absolute minimum necessary to fund a truly effective, sustained comprehensive program" (Show 2001, ii). In light of this, trial lawyer Richard Scruggs's advocacy of the public interest view seems suspect: "We took tobacco on because it was a public health matter. We did not take this case for fees, nor did we intend to raise taxes, or put the state in partnership with tobacco" (Regulation 2000, 47). On the contrary, the data strongly suggest that health was *not* the major concern (at least for those who allocated the tobacco revenues), the trial lawyers did receive enormous fees, in effect cigarette taxes were raised, and the agreement has cartelized the industry with the state as the enforcer.

LEGAL RENT EXTRACTION THROUGH CLASS ACTION LAWSUITS

Can rent extraction theory and empirical methodology be extended to class action lawsuits? Haymond and West (2003) suggest that similar to a politician's ability to threaten legislative action that targets private capital, lawyers are able to threaten private capital with punitive legal action via the class action lawsuit. For a suitable payment (the settlement), the lawyers will withdraw the threat. The result is not quite "money for nothing," as the settlement usually mandates some change in behavior. But often the change in practice may be something the company planned to do anyway, or is simply a token change (to justify the settlement). Just as a politician obtains a property right to impose costs via legislation with his election, lawyers also obtain a property right upon passing the bar.[18] This right was augmented by changes in the Federal Rules of Civil Procedure in 1966. These changes allowed lawyers to sue on behalf of plaintiffs without obtaining the plaintiff's individual consent, and the outcome is binding on all plaintiffs who do not opt out (Hensler 2000, 14). By only requiring representative plaintiffs, the changes significantly reduced the cost and effort to file a class action lawsuit. The Supreme Court in its 1974 *Eisen* decision also contributed to the ease of filing class actions by decoupling the determination of class action status from the actual merits of the case.

None of these changes occurs in a vacuum, and public choice scholarship offers insight into how legal failure that enables rent extraction is possible. Tabarrok and Helland's analysis of state judicial decisions showed a dramatic increase in the size of the award if the defendant was from out-of-state and the state's judges were chosen by partisan election (1999, 186). Trial lawyers are often the largest contributor to judicial elections, and larger awards mean larger fees to both plaintiff and defendant attorneys (160–161). Tabarrok and Helland show that even if judges are not biased, over time the electoral process will favor those who grant larger awards (161). And of course, judges may be well aware of their need for campaign funds and how larger awards may facilitate reelection. Retired Judge Richard Neely writes, "it should be obvious that the in-state local plaintiff, his witnesses, and his friends, can all vote for the judge, while the out-of-state defendant can't even be relied upon to send a campaign donation" (158). Tabarrok and Helland suggest that we can think of a judge's redistribution of wealth from out-of-state defendants to in-state plaintiffs as a way "of providing constituent service" (158).

Further, judicial philosophy that seemingly favors settlement over justice has allowed the class action system to evolve into a system that facilitates extortion. In certifying one class action, Judge Jack Weinstein notes that "the court may not ignore the real world of dispute resolution...a classwide finding of causation may serve to resolve the claims of individuals, in a way that determinations in individual cases would not, by *enhancing the possibility of settlement* among the parties" (emphasis added)."[19] Class action status certainly increases the likelihood of reaching a settlement,[20] but in no way necessarily facilitates a just result. Of course, Judge Weinstein doesn't see it that way: "Prospective litigators have described the procedure (class action lawsuits) as a form of legalized blackmail...I suggest that the monster is neither so large or as terrible as some would have us believe."[21] Risk-averse defendants also prefer a certain settlement over a possible victory; a recent survey of corporate counsel indicated the number one concern is not winning or losing cases, but rather controlling costs (Fulbright 2005, 2).

Jury composition is also a factor in large tort awards. Many of the "judicial hellholes" (see section "Class Action Fairness Act of 2005") are in small, rural areas such as Alabama, Mississippi, and Texas, where the jury pool may be more supportive of large awards against large out-of-state businesses. Helland and Tabarrok (2006) surveyed case data to determine the effects of race and poverty on trial awards. Their results showed damage awards increased dramatically as the poverty rate of blacks in the case's locale increased, and also with Hispanic poverty rates[22] (2006, 46). This provides a strong incentive for trial lawyers to "forum shop" in pursuit of the highest payout, and those forums will often be located in areas with high poverty rates among minorities.

Class action status significantly raises the legal exposure of companies, giving them a strong incentive to settle rather than "bet the business." As Texas' former attorney general John Cornyn states, "Even in the absence of proof, economic pressures are so great that an industry cannot afford to go to trial. They must, out of necessity, try to settle on the best terms they can" (Fund 2000, 10). As Handler suggests, if defendants who maintain their innocence are forced to settle simply because the stakes are so high, their constitutional right to a trial has effectively been denied (Handler 1971, 9). Priest (1997, 547) sums up the issue by noting that it is:

> surely a curious circumstance in a country committed to the rule of law to accept the propositions (1) that class certification alone creates great negotiating power, (2) that that power leads to actual settlements, sometimes large dollar settlements, and, simultaneously, (3) that this great negotiating power can be created without any judicial review of a claim on the merits and, in some cases, without any merit to the claim.

If the legal environment effectively grants lawyers a property right to extract wealth from private capital, it is possible to test through event studies. Nonetheless, distinguishing between the rent extraction hypothesis and the public interest hypothesis is not straight forward. For political rent extraction, if the public interest hypothesis is true and the threat is withdrawn, the company's market value will return in full. Conversely, if the capital value is not returned, then private wealth was extracted. For legal rent extraction, however, many cases may have public interest roots where the capital value is not returned to the level before the class action lawsuit. For instance, if a company were systematically billing customers a few pennies more than it should, then the class action lawsuit that removed this ability would lead to a lower capital value of the company (as the illicit gains are no longer possible). Thus, it is not possible to simply look at the capital value after class action settlement to determine whether legal rent extraction has taken place.

Securities class action lawsuits offer the ability to test for legal rent extraction using event study methodology because they are ostensibly filed on behalf of the shareholders to stop deceptive practices of corporate management. If they are effective at eliminating corrupt practices, this should lead to a higher present discounted value of future earnings as reflected in the stock price. By eliminating corporate management misbehavior, all shareholders would benefit, not just the shareholders who participate in the lawsuit. If, however, the stock price does not return at least to its original level upon the settlement, rent was extracted and the public interest hypothesis is rejected in favor of the rent extraction hypothesis.

Haymond and West (2003) performed an event study with 30 securities class action lawsuits to test the legal rent extraction hypothesis. The hypothesis of legal rent extraction was tested for three distinct event windows (-20 {days prior to the event}, $+10$ {days after the event}), (-5, $+3$), and (-1, $+1$). Academic literature summarized by Beck (1992) concludes that information is reflected in stock prices very quickly (less than 15 minutes), which suggests the shortest event window should fully test the hypothesis. Longer event windows were also tested to guard against possible misspecification of the event dates for either the threat (initial announcement of a class action lawsuit) or the retraction (settlement of the class action lawsuit). The results of their investigation supported the strong form of legal rent extraction for the shortest and longest event window, and supported the weak form of rent extraction for the (-5, $+3$) window.[23] The initial threat of a class action lawsuit resulted in abnormally low stock market returns in 70 percent of the cases with strong statistical significance; the settlement showed either no significant recovery or less than originally lost (Haymond and West 2003, 104–105).

Delegation of Rent Extraction

In Haymond and West's (2003) review of reasons legislators delegate rent extraction to lawyers, they identified several possibilities—after all, why would politicians not extract the rents directly themselves? One reason is legislators maximize returns from both rent creation and rent extraction (McChesney 1997, 22). At the margin, creating rents for lawyers may be more advantageous than direct rent extraction. Trial lawyers have given generously to politicians, leading all other industries during the period 1990–2004.[24] Another reason may be that by allowing lawyers to extract the rents directly, politicians are one step removed from any potential public outrage. Businesses and industries that can be vilified may be a better target for political rent extraction, whereas legal rent extraction may be more effective for those industries with positive reputation but sizable private capital. Nonetheless, more can be said to explain the nature of legal rent extraction and why politicians might delegate this capability.

One reason may be that as politicians create rents for trial lawyers, these rents become a source of potential rent extraction from lawyers. Theoretically, trial lawyers would pay up to the value of the rent to preserve it. Threats to eliminate a rent reduce its capital value, and therefore are fought by the rent's current owner. Once a rent is created, resources will be expended to preserve it, making a fertile area for rent extraction. Tort reform bills become an annual event on Capitol Hill, with trial lawyers contributing to keep their privileged extraction capabilities. On the opposite side, legal rent extraction increases demand for politicians to protect businesses from exploitation. Thus politicians from both parties benefit by delegating rent extraction to lawyers: one party creates rents for trial lawyers and receives campaign contributions and votes; the other party obtains similar rewards to prevent additional rent extraction.[25]

As discussed above, political rent extraction is improved when a particular target can be vilified politically, and is also especially effective against immobile capital (as political processes are cumbersome and slow). In the cases cited above, politicians extracted rent from the tobacco and pharmaceutical industries; neither of these industries had a viable option to relocate capital or to abandon their customer base in favor of differing markets. Politicians portrayed both industries negatively to the public. However, much of the new capital created in today's economy is very mobile and agile, especially in the technology area. Further, these businesses are often little known to the general populace, and much more difficult for a politician to attack. Yet their sizable capital will not fail to attract attention. If politicians are unable to effectively extract rents directly, they may choose to delegate this right to trial lawyers, who may be nimble enough to chase mobile capital. Examples of trial lawyer mobility include forum shopping (seeking the most friendly lawsuit venue) and filing lawsuits against the same defendant in multiple jurisdictions.

In addition to capital mobility, another consideration by politicians for delegating rent extraction may be the degree of organization. McChesney notes that politicians have an incentive to threaten regulation of (and extract rent from) organized groups over unorganized groups due to the lower negotiation costs (1997, 146). He suggests this may also provide an additional reason beyond free riding for groups (especially consumers) to forgo organization. While unorganized, consumers will not be able to fight political threats, leaving their entire consumer surplus at risk. But without organization, there is little incentive for politicians to threaten consumers' surplus, as there would be no effective way for consumers to pay to retain it. So while politicians may prefer to target organized groups for rent extraction, there may be groups that are not organized and have sizable rents susceptible to legal rent extraction.[26] Similarly, high transactions costs may drive politicians to delegate rent extraction. For a politician to target every potential source of private capital may be impracticable, yet this could be delegated to trial lawyers in exchange for other consideration. If this is a significant factor, one would expect to see politicians target the rents of industries and large corporations (preferably monopolies and cartels) while delegating rent extraction of individuals and smaller corporations to trial lawyers.

IMPLICATIONS TO CAPITAL MARKETS

There are many implications to a society that allows legal failure to facilitate private wealth extortion. To the extent citizens recognize that the government allows extortion, public cynicism and distrust/disdain of those who allow and practice extortion will increase.[27] Further, as this behavior is rewarded, we would expect to see more people seek employment in professions that benefit from this activity (lawyers, lobbyists, etc.).[28] Yet victims will not passively accept being extorted. In addition to soliciting political help to protect their capital, victims will take whatever private actions they can to protect their wealth, equating at the margin the costs and benefits of private versus public action. This is analogous to inner city businesses that seek political help to protect their private capital (perhaps by requesting increased police patrols) as well as installing steel bars over their windows to preclude theft. If securities class action lawsuits are seen as extortion, what "steel bars" are corporations putting up to protect their capital?

Public Market Exodus

Litigation costs (to include class actions) are not only an issue for big business—nearly 90 percent of U.S. corporations are involved in some type of litigation, with the average company balancing 37 cases (Fulbright 2005, 1). Securities class action lawsuits continue to be a major concern for U.S. corporations, despite a statistically significant drop in filings in 2005–2006.[29] Nearly 40 percent of companies with revenues of $1 billion or more were served with a class action in 2005 (2005, 5). In a 2006 NERA study, Miller et al. reported 7 of the top 10 largest securities class action settlements were recorded in 2005 and 2006, totaling almost $21 billion (Miller et al. 2006, 1). Further, while some may have hoped for a reduction in rising settlement costs, the values appear to have simply plateaued.[30] Miller et al.'s analysis also suggests an individual corporation faces a nearly 10 percent probability of a securities class action lawsuit over a five-year period (2006, 3). In NERA's 2005 report, Buckberg examined securities class actions since the passage of the Sarbanes-Oxley (henceforth SOX) accounting reforms and concluded that there is no statistically significant change in either the number of filings or the size of settlements (2005, 3). Though much of these results can be attributed to the aftermath of the late 1990s stock market bubble and associated fraud,[31] and there has been a significant reduction in securities class action filings in 2005 and 2006, Miller suggests it is too early to conclude there is now a downward trend (2006, 2).

Given this environment, at the margin, one would expect the high costs of securities class action lawsuits to reduce the number of investors seeking access to the public capital markets, or at least the U.S. public capital markets. If securities class action lawsuits are a method of extortion, then investors will avoid the reach of the extortionist if possible—no different than a citizen avoiding certain portions of the city late at night when walking alone.

Leaving public markets is a costly decision, as companies listing in the United States are reported to have a 1 percent cost of capital advantage over foreign markets, and up to 2.5 percent cost of capital advantage over the private equity market (Interim 2006, 4, 46). Nonetheless, investors are increasingly raising capital outside U.S. public markets, both through private equity and by listing publicly outside the United States. Public concern with the exodus from U.S. public markets led to the formation of the Committee on Capital Markets Regulation in 2006. The committee's purpose was to study the U.S. capital markets to examine whether the United States was losing its competitiveness, and to recommend ways to improve regulation, with an initial report released in November 2006.

The committee noted U.S. market share loss of global initial public offerings (IPOs), with a decline from 50 percent in 2000 to 5 percent in 2005 in terms of overall value, and from 37 percent to 10 percent in the overall number of IPOs (2006, x). The trend only gets worse as 24 of the top 25 IPOs in 2005 and 9 out of the top 10 IPOs in 2006 were placed outside the United States.[32] While foreign investors avoided U.S. public markets, London's share of the global IPO market rose from 5 percent to 25 percent, to include capturing a number of IPOs from companies domiciled in the United States, despite London having many of the same regulatory requirements as the United States (but notably does not allow securities class action lawsuits) (2006, 3).

Similarly, the U.S. private equity market has flourished in the wake of the decline in U.S. public markets. Private equity markets (referred to as Rule 144A markets, for large institutional investors) are free from most U.S. securities regulations, including mandated disclosure requirements and provisions of SOX. The committee noted that foreign investors raised over $83 billion in these private equity offerings in 2005, compared to only $5.3 billion in public offerings. Foreign investors were not alone in the flight to private equity markets; going-private transactions increased to over 25 percent of public takeovers in the past three years (2006, 4–5). Since 2001, venture capitalists exiting their investments have preferred private equity markets to IPOs by over 10 to 1. The implications of this loss of competitiveness are significant; U.S. financial markets account for over 8 percent of GDP, totaling over $1 trillion, and the financial services sector employs over 6 million workers as of 2005 (2006, 1).

Given the significantly lower cost of capital of U.S. public markets, the committee believes that "the finding strongly suggests that the regulatory and litigation burden is an important factor in the choice between public and private markets" (2006, 46). The civil penalties levied on businesses in 2004 were over $4.7 billion, with an additional $3.5 billion in class action lawsuit settlements; the committee concluded the penalties are disproportionately large compared to their benefit. In the United Kingdom, for instance, the overall regulatory penalties for 2004 were only $40.5 million, and as mentioned above, they do not have securities class action lawsuits (neither do many of the other financial competitors of the United States). In addition, litigation costs help drive director and officer insurance costs in United States six times higher than in Europe. While there is no way to tell how much of the loss of U.S. public capital market share is due to regulation and litigation, foreign companies do commonly cite the U.S. class action system as the most important reason not to list in the United States (2006, 11).[33] Allowing legal extortion does have its costs, and "steel bars" are increasingly being raised to protect private capital.

CLASS ACTION FAIRNESS ACT OF 2005

In addition to raising "steel bars," business interests continue to pursue tort reform, although they are often frustrated by the glacial rate of progress. While businesses have contributed to campaigns of those supporting tort reform, trial lawyers have just as munificently supported tort reform's opponents. Further, many reforms passed at the state level (where arguably more reform is needed) have been found to be unconstitutional by state courts. Many state judges are elected, where trial lawyers often provide large campaign donations. In 1999, for instance, the Ohio Supreme Court rejected a three-year-old tort reform package in a 4–3 decision; the four justices voting against the tort reform package had received $1.5 million in campaign donations from trial lawyers, while the opposing judges received only $70,000 (Bandow 1999, 1).[34] The U.S. Chamber of Commerce responded in 2000 with a campaign to raise at least $10 million for elected judges in Alabama, Illinois, Michigan, Mississippi, and Ohio (Stone 2000, 2004). So the tort reform effort seems to go back and forth with trial lawyers opposed to any reform and businesses pushing various legislative solutions, but with little substantively to show.

Nonetheless, the Congress passed and the president signed the Class Action Fairness Act of 2005 (CAFA), which offered meaningful (albeit limited) tort reform in response to some of the more egregious class action abuses. During his signing ceremony, President Bush highlighted two specific abuses that CAFA was intended to address: (1) the practice of "forum shopping" for the most plaintiff-friendly venue and (2) trial lawyers walking away with huge fees while plaintiffs receive next to nothing. The 1990s saw the federal courts increasingly skeptical of class certification, and in 1998 Congress provided limited appellate review of class certification (Hooper 2005, 2). Trial lawyers responded by significantly increasing state class actions, in plaintiff-friendly venues, which critics called "judicial hellholes." From 1998 to 2000, Madison County, Illinois (perhaps the biggest "judicial hellhole"), featured an 1850 percent increase in class action lawsuits (Beisner and Miller 2000, 7). To reduce forum shopping, CAFA changed diversity requirements resulting in more class action suits being tried at the federal level. The previous requirement for federal courts to have jurisdiction over a class action lawsuit was for "complete diversity," meaning none of the plaintiffs could be from the same state as any of the defendants. In a large class action lawsuit, plaintiff's attorneys could rather easily avoid this requirement by naming additional defendants or plaintiffs as required. Under CAFA, if any of the plaintiffs are from a differing state than any of the defendants, then federal jurisdiction may be appropriate (if the aggregate value of the claims exceeds $5 million, and there are at least 100 class members). Most large, multistate class actions will now be tried at the federal level, although large intrastate class actions will remain under state jurisdiction. Securities class action lawsuits were not part of this legislation, as existing law (Securities Litigation Uniform Standards Act of 1998) already ensured most securities class action issues would be tried in federal court.

Another major goal of CAFA was to adjust the settlement approval process to counter the perception (and in many cases reality) of trial lawyers enriching themselves while providing little meaningful benefit to the plaintiffs. Coupon settlements were a particularly popular resolution method for both defendants and plaintiffs lawyers (which would give plaintiffs a coupon for a discount off their next purchase from the defendant). Defendants found that these coupons were seldom redeemed, and if they were, they provided additional sales. Trial lawyers were supportive because they could negotiate larger settlements because of low redemption rates and thus increase their fees. Under CAFA, coupon settlements will face additional review, and the attorney's fees will be based on the value of the coupons redeemed (or the time actually working on the case). Further, all settlements that feature a net loss to the plaintiffs must not be approved unless the court is shown that nonmonetary benefits substantially outweigh any loss. Finally, notification of proposed settlements must be made to state and federal regulators for their review.

As part of the CAFA, the Federal Judiciary Center was required to assess the impact of the law on federal courts. Their initial reviews have found a statistically significant increase in class action lawsuits in the federal courts, both in original filings as well as removals from state court. Prior to CAFA, the federal courts averaged 27 cases/month; after CAFA they averaged 53.4 cases/month (Willging and Lee 2007, 2). Clearly CAFA is having its intended effect, with the transfer of many class action lawsuits from state to federal courts. One business article headline proclaimed that "Judicial Hellholes Are Freezing Over" as new class action filings in Madison County have slowed to a crawl. However, existing class action suits filed prior to CAFA enactment are still being processed, and entrepreneurial trial lawyers are amending old class action suits to avoid the CAFA requirements where possible (Frank 2007).

Does the transfer to federal courts benefit business interests over trial lawyers? At this point, it seems too early to tell, although business was a strong supporter of CAFA. In a Fulbright survey of U.S. and U.K. corporate counsel shortly after the passage of CAFA, almost one-half predicted little impact on businesses from CAFA, with 13 percent predicting an increase in corporate legal costs, and over a quarter believing it would reduce costs. Surprisingly, corporate counsel was much more concerned about electronic discovery and increased regulatory compliance issues (from SOX) than with class action lawsuits. However, as the company's size increased, so did the importance of class action lawsuits; it was the second ranked legal concern of companies with gross revenues over $1 billion (Fulbright 2005, 5–6). Some trial lawyers were less sanguine; James Sturdevant suggests, "The goal of CAFA was to blow up the caseload in the federal court system, so that cases would move more slowly if at all . . . If cases move more slowly, then the conduct or policies of the defendant never get changed" (Yates 2006, 4). But on balance, trial lawyers interviewed believe CAFA tilts the field only slightly for the defendant (Yates 2006, 4).

Economic theory suggests that agents optimize behavior by equating costs and benefits at the margin. If the cost at one margin changes (i.e., the ability to file class action lawsuits in state courts), then trial lawyers should simply increase activity across another margin. As seen above, the Federal Judiciary Center's analysis shows that as the state class action option was eliminated, trial lawyers filed more federal lawsuits. One trial lawyer confirmed this (Yates 2006, 4): "We have seen in our practice more plaintiffs' lawyers filing in federal court. They're recognizing reality— they don't want to be frustrated by the delay of filing in state court, then getting removed to federal court. That's not useful for plaintiffs. They're not trying to be too creative in getting around CAFA." If trial lawyers overcome the class certification hurdle, the increased workload on the federal courts due to CAFA will also motivate judges to encourage settlements, possibly to the benefit of trial lawyers. Further, while CAFA may eliminate venue shopping to "judicial hellholes," class action procedures were not changed. Class action extraction is still possible at both the state and federal levels.[35]

FUTURE RESEARCH

While rent extraction (both political and legal extortion) is strongly supported by empirical investigations to date, more work remains to be done. Legal rent extraction theory could be strengthened by additional empirical investigations. Haymond and West's initial empirical work examined only 30 securities class action cases, with the initial threat period spread out from 1991 to 1998. In the subsequent years, especially with the late 1990s stock market bubble, many more class action lawsuits were filed and settled. This opens the door for at least three areas of additional empirical work. First, the basic theory of legal rent extraction could be tested using event studies methodology for a much larger data set over a longer period of time.[36] Second, the larger data set also allows for comparison within the data. For instance, the SOX bill significantly changed reporting requirements and public regulation. Event studies could determine whether there is a difference in the ability to extract rent post-SOX. Finally, one could sort the individual cases by industry to see whether some industries are more susceptible to legal rent extraction than others .

While securities class action lawsuits have been shown empirically to be consistent with legal rent extraction, a far more likely area of extortion is the mass tort. With securities class action lawsuits, the suit is typically settled for "nuisance" value, at the point where the cost of contesting the lawsuit is expected to exceed the cost of settlement. The company could afford to fight the suit, but it is simply not worth it. In the mass tort case, however, the company's very survival is at stake—the only way to guarantee survival is to settle at the best terms possible. In that environment, extortion seems even more plausible. Yet the mass tort has a legitimate public interest case; there are real victims with injuries who deserve recompense. Separating the legitimate public interest aspects from legal extortion is one of the remaining challenges to demonstrate the theory of legal rent extraction.

For instance, asbestos litigation is seemingly never ending. Despite the cessation of asbestos use in the late 1970s and the decline of cancer deaths since 1992, the number of claims continues to increase. Further, it is estimated that approximately 90 percent of asbestos claimants are unimpaired, and are receiving 65 percent of available compensation. Meanwhile, transactions costs consume roughly two-thirds of the available compensation (White 2003, 48–52). This results in some unimpaired members being rewarded when they will never suffer injury, while other claimants that will develop serious complications in the future will find the trust funds unable to compensate them consistent with their injury.

A 2005 RAND study asked how well the tort system is working for asbestos litigation in the areas of compensation, deterrence, and individualized justice (Carroll 2005, xxviii–xxix). Under compensation, as discussed above, the results are not what a public interest ideal would expect. Under deterrence, Carroll et al. note that as the original producers of asbestos have declared bankruptcy, plaintiffs have sued companies further removed from the actual harm.[37] When businesses are punished independent of the level of harm they create, there is no effective deterrent to shape their behavior—a result not consistent with a public interest hypothesis. In individualized justice, RAND concludes it is a myth in asbestos litigation. If asbestos facts argue against a public interest explanation, is it possible to empirically verify legal rent extraction?

Another area of research could be to test the implications of legal rent extraction. One prediction is that politicians may delegate the right of extortion to lawyers for cases that are more difficult for the politician to reach. As discussed earlier in this chapter, one should find legal rent extraction targeting more mobile capital that cannot be as easily reached via legislative action. If securities class action lawsuits were concentrated among companies with relatively more mobile capital, this would support the theory. LaCroix's analysis (2007, 5) of 2006 filings suggests filings appear to be concentrated in industries that are more dynamic. A more rigorous investigation of what constitutes dynamic and mobile capital could be conducted, with a subsequent empirical investigation of actual securities class action lawsuits to verify this prediction.

CONCLUSION

Unfortunately, extortion is alive and well in the legal system of the United States. While political extortion by rent extraction is more subtle than common criminal undertakings, numerous empirical studies support the rent extraction hypothesis, including the tobacco MSA. The MSA was driven by a combination of political and legal pressure, suggesting the possibility of pure legal rent extraction. While mass tort class action lawsuits are often the most conducive to extortion, securities class action lawsuits offer a cleaner basis for empirical testing. Empirical testing of legal rent extraction provides strong support to theory and evidence of legal failure.

The cost of securities class action lawsuits to businesses is significant in the aggregate, as is the probability of an individual firm facing a lawsuit. Legal rent extraction is objectionable from a moral perspective, as well as a pragmatic one. The Committee on Capital Market Regulation raised significant concerns about the exodus of investors raising funds in the public capital markets in favor of the less-regulated private equity markets (with securities class action lawsuits likely a driving factor). Yet the option of private equity is encouraging, as the market is taking action to eliminate class action extraction in the absence of tort reform. Nevertheless, investors making the decision to seek private equity financing face a significantly higher cost of capital than with public markets, so efforts at legal reform could assist capital formation.

McChesney (1997, 168) asked that if political rent extraction should be eliminated, "would the world be a better place if extortion payments were punished legally or somehow made more difficult?" He concluded that given a politician's ability to threaten privately created wealth, if bribes were not available, the politician could still take and transfer private capital, even if he couldn't extract wealth directly. There is always another margin on which a politician could optimize; for example, eliminating rent extraction might lead to even more socially wasteful rent creation and rent seeking (1997, 170). The only way to avoid these outcomes is to eliminate the politician's power over private capital. Rent extraction just might be the best option in the second-best world in which we live. For legal rent extraction, however, the United States is virtually alone in allowing securities class action lawsuits. Further, changing back to an "opt in" vice "opt out" requirement to be part of a class action (as existing prior to 1966 changes) could provide meaningful reform. Even in the second-best world we live it, it seems we also could eliminate or reduce class action extraction.

Appendix 10.1   2007 State Spending on Tobacco Prevention

State	% of CDC Minimum	State	% of CDC Minimum
Alabama	2.6	Missouri	0
Alaska	76.6	Nebraska	22.5
Arizona	91.8	Nevada	28.2
Arkansas	84.3	New Hampshire	0
California	50.9	New Jersey	24.4
Colorado	101.8	New Mexico	56.2
Connecticut	9.4	New York	89.2
D.C.	6.7	North Carolina	35.2
Delaware	119.4	North Dakota	38
Florida	7.1	Ohio	72.9
Georgia	5.4	Oklahoma	45.8
Hawaii	84	Oregon	16.3
Idaho	8.2	Pennsylvania	46.2
Illinois	13.1	Rhode Island	9.6
Indiana	31.3	South Carolina	8.4
Iowa	33.6	South Dakota	8.1
Kansas	5.5	Tennessee	0
Kentucky	8.8	Texas	5
Louisiana	29.5	Utah	47.3
Maine	131.3	Vermont	64.5
Maryland	61.7	Virginia	34.7
Massachusetts	23.4	Washington	81.3
Michigan	0	West Virginia	38.1
Minnesota	75.8	Wisconsin	32.1
Mississippi	0	Wyoming	79.9
Mean	39.6	Standard Error	4.88

Source: Campaign for Tobacco Free Kids, http://tobaccofreekids.org/
reports/settlements/

NOTES

The views expressed in this chapter are those of the author and do not reflect the official policy or position of the United States Air Force, the Department of Defense, or the U.S. government.

1. In a 2007 report, the Pacific Research Institute estimates the annual overall cost of the U.S. tort system at $865 billion, or $9,827 for a family of four, see http://www.pacificresearch.org/. What percentage of this is frivolous is beyond the scope of this chapter and is left to the reader.
2. The possibility that market forces alone could sufficiently discipline "big business" is almost never considered by advocates of class action lawsuits.
3. Of course, the behavior could be worse than opportunistic, it could be criminal. Milberg Weiss, one of the largest securities class action firms, was indicted for allegedly paying plaintiffs illegally. See http://money.cnn.com/magazines/fortune/fortune_archive/2006/11/13/8393127/index.htm
4. The Committee on Capital Markets Regulation is an independent and bipartisan group comprised of 23 leaders from the investor community, business, finance, law, accounting, and academia. It began its work in 2006 and is directed by

Prof. Hal S. Scott of Harvard Law School. The Committee Co-Chairs are Glenn Hubbard, Dean of Columbia Business School, and John L. Thornton, Chairman of the Brookings Institution.

5. Indeed, the shareholders who benefited the most are those who owned a security during a period of management malfeasance (the misbehavior keeping/raising the stock price to a level it would otherwise not achieve), yet sold the stock before the effects of the malfeasance being made known to the market. Yet these stockholders are no longer there—they are beneficiaries and will pay nothing.

6. Buckberg et al. (2005)found that "settlements increase with the depth of the defendants' pockets. For each 1.0 percent increase in the company's market capitalization on the day after the end of the class period, the typical settlement will increase 0.1 percent" (7). Simmons and Ryan also find that securities class action lawsuits naming an accounting firm as an additional defendant settle for a significantly higher percentage of damages relative to cases not involving accounting allegations (Simmons 2006, 8). Likewise, Miller et al. found that health service sector pays typical settlements one-third higher than any other industry, after controlling for other case characteristics (2006, 9).

7. One such outrageous anecdote (*Hoffman vs. Bank of Boston*) was highlighted in congressional testimony and helped win passage of the Class Action Fairness Act of 2005, see http://www.pointoflaw.com/archives/000967.php

8. Tullock showed the cost of monopoly would not simply be the loss of consumer surplus known as the Harberger triangle. Monopolists would be willing to expend up to the value of the monopoly privilege to obtain it. This "Tullock rectangle" was in addition to the Harberger triangle, a much larger social loss. See http://www.thelockeinstitute.org/journals/luminary_v1_n2_p2.html for a succinct review.

9. As used here, rent creation is simply a politician's response to constituents' rent-seeking behavior. This is not to suggest that the politician creates the original rent; that source is a redistribution from one group to another. But from the rent seeker's perspective, the politician can "create" a rent by transferring it to the rent seeker.

10. Event studies applied to rent extraction are discussed in McChesney (1997), Beck, Hoskins, and Connelly (1992), and Haymond (2001, 2003). For a general discussion of event study methodology, see Brown and Warner (1985).

11. Source originally obtained on the internet and is no longer available. Article available from author upon request.

12. There was one possible exception, as the "Nixon Campaign Fund" could not be positively identified to either political party.

13. Florida was not an isolated case. In Louisiana, a state judge approved $575 million in legal fees that amounted to $6,700/hr because "Louisiana, the tobacco manufacturers and Louisiana private counsel have acted in good faith." See AP (2001).

14. The report, a "meta" study linking eleven other ETS studies, came to its conclusion despite the fact that only one of the original studies had statistical significance, and only at the 90 percent confidence level (Viscusi 1995, 2). In some cases, the studies reviewed came up with answers in the opposite direction. The major problem with this report was the lack of multivariate controls normally done with such studies. Another concern was a lowering of the confidence level from 95 percent (EPA's published guideline for analysis) to 90 percent (an easier standard to meet), which suggests the EPA was looking for an answer.

15. Transcript of *60 Minutes* program, found at http://www.jeffreywigand.com/60minutes.php
16. http://www.waxman.house.gov/issues/health/tobacco_back.htm
17. Or in the "tell us how you really feel" category, Yale Law School's John Langbein said, "These are not real lawsuits. They are taxes on industries by well-coordinated groups of predators. This one happened to be on tobacco; the one before that was directed at breast implants. We are witnessing utter voodoo science, utter witch-craft, manufactured by a cabal of tort lawyers" (Regulation 2000, 45).
18. Note that these costs are independent of any actual settlement or judgment against the company, as the company necessarily must pay attorney's fees to defend against the suit. The suit may also create uncertainty in the financial markets concerning future profitability of the company, lowering its credit rating and thus increasing costs of finance.
19. See In re "Agent Orange Product Liability Litigation," 100 F.R.D. 718, 724 (E.D.N.Y 1983)
20. The Federal Judiciary Center found that class action suits were more than twice as likely to settle as those that contained class allegations but were never certified (Willging 1996, 60)
21. Some Reflections on the "Abusiveness" of Class Actions, 58 F.R.D. 299 (1973).
22. However, the results did vary more, possibly indicating greater variation within persons classified as Hispanic.
23. With the strong form of rent extraction, the rate of return with the threat is abnormally low, but retraction of the threat (settlement) will not result in any appreciable recovery. With the weak form of rent extraction, upon removal of the threat, the stock price will recover some, but not all, of the initial loss.
24. Although dropping to the #2 position in the 2006 cycle, behind only retired individuals. Data from the Center for Responsive Politics, http://www.opensecrets.org/industries/indus.asp?Ind=K01
25. As cited by McChesney, Ralph Nader calls tort reform "a PAC annuity for members of Congress. It's like rubbing the golden lamp" (Abramson 1990, A16).
26. To include producers (that are susceptible to class action lawsuits); not being organized may preclude legislators from being able to threaten the entire producer surplus.
27. To no surprise, public esteem of lawyers and politicians continues to decline. See http://www.forbes.com/leadership/2006/07/28/leadership-careers-jobs-cx_tvr_0728admired.html.
28. The number of registered lobbyists has doubled since 2000, with dramatically higher salaries. See http://www.washingtonpost.com/wp-dyn/content/article/2005/06/21/AR2005062101632.html
29. Cornerstone Research reports that filings in 2006 were down 38 percent from 2005 level, and 43 percent below the 10-year average. They suggest the combination of (1) vigorous enforcement activity by the SEC, (2) stable U.S. stock prices, and (3) the boom/bust filings of the late 1990s are now over could explain the drop in filings (Securities, 2006: 1). The indictment of the large Milberg-Weiss law firm may also be a factor, if other firms also engaged in aggressive plaintiff recruitment and are modifying their behavior to avoid similar outcomes.
30. Miller et al. report that average settlement values for class action lawsuits rose from $13.3 million (1996–2001) to $22.3 million (2002–2005). While increases in average settlement value tend to reflect the largest settlements, median values

have also risen, almost doubling from 1996 to 2005 to $7 million (Miller et al. 2006, 4–5).

31. Worldcom and Enron alone account for over $13 billion of the almost $21 billion (Miller et al. 2006, 1).

32. While many of these IPOs were from China and Russia (and perhaps not meeting our regulatory standards for listing), many others were not. The committee noted "the United States' loss of foreign IPOs is even more severe when attention is restricted to global IPOs from developed countries" (Interim 2006, 3).

33. In NERA's review of the top ten shareholder class action lawsuits in 2006, they noted "the chilling news to non-United States issuers already wary of being embroiled in U.S. litigation, two of those six settlements, those of Nortel Networks of Canada and Royal Ahold N.V. of the Netherlands involved foreign companies" (Miller et al. 2006, 1).

34. This legal conflict of interest is not isolated; when Detroit decided to sue the gun manufacturers, the city's lead private lawyer was one of the biggest donators to the judge assigned the case, much to the chagrin of the gun manufacturers. The city's lawyer saw no problem since his firm donated to "about 90 percent of the judges in Wayne County" and the chief judge's boss was equally unconcerned, "This happens all the time. Who do you think donates to judicial campaigns? It isn't Aunt Susie—it's lawyers" (Olson 2003, 77).

35. Indeed, Madison County still has hundreds of class actions pending that were filed prior to CAFA, and there are thousands nationwide. It will be several years before this case load is exhausted. CAFA also maintains class actions at the state level if two-thirds or the plaintiffs are from the same state as one of the primary defendants. Further, forum shopping at the federal level can still occur as well. See comments from Ted Frank, http://www.fed-soc.org/publications/PubID.165/pub_detail.asp

36. There are currently over eight hundred securities class action lawsuits on the Stanford Securities Class Action lawsuit database from 1996 to 2006. Significantly less than that would meet the criteria for an event study, but would still expand the scope of the original work. See http://securities.stanford.edu/companies.html.

37. Under joint and several liability (also known as the deep pocket rule), if two or more parties contribute to a harm, and one party is incapable of paying, the other party(s) can be held responsible for paying the total cost, independent of the portion of fault.

Chapter 11

Cy Pres and Its Predators

Charles N. W. Keckler

Introduction

When an area of the law involves enormous judicial discretion over an ever-increasing amount of money, the conditions are created for remarkable—and sometimes unseemly—attempts by attorneys to influence that discretion. In the following, I analyze a small data set of recent cy pres distributions by courts of unclaimed funds arising from class actions. Although these funds generally went to "nonprofit" institutions and activities, they were predominantly directed to law-related entities such as law schools, pro bono advocacy organizations, and the like. These are the sort of preferences one expects from lawyers and judges, but not from the preferences of the plaintiffs to whom unclaimed funds are owed. It was the plaintiff preferences that once guided application of cy pres, and the transformation to lawyer preference required a series of legal innovations in the cy pres doctrine that I trace below. More speculatively, this phenomenon helps fuel increases in the underlying rate of litigation, because it is reasonable to assume that now that class action funds can underwrite the desires of judges and lawyers, the courts have an incentive to permit more class litigation. I close with some brief suggestions on how one could legislatively rein in this phenomenon, and restore cy pres to its role of implementing preferences of injured consumers rather than the preferences of lawyers and judges.

First, though, I illustrate the dynamics of this phenomenon by an extended case study of a recent attempt by a court in Illinois to distribute a $7 billion judgment—money that would only materialize if the defendant's liability was upheld on an uncertain appeal. As in many class actions, everyone involved knew that many successful plaintiffs would never bother to get compensated out of the fund—if even 30 percent was distributed to class members it would have been a surprise, and that would have left billions for the court to dispose of, more or less as it pleased, or as suggested by the attorneys. For every 1 percent increase in the probability of being upheld on appeal, the plaintiffs' attorneys could expect to personally gain $18 million

218 CHARLES N. W. KECKLER

in the expected value of their fee award, so they had every incentive to shape the proposed distribution of the unclaimed funds to increase this probability. There are rules about how a court is supposed to handle such funds, the rules of cy pres, but those restrictions have gotten a lot looser over the last few decades, so that a judge can do "almost anything" (Forde 1996) he wants with these funds. Under such loose institutional constraints, we are prompted to question what judges want, how they decide to pursue their wants, and how their desires and rulings can be manipulated by other actors in the legal system.

At the prompting of the attorneys who won the case *Price v. Phillip Morris,* the judge decreed straightaway where all the "extra money" would go if his judgment was sustained, thereby creating incentives for these potential recipients to help the plaintiffs' attorneys in their quest to preserve their big trial win despite scrutiny by higher courts. What was done in *Price* differs only in degree from what now occurs regularly through the application of "modern" cy pres rules. Before the Illinois Supreme Court struck down the verdict (on entirely separate grounds, see *Price v. Philip Morris, Inc.,* 219 Ill. 2d 182, 185 [Ill. 2005]) two years later, class action law teetered at the edge of a very slippery slope, a creation of the rapid increase in the size of class action awards joined with the loosening of the cy pres rules that had formerly limited who could derive benefit from this money. Unchecked, this trend would inject into legal proceedings a scramble of organized interests recruited to lobby for favorable verdicts, because these power brokers would be guaranteed a payment from any award. They are made into legal allies with literally a piece of the action.

Of course, this phenomenon is part of litigation, so there is an opposite view: *"Amici* submit to this Court that Judge Byron's plan for cy pres distribution of the unclaimed compensatory damage funds in this monumental case is a thoughtful, pragmatic, efficient order that is consistent with Illinois precedent and prevailing trends in application of the cy pres doctrine to consumer class action cases" (Brief of Amici Curiae 2005 IL S. Ct. Briefs 96236). Eleven law schools disagree with me: for instance, the foregoing sentiment was expressed in a brief they filed jointly in support of the plaintiffs. One may surmise why these learned institutions considered Judge Byron to have been so "thoughtful": he did, after all, designate each of them as the recipient of 3 percent of any unclaimed funds, which a conservative estimate[1] would place at a hundred million for each school ($2–4 million per full-time faculty member).

Nevertheless, what the law schools stated in their brief was true. The *Price* distribution was indeed in line with "prevailing trends in the application of the cy pres doctrine[.]" Three successive shifts, taking place over the past several decades, have occurred within the antique doctrine of cy pres, resulting in many American courts acquiring broad powers over residual class action funds. Cy pres began life as an idea in the law of charitable trusts (Draba 2004). The first legal innovation, now relatively uncontroversial, was to apply it to class actions funds found to be not distributable, as it had been applied to trust funds found to be not distributable. The second innovation was to initiate cy pres distribution ex ante, before other attempts at distribution and before a judicial decision on the merits or the settlement had been reached. The third innovation was to employ the distribution to maximize the *general* welfare rather than the welfare of the originally intended beneficiaries; both of the latter two rules have encountered considerable (and I will argue, deserved) judicial skepticism.[2] The *Price* verdict depends on all three new rules, in that it applies cy pres to a class action (Rule 1), decides cy pres to be appropriate contemporaneously with the creation of the award fund (Rule 2), and determines recipients on public welfare rather than class benefit criteria (Rule 3). Finally, the specific innovation in *Price* was to immediately specify by name, in advance, the recipients of the future cy pres award. Such preannouncements appear to be common in the *settlements* of lawsuits, but had never occurred before in a *judgment* that has yet to work its way through the appellate courts.

Cy pres is a phrase from the Law French *"cy pres comme possible"* used in the medieval English courts, meaning "as near as possible" (Black's Law Dictionary, 8th ed. 2004). There it was an "equitable doctrine under which a court reforms a written instrument with a gift to charity as closely to the donor's intention as possible, so that the gift does not fail" (415). In the trust context, cy pres is, strictly speaking, a heuristic by which a court attempts to determine the dominant intent of somebody who is now generally long dead and who we know intended for his/her (1) property to go to charity, but (2) in a specific way that has become infeasible, impossible, or illegal. The court has to decide whether the first or the second part of the donor's intent is to dominate, now that (2) cannot be carried out. It may be that "general charitable intent" is likely to have been dominant and should prevail ("as nearly as possible" to the way detailed), or alternatively, if the details were crucial and the donor wasn't interested in charity except in the way detailed, the trust fails and ends up in the hands of heirs (or the government). The court's goal is to optimize preference-satisfaction, by identification of "second-best" solutions, if there is sufficient information to do so.

As the modern class action has emerged over the past 40 years, it has become another instance where courts are asked to find "second-best" solutions in circumstances where the "best" solution, as designated by a legal instrument, cannot be achieved. Given the large number of people, and the small individual amounts of money involved, it is not uncommon for class members to never receive notice of the money owed them, or to never bother to claim it. The end result is frequently "leftover" money in the care of the court that approved the settlement. Depending on the way notice was conducted, and the amount of the individual recoveries, the unclaimed money in the hands of the court can end up being much greater than the claimed money delivered by the class action to particular people. When a balance remains after distribution, the court will direct, cy pres, "the unclaimed fund to its next best compensation use, e.g., for the aggregate, indirect, prospective benefit of the class" (Newberg and Conte 2002: 2, sec 10.17).

Beyond simply applying cy pres to class actions, a practice has emerged over time that allows courts in certain instances to use this rule ex ante rather than ex post. When the court perceives from the outset that individual recoveries would be swamped by administrative costs, it may authorize settlement payments to proceed, from the beginning, by a form of cy pres usually known as "fluid recovery" (Miller and Singer 1997). For instance, suppose a utility charged its past customers late fees that turn out to be unauthorized, and a class action results in an order that they return their ill-gotten gains (see, e.g., *Boyd v. Bell Atlantic-Maryland, Inc.*, 390 Md. 60, 73 [Md. 2005]). Because the fees are small, it may be quite inefficient (for customers or the utility) to engage in extensive proof of past charges in order to claim their share of the money. Instead, a cy pres distribution involving a rate reduction for defendant's *current* customers will at least get some money to most of past customers overcharged, although it gives "windfalls" to those who always paid their bills on time, those who recently became customers, and so forth. The fairly unique provision of court awards to wholly uninvolved third parties entailed by this practice (Krueger and Serotta 2005), and the attenuation of the usual common law relationship between a claim and an identifiable person with a legitimate grievance, has caused some courts to be hesitant to implement this form of cy pres (see *Simer v. Rios*, 661 F.2d 655, 675 [7th Cir. 1981]).

It is important to keep in mind that the only true analogy between estates and class action funds is that in both a court approximates as closely as possible an asset allocation that, for some reason, cannot be done exactly. In class actions, the preferences being maximized are not those of the original source of money, but of the original *recipients*. Moreover, these preferences are not charitable but proprietary: each plaintiff is a partial owner of the class funds and his preference satisfaction can be presumed to track how much of his potential share he actually recovers.

A MODEL OF TRADITIONAL CY PRES

The logic of class action cy pres is amenable to formal treatment, which is helpful in establishing the baseline of how the command of cy pres can be taken as quite objective and *nondiscretionary*, when one takes its meaning seriously and literally. A class action creates a fund of size A, which is to be delivered in a number of separate payments to the members of class C.[3] The amount of A actually directed as payment to the class we can call P. Putatively this is all of A, minus the costs of the distribution. We can call this the "mandatory" distribution, because it is the distribution whose shape is mandated by the definition agreed upon by the parties during settlement and/or used by the court in rendering judgment. Or to put it more straightforwardly, the money judgment is simply sent to all the people to whom it was awarded, sometimes equally and sometimes by more complex formulae that track the various levels of injury different plaintiffs have experienced. Suppose, for example, a taxicab company has overcharged some passengers in the past, and a court finds they are entitled to restitution.[4] Class C is defined as having, as its members, passengers who rode certain routes between certain dates (in period years in the past), and were overcharged; they are entitled to the specific amounts they personally were overcharged.

Under the mandatory distribution of total class award A, the ith class member receives payment p_i, his share of A, a_i, minus his share of transaction costs (payable from the fund for locating and transmitting the money to its intended recipients). These costs, k_i, in aggregate K, include those that are constant (like postage) and others that increase as it becomes more difficult to locate a subset of class members who do not voluntarily come forward or who are otherwise harder to contact. The goal, then, is to maximize aggregate net benefit to the class, P, which is equal in a mandatory distribution to $A - K$.

Minimally, it is impossible (in a way roughly analogous to impossible charity) to deliver a non-negative class action payment, p_i, to a class member if $a_i < k_i$. Because some members are harder to find than others and because people are less likely come forward on their own when the payment due them is small, unclaimed funds frequently remain after an initial mandatory distribution. These unclaimed funds are due to a subset of C for whom a_i may be small and k_i high, and cannot be efficiently distributed via the class definition. In the example, taxi service normally occurs on an anonymous cash-transaction basis, making contact with most passengers/plaintiffs extremely difficult. A small subset of business passengers keeps taxi receipts and so might be able to prove both class membership and damages at efficiently low cost—but for most of the class this will not be feasible. It is also possible that it will be immediately apparent at the time the fund is created that a mandatory distribution would eat up most of the payments.

Whether ex ante or ex post, therefore, the court may consider designating the group of recipients in some more efficient way, with efficiency being specified here as maximizing the quantity P. So, for example, it might compel a defendant taxicab company to lower its meter rates for some period of time, and therefore monetarily benefit some of its future passengers, a set of people who can be presumed to overlap with the set of anonymous past passengers to whom it owes money. It is important to note that P always remains tied to the original class definition of C; the relevant maximand is how much net money flows to individuals who are members of the legally defined class. However, if identifying members of this class is sufficiently costly, it may often be the case that the monetary benefit to members of class C is actually maximized by directing a portion of award A to an overlapping set of persons, D, whose membership can be identified at much lower cost. Although there is only one class C, there are many possible distributions D, from which the court must choose, according to the principle:

(1) Choose $D \mid \max P$, where $K(D) < K(C)$

For simplicity, since the goal here is to sketch a baseline for cy pres, rather than to give a complete arithmetical treatment, assume that payments for all members of a distribution are equal and per capita. That is, under mandatory distribution, payments were equal to the number of class members, N, dividing up a constant A and bearing an equal amount of costs, so that $p_i = (A - K)/N$. Then, the relationship of any discretionary distribution D to the net payments to the class can be basically determined by the extent to which D is equivalent to the set defined in class litigation, C. A set D can be nonequivalent by including some people who were not in the class, and "windfall" payments to these persons dilute the payments to members of C. In set notation, this group is defined as the intersection of D and not C (or C'), $D \cap C'$. In addition a set can be nonequivalent by leaving out certain members of the class who are owed money. This group of class members consists of the elements of C who are not part of D, or $C \cap D'$.

Call $S1$ the size of set $D \cap C'$, and $S2$ the size of $C \cap D'$. This leads to the useful, if elementary, point that if the size of the class was N, then the size of set $D = N + S1 - S2$. If C and D were equivalent, $S1$ and $S2$ would both be zero (they would be empty sets), which leads to another formulation of command of traditional cy pres, in which the goal is minimize costs to the class and nonequivalency of the distribution, given that there is a fixed pool of awarded funds available, and P is inversely proportional to $S1$, $S2$, and K:

(2) Choose $D \mid \min(S1, S2, K)$

The total benefit to the class will be determined in part by the number of class members who receive payments $(N - S2/N) * (A - K)$. Because this discussion assumes equal payments to all recipients, there will be less money to go around if D is a larger group than C, which occurs when $S1 > S2$. The payment to a class member will normally *not be higher* than A/N, even if $S2 > S1$. The original award, divided equally among members of the original class, is the maximum a member of the class is actually owed; a class member holds no special entitlement as to funds where payments exceed this quantity and in such cases the excess payment is not be counted to the satisfaction of class distribution obligations. More generally, all of the payments received as "windfall" recipients—not members of C—cannot be counted as part of P. Like excess payments to class members, payments to nonclass members are just the price paid (when cy pres is done efficiently) for reduced costs of distribution.

Benefit to the class will reflect a standard payment based on the award, A, net the new costs, K, divided among the $N + S1 - S2$ class members and the nonclass members included in the distribution. $N - S2$ class members will receive this payment to yield the aggregate payment. Therefore, a cy pres distribution D will yield the following benefit P to class members:

(3) If $S1 > S2$: $P = \dfrac{(A - K)}{N - S2 + S1} \cdot (N - S2)$

Simplifying and rearranging (3), which probably characterizes most circumstances,[5] generates complete distribution without explicit overcompensation, and the goal of the court should be to find a D and associated cost K so that:

$$(4) \quad \text{Max } P \,|\, P = (A - K) \cdot \left(\frac{N - S2}{N - S2 + S1} \right)$$

In order for cy pres to be proper, $P|D > P|C$, and indeed $P|D$ must be greater than any other possible alternative distribution.[6] Without overburdening the treatment here, it is readily apparent that P increases with A, which is generally fixed, and declines with K. P varies with $S1$ and $S2$ so that we can restate (2) as

$$(5) \quad \frac{\partial P}{\partial S1} < 0, \frac{\partial P}{\partial S2} < 0, \frac{\partial P}{\partial K} < 0$$

This produces the not very surprising result that the task of the distributor (trustee, class counsel, or judge), under the traditional cy pres rule, is to jointly minimize the number of class members left out and the number of nonmembers paid, all while reducing costs as much as possible. An omniscient and benevolent judge would be able and willing to maximize Equation (4).

MODERN CY PRES PRACTICE

However, an important doctrinal innovation has substantially altered the basis of the above model by suggesting that judges acting cy pres need no longer maximize P, but may instead "devote the funds to a broader public service in order to *maximize the benefit to society*" (Shepherd 1972; emphasis added). Thus, courts now approve settlements such as that in the Microsoft antitrust cases, where potentially hundreds of millions of dollars in software license overcharges are directed cy pres into providing equipment for low-income California public school districts (McKee 2006, *In re Microsoft I-V Cases*, 135 Cal. App. 4th 706, 713 [Cal. Ct. App. 2006]). A court under this rubric may effectively act as a grant-making entity funding "worthy" proposals it solicits to help it dispose of a litigation-created fund. For instance, in the settlement of a federal case involving market manipulation in the bottling industry, the court advertised for suggestions from the public as to the use of the funds, and ultimately funded a newsletter for an AIDS advocacy organization, production of video skits to aid in teaching legal ethics, a display of glass art at a San Jose museum, and 12 other "winning" projects (*Superior Beverage v. Owens-Illinois*, 827 F.Supp. 477, 487–488 [N.D. Ill. 1993]). Alternatively, the court may simply delegate grant-making to a new charitable foundation or existing nonprofit that will then distribute the funds over time (McCall et al. 1995).

Unlike a second-best solution tied to the baseline of enriching the plaintiff class, a maximized benefit to "society" is inherently vague because (1) it is no longer about benefit to an identifiable group of persons and (2) benefit is no longer defined as transfers of money, but about the generation of value or utility. It is readily apparent that such a principle of distribution is antithetical to the traditional model of cy pres summarized in Equations (1)–(5), and based on an entirely different legal theory of entitlement. For instance, the use of such a large reference class would fail to minimize $S1$; in fact it maximizes it, because to seek to benefit the "public" means to make D as large as possible, and thus it also makes $D \cap C'$ as large as possible. If we instead took D to be the direct recipients of monetary transfers, which is more consistent with the above treatment, it would usually be the case that no class member is such a recipient, and when all class members are excluded from D, $S2 = N$, its maximum, rather than its minimum value.

Although redefining the class as the public may lead to a low value for K, and thus much of award A goes "out the door" into the hands of recipients, the supposed superiority of this approach comes from simply ignoring what we called above $S1$ and $S2$, the measures of how much the recipient group tracks the legal class. Suppose the members of D, narrowly defined as monetary beneficiaries, receive different payments, $m_1, m_2, m_3 \ldots m_n$, until $A - K$ is exhausted. The social welfare principle would then be

(6) Choose $D \mid \max\ U$, where $U = f(m_1, m_2, m_3 \ldots m_n)$

This assumes, of course, that there no potential recipient outside of D who could transform wealth into utility better than those already chosen. Moreover, it is presumably the case, in line with basic welfare economics, that marginal changes of money among recipients could yield no greater public utility such that:

(7) Choose $D \mid \dfrac{\partial U}{\partial m_1} = \dfrac{\partial U}{\partial m_2} = \dfrac{\partial U}{\partial m_3} = \ldots \dfrac{\partial U}{\partial m_n}$

The difficulties of actually demonstrating that a social welfare enhancing distribution satisfies the conditions of Equations (6) and (7) are manifest. In practice, judges are left to their own-preference satisfaction as to in whose hands the money is "best" placed to the most "good," as they have no describable function to maximize. Developing a function for "society" along the lines of, for instance, Equation (4) is beyond the scope of this chapter and perhaps scientific possibility as well (see Hayek 1991, 73–74). Furthermore, even a good-faith effort to maximize "the benefit to society" at best means maximizing the utilities of people within it, and the weights assigned to these utilities will not be even, but instead will vary according to the preferences, perceptions, and interests of the legal actors proposing and approving the distribution.

Combining two recent innovations, a social welfare reorientation with the ex ante designation of a cy pres distribution, is likely to be particularly powerful in injecting personal judicial preferences into judicial decision-making. Together, these allow the distribution of funds to whomever is deemed worthy, and a fund can be proposed that will be precommitted to worthy causes—and the judge may be given discretion as to what will qualify as worthy. This has obvious tactical advantages for the lawyers who require a judge's approval at two stages–class certification and then approving a settlement agreement that terminates the action. It is certainly quite plausible that a judge could be swayed, perhaps unconsciously, into allowing either the action to proceed, and/or the fund from it created, if he knows that the results will be for the judge's own notions of the "public good" rather than merely involve the movement of money between private parties. The Microsoft settlement, for instance, had to overcome an objection that it shortchanged its actual past customers, and that the company had "bought justice" in the form of judicial approval of overly favorable settlement, by including, ex ante, significant cy pres subsidization of the California public schools (McKee 2006). A judge might define the public good and pick the charities; where the lawyers instead have chosen them, rational lawyers will in any event propose those cy pres recipients most likely to meet with judicial favor, thereby making settlement disapproval or class de-certification that much more painful for the deciding jurist.

PRICE V. PHILLIP MORRIS

The actual innovation of *Price,* a fourth expansion of cy pres, can now be understood in context. The lawyers preannounced by name the prospective recipients of the funds in the context of judgment rather than a settlement. This shows sophisticated use of public choice reasoning, because it attempts to sway the decision on the *merits* of the case, by presenting appellate judges negative consequences if they upset the verdict. In settlement too, the defendant and class attorneys are in agreement and the only concern is that the interests of the class *might* be divergent from its self-appointed agent. A trial verdict still be fought over is obviously at odds with the interests of the defendant, making any biasing effect more consequential. And by naming the cy pres recipients, more than a judge's general charitable instincts are aroused. Since there were now specific interest groups that would have gotten the money—contingent on plaintiffs being successful of course—the lawyers created virtual "co-plaintiffs" (technically, "co-appellees" with an interest in defending the verdict). These groups can now (and did in *Price*) represent their interests through formal submission of amicus briefs before higher courts, in order to lobby for a proplaintiff result, and this lobbying can be effective (Kearney and Merrill 2000). Moreover, the choice of interests they created was not random; nor can it be described by the traditional cy pres rules, nor, really, by maximization of social welfare. Instead, by making its de facto beneficiaries the most legally sophisticated and influential actors in

Illinois, the preannouncement was designed to win the case and maximize likelihood of affirmation on appeal, thus bringing the fund into existence.

Price was not obviously suitable for either class action status or liability (Yahya 2005); the litigation outcome was ex ante in doubt, although in the end a divided (4–2) Illinois Supreme Court rejected the lawsuit (*Price v. Philip Morris, Inc.,* 219 Ill. 2d 182, 185 [Ill. 2005]). The basic premise of the action was the claim that consumers of "light" cigarettes were deceived into thinking they were buying a "safer" cigarette; personal injury was not considered—consumers simply sought restoration of the money they had allegedly been misled into spending. The arguments, and the complexities of calculating damages, are not the primary concern here.[7] *Price* involved only consumers in Illinois and "only" $10.1005 billion of the defendant's money. The way the money was distributed, rather than size of the verdict per se, is of most interest. First, $3 billion was designated as punitive damages and made payable directly to the state of Illinois; this payout led the plaintiff's lawyer (who shared in the attorney fees of $1.78 billion) to "believe Governor Blagojevich will be standing right beside me in [the appellate court]" (Howard and Hampel 2003, C1).[8] This left $5.33 billion (three times attorneys' fees) to be paid out, potentially to plaintiffs, but failing that, to a designated list of charities.

There was no legal necessity in specifying who "might" get money years in the future if there happened to be unclaimed funds. Any disposition of "leftovers" could never have begun until after appeals were finished (this took two and half years), and after an attempt at giving at least part of the money to cigarette customers. Indeed, creating this list it was legally innovative, and arguably superfluous, so why did the judge allow it? In a romantic perspective on the law, one where the parties struggle solely to find the "right" answer to legal dilemmas, the incentive for this "extra" effort by the lawyers and the judge would be mysterious; the lawyer's fees were fixed regardless of how much of the fund was left unclaimed (a fact worthy of reform in itself). And the judge was not required to craft an opinion on uncontested questions that might or might not arise years after postjudgment.

The solution to the "mystery," of course, is that the lawyers' fees were not fixed: they would either get 25 percent of $7.1005 billion, or they would get 25 percent of nothing, which is considerably less. Their expected gain could therefore be calculated to $1.775 billion $* (1 - R)$, where $0 < R < 1$ is the probability of reversal, and they knew that R was not negligible ($R > 0$). Every percentage point they could reduce R was worth almost $18 million in expected gain, so any effective postjudgment efforts, such as recruitment of appellate allies, who may change the odds of victory at least 1 or 2 percent by their efforts (Kearney and Merrill 2000), yield a very high rate of return. The strongest effect on R is likely to have proceeded by the effects of marshalling public sentiment and especially, judicial sentiment in favor of the verdict, making it electorally and personally painful for judges to reverse an artfully designed payout to sympathetic and powerful recipients.

Who then was made an involuntary beneficiary in this decree, and does the selection of these plaintiffs comport with the predicted goal of minimizing R (rather than maximizing payment to the class, or benefit to society). The Illinois Bar Foundation was given 46 percent, eleven law schools were to share 33 percent, 9 percent was directed for legal aid services for the poor, 6 percent went to the American Cancer Society, 3 percent was given over to domestic violence programs, and the last 3 percent went straight back to the Illinois judiciary to fund its program of "drug courts." The Bar Foundation, which is the charitable arm of the state bar association, was to administer the distribution of the entire surplus using its 46 percent direct share to cover administrative costs, and to support any charitable activities it chose.

For scale, assume a minimum for the projected surplus of about $3.7 billion.[9] This presumes, optimistically, that the million or so members of a class of smoker-claimants might recover several hundred dollars of economic damages to refund past purchases of light cigarettes. Meanwhile the people of Illinois, through the separate $3 billion in punitive damages, receive over $200 per person on average, and the average lawyer in Illinois, through the bar foundation, receives a potential benefit of approximately $30,000. Legal aid groups get over $300,000,000, the American Cancer Society gets over $200,000,000, and programs against domestic violence get at least $100,000,000, as does the judiciary itself. Meanwhile each law school in Illinois (plus the two in neighboring St. Louis) is made the recipient of in excess of $100,000,000.[10] One effect of the latter "grant" may be that what was the biggest civil case in Illinois history prompted what appears to be absolutely no commentary from faculty of the local law schools. One can easily surmise that faculty, even if they were dubious about aspects of the case, would be understandably conflicted, given the alliance of their institutions with the plaintiffs' cause. Any doubts they expressed openly could easily have interfered with what would have been an enormous boon to their students, colleagues, and themselves.

Although amicus support and neutralization of academic criticism were likely of some additional value in *Price*, the main effect of crafting a "social welfare" cy pres distribution is via its influence on the judge or judges who will decide whether to accept the proposed disposition of the case, including, crucially the cy pres distribution D that is tied to that disposition. This is true of class actions more generally, including settlements requiring judicial approval, and characterizes any proposals for cy pres that are unmoored to class member payment, viz. in Equation (4). Their function is to appear attractive to the judicial decision-maker and thereby make a judge reluctant to interpose a legal ruling that will "deny" charities and government cash. A simple model might be to take U as the utility of the judge (or a "swing" member of a multijudge appellate body); U_A is his utility if he affirms a legal decision or settlement and U_R will be his utility if he reverses or rejects it. The goal of the plaintiff's attorney is to maximize the difference $U_A - U_R$ and his tool available to do this is choice of a D consisting of payments m_1, m_2, $m_3, \ldots m_n$ to recipients sharing in an aggregate 100 percent of the unclaimed funds. If we assume that U_R is relatively constant, because it is based on the status quo ante, then we can model the choice of distribution much as was done in Equation (6), only this time we are more realistically looking at the utility of *judge*, rather than society as whole:

(8) max $U_A = f(\mathbf{D})$

Performing a search for cy pres and "distribution" and "class action" for relevant material produced 19 federal district cases where it was possible to tell where the funds went.[11] Many other settlements use cy pres for some or all funds involved—there is no literature on the prevalence of the phenomenon—but dispositions, especially in state courts, are rarely reflected in electronic databases. All the cases in my small sample, like almost all class actions (but unlike *Price*), involved settlement agreements approved by the court. The primary distinction was between settlements that immediately, ex ante, designated a cy pres recipient of defendant funds and those where the parties returned to the court months to years after the initial settlement, in order to dispose, ex post, of remaining unclaimed funds.

A total of 52 designees were named either before or after settlement; 30 of these turn out to be law-related charities such as law schools, legal aid societies, or the local bar association. Lawyers received cy pres payments in 13 of the 19 cases, and in six of the seven cases issued since the start of 2006.[12] This result is quite similar to Forde's (1996) separate list of mostly unreported dispositions. In his description of 20 different cases, 14 of them directed the funds to associations of lawyers. In this respect, also, *Price* is unexceptional—91 percent of the surplus funds were directed to lawyers.

Even if one is willing to grant that subsidization of legal activity might be socially beneficial, it seems difficult to argue this it is the *most* socially useful expenditure of "free money." It is, however, the one that apparently comes foremost to the minds of lawyers (including judges) when they control the disposition of such funds. It would appear that in the cy pres context, "the next best thing" to a lawyer getting money himself is for other lawyers to get it. Arguably this is an object lesson in attempts to perform the impossible task of redistributing wealth to maximize social welfare; it is all too likely that lacking any objective maximand, the money will gravitate toward those closest in proximity to the decision-makers controlling the means of distribution.[13]

This pattern is broadly consistent with the literature on what judges are thought to personally maximize, which, beyond income, are thought to include popularity, prestige, public interest, and reputation (Posner 1993). The salient group whose esteem is most relevant to judges is presumably other judges, together with practicing lawyers within their jurisdiction (Schauer 2000). Judges acting cy pres can provide resources directly to the local bench and bar and thereby gain esteem in the group most relevant to them. As important, if it becomes known that a judge has blocked funds that could have gone to this group, a certain amount of collegial resentment could well be anticipated. More generally, a judge's sense of the "public interest" when exercising discretionary distribution of funds probably mirrors, unsurprisingly, the kinds of donations a lawyer would make with *his own* time and money. That is, we find in both circumstances a focus on such causes as pro bono professional services to the poor, law reform activities, and the like, the charitable behavior the judge's professional background equips him to understand and consider worthy.

The simplest and most cynical answer for why judges prefer give money to lawyers is that lawyers often give money to judges (Tabarrok and Helland 1999). In more formal terms, U_A is dependent on the judge's income, I_J, and I_J is itself a positive function of a vector of income of other lawyers, I_L, because by one means or another, some percentage of local attorney income redounds to the judge. Income increases on a random group of recipients, I_G, given the same total amount of money, would naturally have less of an effect on judicial income.

(9) $U_A = f(I_J, I_L), \partial I_J / \partial I_L > \partial I_J / \partial I_G$

The income of state judges (including those in Illinois) is dependent on elections, while some other state judges depend on appointments by selection committees consisting of other lawyers (Hanssen 2002). In order to win a future election or appointment, the judge's conduct in office is designed to please (or at least not to offend) key interest groups that have a disproportionate influence in the voting process (Rubin 2005). For judicial elections, it is likely that voters ultimately decide based on media funded by lawyers donating to a judge's campaign, and on newspaper endorsements, with the newspapers in turn relying on the one group that actually knows and cares something about the race: lawyers, especially that subgroup of trial lawyers representing interests that may come before the relevant court. When judges are not elected, the organized bar controls completely and openly (Hanssen 2002). So it is lawyers—and not even many of those—who shape almost all opinion in a judicial selection, both through their "objective" assessment of the judicial candidate's quality and through their money. Other lawyers are also largely responsible for financing judicial campaigns. The judge who issued the *Price* decree, for instance, was the prior recipient of a significant campaign donation by the plaintiffs' lawyer (Lenzer and Miller 2003). If they were not constrained by strong norms and institutions, judges would be in the position to be captured by the interests of attorneys, almost as if they were running for union rep rather than a public interest office.

Yet the income hypothesis poorly matches the facts. Federal judges show a strong lawyer preference in cy pres distribution, which is equally in evidence in *Price* and the mixed federal/state sample of cases in Forde (1996). Federal district judges, however, have essentially a fixed income; their jobs are "carefully designed to insulate the judges from the normal incentives and constraints that determine the behavior of rational actors" (Posner 2005).

Therefore, attribution of a direct, self-dealing motivation is implausible for either state or federal judges. A more parsimonious explanation would be that distributing judges are acting like legislators whose utility function is determined by weighted aggregation of the welfare of the interest groups which they perceive themselves as representing, constrained by a need to maintain a reputation for honesty and integrity within a relevant audience (Coate and Morris 1995). Public interest lawyering is a natural target for judicial charity, although like any charity there is a tendency to favor one's own, an element of self-promotion, and an opportunity to advance one's personal vision of society.[14]

In summary, the increase in judicial discretion over cy pres funds, from a straightforward and formalizable principle that maximized plaintiff recovery, to what is in some cases a free-ranging attempt by courts to implement social utility, has resulted in the enrichment of lawyer-dominated and favored groups through the frequent judicial equation of public interest law with the public interest itself. This implementation of judicial charitable preferences has come at the expense of either (1) the plaintiff themselves, if the case would have resulted in a fund whether or not charitable cy pres was contemplated, or (2) if the case would not have succeeded without this incentive, at the expense of the defendant, of the public bearing the externalities of a more favorable climate for class action litigation. Even if a case has merit at trial as a class action, it thoroughly distorts the appellate review process to incorporate into a judgment preannounced charitable beneficiaries of the funds that may be created, as was done in *Price*. Once one abandons a romantic view of judging, and understands that judges—particularly, but not only those subject to election—are inevitably sensitive to political and public pressure, allowing them to be subject to proposals to use cy pres for specific "public benefits" creates an obvious threat to the objectivity of their legal judgment. That the distortion of objectivity is likely to operate only semiconsciously, and as part of a good-faith effort to maximize public benefit as they perceive it, does not completely mitigate this concern.

Some Suggestions for Improvement

The first suggestion for reform of cy pres law is simple transparency. Despite the presumably prevalent nature of unclaimed funds requiring some discretionary disposition—often through cy pres—the evidence on these allocations is not easily obtainable. Cy pres payments are made by trial courts, whose material is poorly represented in legal databases. From an economic perspective, in which the primary feature of a legal decision is the state backed redistribution of wealth, this is quite unfortunate. Although we might have access to the reasons why the state chooses to dispossess the defendant of money, we rarely can see where the money is ultimately directed. For reasons of policy (as well as those of research), therefore, courts and database providers should make available and searchable court-approved distributions of funds, at least to the same extent they disseminate the opinions that create these funds.

Substantively, the presumption should be restored that a court's purpose, acting cy pres, is to distribute funds preferentially to class members, even if administrative difficulties mean this can only be a weak preference. The existence of class preference provides an objective benchmark, via Equation (4), and a check on the natural tendency of even the best people to inject their personal preferences into monetary distribution. More importantly, relaxing the class benefit presumption so that a judge knows he may eventually "do good" with class funds has some potential to encourage findings of defendant liability or approval of settlements. Ex ante designation of a cy pres class is not intrinsically problematic; however, when a "social welfare" cy pres fund is created prior to judgment or settlement, the potential for the creation of interest groups, as well as for appeal to personal judicial preferences, is severely magnified. Lawyers seeking judicial approval use the charitable contribution as a sweetener for the decision-maker and put him a difficult bind by finding something he cares about—besides doing justice according to the law—and injecting it into his decision. The actual naming of prospective beneficiaries, as in *Price*, actively encourages this unseemly lobbying of the judiciary by lawyers and potential recipients, and serves no useful legal function.

In many consumer and antitrust cases—the bulk of class actions producing unclaimed funds—a price reduction, or a coupon or voucher, is an "uncreative" but appropriate solution. Any concerns that this would either enhance market dominance by the defendant (DeJarlais 1987) or tie consumers to goods now revealed as defective can be relatively easily corrected by a court requiring the issue of a *general coupon* good for the both the defendant's products and those of any competitors (*In re Microsoft I-V Cases*, 135 Cal. App. 4th 706, 713 [Cal. Ct. App. 2006]). In the light cigarette cases, such as *Price*, vouchers could be made available for free or reduced price cigarettes of any brand. A more politically palatable alternative might involve the settlement funding a "tax holiday" of state cigarette taxes. Escheat of settlement funds to the state, in exchange for a revenue-neutral remission of sales or other taxes, directed to goods or services used preferentially by class members, is in fact a generalizable solution potentially applicable in many circumstances.[15]

To provide proper incentive for finding such solutions, attorney compensation should be a function not of the size of the cy pres distribution, but of how much of the money actually gets to the class members. Due to the Class Action Fairness Act, for certain federal cases involving coupon payments, this restriction on attorney payment already holds true, 28 U.S.C. 1713(e), and the logic of this provision should be extended more generally, including to cases in state courts. This would avoid the absurd prospect of lawyers being paid pro rata based on how much a judge decides to give to his favorite charity. As a related reform, it would be prudent to simply place a presumption against any award to lawyers as grantees, unless the case somewhat related to legal services.[16]

Even if approving a charitable gift, the judge should also avoid turning herself into a personal foundation with capacity to pick and choose the objects of its beneficence (Draba 2004); it will usually be better that the money be presumptively directed to a generalized charity, such as the local United Way active in the area or areas occupied by the majority of the plaintiffs. And this would only be preferable if plaintiffs were hidden practically randomly throughout a jurisdiction. If plaintiffs can be identified more readily than this, in most cases a targeted voucher or tax credit will provide more benefit to the class, thus more closely approximating—cy pres—what would occur outside a class action structure, namely, the discharge of a debt the defendant owes his creditors, rather than any debt he owes "society."

NOTES

1. This figure sets the high end of the *claimed* funds at 30 percent, yielding an estimate for the cy pres fund at $.70 * .75 * 7.1005$ billion = \$3.7 billion, deducting, as the court ordered, 25 percent of the award for attorney fees. Such estimates are speculative, and there is limited quantitative material in this area. However, Hensler and her collaborators (2000, ch. 15), tracked recovery rates at 27 percent and 29 percent in two roughly comparable consumer class actions. Another estimate given by Hensler et al. is for another famous cy pres case, *State v. Levi-Strauss Co.* 715 P.2d 564 [Cal. 1986]) where "14 to 33 percent" was the estimated rate of claims (discussed 2000, ch. 3).

2. For example, see, *Fogie v. THORN Ams., Inc.*, 190 F.3d 889, 904 [8th Cir. 1999], rejecting a plan that lacked an initial attempt at distribution to class members, by noting "the District Court acted prematurely in ordering the creation of a cy pres fund." The same court of appeals later rejected distribution to a public interest law group that regularly garners cy pres monies because it lacked "any connection between its purposes and the subject matter of this class action lawsuit" (*Airline Ticket Comm'n Antitrust Litig. Travel Network v. United Air Lines*, 307 F.3d 679, 681–682 [8th Cir. 2002]).

3. Formally, any "class" of plaintiffs is a subset of the general population (the set of all people). The formal and careful definition of the class is worked out during the course of class action litigation, and each plaintiff is a member of that set.

4. This example is taken from an well-known cy pres case, *Daar v. Yellow Cab. Co.*, 135 Cal.2d. 695 [Cal. 1967].

5. Alternatively, where the recipient group is smaller than the class, $S1 < S2$: $P = \frac{A}{N} \cdot (N - S2)$, which can be rearranged perhaps more intuitively, as $P = A - S2\frac{A}{N}$. That is, the payment to the class consists of the net money available for distribution (A), less the payments that should have gone to those members of C not included in D (those in $S2$). This money ends up being "lost" by disbursements to nonclass members and by excessive compensation to those class members remaining in D. In the above formula, this "excess" is assumed to be sufficient so as to be greater than K, so all class members lucky enough to receive a payment at all ($D \cap C$) receive the full value of their claim (A/N), and more. (If the average payment is between $A - K/N$ and A/N a slightly more complex formula for P ensues.) This proviso about the relative size of the class and the distribution means a settlement or judgment could not simply give the entire recovery to the named plaintiff and call it benefiting "the class."

6. The reason for this is that what the cy pres court is commanded to come "as near as possible" to is to the distribution of 100 percent of the legal award A, exclusive of costs, and A is the maximum value which P can take.

7. It is worth noting that the damages are being relitigated in federal court in New York at this writing, with claimed damages in the range of $200 billion, to be distributed, as one might predict, cy pres, rather than to consumers (*Schwab v. Philip Morris USA, Inc.*, 2005 U.S. Dist. LEXIS 27469 [E.D.N.Y. 2005]).

8. This comment illustrates that punitive damages can also be used to recruit allies for lobbying verdicts, if those punitive damages are payable to the state, and there is some evidence this has encouraged more punitive awards (Schwartz, Behrens, and Silverman 2003). Whether it has encouraged primary findings of liability (i.e., actually biased substantive justice) is less clear but worthy of further study. Presumably, judges whose preferences include expanded government revenue are influenced positively, and may receive pressure from revenue hungry members of the executive and legislative branch, and to some extent the more diffuse public. In Ohio, apparently, judges have discretion to distribute punitive awards to any "place that will achieve a societal good (535). In the latter circumstance, the public choice analysis of punitive damages award would fully parallel that of cy pres distributions.

9. See note 1, *supra*.

10. Particularly for some of the proposed recipient schools, a $100 million in court "charity" would be much larger than they have ever received from normal charitable sources. For instance, the largest gift apparently ever received by Loyola University Law School is a comparatively tiny $5 million, and the largest gift to Chicago-Kent School of Law, from a living alumnus, is a mere $1 million (Day 2006).

11. Data are available from the author, and can easily be replicated through a search in Lexis-Nexis; the search and count of cases, was conducted in May 2007 with the most recent case being *Nienaber v. Citibank* (2007 U.S. Dist. LEXIS 20581 [D.S.D. 2007]).

12. The one exception, *In re Compact Disc Minimum Advertised Price Antitrust Litig.*, 236 F.R.D. 48 (D. Me. 2006), overseen by Judge Hornby in Maine, shows considerable diligence to find some way for the remaining money to be spent to the benefit of the plaintiff class, overcharged members of "music clubs"; much of it was given to cleaning up old (out of copyright) recordings and making them freely available on the Internet to music lovers, of which the plaintiff class was presumably a subset.

13. Interesting in this regard is a comment made about the *Price* verdict by a retired judge: "It all sounds very nice to give to charities and the state, but that's just not good legal logic in my opinion. That's almost like a form of communism." (Vock 2003).

14. On occasion, judges have been sufficiently sensitive enough to this temptation to reject "social welfare" cy pres or particular distributions. For example, one federal judge threw out a proposal to settle a nationwide class action by payment to local Philadelphia charities, including the University of Pennsylvania law school, noting "the Court is sensitive to the appearance of conflict in selecting as the beneficiary of the fund an institution with [which it has] long-established ties" (*Schwartz v. Dallas Cowboys Football Club, Ltd.*, 362 F. Supp. 2d 574, 577 [D. Pa. 2005]). If the foregoing was correct, of course, this recipient had been chosen for that very reason, and the judge was right to be skeptical.

15. A targeted tax credit or cut is distinct and superior to a common option for cy pres, escheat of unclaimed funds to the state. Obviously, this amounts to nothing less than a 100 percent tax imposed on a plaintiff award, and it is hard to believe any plaintiff would perceive this solution as a second-best satisfaction of their preferences.

16. Unfortunately, but not surprisingly, the legislative trend is the other way. Two recent statutes on cy pres, N.C. Gen. Stat. § 1–267.10, and Calif Civ. Code § 384, make special exceptions from normal cy pres reasoning for nonprofit legal services, stating that distributions to them are to be presumptively lawful. This industry favoritism, enacted by lawyer-legislators, appears to be a classic legislative rent.

CHAPTER 12

LICENSING LAWYERS: FAILURE IN THE PROVISION OF LEGAL SERVICES

Adam B. Summers

That in every profession the fortune of every individual should depend as much as possible upon his merit, and as little as possible upon his privilege, is certainly for the interest of the public.

Adam Smith, Letter to William Cullen, September 20, 1774

INTRODUCTION

The legal profession, like so many others these days, is heavily regulated. Not just anyone can call him/herself a lawyer and offer legal services to the public. In every state in the nation, one must first obtain a license from the state. Requirements may include passing the state bar examination, membership in the state bar association, completing an approved formal legal education, paying various fees, satisfying a "moral character" determination, passing the Multistate Professional Responsibility Exam, and earning a certain minimum number of Continuing Legal Education credits after initial admission to the bar. In many states, to qualify as a lawyer, one must incur the costs of attending a law school accredited by the American Bar Association (ABA) just to be eligible to sit for the bar exam. Other regulations include restrictions on the advertisement of legal services and a general lack of reciprocity, or allowing an individual who has satisfied the licensing laws of another state to practice without retaking the bar exam and satisfying other regulations in the new state. Past regulations included total bans on advertising and mandatory minimum fee schedules for legal services.

These regulations and institutional barriers are ostensibly designed to protect consumers from substandard practitioners and preserve the reputation of the profession (feel free to insert your own lawyer joke here), but they ultimately restrict and distort the supply of attorneys, reduce competition, raise prices for legal services, reduce consumer choice, and limit access to the legal system, particularly to those with low or moderate incomes. This chapter analyzes the arguments in favor of licensing requirements and weighs them against the drawbacks of regulation. I also attempt to show how market forces in the supply of legal services, without regulations, would operate.

A Brief History of Legal Services Regulation

Lawyers in the United States were not always as heavily regulated as they are today. Attorneys first organized through voluntary local bar associations in cities and counties. During the colonial period, some local bar associations were able to impose some degree of control over who could become a lawyer, but most restrictions on the practice of law were abolished after the American Revolution, and by the time of the Civil War, "no significant restrictions remained, and several states had statutes or even constitutional provisions specifically stating that every citizen was entitled to practice law" (Leef 1998, 18). The growing political influence of the legal profession led it to push states to establish minimum education requirements for bar membership beginning in the late nineteenth century. By 1902, 27 of the 45 states had enacted such measures (Leef 1998, 18).

Over time, the concept of a unified, or integrated, bar took hold as a means of better controlling professional standards throughout an entire state's jurisdiction. This started with the unification of the North Dakota bar in 1921 (The Florida Bar 2005). Today, 33 of the country's 51 state bars (including the District of Columbia) are unified (American Bar Association 2007b).

In states with unified bars, one must be a member of the state bar association to practice law. This requirement affords these bar associations a great deal of power, including unique funding and lobbying opportunities (Barton 2007, 463). As noted in chapter 9, the involvement of the state supreme courts in bar unification—and thus the regulation of lawyers—ushered in an era of increased regulation and barriers to entry into the profession.

Unauthorized Practice of Law

The movement to prohibit "unauthorized practice of law" (UPL) took on new life beginning in 1930 when the ABA established its Committee on Unauthorized Practice of Law. Many state and local bar associations soon followed suit and began to lobby for statutes banning the "unauthorized" provision of legal services, which led to requirements that only licensed attorneys could practice law (Leef 1998, 19). UPL statutes are notoriously—and almost certainly intentionally—vague, which means that it is up to the judiciary to decide which services are the province of the legal profession and which are "unauthorized." Since judges come from the legal profession, they are predisposed to be sympathetic to the interests of lawyers seeking redress under UPL restrictions. UPL prohibitions are typically justified as a means of protecting consumers from incompetent or unscrupulous practitioners. It is necessary, proponents argue, for the profession to establish some minimum set of standards so that the public can be confident that they will receive good services from well-qualified lawyers.

But there are also strong economic motivations to restrict the entry of individuals into the profession. By limiting the number of people who can become lawyers, the profession can limit the competition for its services. It is no coincidence, for example, that the push for UPL legislation came during the onset of the Great Depression, when there was a perceived need to settle "the anxieties of lawyers about their livelihoods," and restrictions on who could provide legal services were seen as a way to preserve the profession (Christensen 1980, 214). These economic incentives, not the public interest, are the true motivation of licensing regulations. In addition, as this chapter seeks to demonstrate, even the service quality and consumer welfare arguments are highly suspect, as regulations tend to do much more harm than good to consumers.

THE ASYMMETRIC INFORMATION ARGUMENT

Some argue that because the law is so complex, and thus that the information gap between the consumer and the attorney can be so large, we must rely on members of the profession to set and enforce quality standards. The implicit supposition is that lawyers are above self-interest and that, when the needs of the client and their own needs conflict, they will always sacrifice themselves for the sake of the client. But lawyers act in their own self-interest, just as everybody else does.

The argument also implies that there are no other ways for consumers to obtain meaningful information about lawyers and the services they provide. It is just too difficult for people who do not know the law to figure these things out on their own. Yet, despite the fact that most people are not electronics engineers, they still manage to figure out which features they need when they purchase a television or DVD recorder. You may not be a computer science major, but that doesn't stop you from determining which computer and software best meet your needs. In the absence of mandatory licensing, there are numerous sources of information for consumers because there is tremendous demand for this information. There is no reason to believe things would be any different for legal services.

To say the least, the fact that lawyers effectively establish monopoly regulatory authority over their profession raises serious conflict of interest concerns and, as we shall see later, mandatory licensing tends to make consumers even *worse* off than in the absence of licensing restrictions, particularly when compared to voluntary certification.

CONFLICT OF INTEREST

Some mistakenly believe that business interests and regulation are contradictory concepts. In fact, oftentimes, quite the opposite is true. Business interests long ago learned that, like other interest groups, they could lobby politicians to use the coercive power of government to their advantage. This is known as the "capture theory" of regulation, since the private sector—in this case, attorneys—captures the regulatory enforcement powers of the government to use toward its own ends, such as rigging regulations to benefit incumbent practitioners at the expense of new (or potential) competitors. Of course, if this regulatory machine did not exist in the first place, business interests would have no recourse but to compete fairly in the market like everyone else.

Occupational licensing is especially ripe for this type of special-interest lobbying because much of the information relevant to regulated businesses or industries, such as the legal profession, is technical and politicians cannot possibly know all the intricate details of running every kind of business in every industry. Since the politicians are not experts in all the industries they regulate, they rely on those being regulated for such information (Hood 1992). Moreover, they typically leave the regulation up to a board composed mostly or entirely of those being regulated. In the case of attorneys, this role is filled by the state bar associations. Incumbent lawyers dominate the creation and enforcement of regulations because they control the licensing boards. Most licensing board members, thus, have a blatant conflict of interest.

Some argue that it is necessary to have representatives of the licensed profession on the board because lawyers, for example, best understand the business of the law and are, therefore, the best suited to regulate other lawyers. But, as economist and syndicated columnist Walter Williams (2000) counters, "with that kind of reasoning, we would have made Al Capone Attorney General—after all, who can best regulate criminals but other criminals?" In other words, lawyers might know the legal business well, but if they have the ability to use the regulatory power of government to their advantage, they might also be most likely to take advantage of the system. Or, as Benjamin Barton notes in chapter 9: "As a general rule foxes make poor custodians of henhouses."

THE MYTH OF QUALITY ASSURANCE

> I am myself persuaded that licensure has reduced both the quantity and quality of medical practice; that it has reduced the opportunities available to people who would like to be physicians, forcing them to pursue occupations they regard as less attractive; that it has forced the public to pay more for less satisfactory medical service, and that it has retarded technological development both in medicine itself and in the organization of medical practice. I conclude that licensure should be eliminated as a requirement for the practice of medicine.
> Milton Friedman, *Capitalism and Freedom* 1962 [1982], 158

While Milton Friedman's analysis was of the impact of licensing laws on the practice of medicine, it applies equally well to legal services. Despite the aforementioned conflict of interest concerns, we are assured that the legal profession must be regulated so that it can ensure a high quality of services and ethics. However, licensing's record at protecting the public is dubious at best, and often even makes things worse. A 2001 report by the Canadian Office of Fair Trading presented a summary of 15 academic studies on the effects of occupational regulation on product and service quality for a variety of professions, including law. The effect was neutral in seven cases, mixed in one case, negative in five cases, and positive in only two cases (LECG 2000, 22). In addition, a 1990 Federal Trade Commission (FTC) report titled "The Costs and Benefits of Occupational Regulation" found that occupational regulations frequently increase prices and impose significant costs on consumers without improving the quality of professional services (Cox and Foster 1990).

There are a number of reasons why the quality of legal services may actually be *diminished* by licensing requirements:

- *Less Pressure to Compete*: Since it is more difficult to work if one has to satisfy costly or time-consuming requirements to obtain a law license, fewer people will become attorneys than would exist in an unregulated world. Less competition for licensees means less pressure to offer higher quality or lower prices to attract business. Thus, licensed attorneys will be more inclined to pocket more of their profits and invest less in developing higher quality or innovative services. Since lawyers have less incentive to provide high-quality services under a regulated system, occupational licensing laws such as UPL statutes actually make consumers worse off. (Note that in a laissez-faire, license-free market, even if only some consumers shop around for high-quality legal services, this pressures sellers to maintain high quality, which benefits all consumers.) (Young 1987).
- *Improper Training Requirements*: Established standards may sound all well and good, but what if you establish the wrong standards? Conditions and required knowledge may vary from place to place and from the practice of one area of the law to the next, but with a single rigid set of standards, licensed attorneys may be forced to spend time and money gaining irrelevant knowledge and skills in law school. Moreover, highly trained lawyers must perform routine tasks that could be done by less-qualified workers at less expense to consumers, leaving them with less time to devote to honing high-quality, specialized skills.[1] Licensing, therefore, discourages specialization and makes licensees less effective and less able to serve their customers. In addition, minimum and continuing education standards force lawyers to focus narrowly on meeting arbitrary licensing requirements, which may or may not be relevant to their business and their customers' needs. This prevents them from specializing and exploring new and "unapproved" practices that might allow them to better serve their customers. Such narrow-mindedness has led some bar associations, for example, to ban low-cost legal clinics (Young, "Occupational Licensing").
- *Club Mentality*: While bar associations ardently prosecute unlicensed attorneys (regardless of whether or not there is reason to believe there is any issue of incompetence or fraud), they are typically much more hesitant

to discipline one of their own (Rhode 2002). The courts, ruled by judges who were once lawyers themselves, are similarly disinclined to dole out punishment to lawyers accused of negligent practice (Barton 2007). Making public the indiscretions of a licensed worker brings unwanted negative publicity and, like a union whistleblower, "is often viewed as disloyalty to the professional community" (Young, "Occupational Licensing"). Thus, not only are unscrupulous or incompetent licensees not punished, they are allowed to continue their work and the public is left in the dark about the hazards of doing business with them.

- *False Sense of Security*: Because of the reluctance of bar associations to discipline negligent licensees for their transgressions and the possible mismatch between licensing standards and actual practical job requirements, the state's seal of approval gives consumers a false sense of security about the competence of licensees. This causes people to be less critical, and possibly less demanding, of those with whom they do business than they otherwise would be. As an *Orange County Register* editorial observed, "Without the false sense of security licensing boards provide, consumers might be encouraged to shop more intelligently for a range of services" (*Orange County Register* 2004). Moreover, since licensing boards are not wont to punish their licensees for negligence, consumers are left even more open to abuse by licensees.

LICENSING LAWS: PROTECTING THE PUBLIC INTEREST OR SPECIAL INTERESTS?

> The truth is that legislatures and Courts have made lawyers a privileged class, and have thus given them facilities, of which they have availed themselves, for entering into combinations hostile, at least to the interests, if not to the rights, of the community—such as to keep up prices, and shut out competitors.
> Lysander Spooner, "To the Members of the Legislature of Massachusetts."
> *Worcester Republican*, August 26, 1835

If licensing laws do not serve to improve public safety and protect consumers, what purpose do they serve and how do they come to be? Whenever new legislation is passed, the discerning, pocketbook-protecting, healthily skeptical observer will always ask, "Who benefits?" While the public may not benefit from licensing laws, existing trade interests sure do. As policy analyst Jack P. McHugh (2003) observed: "The dirty little secret about state licensure is that the people who lobby for it are usually the stronger competitors of those who would be licensed. Their goal is not to protect the public, but instead to raise barriers to new competitors who might cut prices and lower profits."

Unfortunately, the history of licensing laws reveals that they are regulations born of special interests, not the public interest. Lawyers, like other workers and businesses, have a financial interest in minimizing their competition. More competition means consumers have more sellers to choose from to find a good deal, and can more easily switch from one seller to another if their standards are not met. In order to maintain and increase their customer base—and thus their profits—firms (and, by extension, their employees) are pressured to keep prices low and the quality of goods and services high. The more competition there is in the marketplace, the stronger these incentives are. If, however, businesses are able to artificially reduce their competition (not by outcompeting them with lower prices or better services, but rather by arbitrarily raising the cost of doing business and pricing them out of the market through government regulation), they will be better able to raise prices and realize greater profits.

As evidence of the artificial barriers to entry erected by licensing regulations, consider that licensing reduces the rate of job growth within an industry by 20 percent (Kleiner 2006, 146, 149). In other words, if an occupation grew by 10 percent during a given period under a government licensing regime, it would have grown by 12 percent over the same period in the absence of licensing. Since there are fewer practitioners under licensing, there is less competition, which allows the licensed practitioners to charge higher prices and earn higher wages than they otherwise could. The additional profits trade interests can achieve through licensing laws are significant. A number of studies analyzing the impact of licensing on prices and wages on various industries have shown that there is a strong correlation between occupational restrictions and higher prices for consumers (LECG 2000, 27). An analysis by Morris M. Kleiner (2006, 94, 149), AFL-CIO chair of labor policy and public affairs professor at the University of Minnesota, estimated that licensing increases earnings for a number of occupations, including lawyers, by 10 percent to 12 percent, although this may vary widely depending on the occupation and how strict the regulations are. And Mario Pagliero (2004) found that tougher licensing regulations increase the starting earnings of "new" lawyers in the United States by nearly 37 percent.

The way that licensing laws are enforced also speaks to their true purpose of establishing barriers to entry and restricting competition. Consider the following examples of UPL "violations." Rosemary Furman was a legal secretary in Florida. During 1976 and 1977, she was the owner of Northside Secretarial Services, a business that executed uncontested divorces and offered services for other straightforward legal matters, primarily to low-income women. In order to address the needs of this clientele, Furman charged no more than $50 for her services. The Florida Bar sued Furman for unauthorized practice of law in 1977. Even though the Florida Supreme Court determined that she had not advertised herself as a lawyer, had not harmed any client, and was performing a needed service for poor clients who might not otherwise be able to afford access to the legal system, it found that her activities constituted a practice of law and thus violated the state's UPL prohibition. Furman was sentenced to four months in jail in 1982, but was then pardoned by the governor.

Brian and Susan Woods also found themselves at odds with the bar when they sued the school board in Akron, Ohio, on behalf of their autistic son, Daniel, in an attempt to get the school district to adequately provide for his educational needs. They had decided to handle the case themselves after determining that they could not afford to hire an attorney. One lawyer had offered them an estimate of $60,000 for their case. After a lengthy court battle, the case was settled in 2002 when the district agreed to several concessions, including sending Daniel to a private school, and a $160,000 award. The Cleveland Bar Association responded by charging the Woodses with unauthorized practice of law and threatening them with a $10,000 fine, arguing that while the Woodses could represent themselves, they could not act as attorneys for their son. According to Mr. Woods, the bar association was trying to intimidate him in order to prevent other cases of parents representing their children, rather than paying tens of thousands of dollars in fees to lawyers. In the face of negative publicity and a slim chance of success in the courtroom (the Ohio Supreme Court had noted that it did not appear the Woodses had engaged in unauthorized practice of law and ordered the bar association to demonstrate why the case should not be dismissed), the bar eventually backed down.

VIOLATING ECONOMIC LIBERTY

> That is not a just government, nor is property secure under it, where arbitrary restrictions, exemptions, and monopolies deny to part of its citizens that free use of their faculties, and free choice of their occupations.
>
> James Madison, "Property," *National Gazette*, March 29, 1792

While occupational licensing laws are sometimes thought of as little more than a nuisance (except by those to whom they deny employment), they "infringe on one of our most precious, but oft-forgotten, civil rights: the right to engage in the occupation of one's choice without arbitrary or irrational government interference" (Keller 2003).

The importance of the ability to earn one's own living unhindered by the state and to voluntarily do business with whomever one chooses cannot be overstated. It goes to the very root of living in freedom. As economist and author Murray Rothbard (1973, 42) explained, "If a man has the right to self-ownership, to the control of his life, then in the real world he must also have the right to sustain his life by grappling with and transforming resources." In other words, if we are to have the unalienable right to life, then we must also have the right to sustain our lives through the use of our labor. Added Rothbard (1973, 28),

> Since each individual must think, learn, value, and choose his or her ends and means in order to survive and flourish, the right to self-ownership gives man the right to perform these vital activities without being hampered and restricted by coercive molestation.

The copious licensing laws on the books today in every state of the union are testament to the disdain legislators and judges alike have shown to this freedom to work. Such was not always the case, however. As noted previously, there were few licensing laws in the early days of the nation, and several states had statutes or constitutional provisions affirming every citizen's right to practice law. Federal judges once struck down state laws restricting the right to engage in one's chosen occupation without government interference with regularity. During the U.S. Supreme Court's "Lochner Era" from 1905 to 1937, for example, the high court repeatedly rebuffed state attempts to infringe upon this right (Sandefur 2002, 69).

Indeed, the federal courts have often adopted the Rothbardian notion of the right to earn a living:

- "The right to hold specific private employment and to follow a chosen profession free from unreasonable governmental interference comes within the 'liberty' and 'property' concepts of provisions of the Fifth Amendment to the Federal Constitution that no person shall be denied liberty or property without due process of law." (*Greene v. McElroy*, 360 U.S. 474, 492 [1959]).
- "[T]he Fourteenth Amendment protects an individual's right to practice a profession free from undue and unreasonable state interference...." (*Gabbert v. Conn*, 131 F.3d 793, 800–801 [CA9 1997]).
- "[T]he right to work for a living in the common occupations of the community is of the very essence of personal freedom and opportunity that it was the purpose of the [Fourteenth] Amendment to secure." (*Truax v. Corley*, 814 F.2d 223, 227 [5th Cir. 1987]).

State courts have likewise recognized this right:

- The California Supreme Court deemed the right to earn a living a "fundamental" one. (*Conway v. State Bar*, 47 Cal. 3d 1107, 1134 n. 7 [1989]).
- Texas courts have found that citizens "[have] a vested property right in making a living." (*Smith v. Decker*), (158 Tex. 416 [1958]).
- New York courts asserted: "Monopolistic restrictions on the right to earn a living are odious devices." (*Di Carlo v. State Liquor Auth.*, 54 Misc. 2d 482 [1967], at 485).
- The Florida Supreme Court held that "[t]he fundamental right to earn a livelihood in pursuing some lawful occupation is protected in the Constitution, and in fact, many authorities hold that the preservation of such right is one of the inherent or inalienable rights protected by the Constitution." (*State ex rel. Hosack v. Yocum*, 136 Fla. 246, 251 [1939]).
- The North Carolina Supreme Court found that individual liberty "does not consist simply of the right to be free of arbitrary physical restraint or servitude, but... 'includes the right of the citizen to be free to use his faculties in all lawful ways; to live and work where he will; to earn his livelihood by any lawful calling; to pursue any livelihood or vocation....' " (*State v. Balance*, 229 N.C. 764, 51S.E.2d 731, 734 [1949], quoting Am. Jur. Constitutional Law § 329).

The courts have also been rather inconsistent, however, sometimes ignoring or denying precedents that upheld the right to earn a living unfettered by government (Sandefur 2002, 88). The point is not that anyone is *entitled* to any particular job, only that everyone has the right to pursue a career of his or her choice free from government obstruction. Occupational licensing laws violate this freedom.

EFFECTS ON THE POOR

Economic regulation such as occupational licensing laws, minimum wage laws, and zoning laws tend to hurt the very people that the government purports to be "protecting" with its regulations. Such regulations disproportionately harm the poor and minorities, who generally have less work experience and fewer employment opportunities than the rest of the population. Laws that make it more difficult for them to obtain certain jobs or start their own businesses only make it that much harder for them to work their way up the economic ladder.

The poor, who are in most need of economic opportunity and who can least afford to jump through regulatory hoops, are repudiated by prohibitively costly licensing requirements. This is not to suggest that, in the absence of licensing laws, poor, unskilled workers would suddenly flood the legal profession and be qualified to provide complex legal services. But there are certain segments of the law that do not require years of expensive legal education in order to perform quality services. For these more routine legal matters, people who otherwise would not be able to afford to go to a fancy law school would be able to obtain the lesser training necessary to provide those services, affording greater employment opportunities to those with low or moderate incomes or less experience.

If the job entry restrictions were not enough, the poor are doubly hit by licensing laws since the reduced competition and higher business costs that result from licensing force them to pay higher prices for legal services, and oftentimes prohibit them from gaining access to the legal system altogether. According to the 1993 ABA Comprehensive Legal Needs Study, despite the fact that approximately half of all low- and moderate-income American households surveyed reported facing a civil legal matter, 71 percent of situations faced by low-income households and 61 percent of situations faced by moderate-income households were not addressed by the justice system. When faced with a potential legal need, 38 percent of low-income households and 26 percent of moderate-income households took no action at all. The survey revealed that cost concerns were the second most popular reason for not seeking legal assistance (behind the perception that legal assistance would not help) for low-income households, and the fourth most common reason for moderate-income households (American Bar Association 2004). As Justice Denise R. Johnson (1998, 488) argues,

> Lawyers have made themselves a scarce resource, and it is difficult to sustain the argument that the poor are being protected by not receiving any legal

advice at all. For clients who are poor, uneducated, and powerless, and who may have language and cultural barriers that distance them even farther from access to justice, an adviser with a limited range of skills or knowledge is preferable to no adviser at all.

By imposing costs on those least able to afford them, licensing laws have hurt the people and communities that need economic liberty the most. Rather than discouraging entrepreneurship and locking the poor out of the labor market, government should focus on reducing poverty and improving citizens' quality of life by simply getting out of the way and removing the barriers it has erected to economic freedom.

REGULATING BUSINESS PRACTICES

UPL statutes are hardly the only restrictions placed on those wishing to practice law. There are numerous regulations on their business practices as well. Chief among these were the establishment of mandatory minimum fee schedules, the restriction—and even outright prohibition—on advertising and client solicitation, and strict rules regarding client referrals. It was not until the 1970s that these restrictions began to be relaxed.

Mandatory Minimum Fee Schedules

There was never any real pretense about the minimum price lists enforced by the bar associations. Their purpose was simply economic protectionism. The Virginia State Bar, for example, supported the schedules on the grounds that through competition "lawyers have been slowly, but surely committing economic suicide" (Virginia State Bar 1962, 3, App. 20). In 1975, the U.S. Supreme Court put an end to the restrictions when it ruled in its *Goldfarb v. Virginia State Bar* (421 U.S. 773 [1975]) decision that the imposition of minimum price lists by state bar associations constituted a violation of the Sherman Antitrust Act.

Advertising Restrictions

Contrary to minimum fee schedules, advertising restrictions were purportedly justified in the name of protecting the consumer. The naked commercialization and solicitation of business were seen as unprofessional and unseemly and a general ban on advertising remained in effect between 1908 and 1977 (Lang and Marks 1980). That never seemed to stop lawyers from networking with high net worth potential clients on the golf course or in other social settings, however. As attorney David W. Singer argues,

> It's so hypocritical. These guys market at the country club but they call marketing on television crass and demeaning to the profession. You see tasteless advertisements, yeah, maybe for a while, but the marketplace will induce those lawyers to pull those ads because they won't be effective. (Ballard 2002)

A victory for competition in the legal services market came in 1977 in the form of the 5–4 Supreme Court decision in *Bates v. State Bar of Arizona* (433 U.S. 350 [1977]) that state prohibitions on the advertisement of legal services violated lawyers' freedom of speech, so long as the advertisements were not false or deceptive. John R. Bates and Van O'Steen had had the gall to set up a low-cost legal clinic in Arizona in 1974. Since the legal services to be provided were designed to serve those with low or moderate incomes who did not qualify for government-funded legal aid, profit margins were very small. Bates and O'Steen thus needed a lot of clients to make a living and saw advertising as the answer, so they placed an advertisement for the clinic in the *Arizona Republic*. As O'Steen recalls, "We said we expected that consumer-based law firms would grow much larger, thereby opening the legal system to people who otherwise have no access and that growth would be based on advertising. And that has happened" (Ballard 2002).

Advertising restrictions did not end immediately with the *Bates* decision, however. Legal attacks on *Bates* continued for two decades and states maintained some limitations on advertising. According to the U.S. Federal Trade Commission (FTC),

> By 1980, 23 of the 50 states restricted the geographical scope of lawyer advertising (thus effectively prohibiting national advertising), seven prohibited the advertising of contingency fees (a system commonly used in personal injury cases where a lawyer accepts a percentage of whatever money is recovered as a fee in lieu of an hourly or fixed rate), 25 insisted that advertisements be dignified, 36 prohibited the use of trade names, and 15 prohibited television advertising. (U.S. Federal Trade Commission 2004, 8)

A 1984 FTC study (Jacobs et al. 1984) analyzed the impact of advertising restrictions on the price and quality of legal services. It found that the costs of legal services such as personal injury, divorces, bankruptcies, and simple wills were significantly higher in states that restricted advertising. Moreover, empirical evidence demonstrated that advertising did not necessarily reduce service quality, and the report noted that increased competition should lead to improved service quality as well as lower prices. A 1980 study (Bond et al. 1980) found that advertising restrictions alone resulted in price increases between 5 percent and 11 percent. Furthermore, the relaxation of advertising restrictions in the United States has been shown to facilitate the growth of alternate service providers and possibly increase demand for some kinds of legal services (Andrews 1980).

Not only does advertising lead to greater competition, lower prices, and, in the case of patrons of low-cost clinics, increased access to the legal system, it also provides consumers with valuable information about the qualifications of attorneys and the kinds of legal services available to them. Even the ABA now recognizes that "policies that restrict lawyers' ability to market have the concomitant effect of diminishing the information that is available to the public about their options for obtaining legal services" (American Bar Association 2003).

LACK OF RECIPROCITY

Controls over the mobility of labor in the market for legal services are another means of reducing competition and the supply of attorneys. This is due primarily to a lack of reciprocity, or the recognition of the license of an attorney from another state without requiring him or her to pass the local state's bar examination. Many large states refuse to offer reciprocity, so it is seldom used.

By making it difficult for lawyers to move from one jurisdiction to another without having to jump through a whole new set of regulatory hoops, the profession suppresses the number of people entering the practice of law. This form of cartelization produces predictable results: less competition and higher prices. According to an analysis of occupational restrictions on lawyers by FTC economist Steven Tenn (2000), low rates of interstate immigration and emigration, a common effect of licensing, were associated with higher wages.

These restrictions are not limited to differing licensing requirements from one state to the next. The rules on foreign attorneys (and other professionals) practicing in the United States are a significant burden as well. As economist Dean Baker (2006, 19), co-director of the Center for Economic and Policy Research, explains,

> Trade pacts have done little or nothing to remove the extensive licensing and professional barriers that prevent foreign doctors, lawyers, economists, and journalists from competing on equal footing with their counterparts in the United States.... If U.S. trade negotiators approached the highly paid professions in the same way they approached the auto industry...they would be asking the trade negotiators from Mexico, India, or China what obstacles prevent them from sending hundreds of thousands of highly skilled professionals to the United States.

THE PROBLEM WITH LAW SCHOOLS (ABA ACCREDITATION STANDARDS)

The occupational regulation of lawyers starts long before one sits down to take the bar exam. It starts with legal education. Here, too, the ABA exerts strong and rigid control over the standards of the profession. In most states, one must attend an ABA-accredited law school to even be eligible to take the bar examination (American Bar Association 2007a, 6), and the ABA's Council of the Section of Legal Education and Admissions to the Bar is the only national accrediting organization for law schools (U.S. Department of Justice 2006).

This structure has allowed the ABA to dictate everything from the three-year length of law school programs to course offerings, to tenure and other standards for faculty, to the requirement that law schools be nonprofit, to the number and kind of volumes that must be housed in a school's law library. In 1995, the Department of Justice filed an antitrust suit against the ABA alleging that the ABA's law school accreditation process had been misused by law school personnel with a direct economic interest in the outcome of accreditation reviews, resulting in anticompetitive conduct. The following year, the U.S. District Court for the District of Columbia "entered an agreed-upon final judgment prohibiting the ABA from fixing faculty salaries and compensation, boycotting state-accredited law schools by restricting the ability of their students and graduates to enroll in ABA-approved schools, and boycotting for-profit law schools" (U.S. Department of Justice 2006).

California is an interesting example of lawyer regulation. Unlike many states, California does not require the aspiring lawyer to attend an ABA-approved law school to sit for the bar examination. On the other hand, the state's grueling, three-day-long bar exam is widely considered the most difficult in the nation. For the past 10 years, the pass rate has been less than 50 percent. In a comment posted in response to a *Wall Street Journal* article on occupational licensing (Fund 2007), a California attorney describes his frustration with the ABA's control over legal education standards and the effect of these restrictions on competition:

> I'm a lawyer with 12 years of unblemished practice in California. Because I attended a California State Bar-approved law school and not an American Bar Association law school, I am not even permitted to sit for the bar examination in some 20 states, including Utah, where I would like to live. In California, there are many lawyers who would like to unlicense those thousands of us who didn't attend ABA-approved law schools. The practice of limiting competition exists in many forms and hearts, not just with the regulators.

The ABA's monopoly power and micromanagement strongly discourages experimentation and innovation in the provision of legal education. As Rachel F. Moran (2006, 383), UC Irvine law school professor and president of the Association of American Law Schools, observes of the current state of legal education,

> The dominant paradigm is one of cooperation rather than competition. In fact, norms of uniformity and standardization have dominated the world of legal education, substantially limiting law schools' ability to compete against one another.... Given this framework of comprehensive rules and regulations, no law school has been able to pursue radical innovations without jeopardizing its accreditation, its reputation, and its future. In a world of highly constrained competition, schools have few ways to improve their standing through strategies that upset the prevailing wisdom about how best to deliver legal educa-tion.... With full-bodied competition curbed by the accreditation process, schools rely on gaming to influence the [*U.S. News & World Report* law school] rankings rather than strike out in novel directions to gain prominence.

Who is to say, for example, that a three-year formal education is the proper amount of training? And for whom? Surely, certain areas and specializations require less formal training than others. Depending on what aspects of the law one intends to practice, some may need the benefit of extensive class-room training, while others will get most of their training on the job. An open market for legal education would allow for all of these disparate needs to be met.

Then there is the issue of the content of the legal instruction. While law schools provide a solid overview of jurisprudence, major legal decisions, and legal research and writing, as well as elective courses, this broad introduction to the law does not necessarily mean that a law school graduate is highly qualified to practice the law. After all, law schools are designed primarily to teach students how to pass their bar examinations, not necessarily to instruct them in the practical knowledge germane to their future lines of work. Even the ABA concedes this point:

> While the profession has moved away from "apprenticeship" programs, it is widely acknowledged that current forms of legal education do not adequately prepare graduates to immediately enter the practice of law. Large firms, accepting this reality, have created a system whereby new associates are gradually given higher levels of responsibility as they develop their real-world skills. But there is no analogous system in the solo and small firm community of personal legal services lawyers. (American Bar Association 2003)

Law school curricula rarely address many of the areas of the law needed most by those with low or moderate incomes. For example, "[s]chools do not generally teach, and bar exams do not test, ability to complete routine forms for divorces, landlord-tenant disputes, bankruptcy, immigration, welfare claims, tax preparation, and real estate transactions" (Rhode 1996, 709). The fact is most of a lawyer's necessary training will be provided through real-world experience on the job. Moreover, laws and the demands for legal services change. Where there is no competition and no real consumer choice (in this case, the choice of prospective law students), there is no way to adapt to these changes and there can be no discovery of the optimal set of legal education services to be provided.

Before the ABA gained such control over the law schools, there were many education options for aspiring attorneys. Some lawyers, like Abraham Lincoln, were self-taught. Others, like Clarence Darrow, learned by serving as apprentices to practicing lawyers. Those seeking a more formal education could choose from full-time and part-time schools that offered instructional programs ranging from one year to three years (Leef 1998, 18, 24). The fact that "very few law schools offered three-year programs before they were mandated is evidence that the mandate is inefficient. It compels what is for many an overinvestment in legal education" (Leef 1998, 28).

Thus, not only do the high costs and lengthy program requirements of law schools restrict the supply of lawyers, they further distort supply by forcing many to undertake more legal education than necessary. This encourages students to pursue those areas of the law (such as corporate law) where law school credentials are held in especially high esteem, and neglect more routine services that require lesser formal education.

None of this would be so serious a problem if not for the ABA's virtual monopoly on legal education. If the market for legal education were truly free and ABA accreditation standards were not mandatory, law schools not meeting the demands of the public and aspiring law students would be forced to adapt their standards and programs of instruction or else lose their business to new rival schools that would meet these needs. As was the case before ABA control of the law schools, various programs of instruction would arise to meet varying needs and career paths. Similarly, it is fine for the state bar associations to offer a bar examination and establish their own standards for admission to their organization, but they should not be the sole standard-setters within their jurisdictions and membership should be voluntary.

THE ALTERNATIVE: PRIVATE CERTIFICATION

The belief that consumers are left unprotected if the government does not step in to regulate is a common misconception. In fact, the private sector does at least as good a job as the government in protecting consumers. Skeptics tend to neglect two crucial elements that serve to protect consumers and encourage the delivery of high-quality products: business reputation and a legal system that consistently protects property rights.

The significance of the reputation of a business or a worker cannot be overstated. Reputation is perhaps the most important, and least discussed, aspect of doing business. What would happen for example, if certain state governments stopped licensing exterminators, chiropractors, and barbers? Would people be living in bug-infested dwellings and running around with bad backs and bad haircuts? Of course not. People would find a way to manage without government regulation. When looking for a place to get your hair cut, you probably just ask your friends for a good referral. As it turns out, legal services are not all that different. According to an ABA survey, approximately one-third of people seeking a lawyer did so on the recommendation of a friend, and an additional one-third already knew a lawyer (American Bar Association 2004). Herein lies the function of the free market: businesses have an incentive to provide the goods and services customers want at the best possible price and quality. Bad service is just as much a killer for business as high prices (Summers 2004, 32).

Word of mouth is not the only means of assessing a business's reputation, however. Private certification organizations also provide consumers with information about the product and service quality they can expect from certain sellers. There are a couple of different ways to provide such an evaluation. One model is to simply use the reputation of the certifying organization to determine whether or not a product is "good." Since some certification organizations may be better than others, this determination may vary. Again, competition here is beneficial to the consumer, as it leads to more informed valuations of the quality of legal services. The ABA can certainly continue to certify law schools, and the state and local bar associations can continue to establish standards for those members who decide to join them, but they should not be the only ones to set the standards. Competition among various rating agencies will lead them to try to outdo each other by providing the most accurate information and establishing higher standards for certification.

A second certification model allows for different levels of quality. Walter Williams (2000) explains the process as follows: "A person can take a test—if he scores a 90, he has the right to declare himself a 'class A' practitioner; if he scores an 80, he has the right to call himself 'class B.' Such a method would give consumers information about quality while leaving them free to choose." Unlike the single standard—predetermined by the government—of occupational licensing, these multiple standards provide a greater array of information to consumers and allow them to make better decisions based on their individual quality, price, and risk preferences.[2]

Where government (compulsory) certification restricts the number of practitioners, voluntary certification actually increases it. In a study on the effects of occupational regulation on service quality, Sidney L. Carroll and Robert J. Gaston (1981, 970) observed: "certification (voluntary licensing) seems to increase the number of licenses compared to both no licensing and compulsory licensing." Rather than shying away from unnecessary and overly burdensome state-imposed requirements, practitioners are eager to obtain reasonable and relevant certifications to signal to customers that they provide high-quality services.

State bar associations are already offering board certification for attorneys wishing to demonstrate expertise in various areas of the law. Why not just make such voluntary certification the standard for all types of law?

The existence of so many consumer organizations and businesses that provide information about products and businesses is a testament to the success of private certification. The Better Business Bureau enforces quality standards on its member businesses and charitable organizations and allows consumers to register complaints or view reports of past complaints and their outcomes. It will even act as a mediator to try to resolve disputes between customers and member businesses. Underwriters Laboratories offers private certification for numerous consumer products, including medical appliances, automotive products, electrical appliances, chemicals, and alarm systems. *Good Housekeeping* magazine awards its Good Housekeeping Seal of Approval to products advertised in the magazine only after extensive quality testing by the Good Housekeeping Research Institute, and it offers consumers a two-year warranty on products that have earned the Seal (*Good Housekeeping*, "About the Good Housekeeping Seal"). *Consumer Reports* has developed a business around providing customers with accurate information and sound reviews on a wide variety of products—from cars to computers to travel arrangements to home appliances. Industry groups such as the American Dental Association also certify consumer products.

Within the legal profession, the American Arbitration Association (AAA) serves as a private resource for those looking to avoid costly and time-consuming litigation. The AAA offers alternative dispute resolution (ADR) services such as arbitration and mediation, as well as ADR training and education services, and the design and development of ADR systems for corporations, unions, government agencies, law firms, and the courts. It maintains a roster of over 7,000 arbitrators and mediators located throughout the world, who must undergo the organization's screening and training process. The organization has established its own Code of Ethics, as well as Rules and Procedures tailored to arbitrations and mediations for different types of cases, including commercial, consumer, employment, and labor rules (American Arbitration Association). The AAA is but one of a number of private ADR organizations, not to mention numerous individual arbitrators and mediators offering their dispute resolution services.

As with barbers, consumer electronics product dealers, and attorneys, arbitrators rely heavily on their reputations in order to make a living. An arbitrator must maintain a reputation of neutrality, fairness, and good judgment if he is to attract clients. This added market incentive may make arbitrators better adjudicators than judges in government-controlled legal institutions.[3] As legal philosopher Lon Fuller (1981, 110–111) reasons, "Being unbacked by state power...the arbitrator must concern himself directly with the acceptability of his award. He may be at greater pains than a judge to get his facts straight, to state accurately the arguments of the parties, and generally to display in his award a full understanding of the case." Or, to put it more bluntly, "A free-market arbiter depends for his livelihood on his skill and fairness at settling disputes. A governmental judge depends on political pull" (Tannehill and Tannehill 1970, 67).

Market incentives for private ADR are also superior to the incentives of public courts in the area of innovation. Since private providers of dispute resolution services have strong incentives to minimize costs and maximize profits if they want to stay in business—and the courts do not—they are prone to experimentation to best serve the differing needs of their clients (Caplan and Stringham 2007, Hadfield 2006). Private-sector providers have a large advantage over the courts here because their decentralized nature means that numerous private providers can simultaneously offer a wide variety of services and the cost of a failed product is relatively low. The public nature of the courts, however, means that any experimentation or change in the system applies to everyone, so failure costs are extremely high (Caplan and Stringham 2007, 14–16). Moreover, even private-sector attorneys are limited in their ability to develop and offer innovative legal services by the shackles of professional regulation. According to University of Southern California law and economics professor Gillian K. Hadfield (2008, 141),

> Professional regulation limits what may be offered as a legal product or service, homogenizes the pool of potential innovators in terms of training and risk-orientation, prohibits the corporate practice of law, severely restricts the available financing for large-scale legal ventures and constrains the capacity to exploit economies of scope and scale in developing better methods of producing what business clients ultimately need.

Despite market incentives and the efforts of certifying organizations, there will always be cases of worker negligence. But legal malpractice occurs already under the current licensing scheme. When consumers are harmed by poor workmanship, faulty products, or dishonest businessmen, the courts serve as a final resort to ensure that the consumer is compensated for the harm done. If all else fails, the legal system provides an additional incentive for businesses to provide high-quality goods and services. If you are injured by a defective product, you can sue the manufacturer for negligence and perhaps fraud. If the stigma of being tried and convicted for selling faulty products is not enough to deter shady business practices, the economic effects of a guilty verdict certainly are. Any company foolish enough to hawk faulty and dangerous goods would quickly be put out of business by legal judgments (Summers 2004, 32–33). And any attorney who consistently provides shoddy legal services can expect the need to find a new line of work.

CONCLUSIONS

While occupational licensing regulations and unauthorized practice of law statutes are billed as a means of protecting the public from negligent, unqualified, or otherwise substandard practitioners, in reality, they are simply a means of using government regulation to serve narrow economic interests. Numerous studies have revealed little, if any, improvement in service quality from compulsory licensing. Oftentimes, licensing laws actually *reduce* service quality, as consumers make decisions based on a false sense of security regarding a licensee's state- or bar-association-sanctioned qualifications, and the artificially high prices caused by licensing causes more people to perform their own legal services that they may not be qualified to undertake, or forego legal action altogether when it is called for.

Some have argued that because the law is so complex, and the gap between the consumer's and attorney's knowledge of the law is so great, we must have other lawyers determine and enforce proper quality standards. Besides being incredibly paternalistic, this notion ignores the fact that people are constantly purchasing products and services of which they initially have no specialized knowledge and finding ways to inform themselves. So long as there is demand for such information, it will be provided in a free market.

Unauthorized practice of law prohibitions, regulations on business practices such as advertising restrictions, the lack of reciprocity agreements among jurisdictions, and the virtual monopoly control of legal education by the ABA are designed not to protect consumers, but rather to protect existing business interests from competition. This suppression of competition damages the business climate, stifles innovation, and allows licensed lawyers to charge higher fees for services than they would be able to in a truly free market.

Regulatory barriers to entry deny many the freedom and opportunity to earn an honest living in the occupation of their choosing. It is not only would-be workers and entrepreneurs who are hurt by licensing laws, however. The rigid, one-size-fits-all standards imposed by the government (and supported by state bar associations) also harm consumers by reducing consumer choice. Individuals have different wants and needs, and even different levels of risk tolerance. They are better able to determine their own needs and protect their own interests than politicians or bureaucrats far removed in the halls of the state capitol or city hall. In the event of someone being taken advantage of or otherwise wronged by a dishonest or incompetent lawyer, the courts are available to punish wrongdoers and make the victims whole.

In light of the enormous economic losses to society inflicted by occupational licensing regulations, and the destructive effects these laws have on consumers and aspiring lawyers—not to mention individual liberty in general—*UPL statutes and other mandatory licensing regulations should be abolished.* Private-sector alternatives such as voluntary certification and reputational information would allow consumers to obtain valuable information about attorneys and legal services while leaving them free to choose to do business with those who best meet their needs. In a true free market for legal services, one could expect greater specialization, more low-cost legal clinics, and more innovative forms of alternative dispute resolution, such as expanded use of arbitration and mediation services. The powerful free-market incentive to maintain a solid business reputation and the existence of the legal system to address malpractice or other wrongdoing are all that is needed to protect consumers.

NOTES

1. The emergence of the paralegal field and companies that provide low-cost legal document services for routine, uncontested matters such as divorce, real estate, bankruptcy, and wills has mitigated this somewhat, but imagine how much more specialization (and the resulting lower prices for consumers) would occur in the absence of strict licensing laws.
2. For a more detailed discussion and analysis of the role and importance of reputation in business and social relations, particularly in the absence of governmental regulation, see Daniel B. Klein, ed., *Reputation: Studies in the Voluntary Elicitation of Good Conduct* (Ann Arbor, MI: University of Michigan Press, 1997).
3. For more on the history and success of private arbitration, see Bruce L. Benson, "How to Secede in Business Without Really Leaving: Evidence of the Substitution of Arbitration for Litigation," in *Secession, State and Liberty*, ed. David Gordon, (New Brunswick, NJ: Transaction Publishers, 1998); Bruce L. Benson, "Arbitration," in *Encyclopedia of Law and Economics, Vol. 5*, ed. Boudewijn Bouckaert and Gerrit De Geest, (Cheltenham, UK: Edward Elgar, 2000), 159–193; Bryan Caplan and Edward P. Stringham, *Privatizing the Adjudication of Disputes*, Independent Institute Working Paper Number 69, October 17, 2007, http://www.independent.org/pdf/working_papers/69_private.pdf (accessed February 3, 2010); and Murray N. Rothbard, "Society Without a State," Speech before the American Society for Political and Legal Philosophy, Washington, D.C., December 28, 1974, available online at http://mises.org/story/2429 (accessed February 3, 2010).

BIBLIOGRAPHY

CHAPTER 1

Baumol, William J. 2002. *The Free Market Innovation Machine*. Princeton, NJ: Princeton University Press.

Benson, Bruce. 1990. *The Enterprise of Law: Justice without the State*. San Francisco, CA: Pacific Research Institute.

———. 2005. The Mythology of Holdout as Justification for Eminent Domain and Public Provision of Roads. *The Independent Review*, 10(2): 165–194.

Bebchuk, Lucian Arye, Jesse M. Fried, and David I. Walter. 2002. Managerial Power and Rent Extraction in the Design of Executive Compensation, NBER Working Paper No. 9068.

Boettke, Peter J., Christopher J. Coyne, and Peter T. Leeson. 2007. Saving Government Failure Theory from Itself: Recasting Political Economy from an Austrian Perspective. *Constitutional Political Economy*, 127–143.

Buchanan, James M. 1979 [1999]. Politics without Romance, in *The Collected Works of James M. Buchanan*, vol. 1, *The Logical Foundations of Constitutional Liberty*, 45–59. Indianapolis, IN: Liberty Fund.

———. 2003. What Is Public Choice Theory? *Economics Education Bulletin*, XLIII(5): 1–4.

———. 2005. Three Amendments: Responsibility, Generality, and Natural Liberty. *Cato Unbound*, 1, December (www.catounbound.org).

Caplan, Bryan. 2007. *The Myth of the Rational Voter*. Princeton, NJ: Princeton University Press.

Cole, Daniel H. and Peter Z. Grossman. 2005. *Principles of Law and Economics*. Englewood Cliffs, NJ: Prentice-Hall.

Cooter, Robert and Thomas Uhlen. 2004. *Law and Economics*, 4th Ed. Boston, MA: Addison-Wesley.

Cowen, Tyler. 2005. Self-deception as the Root of Political Failure. *Public Choice*, 124(3/4): 437–451.

Dixit, Avinash. 2004. *Lawlessness and Economics: Alternative Modes of Governance*. Princeton, NJ: Princeton University Press.

Ellickson, Robert. 1991. *Order without Law: How Neighbors Settle Disputes*. Cambridge, MA: Harvard University Press.

Farmer, Amy and Paul Pecorino. 1999. Legal Expenditure as a Rent Seeking Game. *Public Choice*, 100: 271–288.

Greif, Avner. 2008. Contract Enforcement and Institutions among the Maghribi Traders: Refuting Edwards and Ogilvie, manuscript available online at http://ssrn.com/abstract=1153826. Accessed September 1, 2008.

Hanssen, F. Andrew. 2002. On the Politics of Judicial Selection: Lawyers and State Campaigns for the Merit Plan. *Public Choice*, 110(1–2): 79–97.

Helland, Eric and Alexander Tabarrok. 2003. Race, Poverty, and American Tort Awards: Evidence from Three Data Sets. *Journal of Legal Studies*, 32: 27–58.

———. 2005. *Judge and Jury: American Tort Law on Trial*. Oakland, CA: The Independent Institute.

Hummell, Jeffrey Rogers. 1996. *Emancipating Slaves, Enslaving Free Men*. Chicago, IL: Open Court.

Lopéz, Edward J. R. Todd Jewell, and Noel D. Campbell. 2009. Pass a Law, Any Law, Fast! State Legislative Responses to the *Kelo* Backlash," *Review of Law & Economics* 5(1), 101–135.

Mansfield, Harvey C. 1998. *The Prince by Niccoló Machiavelli*. Translated and with an Introduction by Harvey C. Mansfield, 2nd ed. Chicago, IL: University of Chicago Press.

McChesney, Fred S. 1987. Rent Extraction and Rent Creation in the Economic Theory of Regulation. *Journal of Legal Studies*, 16: 101.

———. 1997. *Money for Nothing: Politicians, Rent Extraction, and Political Extortion*. Cambridge, MA: Harvard University Press.

Mueller, Dennis C. 1989. *Public Choice II*. Cambridge, MA: Cambridge University Press.

Mulherin, J. Harold. 2005. Corporations, Collective Action, and Corporate Governance: One Size Does Not Fit All. *Public Choice*, 124(1/2): 179–204.

North, Douglass C. and Barry R. Weingast. 1989. Constitutions and Commitment: The Evolution of Institutions Governing Public Choice in Seventeenth Century England. *Journal of Economic History*, XLIS (4) (December): 803–832.

Olson, Walter K. 2003. *The Rule of Lawyers: How the New Litigation Elite Threatens America's Rule of Law*. New York: St. Martin Press.

Osborne, Evan. 2002. What's Yours Is Mine: Rent Seeking and the Common Law. *Public Choice*, 111: 399–415.

Pincione, Guido and Fernando R. Tesón. 2006. *Rational Choice and Democratic Deliberation*. Cambridge, MA: Cambridge University Press.

Pipes, Richard. 1999. *Property and Freedom*. New York: Knopf.

Posner, Richard S. 1988. *Economic Analysis of the Law*. Chicago, IL: University of Chicago Press.

Reksulak, William F. Shughart, and Robert D. Tollison. 2004. Economics and English: Language Growth in Economic Perspective. *Southern Economic Journal*, 71(2): 232–259.

Rubenfeld, Jed. 1993. Usings. *Yale Law Review*, 102(5)(March): 1077–1163.

Rubin, Paul H. 2005. Public Choice and Tort Reform. *Public Choice*, 124(1–2): 223–236.

Rubin, Paul H., Christopher Curran, John F. Curran. 2001. Litigation versus Legislation: Forum Shopping by Rent Seekers. *Public Choice*, 107: 295–310.

Shughart, William F. and Robert D. Tollison. 2005. The Unfinished Business of Public Choice. *Public Choice*. 124(1/2): 237–247.

Tabarrok, Alexander and Eric J. Helland. 1999. Court Politics: The Political Economy of Tort Awards. *Journal of Law and Economics*, XLII:157–188.

Tullock, Gordon. 1975. The Transitional Gains Trap. *Bell Journal of Economics*, 6(2): 671–678.

Wagner, Richard. 2004. Meddlesome Preferences and Rent Extraction: The Tobacco Shakedown, in Charles K. Rowley (ed.). *The Encyclopedia of Public Choice,* Kluwer Academic Press, 378.

CHAPTER 2

Alexander, Michael. 2002. *A History of Old English Literature.* Ontario: Broadview Press.

Anderson, Terry and P. J. Hill. 1979. An American Experiment in Anarcho-Capitalism: The *Not* So Wild, Wild, West. *Journal of Libertarian Studies,* 3: 9–29.

Axlerod, Robert. 1984. *The Evolution of Cooperation.* New York: Basic Books.

Barnett, Randy E. 1998. *The Structure of Liberty.* Oxford: Oxford University Press.

Benson, Bruce L. 1989. The Spontaneous Evolution of Commercial Law. *Southern Economic Journal,* 55(January): 644–661.

———. 1990. *The Enterprise of Law: Justice Without the State.* San Francisco, CA: Pacific Research Institute for Public Policy.

———. 1991. Reciprocal Exchange as the Basis for Recognition of Law: Examples from American History. *Journal of Libertarian Studies.* 10(Fall): 53–82.

———. 1994. Are Public Goods Really Common Pools? Considerations of the Evolution of Policing and Highways in England. *Economic Inquiry,* 32(April): 294–271.

———. 1998. *To Serve and Protect: Privatization and Community in Criminal Justice.* New York: New York University Press for The Independent Institute.

Berman, Harold J. 1983. *Law and Revolution: The Formation of the Western Legal Tradition.* Cambridge, MA: Harvard University Press.

Blair, Peter Hunter. 2003. *An Introduction to Anglo-Saxon England,* 3rd ed. Cambridge, UK: Cambridge University Press. Cambridge University Press for The Independent Institute.

Brubaker, Earl R. 1988. Free Ride, Free Revelation, or Golden Rule? in Tyler Cowen, (ed.). *The Theory of Market Failure,* 93–110. Fairfax, VA: George Mason University Press.

Buchanan, James M. 1975. *The Limits of Liberty.* Chicago, IL: University of Chicago Press.

———. 1999. Politics without Romance, in *The Collected Works of James M. Buchanan,* vol. 1, *The Logical Foundations of Constitutional Liberty,* 45–59. Indianapolis, IN: Liberty Fund.

———. 2004. Heraclitian Vespers, in J. Pitt, D. Salehi-Isfahami, and D. Echel (ed.). *The Production and Diffusion of Public Choice Policy Economy,* 263–271. Malden, MA: Blackwell Publishing.

Buchanan, James M. and Gordon Tullock. 1962. *The Calculus of Consent: Logical Foundations of Constitutional Democracy.* Ann Arbor, MI: University of Michigan.

Cam, Helen Maud. 1963. *The Hundred and the Hundred Rolls.* London: Merlin Press.

Caplan, Bryan and Edward Stringham. 2005. Mises, Bastiat, Public Opinion, and Public Choice. *Review of Political Economy,* 17(1): 79–105.

———. 2008. Privatizing the Adjudication of Disputes. *Theoretical Inquiries in Law* 9(2): 503–528.

Coase, Ronald. 1974. The Lighthouse in Economics. *Journal of Law and Economics,* 17(October): 357–376.

De Jasay, Anthony. 1989. *Social Contract, Free Ride: A Study of the Public Goods Problem*. Oxford: Clarendon Press.

Dixit, Avinash K. 2004. *Lawlessness and Economics: Alternative Modes of Governance*. Princeton, NJ: Princeton University Press.

Ekelund, Robert and Cheryl Dorton. 2003. Criminal Justice Institutions as a Common Pool: The 19th Century Analysis of Edwin Chadwick. *Journal of Economic Behavior and Organization*, 50: 271–294.

Ellickson, Robert C. 1991. *Order without Law: How Neighbors Settle Disputes*. Cambridge, MA: Harvard University Press.

Foreign Policy and the Fund for Peace. 2007. *2007 Failed State Index*, available online at http://www.fundforpeace.org/web/index.php?option=com_content&task=view&id=229&Itemid=366.

Friedman, David. 1979. Private Creation and Enforcement of Law: A Historical Case. *Journal of Legal Studies*, 8(March): 399–415.

———. 1989. *The Machinery of Freedom: Guide to a Radical Capitalism*, 2nd ed. La Salle, IL: Open Court.

———. 1994a. A Positive Account of Property Rights. *Social Philosophy and Policy*, 11: 1–16.

———. 1994b. Law as a Private Good: A Response to Tyler Cowen on the Economics of Anarchy. *Economics and Philosophy*, 10: 319–327.

Fuller, Lon L. 1964 (rev ed.). *The Morality of Law*. New Haven, CT: Yale University Press.

Goldin, Kenneth S. 1988. Equal Access vs. Selective Access: A Critique of Public Goods Theory, in Tyler Cowen (ed.). *The Theory of Market Failure*, 69–92. Fairfax, VA: George Mason University Press.

Grief, Avner. 1989. Reputation and Coalitions in Medieval Trade: Evidence from the Geniza Documents. *Journal of Economic History*, 49(4): 857–882.

———. 1994. Cultural Beliefs and the Organization of Society: A Historical and Theoretical Reflection on Collectivist and Individualist Societies. *Journal of Political Economy*, 102: 912–950.

Gunning, Patrick. 1972. Towards a Theory of the Evolution of Government, in Gordon Tullock (ed.). *Explorations in the Theory of Anarchy*, 19–25. Blacksburg, VA: Center for the Study of Public Choice.

Hasnas, John. 2008. The Obviousness of Anarchy in Roderick T. Long and Tibor R. Machan (eds.) *Anarchism/Minarchism: Is a Government Part of a Free Country*. Burlington, VT: Ashgate Publishing Company.

Holcombe, Randall G. 2007. Is Government Inevitable? Reply to Leeson and Stringham. *The Independent Review*, 9(4): 551–557.

———. 1997. A Theory of the Theory of Public Goods. *Review of Austrian Economics*, 10(1): 1–22.

Hummel, Jeffrey Rogers. 2001. The Will to Be Free: The Role of Ideology in National Defense. *The Independent Review*, 5(4): 523–537.

Lacey, Robert and Danny Danziger. 1999. *The Year 1000: What Life Was Like at the Turn of the First Millenium*. Boston, MA: Little, Brown.

Landa, Janet T. 1981. A Theory of the Ethnically Homogenous Middlemen Group: An Institutional Alternative to Contract Law. *Journal of Legal Studies*, 10(2): 349–362.

Laster, Richard E. 1970. Criminal Restitution: A Survey of Its Past History and an Analysis of Its Present Usefulness. *University of Richmond Law Review*, 5: 71–80.

Leeson, Peter T. 2006. Cooperation and Conflict: Evidence on Self-Enforcing Arrangements and Heterogeneous Groups. *American Journal of Economics and Sociology*, 65(4): 891–907.

———. 2007a. An-*arrgh*-chy: The Law and Economics of Pirate Organization. *Journal of Political Economy*, 115(6): 1049–1094.

———. 2007b. The Laws of Lawlessness, Working Paper. George Mason University.

———. 2007c. Trading with Bandits. *Journal of Law and Economics*, 50(2): 303–321.

———. 2008a. How Important Is State Enforcement for Trade? *American Law and Economics Review*, 10(1): 61–89.

———. 2008b. Social Distance and Self-Enforcing Exchange. *Journal of Legal Studies*, 37(1): 161–188.

Leeson, Peter T. and Edward Stringham. 2005. Is Government Inevitable? *The Independent Review*, 9(4): 543–549.

Liggio, Leonard P. 1977. The Transportation of Criminals: A Brief Political-Economic History, in Randy E. Barnett and John Hagel III (ed.). *Assessing the Criminal: Restitution, Retribution, and the Legal Process*, 274–294. Cambridge MA: Ballinger Press.

Little, Peter. 2003. *Somalia: Economy without State*. Bloomington, IN: Indiana University Press.

Loyn, H. R. 1984. *The Governance of Anglo-Saxon England, 500–1087*. Stanford, CA: Stanford University Press.

Lyon, Bruce. 1980. *A Constitutional and Legal History of Medieval England*, 2nd ed. New York: W.W. Norton.

Macaulay, Stewart. 1963. Non-Contractual Relationships in Business: A Preliminary Study. *American Sociological Review*, 28: 55–70.

Milgrom, Paul R., Douglas C. North, and Barry R. Weingast. 1990. The Role of Institutions in the Revival of Trade: The Law Merchant, Private Judges, and the Champagne Fairs. *Economics and Politics*, 2(March): 1–23.

Morris, William. 1910. *The Frankpledge System*. New York: Longmans, Green, and Co.

Nye, John. 1997. Thinking About the State: Property Rights, Trade, and Changing Contractual Arrangements in a World with Violent Coercion, in John Drobak and John Nye (eds.). *Frontiers of the New Institutional Economics*. London: Academic Press.

Ostrom, Elinor. 1990. *Governing the Commons: The Evolution of Institutions for Collective Action*. Cambridge, UK and New York: Cambridge University Press.

Peden, Joseph R. 1977. Property Rights in Celtic Irish Law. *Journal of Libertarian Studies*, 1: 81–95.

Plantey, Alain. International Arbitration in a Changing World, in . A.J. van den Berg (ed.). *International Arbitration in a Changing World*. 67–84. Deventer: Kluwer Law and Taxation Publishers.

Plucknett, T. F. T. 1956. *A Concise History of the Common Law*, 5th ed. Boston, MA: Little, Brown.

Polanyi, Michael. 1951. *The Logic of Liberty*. Chicago, IL: University of Chicago Press.

Pollock, Frederick and Frederick W. Maitland. 1899. *The History of English Law*, 2nd ed. 2 vols. Cambridge: Cambridge University Press.

Popisil, Leonard. 1974. *Anthropology of Law: A Comparative Theory*. New York: Harper & Row.

Sawyer, P.H. 1965. The Wealth of England in the Eleventh Century. *Transactions of the Royal Historical Society,* 5th Ser., 5: 145–164.

Schmidtz, David. 1991. *The Limits of Government Action: An Essay on the Public Goods Argument.* Boulder, CO: Westview Press.

Seebohm, Frederic. 1902. *Tribal Custom in Anglo-Saxon Law.* New York: Longmans, Green, and Co.

Sobel, Russell S. and Brian J. Osoba. Youth Gangs as Pseudo-Governments: Implications for Violent Crime. *Southern Economic Journal.* Forthcoming.

Solvason, Birgir T. R. 1992. Ordered Anarchy: Evolution of the Decentralized Legal Order in the Icelandic Commonwealth. *Journal des Economists et des Etudes Humanes,* 3(June/September): 333–351.

———. 1993. Institutional Evolution in the Icelandic Commonwealth. *Constitutional Political Economy,* 4: 97–125.

Stenton, F. M. 1950. *Anglo-Saxon England, 500–1087.* Oxford: Clarendon Press.

Stephen, James. 1883. *A History of the Criminal Law of England.* Reprint, New York: Burt Franklin, 1963.

Stringham, Edward (Ed.) 2005. *Anarchy, State, and Public Choice.* Cheltenham, UK: Edward Elgar.

———. 2007. *Anarchy and the Law: The Political Economy of Choice.* Somerset, NJ: Transaction Publishers for The Independent Institute.

Sugden, Robert. 1986. *The Economics of Rights, Cooperation, and Welfare.* Oxford: Basil Blackwell.

Tullock, Gordon (Ed.) 1972. *Explorations in the Theory of Anarchy.* Blacksburg, VA: Center for the Study of Public Choice.

———. 1974. *Further Explorations in the Theory of Anarchy.* Blacksburg, VA: Center for the Study of Public Choice.

Umbeck, John R. 1981. *A Theory of Property Rights with Application to the California Gold Rush.* Ames, IA: Iowa State University Press.

Warren, W. L. 1987. *The Governance of Norman and Angevin England, 1086–1272.* Stanford, UK: Stanford University Press.

Whitelock, Dorothy. 1952. *The Beginnings of English Society.* Harmondsworth, UK: Penguin Books.

Williamson, Oliver E. 1975. *Markets and Hierarchies: Analysis and Anti-Trust Implications.* New York: Free Press.

———. 1983. Credible Commitments: Using Hostages to Support Exchange. *American Economic Review,* 83(September): 519–540.

Zywicki, Todd. 2004. The Rise and Fall of Efficiency in the Common Law: A Supply-Side Analysis. *Northwestern University Law Review,* 97: 1551–1633.

CHAPTER 3

Alesina, Alberto, Arnaud Devleeschauwer, William Easterly, Sergio Kurlat, and Romain Wacziarg. 2003. Fractionalization. *Journal of Economic Growth,* 8(2) (June): 155–194.

American Bar Foundation. 2004. *The Lawyer Statistical Report: The U.S. Legal Profession in 2000.* Chicago, IL: American Bar Foundation.

American Judicature Society. 2007. Initial Selection: Courts of Last Resort. Des Moines, IA: American Judicature Society. Online: www.ajs.org/js/LastResort.pdf.

Baicker, Katherine and Nora Gordon. 2006. The Effect of State Educational Finance Reform on Total Local Resources. *Journal of Public Economics,* 90(8–9) (September): 1519–1535.

Besley, Timothy and Abigail Payne. 2003. Judicial Accountability and Economic Policy Outcomes: Evidence from Employment Discrimination Charges. Mimeo.

Caplan, Bryan. 2007. *The Myth of the Rational Voter: Why Democracies Choose Bad Policies*. Princeton, PA: Princeton University Press.

Christianson, Scott. 2004. *Innocent: Inside Wrongful Conviction Cases*. New York: New York University Press.

Council of State Governments. 2004. *The Book of the States*. Lexington, VA: Council of State Governments.

Cross, Frank B. and Emerson H. Tiller. 1998. Judicial Partisanship and Obedience to Legal Doctrine: Whistleblowing on the Federal Court of Appeals. *Yale Law Journal*, 107: 2155–2176.

Dyke, Andrew. 2007. Electoral Cycles in the Administration of Criminal Justice. *Public Choice*, 133(3–4) (December): 417–437.

Farber, Daniel A. and Suzanna Sherry. 1990. *A History of the American Constitution*. St. Paul, MN: West.

Garrett, Thomas A. and Russell S. Sobel. 2003. The Political Economy of FEMA Disaster Payments. *Economic Inquiry*, 41(3) (July): 496–509.

Glaberson, William. 2005. Cases Against Rivals Were Justified, Hynes Said, *The New York Times*, January 6.

Glaeser, Edward. 2006. Inequality, in Barry Weingast and Donald Wittman (eds.). *The Oxford Handbook of Political Economy*. Cambridge: Oxford University Press.

Glaeser, Edward, Jose Scheinkman, and Andrei Shleifer. 2003. The Injustice of Inequality. *Journal of Monetary Economics*, 50(1) (January): 199–222.

Grose, Christian R. 2007. Cues, Endorsements, and Heresthetic in a High-profile Election: Racial Polarization in Durham, North Carolina? *PS: Political Science and Politics*, 40(2) (April): 325–332.

Hanssen, F. Andrew. 2000. Independent Courts and Administrative Agencies: An Empirical Analysis of the States, *Journal of Law, Economics, and Organization*, 16: 534–571.

———. 2002. On the Politics of Judicial Selection: Lawyers and State Campaigns for the Merit Plan, *Public Choice*, 110(January): 79–97.

———. 2004. Learning about Judicial Independence: Institutional Change in the State Courts. *Journal of Legal Studies*, 33(June): 431–473.

Helland, Eric and Alexander Tabarrok. 2002. The Effect of Electoral Institutions on Tort Awards, *American Law and Economics Review*, 4: 341–70.

———. 2006. *Judge and Jury: American Tort Law on Trial*. Oakland, CA: The Independent Institute.

Koppl, Roger. 2005. How to Improve Forensic Science. *European Journal of Law and Economics*, 20(3) (November): 255–286.

Kubik, Jeffrey D. and John R. Moran. 2003. Lethal Elections: Gubernatorial Politics and the Timing of Executions. *Journal of Law & Economics*, 46(1) (April): 1–26.

Lapinski, Alex. 2001. Incumbent Abraham Is Confident of Re-election as City's District Attorney. *The Daily Pennsylvanian*, November 6.

Link, Bradley. 2004. Had Enough in Ohio? Time to Reform Ohio's Judicial Selection Process. *Cleveland State Law Review*, 51: 123–152.

Murray, Jeff. 2007. DA Hopefuls Make Pitches to Two Clubs, *Elmira Star-Gazette*, August 22.

Neff, Joseph and Anne Blythe. 2007. Panel Disbars Duke Lacrosse Prosecutor. *Raleigh News & Observer*, June 16.

Radin, E. D. 1964. *The Innocents.* New York: William Morrow.

Schanzenbach, Max. 2005. Racial and Sex Disparities in Prison Sentences: The Effect of District-Level Judicial. *Journal of Legal Studies,* 34(1) (January): 57–92.

Sobel, Russell S. and Joshua C. Hall. 2007. The Effect of Judicial Selection Processes on Judicial Quality: The Role of Partisan Politics. *Cato Journal,* 27(1) (Winter): 69–82.

Smith, Joseph and Emerson Tiller. 2002. The Strategy of Judging: Evidence from Administrative Law. *Journal of Legal Studies,* 31: 61–82.

Tabarrok, Alexander and Eric Helland. 1999. Court Politics: The Political Economy of Tort Awards, *Journal of Law and Economics,* 42 (April): 157–188.

———. 2003. Race, Poverty, and American Tort Awards: Evidence from Three Data Sets. *Journal of Legal Studies,* 32(1) (2003): 27–58.

U.S. Bureau of the Census. 2004. *Statistical Abstract of the United States 2004–05.* Washington, DC: Government Printing Office.

U.S. Chamber of Commerce. 2004. *State Liability Systems Ranking Study.* Washington, DC: U.S. Chamber of Commerce.

West, William F. 2007. Nifong Apologizes to 3 Players; DA Also Takes Issue With Some of AG's Sharp Criticism, *Durham Herald-Sun,* April 13.

Wittman, Donald A. 1995. *The Myth of Democratic Failure: Why Political Institutions Are Efficient.* Chicago, IL: University of Chicago Press.

CHAPTER 4

ABC News. 2009. Arson Execution Update, broadcast on *Nightline* October 5. http://abcnews.go.com/video/playerIndex?id=8740108 (accessed October 8, 2009).

Baicker, Katherine and Mirelle Jacobson. 2007. Finders Keepers: Forfeiture Laws, Policing Incentives, and Local Budgets. *Journal of Public Economics,* 91(11): 2113–2136.

Benson, Bruce. 1998. Crime Control Through Private Enterprise. *The Independent Review,* 2(3): 341–371.

Benson, Bruce and David Rasmussen. 1995. Predatory Public Finance and the Origins of the War on Drugs. *The Independent Review,* 1: 163–195.

Benson, Bruce, David Rasmussen, and David Sollars. 1995. Police Bureaucracies, Their Incentives, and the War on Drugs. *Public Choice,* 83: 21–45.

Beyler, Craig L. 2009. Analysis of the Fire Investigation Methods and Procedures Used in the Criminal Arson Cases Against Ernest Ray Willis and Cameron Todd Willingham, Report submitted to the Texas Forensic Science Commission, August 17, 2009. Downloaded August 16, 2009, from http://www.docstoc.com/docs/document-preview.aspx?doc_id=10401390.

Blackstone, William. 1765–1769. Commentaries on the Laws of England. http://www.lonang.com/exlibris/blackstone/.http://www.lonang.com/exlibris/blackstone/

Breton, Albert and Ronald Wintrobe. 1982. *The Logic of Bureaucratic Control.* Cambridge: Cambridge University Press.

Bromwich, Michael R. 2005. Second Report of the Independent Investigator for the Houston Police Department Crime Laboratory and Property Room. http://www.hpdlabinvestigation.org/reports/050531report.pdf (accessed May 24, 2007).

Budowle, Bruce, JoAnn Buscaglia, and Rebecca S. Perlman. 2006. Review of the Scientific Basis for Friction Ridge Comparisons as a Means of Identification: Committee Findings and Recommendations. *Forensic Science Communications* 8.

http://www.fbi.gov/hq/lab/fsc/backissu/jan2006/research/2006_01_
research02.htmon (accessed July 31, 2007).

Bureau of Justice Statistics. 2005. *Federal Criminal Case Processing, 2002.* Bureau of Justice Statistics.

———. 2006. *Compendium of Federal Justice Statistics, 2004.* Bureau of Justice Statistics.

———. 2007. Felony Sentences in State Courts, 2004. *Bulletin,* July, NCJ 215646. http://bjs.ojp.usdoj.gov/content/pub/ascii/fssc04.txt. Accessed December 29, 2009.

Bureau of Prisons. 2002. Annual Determination of Average Cost of Incarceration. *Federal Registry,* March 19, 2002, 67(53): 12586.

Butos, William and Roger Koppl, 2003. Science as a Spontaneous Order: An Essay in the Economics of Science, in H.S. Jensen, M. Vendeloe, and L. Richter (eds.). *The Evolution of Scientific Knowledge.* Cheltenham: Edward Elgar.

Butos, William and Thomas McQuade. 2006. Government and Science: A Dangerous Liaison? *The Independent Review,* 11(2): 177–208.

California Investigation Services website. http://www.cali-pi.com/fingerprint.html (accessed May 9, 2007).

Cole, Simon. 2005. More Than Zero: Accounting for Error in Latent Fingerprint Identification. *Journal of Criminal Law & Criminology,* 95(3): 985–1078.

Crime Lab Report. 2009. Post-conviction Activists 'Contaminate' Evidence in Texas. http://www.crimelabreport.com/library/monthly_report/9–2009.htm (accessed October 8, 2009).

Dror, Itiel and David Charlton. 2006. Why Experts Make Errors. *Journal of Forensic Identification,* 56(4): 600–616.

Durose, Matthew and Patrick A. Langan. 2004. *Felony Sentences in State Courts, 2002.* Bureau of Justice Statistics.

FBI Director. 2002. *An Audit of Houston Police Department Crime Laboratory-DNA/Serology Section,* December 12–13.

Feigenbaum, Susan and David M. Levy. 1996. The Technical Obsolescence of Scientific Fraud. *Rationality and Society,* 8: 261–276.

Giannelli, Paul C. 1997. The Abuse of Evidence in Criminal Cases: The Need for Independent Crime Laboratories, *Virginia Journal of Social Policy & the Law,* 4: 439–478.

Gillispie, Mark and Lila J. Mills. 2004. Suspended Crime-Lab Technician Lands a Job, *The Plain Dealer,* August 22.

Glenn, Michael. 2006. Under the microscope: HPD's evidence closely watched the time around, *Houston Chronicle,* July 11. http://www.chron.com/disp/story.mpl/special/crimelab/4038116.html (accessed May 24, 2007).

Grann, David. 2009. Trial by Fire, *The New Yorker,* September 7. http://www.newyorker.com/reporting/2009/09/07/090907fa_fact_grann?currentPage=all (accessed September 7, 2009).

Haber, Lyn and Ralph N. Haber. 2004. Error Rates for Human Latent Fingerprint Examiners, in N. Ratha and R. Bolle (eds.). *Automatic Fingerprint Recognition Systems.* New York: Springer-Verlag.

———. 2008. Experiential or Scientific Expertise, *Law, Probability and Risk,* 7(2): 143–150.

Harmon, Rockne and Bruce Budowle. 2006. Letter to the Editor. *Science* 311: 607.

Hume, David. 2005. *Essays Moral, Political, Literary.* Liberty Fund. http://oll. libertyfund.org/EBooks/Hume_0059.pdf (accessed June 18, 2007).

Kaye, Randi. 2009. Did Texas Execute Innocent Man? CNN report. http://www. cnn.com/video/#/video/crime/2009/10/04/kaye.execution.coverup.cnn (accessed October 8, 2009).

Kennedy, Donald. 2003. Forensic Science: Oxymoron? *Science,* 302: 1625.

Khanna, Roma. 2006. Crime Lab's DNA Section, Shut in '02, Will Reopen, *Houston Chronicle,* June 21. http://www.chron.com/disp/story.mpl/special/crimelab/ 3988198.html (accessed May 24, 2007).

Koppl, Roger. 2005. How to Improve Forensic Science. *European Journal of Law and Economics,* 20(3): 255–286.

———. 2006. Democratic Epistemics: An Experiment on How to Improve Forensic Science. *Papers on Economics and Evolution,* Max Planck Institute of Economics, Evolutionary Economics Group, #0609.

———.2007. Diversity in Forensics: Diversity in Hiring is Not Enough. *Medicine, Science and the Law,* 47(2): 117–124.

Koppl, R., R. Kurzban, and L. Kobilinsky. 2008. Epistemics for Forensics. *Episteme: Journal of Social Epistemology,* 5(2): 141–159.

Krane, Dan et al. 2008. Sequential Unmasking: A Means of Minimizing Observer Effects in Forensic DNA Interpretation. *Journal of Forensic Sciences,* 53(4): 1006–1007.

Makowsky, Michael and Thomas Stratmann. 2007. Political Economy at Any Speed: What Determines Traffic Citations? SSRN Manuscript. http://papers.ssrn.com/ s013/Delivery.cfm/SSRN_ID964958_code518367.pdf?abstractid= 961967&mirid=1

McMullan, Donald. 2009. Letter to Leigh Tomlin, Commission Coordinator, Texas Forensic Science Commission, September 29. http://static.cnhi.zope.net/ corsicanadailysun/images/City_of_Corsicana_response.pdf (accessed October 8, 2009).

Mills, Steve and Maurice Possley. 2001. Report Alleges Crime Lab Fraud Scientist Is Accused of Providing False Testimony, *Chicago Tribune,* January 14.

———. 2004. Texas Man Executed on Disproved Forensics: Fire that Killed his 3 Children Could Have Been Accidental, *Chicago Tribune,* December 9.

NAS Committee on Identifying the Needs of the Forensic Sciences Community. 2009. *Strengthening Forensic Science in the United States: A Path Forward.* Washington, D. C. : The National Academies Press.

Neufeld, Peter. 2005. The (Near) Irrelevance of *Daubert* to Criminal Justice and Some Suggestions for Reform. *American Journal of Public Health,* 95(supplement 1): S107–S113.

Niskanen, William. 1971. *Bureaucracy and Representative Government,* Chicago, IL: Aldine-Atherton.

Office of the Inspector General, United States Department of Justice. 1997. The FBI Laboratory: An Investigation into Laboratory Practices and Alleged Misconduct in Explosives-Related and Other Cases. http://www.usdoj.gov/oig/special/97– 04a/index.htm.

———. 2004. The FBI Laboratory: A Review of Protocol and Practice Vulnerabilities. http://www.usdoj.gov/oig/special/0405/final.pdf.

———. 2006. A Review of the FBI's Handling of the Brandon Mayfield Case: Unclassified Executive Summary. http://0225.0145.01.040/oig/special/s0601/ PDF_list.htm.

Office of the Inspector General, United States Department of Justice. 2008. Review of the Office of Justice Programs' Paul Coverdell Forensic Science Improvement Grants Program. http://www.usdoj.gov/oig/reports/OJP/e0801/final.pdf.

Peterson, Joseph L. and Matthew J. Hickman. 2005. *Census of Publicly Funded Forensic Crime Laboratories, 2002.* Bureau of Justice Statistics.

Peterson, Joseph L. and Penelope N. Markham. 1995a. Crime Lab Proficiency Testing Results, 1978–1991, I: Identification and Classification of Physical Evidence, *Journal of Forensic Sciences,* 40(6): 994–1008.

———. 1995b. Crime Lab Proficiency Testing Results, 1978–1991, II: Resolving Questions of Common Origin, *Journal of Forensic Sciences,* 40(6): 1009–1029.

Possley, Maurice and Ken Armstrong. 1999. Lab Tech in Botched Case Promoted: Testimony Helped Wrongly Convict Man of Rape, *Chicago Tribune,* 19 March.

Pyrek, Kelly M. 2007. *Forensic Science Under Siege: The Challenges of Forensic Laboratories and the Medico-Legal Death Investigation System.* Amsterdam, Boston, and other locations: Academic Press.

Risinger, Michael, Michael J. Saks, William C. Thompson, and Robert Rosenthal. 2002. The Daubert/Kumho Implications of Observer Effects in Forensic Science: Hidden Problems of Expectation and Suggestion. *California Law Review* 90: 1–56.

Roberts, Paul Craig. 2003. The Causes of Wrongful Conviction. *The Independent Review,* 7(4): 567–574.

Rubinstein, Joshua S., David E. Meyer, and Jeffrey E. Evans. 2001. Executive Control of Cognitive Processes in Task Switching. *Journal of Experimental Psychology: Human Perception and Performance,* 27(4): 763–797.

Seminole County Sheriff's Office. 2007. *Administrative Review* PC-07–0018, dated June 4, 2007. This review was prepared by Professional Standards Investigator Joy Williams.

Smith, Adam. 1981. *An Inquiry into the Nature and Causes of the Wealth of Nations.* Indianapolis, IN: Liberty Fund.

Solomon, John. 2007. FBI's Forensic Test Full of Holes: Lee Wayne Hunt in one of hundreds of defendants whose convictions are in question now that FBI forensic evidence has been discredited, *Washington Post,* November 18.

State of Maryland v. Bryan Rose, Memorandum Decision, October 19, 2007, Circuit Court for Baltimore County, K06–545.

Stutzman, Rene. 2007a. Are Innocent Imprisoned? Fingerprint Errors Found, *Orlando Sentinel,* May 4.

———. 2007b. Fingerprint Scandal Costs Analyst Her Job, *Orlando Sentinel,* June 7.

SWGFAST (Scientific Working Group on Friction Ridge Analysis, Study and Technology). 2002a. Friction Ridge Examination Methodology for Latent Print Examiners. http://www.swgfast.org/Friction_Ridge_Examination_Methodology_for_Latent_Print_Examiners_1.01.pdf (accessed June 11, 2007).

———. 2002b. Quality Assurance Guidelines for Latent Print Examiners. http://www.swgfast.org/Quality_Assurance_Guidelines_for_Latent_Print_Examiners_3.0.pdf (accessed June 11, 2007).

Tullock. Gordon. 1965. *The Politics of Bureaucracy.* Washington, DC: Public Affairs Press.

Walstad, Allan. 2003. Science as a Market Process. *The Independent Review* 7(1): 5–45.

Williamson, T. March 12, 2007. Memorandum to Captain Randy Pittman. Available from the author.

CHAPTER 5

Ades, Alberto and Rafael di Tella. 1999. Rents, Competition, and Corruption. *American Economic Review* 89: 982–993.

Adserà, Alicia, Carles Boix, and Mark Payne. 2003. Are You Being Served?: Political Accountability and Quality of Government. *Journal of Law, Economics and Organization*, 19: 445–490.

Alt, James E., David Dreyer Lassen. 2003. The Political Economy of Institutions and Corruption in American States. *Journal of Theoretical Politics*, 15: 341–365.

———. 2008. Political and Judicial Checks on Corruption: Evidence from American State Governments. *Economics and Politics*, 20(1): 33–61.

Barro, Robert J. 1973. The Control of Politicians. *Public Choice*, 14: 19–42.

Banfield, Edward C. 1979. Corruption as a Feature of Governmental Organization, in M. Ekpo, (ed.). *Bureaucratic Corruption in Sub-Saharan Africa: Toward a Search for Causes and Consequences*. Washington DC: University Press of America.

Besley, Timothy and Abigail Payne. 2003. Judicial Accountability and Economic Policy Outcomes: Evidence from Employment Discrimination Charges. The Institute for Fiscal Studies, WP03/11.

Boylan, Richard T. and Cheryl X. Long. 2003. Measuring Public Corruption in the American States: A Survey of State House Reporters. *State Politics and Policy Quarterly*, 3: 420–438.

Cordis, Adriana S. 2009. Judicial Checks on Corruption in the United States. *Economics of Governance*, 10: 1203–1250.

Easterly William and Ross Levine. 1997. Africa's Growth Tragedy: Policies and Ethnic Divisions. *Quarterly Journal of Economics*, 112: 1203–1250.

Feld, Lars and Stefan Voigt. 2003. Economic Growth and Judicial Independence: Cross-Country Evidence using a New Set of Indicators. *European Journal of Political Economy* 19: 497–527.

Ferejohn, John. 1986. Incumbent Performance and Electoral Control. *Public Choice* 50: 5–26.

Glaeser, Edward and Raven E. Saks. 2004. Corruption in America, NBER Working Paper 10821, September.

Gwartney, James, Robert Lawson, and William Easterly. 2007. *Economic Freedom of the World Annual Report*.

Hall, Melinda Gann. 1987. Constituent Influence in State Supreme Courts: Conceptual Notes and a Case Study. *Journal of Politics*, 49: 1117–1124.

———. 2001. State Supreme Courts in American Democracy: Probing Myths of Judicial Reform. *American Political Science Review*, 95: 315–330.

Hamilton, Alexander, James Madison, and John Jay. [1788] 2004. *The Federalist Papers*, J.R. Pole (ed.). Indianapolis: Hackett Publishing Company.

Hanssen, F. Andrew. 2002. On the Politics of Judicial Selection: Lawyers and State Campaigns for the Merit Plan. *Public Choice* 110: 79–97.

Hanssen, F. Andrew. 2004. Is There a Politically Optimal Level of Judicial Independence? *American Economic Review*, 94: 712–729.

Hayek, Friedrich A. von. 1960. *The Constitution of Liberty*. Chicago, IL: University of Chicago Press.

Henisz W. and B. Zelner. 2005. Codebook of the Political Constraint Index (POLCON) Dataset.

Kalt, Joseph P. and Mark A. Zupan. 1990. The Apparent Ideological Behavior of Legislators: Testing for Principal-agent Slack in Political Institutions. *Journal of Law and Economics* 33: 103–131.

Kaufmann D., Aart Kraay, and Massimo Mastruzzi. 2007. Governance Matters VI: Aggregate and Individual Governance Indicators 1996–2006, World Bank Policy Research Working Paper 4280.

Kunicovà, Jana and Susan Rose-Ackerman. 2005. Electoral Rules as Constraints on Corruption. *British Journal of Political Science*. 35: 573–606.

La Porta, Rafael, Florencio López-de-Silanes, Andrei Shleifer, and Robert W. Vishny. 1999. The Quality of Government. *Journal of Law, Economics and Organization*, 15: 222–279.

La Porta, Rafael, Florencio López-de-Silanes, Cristian Pop-Eleches, and Andrei Shleifer. 2004. Judicial Checks and Balances. *Journal of Political Economy*, 112: 445–470.

Lederman, D., N. Loayza, and R. Reis Soarez. 2005. Accountability and Corruption. Political Institutions Matter. *Economics and Politics*, 17: 1–35.

Lopéz, Edward J. R. Todd Jewell, and Noel D. Campbell. 2009. Pass a Law, Any Law, Fast! State Legislative Responses to the *Kelo* Backlash," Review of *Law & Economics* 5(1), 101–135.

Maddex, Robert L. 1995. *Constitutions of the World*. Washington, DC: Congressional Q.

Maskin, Eric, and Jean Tirole. 2004. The Politician and the Judge: Accountability in Government. *American Economic Review*, 94: 1034–1054.

Matsusaka, J. G. 1992. Economics of Direct Legislation. *Quarterly Journal of Economics* 107: 541–571.

———. 1995. Fiscal Effects of the Voter Initiative: Evidence from the Last 30 Years. *Journal of Political Economy*, 103: 587–623.

———. 2004. *For the Many or the Few*. Chicago, IL: University of Chicago Press.

Mauro, Paolo. 1995. Corruption and Growth. *Quarterly Journal of Economics*, 110: 681–712.

Meier, Keneth J. and Thomas M. Holbrook. 1992. I Seen My Opportunities and I Took 'Em: Political Corruption in the American States. *Journal of Politics*, 54: 135–155.

Persson, Torsten, Gerard Roland, and Guido Tabellini. 1997. Separation of Powers and Political Accountability. *Quarterly Journal of Economics*, 112: 1163–1202.

Romer, Thomas and Howard Rosenthal. 1979. Bureaucrats versus Voters: On the Political Economy of Resource Allocation by Direct Democracy. *Quarterly Journal of Economics*, 93: 563–587.

Rose-Ackerman, Susan. 1975. The Economics of Corruption. *Journal of Public Economics*, 4: 187–203.

———. [1999] 2006. *Corruption and Government. Causes, Consequences, and Reform*, New York: Cambridge University Press.

Shleifer, Andrei and Robert W. Vishny. 1993. Corruption. *Quarterly Journal of Economics*, 108: 599–617.

Sobel, Russell S. and Joshua C. Hall. 2007. The Effect of Judicial Selection Process on Judicial Quality: The Role of Partisan Politics. *Cato Journal*, 27: 69–82.

Svensson, J. 2005. Eight Questions about Corruption. *Journal of Economic Perspectives*, 19: 19–42.

Tabarrok, Alexander and Eric Helland. 1999. Court Politics: The Political Economy of Tort Awards. *Journal of Law and Economics*, 42: 157–188.

Tocqueville, Alexis de. [1835] 1954. *Democracy in America.* New York: Vintage.

Treisman, Daniel. 2000. The Causes of Corruption: A Cross-National Survey. *Journal of Public Economics*, 76: 399–457.

Waisman, Gisela. 2005. *Complementary Controls of Corruption.* IIES: Stockholm University.

Weingast, Barry. 1995. The Economic Role of Political Institutions: Market-preserving Federalism and Economic Growth. *Journal of Law, Economics, and Organization* 11: 1–31.

Welch, Susan and John R. Hibbing. 1997. The Effects of Charges of Corruption on Voting Behavior in Congressional Elections. *Journal of Politics*, 59: 226–239.

CHAPTER 6

American Judicature Society. Judicial Selection in the States: Appellate and General Jurisdiction Courts. http://www.ajs.org/selection/Jud%20Sel%20Chart-Oct% 202002.pdf.

Becker, Gary S. 1968. Crime and Punishment: An Economic Approach. *The Journal of Political Economy*, 76(2): 169–217.

Besley, Timothy and Anne Case. 2003. Political Institutions and Policy Choices: Evidence from the United States. *Journal of Economic Literature*, 41(1): 7–73.

Besley, Timothy and Stephen Coate. 2000a. Elected versus Appointed Regulators: Theory and Evidence, NBER Working Paper 7579.

———. 2000b. Issue Unbundling via Citizens' Initiatives, NBER Working Paper 8036.

Brace, Paul and Melinda Gann Hall. 1990. Neo-institutionalism and Dissent in State Supreme Courts. *Journal of Politics*, 52: 54–70.

———. 1993. Integrated Models of Judicial Dissent. *Journal of Politics*, 55: 914–935.

———. 1995. Studying Courts Comparatively: The View from the American States. *Political Research Quarterly*, 48: 5–29.

Bureau of Justice Statistics. *Annual Survey of Jails: Jurisdiction-Level Data.* (serial, computer file). Washington, DC: Department of Justice, Office of Justice Programs, Bureau of Justice Statistics.

Bushway, Sean and Ann Morris Piehl. 2001. Judging Judicial Discretion: Legal Factors and Racial Discrimination in Sentencing. *Law & Society Review*, 35(4): 733–764.

Canon, Bradley C. and Dean Jaros. 1970. External Variables, Institutional Structure and Dissent on State Supreme Courts. *Polity*, 4: 185–200.

Clinton, William Jefferson. 2001. Erasing America's Color Lines, *New York Times*, January 15.

Crain, Mark W. and Robert E. McCormick. 1984. Regulators as an Interest Group, in James M. Buchanan and Robert D. Tollison (eds.). *The Theory of Public Choice II.* Ann Arbor, MI: University of Michigan Press.

DiIulio, John J., Jr. 1996. Prisons Are a Bargain, by Any Measure, *New York Times*, January 16.

Donohue, John and Steven Levitt. 2001. The Impact of Race on Policing, Arrest Patterns, and Crime. *Journal of Law and Economics*, 44: 2, 367–394.

Dominitz, Jeff. 2003. How Do the Laws of Probability Constrain Legislative and Judicial Efforts to Stop Racial Profiling? *American Law and Economics Review*, 5(2): 412–432.

Greene, William H. 2000. *Econometric Analysis*. Upper Saddle River, NJ: Prentice Hall.

Hall, Melinda Gann. 1995. Justices as Representatives: Elections and Judicial Politics in the American States. *American Politics Quarterly*, 75: 136–151.

Hall, Melinda Gann and Paul Brace. 1996. Justices' Responses to Case Facts: An Interactive Model. *American Politics Quarterly*, 24(2): 237–261.

Hanssen, F. Andrew. 1999. The Effect of Judicial Institutions on Uncertainty and the Rate of Litigation: The Election Versus Appointment of State Judges. *Journal of Legal Studies*, 28(1): 205–232.

———. 2001. Is there a Politically Optimal Level of Judicial Independence? Stanford Law School, John M. Olin Working Paper 218.

Heckman, James. 1976. The Common Structure of Statistical Models of Truncation, Sample Selection and Limited Dependent Variables and a Simple Estimator for Such Models, *Annals of Economic and Social Measurement*. 5: 475–492.

Helland, Eric and Alexander Tabarrok. 1999. Court Politics: The Political Economy of Tort Awards. *Journal of Law and Economics*, 42(1): 157–188.

———. 2000. Runaway Judges? Selection Effects and the Jury. *Journal of Law, Economics, and Organization*, 16(2): 306–333.

———. 2002. The Effect of Electoral Institutions on Tort Awards. *American Law and Economics Review*, 4(2): 341–370.

Jensen, Jennifer M. and Thad Beyle. 2003. Of Footnotes, Missing Data, and Lessons for 50-State Data Collection: The Gubernatorial Campaign Finance Project, 1977–2001. *State Politics and Policy Quarterly* 3: 203–214.

Knowles, John, Nicola Persico, and Petra Todd. 2001. Racial Bias in Motor-Vehicle Searches: Theory and Evidence. *Journal of Political Economy*, 109(1): 203–229.

Levitt, Steven D. 1997. Using Electoral Cycles in Police Hiring to Estimate the Effect of Police on Crime. *American Economic Review*, 87(3): 270–290.

Mustard, David B. 2001. Racial, Ethnic, and Gender Disparities in Sentencing: Evidence from the U.S. Federal Courts. *Journal of Law and Economics*, 44(1): 285–314.

Peltzman, Sam. 1976. Toward a More General Theory of Regulation. *Journal of Law and Economics*, 19(2): 211–240.

Posner, Richard. 1994. What Do Judges and Justices Maximize? (The Same Thing Everybody Else Does). *Supreme Court Economic Review*, 3(1): 1–41.

Shepherd, Joanna M. 2002. Fear of the First Strike: The Full Effect of California's Two- and Three-Strikes Legislation. *The Journal of Legal Studies*, 31(1): 159–201.

Skogan, Wesley G. and Tracey L. Mears. 2004. Lawful Policing. *Annals of the American Academy of Political and Social Science*, 593: 66–83.

Stigler, G. J. 1971. The Theory of Economic Regulation. *Bell Journal of Economics and Management Science*, 2(1): 3–21.

U.S. Dept. of Justice, Bureau of Justice Statistics. State Court Processing Statistics, 1990, 1992, 1994, 1996, and 1998: Felony Defendants in Large Urban Counties [Computer file]. Conducted by Pretrial Services Resource Center [producer], 2001. 3rd ICPSR ed. Ann Arbor, MI: Inter-university Consortium for Political and Social Research [distributor], 2002.

Wright, Ronald F. 1998. Three Strikes Legislation and Sentencing Commission Objectives. *Law and Policy*, 18: 429.

CHAPTER 7

Aladjem, David R.E. 1988. Public Use and Treatment as an Equal: An Essay on *Poletown Neighborhood Council v. City of Detroit* and *Hawaii Housing Authority v. Midkiff. Ecology Law Quarterly,* 15: 671–74.

Benson, Bruce L. 2005. The Mythology of Holdout as Justification for Eminent Domain and the Public Provision of Roads. *The Independent Review,* 10: 165–194.

Bukowczyk, John. 1984. The Decline and Fall of a Detroit Neighborhood: *Poletown v. GM and the City of Detroit. Washington & Lee Law Review,* 41: 49–68.

Calabresi, Guido and A. Douglas Melamed. 1972. Property Rules, Liability Rules and Inalienability Rules: One View of the Cathedral. *Harvard Law Review,* 85: 1089–1128.

Caplan, Bryan Douglas. 2007. *The Myth of the Rational Voter: Why Democracies Chose Bad Policies.* Princeton, PA: Princeton University Press.

Carpenter, Dick M. II and John K. Ross. 2007. Victimizing the Vulnerable: The Demographics of Eminent Domain Abuse. Washington, DC: Institute for Justice. http://www.ij.org/pdf_folder/other_pubs/Victimizing_the_Vulnerable.pdf.

Carpini, Michael X. and Scott Keeter. 1996. *What Americans Know About Politics and Why It Matters.* New Haven, CT: Yale University Press.

Claeys, Eric R. 2004. Public Use Limitations and Natural Property Rights. *Michigan State Law Review,* 877–928.

Cohen, Lloyd R. 1991. Holdouts and Free Riders. *Journal of Legal Studies,* 20: 351–359.

Dana, David A. and Thomas Merrill. 2002. *Property: Takings.* New York: Foundation Press.

Eagle, Steven J. ed. 2005. *Regulatory Takings.* Newark, NJ: LexisNexis.

Ely, James W., Jr. 2003. Can the "Despotic Power" be Tamed? Reconsidering the Public Use Limitation on Eminent Domain. *Probate & Property,* 17: 31–36.

Epstein, Richard A. 1992. Property, Speech and the Politics of Distrust. *University of Chicago Law Review,* 59: 41–89.

Fischel, William A. 1995. *Regulatory Takings.* Cambridge, MA: Harvard University Press.

———. 2001. *The Homevoter Hypothesis.* Cambridge, MA: Harvard University Press.

Frieden, Bernard J. and Lynne B. Sagalyn. 1989. *Downtown, Inc: How America Rebuilds Cities.* Cambridge, MA: MIT Press.

Fullilove, Mindy Thompson. 2004. *Root Shock: How Tearing Up City Neighborhoods Hurts America, and What We Can Do About It.* New York: One World/Ballatine Books.

Gans, Herbert J. ed. 1982. *The Urban Villagers: Group and Class in the Life of Italian-Americans.* New York: Free Press of Glencoe.

Garnett, Nicole. 2006. The Neglected Political Economy of Eminent Domain. *Michigan Law Review,* 105: 101–150.

Gillette, Howard, Jr. 1995. *Between Justice and Beauty: Race, Planning, and the Failure of Urban Policy in Washington, D.C.* Baltimore, MD: John Hopkins University Press.

Hilzenrath, David S. 1993. Disney's Land of Make Believe: Acquisition Agent Used Ruse to Prevent Real Estate Speculation, *The Washington Post*, November 12.

Jacobs, Jane. 1961. *Death and Life of Great American Cities*. New York: Random House.

Jones, Bryan D., Lynn W. Bachelor, and Carter Wilson. 1986. *The Sustaining Hand: Community Leadership and Corporate Power*. Lawrence, KS: University Press of Kansas.

Kelly, Daniel B. 2006. The "Public Use" Requirement in Eminent Domain Law: A Rationale Based on Secret Purchases and Private Influence. *Cornell Law Review*, 92: 1–33.

Kochan, Donald J. "Public Use" and the Independent Judiciary: Condemnation in an Interest-Group Perspective. *Texas Review of Law & Politics*, 3: 49–90.

Merrill, Thomas W. 1986. The Economics of Public Use. *Cornell Law Review*, 72: 61–85.

Michael, Marie. 2001. Detroit at 300: New Seeds of Hope for a Troubled City. *Dollars & Sense*, 236: 24–27.

Mueller, Dennis C. 2003. *Public Choice III*. Cambridge, NY: Cambridge University Press.

Munch, Patricia. 1976. An Economic Analysis of Eminent Domain. *Journal of Politics and Economics*, 84: 473–488.

Noll, Roger G. and Andrew S. Zimbalist. 1997. *Sports, Jobs, and Taxes: The Economic Impact of Sports Teams and Stadiums*. Washington, DC: Brookings Institution Press.

Pinker, Steven. 1999. *How the Mind Works*. New York: W.W. Norton.

Posner, Richard A. ed. 1977. *Economic Analysis of Law*. Boston, MA: Little, Brown.

Pritchett, Wendell E. 2003. The "Public Menace" of Blight: Urban Renewal and the Private Uses of Eminent Domain. *Yale Law & Policy Review*, 21: 1–47.

Radin, Margaret Jane. 1988. The Liberal Conception of Property: Cross Currents in the Jurisprudence of Takings. *Columbia Law Review*, 88: 1667–1691.

Sandefur, Tim. 2003. A Natural Rights Perspective on Eminent Domain in California: A Rationale for Meaningful Judicial Scrutiny of "Public Use." *Southwestern University Law Review*, 32: 569–651.

Schelling, Thomas C. 1960. *The Strategy of Conflict*. Cambridge, MA: Harvard University Press.

Somin, Ilya. 1998. Voter Ignorance and the Democratic Idea. *Critical Review*, 12: 413–419.

———. 2004a. Overcoming *Poletown: County of Wayne v. Hathcock*, Economic Development Takings, and the Future of Public Use. *Michigan State Law Review*, 1005–1039.

———. 2004b. Michigan Should Alter Property Grab Rules, *Detroit News*, January 8.

———. 2004c. Political Ignorance and the Countermajoritarian Difficulty: A New Perspective on the Central Obsession of Constitutional Theory. *Iowa Law Review*, 89: 1287–1371.

———. 2004d. Posner's Democratic Pragmatism. *Critical Review*, 16: 1–14

———. 2004e. *Political Ignorance Is No Bliss*. Washington, DC: Cato Institute Policy Analysis No. 525.

———. 2007a. Controlling the Grasping Hand: Economic Development Takings After *Kelo*. *Supreme Court Economic Review*, 15: 183–271.

Somin, Ilya. 2007b. The Limits of Backlash: Assessing the Political Response to *Kelo*. George Mason Law & Economics Research Paper No. 07–14. http://papers.ssrn.com/s013/papers.cfm?abstract_id=976298.

Smith, Adam. ed. 1976. *An Inquiry Into the Nature and Causes of the Wealth of Nations*. Chicago, IL: University of Chicago Press.

Teixeira, Ruy A. 1992. *The Disappearing American Voter*. Washington, DC: Brookings Institution Press.

Tullock, Gordon. 2002. *Government Failure: A Primer in Public Choice*. Washington, DC: Cato Institute.

Verba, Sidney and Kay Lehman Schlozman and Henry E. Brady. 1995. *Voice and Equality*. Cambridge, MA: Harvard University Press.

Wheeler, Michael. rev. ed. 2000a. *Disney (A): From Disneyland to Disney World- Learning the Art of Land Assembly*, Harvard Business School, Case Study No. 9-898-018.

———. 2000b. *Disney (B):The Third Battle of Bull Run*, Harvard Business School, Case Study No. 9–898-019.

Wolfinger, Raymond E. and Steven J. Rosenstone. 1980. *Who Votes?* New Haven, CT: Yale University Press.

Wylie, Jeanie. 1989. *Poletown: Community Betrayed*. Urbana, IL: University of Illinois Press.

CHAPTER 8

Benson, Bruce L. 2005. The Mythology of Holdout as a Justification for Eminent Domain and Public Provision of Roads. *The Independent Review*, 10(2): 165–194.

Black, Henry Campbell. 1979 [1891]. *Black's Law Dictionary with Pronunciations*, 5th ed. Minneapolis, MN: West Publishing Company.

Buchanan, James M. 1969. *Cost and Choice: An Inquiry in Economic Theory*. Chicago, IL: Markham Publishing Company.

———. 1979. *What Should Economists Do?* Indianapolis, IN: Liberty Press.

Ellickson, Robert C. 1973. Alternatives to Zoning: Covenants, Nuisance and Rules as Land Use Controls. *University of Chicago Law Review*, 68(1).

Epstein, Richard A. 1985. *Takings: Private Property and the Power of Eminent Domain*. Cambridge, MA: Harvard University Press.

———. 1995. *Simple Rules for a Complex World*. Cambridge, MA: Harvard University Press.

Greenhut, Steven. 2004. *Abuse of Power: How the Government Misuses Eminent Domain*. Santa Ana, California: Seven Locks Press.

Holcombe, Randall G. 2002. Political Entrepreneurship and the Democratic Allocation of Economic Resources. *Review of Austrian Economics*, 15(2/3): 143–159.

Honderich, Ted. 1995. *Oxford Companion to Philosophy*. New York: Oxford University Press.

Hülsmann, Jörg Guido. 2003 [1960]. Introduction: Ludwig von Mises. *Epistemological Problem of Economics*. Auburn Alabama: Ludwig von Mises Institute.

———. 2004. The A Priori Foundations of Property Economics. *Quarterly Journal of Austrian Economics*, 7(4): 41–68.

Knetsch, Jack. 1983. *Property Rights and Compensation: Compulsory Acquisitions and Other Losses*. Toronto, Canada: Butterworths, Inc.

Knetsch, Jack and Thomas Borcherding. 1979. Expropriation of Private Property and the Basis for Compensation. *University of Toronto Law Journal*, 29: 237–252.

Krier, James E. and Christopher Serkin. 2004. Public Ruses. *Michigan State Law Review* 859: 867.

Locke, John. 1948 [1688]. An Essay Concerning the True Original Extent and End of Civil Government in J.W. Gough, ed., *The Second Treatise of Civil Government and a Letter Concerning Toleration.* Oxford: Basil Blackwell.

López, Edward J. and Sasha M. Totah. 2007. *Kelo* and Its Discontents. *The Independent Review,* 11(3): 397–416.

Merrill, Thomas. 2005. Brief for the American Planning Association et al. as Amici Curiae Supporting Respondents at 28, *Kelo v. City of New London,* 125 S. Ct. 2655 (No. 04108), 2005 WL 166929.

Mises, Ludwig von. [1949] 1998. *Human Action: A Treatise on Economics: The Scholar's Edition.* Auburn, AL: Ludwig von Mises Institute.

———. [1960] 2003. *Epistemological Problem of Economics.* Auburn, AL: Ludwig von Mises Institute.

Mitchell, Robert Cameron and Richard T. Carson. 1989. *Using Surveys to Value Public Goods: The Contingent Valuation Method.* Washington, DC: Resources for the Future.

North, Gary. 1992. *The Coase Theorem: A Study in Economic Epistemology.* Tyler, Texas: ICE Press.

Nozick, Robert. 1974. *Anarchy, State and Utopia.* New York: Basic Books.

Paul, Ellen Frankel. 1987. *Property Rights and Eminent Domain.* New Brunswick, NJ: Transaction Publishers.

Pollot, Mark. L. 1993. *Grand Theft and Petit Larceny: Property Rights in America.* San Francisco, CA: Pacific Research Institute for Public Policy.

Reisman, George. 1996. *Capitalism: A Treatise on Economics.* Ottawa, IL: Jameson Books.

Robbins, Lionel. 1932. *An Essay on the Nature and Significance of Economic Science.* London: Macmillan.

Rothbard, Murray N. 1997. Toward a Reconstruction of Utility and Welfare Economics, in Murray N. Rothbard, ed., *The Logic of Action: Money, Method and the Austrian School,* 211–254. Cheltenham: Edward Elgar.

———. 1998 [1982]. *Ethics of Liberty.* New York: New York University Press.

———. 2004. *Man, Economy and State with Power and Market.* Auburn, AL: The Ludwig von Mises Institute.

Sutter, Daniel. 2002. The Democratic Efficiency Debate and Definitions of Political Equilibrium. *Review of Austrian Economics,* 15(2/3): 199–209.

CHAPTER 9

Alpert, Thomas W. 1982. The Inherent Power of the Courts to Regulate the Practice of Law: An Historical Analysis. *Buffalo Law Review,* 32: 525–552.

American Bar Association and Federal Bar Association. 2001. *Federal Judicial Pay Erosion: A Report on the Need for Reform.* Washington, DC: ABA.

American Bar Association. Center for Professional Responsibility. 2008. *ABA Model Rules for Professional Conduct.* Chicago: ABA. http://www.abanet.org/cpr/mrpc/mrpc_toc.html.

Armitage, Kelley. 2002. Denial Ain't Just a River in Egypt: A Thorough Review of Judicial Elections, Merit Selection and the Role of State Judges in Society. *Capital University Law Review,* 29: 625–655.

Bainbridge, Stephen M. and G. Mitu Gulati. 2002. How Do Judges Maximize? (The Same Way Everybody Else Does—Boundedly): Rules of Thumb in Securities Fraud Opinions. *Emory Law Journal,* 51: 83–151.

Barton, Benjamin H. 2001. Why Do We Regulate Lawyers? An Economic Analysis of the Justifications for Entry and Conduct Regulation. *Arizona State Law Journal*, 33: 429–490.

———. 2003. An Institutional Analysis of Lawyer Regulation: Who Should Control Lawyer Regulation—Courts, Legislatures, or the Market? *Georgia Law Review*, 37: 1167–1250.

———. 2005. The ABA, the Rules, and Professionalism: The Mechanics of Self-Defeat and a Call for a Return to the Ethical, Moral, and Practical Approach of the Canons. *North Carolina Law Review*, 83: 411–480.

———. 2007. Do Judges Systematically Favor the Interests of the Legal Profession? manuscript available at http://ssrn.com/abstract=976478.

Benham, Lee. 1972. The Effect of Advertising on the Price of Eyeglasses. *Journal of Law and Economics*, 15: 337–352.

Best, Arthur. 2004. *Wigmore on Evidence*. New York: Aspen Publishers.

Calfee, John E. 1997. *Fear of Persuasion: A New Perspective on Advertising and Regulation*. London: Agora.

Cleary, Edward W. 1972. *McCormick's Handbook of the Law of Evidence*, 2nd ed. St. Paul: West.

Colombo, Ronald J. 1998. Forgive Us Our Sins: The Inadequacies of the Clergy-Penitent Privilege. *NYU Law Review*, 73: 225–252.

The Council of State Governments. 1978. *State Court Systems*. Lexington, KY: Council of State Governments.

Dawson, John P. 1960. *A History of Lay Judges*. Cambridge, MA: Harvard University Press.

DeWitt, Clinton. 1958. *Privileged Communications between Physician and Patient*. Springfield, IL: Charles C. Thomas.

Dowling, Henry M. 1935. The Inherent Power of the Judiciary. *American Bar Association Journal*, 21: 635–639.

Drinker, Henry S. 1953. *Legal Ethics*. New York: Columbia University Press.

Eggertsson, Thrainn. 1996. A Note on the Economics of Institutions, in Lee J. Alston, Thrainn Eggertsson, and Douglass C. North (eds.). *Empirical Studies in Institutional Change*. 6–24. Cambridge, MA: Cambridge University Press.

Fischel, Daniel R. 1998. Lawyers and Confidentiality. *University of Chicago Law Review*, 65: 1–33.

Georgetown Law Journal. 2006. Custodial Interrogations. *Georgetown Law Journal Annual Review of Criminal Procedure*, 35: 162–186.

Helland, Eric A. and Alex Tabarrok. 2002. The Effect of Electoral Institutions on Tort Awards. *American Law and Economics Review*, 4: 341–370.

———. 2006. *Judge and Jury: American Tort Law on Trial*. Oakland CA: Independent Institute.

Imwinkelried, Edward J. 2002. *The New Wigmore: A Treatise on Evidence, Evidentiary Privileges*. New York: Aspen Law & Business.

———. 2004. Questioning the Behavioral Assumption Underlying Wigmorean Absolutism in the Law of Evidentiary Privileges. *University of Pittsburgh Law Review*, 65: 145–182.

———. 2005. *Evidentiary Foundations*, 6th ed. Newark, NJ: LexisNexis/Matthew Bender.

Ippolito, Pauline M. and Alan Mathios. 1990. Information, Advertising and Health Choices: A Study of the Cereal Market. *RAND Journal of Economics*, 21: 459–480.

Johnson, Alex M. 1991. Think Like a Lawyer, Work Like a Machine: The Dissonance between Law School and Law Practice. *Southern California Law Review*, 64: 1231–1260.

Klein, Susan R. 2003. No Time for Silence. *Texas Law Review*, 81: 1337–1360.

Lipton, Ashley Saunders. 2005. Know Your Testimonial Objections, *Trial Magazine*, July.

Lunney, Leslie A. 1999. The Erosion of Miranda: Stare Decisis Consequences. *Catholic University Law Review*, 48: 727–800.

McKean, Dayton. 1963. *The Integrated Bar*. Boston, MA: Houghton Mifflin.

Merritt, Deborah J., Lowell L. Hargens, and Barbara F. Reskin. 2001. Raising the Bar: A Social Science Critique of Recent Increases to Passing Scores on the Bar Exam. *University of Cincinnati Law Review*, 69: 929–968.

Mitchell, Mary H. 1987. Must Clergy Tell? Child Abuse Reporting Requirements versus the Clergy Privilege and Free Exercise of Religion. *Minnesota Law Review*, 71: 723–825.

Montone. John J. 1995. In Search of Forgiveness: *State v. Szemple* and the Priest-Penitent Privilege in New Jersey, *Rutgers Law Review*, 48: 263–311.

Moore. Nancy J. 1989. The Usefulness of Ethical Codes. *Annual Survey of American Law*, 1989: 7–21.

Morris, Tarra L. 2005. The Dog in the Manger, The First Twenty-Five Years of War on IOLTA. *Saint Louis University Law Journal*, 49: 605–631.

Posner, Richard A. 1993. What do Judges and Justices Maximize? (The Same Thing Everybody Else Does). *Supreme Court Economic Review*, 3: 1–41.

Provine, Doris Marie. 1986. *Judging Credentials: Nonlawyer Judges and the Politics of Professionalism*. Chicago, IL: University of Chicago Press.

Radtke, Terry. 1998. The Last Stage of Professionalizing the Bar: The Wisconsin Bar Integration Movement, 1934–1956. *Marquette Law Review*, 81: 1001–1027.

Rhode, Deborah L. 1981. Why the ABA Bothers: A Functional Perspective on Professional Codes. *Texas Law Review*, 59: 689–721.

———. 2002. The Profession and the Public Interest. *Stanford Law Review*, 54: 1501–1522.

Rubin, Paul H. 2005. Public Choice and Tort Reform. *Public Choice*, 124: 223–236.

Sagoff, Mark. 1997. Muddle Or Muddle Through? Takings Jurisprudence Meets The Endangered Species Act. *William and Mary Law Review*, 38: 825–993.

Schotland, Roy A. 1985. Elective Judges' Campaign Financing: Are State Judges' Robes the Emperor's Clothes of American Democracy? *Journal of Law and Politics*, 2: 57–167.

Segal, Jeffrey A. and Harold J. Spaeth. 1993. *The Supreme Court and the Attitudinal Model*. New York: Cambridge University Press.

Serkin, Christopher. 2004. Valuing Interest: Net Harm and Fair Market Value in *Brown v. Legal Foundation of Washington*. *Indiana Law Review*, 37: 417–436.

Shuman, Daniel W. 1985. The Origins of the Physician-Patient Privilege and Professional Secret. *Southwestern Law Journal*, 39: 661–687.

Smith, Christopher E. 1995. *Judicial Self-Interest: Federal Judges and Court Administration*. Westport, CT: Praeger.

Strong, John W., ed. 1999. *McCormick on Evidence*. St. Paul: West.

Sullivan, Kathleen M. 1998. The Intersection of Free Speech and the Legal Profession: Constraints on Lawyers' First Amendment Rights. *Fordham Law Review*, 67: 569–588.

Sunderland, Edson R. 1953. *History of the American Bar Association and Its Work*. Chicago, IL: American Bar Association.

U.S. Department of Justice. Office of Justice Programs. Bureau of Justice Statistics. 1998. *State Court Organization*. Washington, DC: U.S. Government Printing Office.

Vermeule, Adrian. 2007. Should We Have Lay Justices? *Stanford Law Review*, 59: 1569–1611.

Volokh, Eugene. 2003. Freedom of Speech and Intellectual Property: Some Thoughts After Eldred, 44 Liquormart, and Bartnicki. *Houston Law Review*, 40: 697–748.

Weissbrodt, David, Ferhat Pekin, and Amelia Wilson. 2006. Piercing the Confidentiality Veil: Physician Testimony in International Criminal Trials against Perpetrators of Torture. *Minnesota Journal of International Law*, 15: 43–109.

Wigmore. John Henry. 1961. *Evidence in Trials at Common Law, McNaughton Revision*. Boston, MA: Little, Brown.

Wolfram, Charles W. 1986. *Modern Legal Ethics*, St. Paul: West.

———. 1989. Lawyer Turf and Lawyer Regulation—The Role of the Inherent-Powers Doctrine. *University of Arkansas Little Rock Law Journal*, 12: 1–23.

Yellin, Jacob M. 1983. The History and Current Status of the Clergy-Penitent Privilege. *Santa Clara Law Review*, 23: 95–108.

CHAPTER 10

Abramson, Jill. 1990. Product-Liability Bill Provides Opportunity for Long-Term Milking of PACs by Congress, *Wall Street Journal*, June 21, A16.

Bandow, Doug. 1998. Medicaid "Reimbursement" Litigation: Is the Issue really About Principle or Is It Money? *ALEC Policy Digest*, 1.

———. 1999. Buying Justice: Plaintiffs' Lawyers Reap Huge Dividends by Investing in Judges and Politicians, *CATO Daily Commentary*, 28 December. http://www.cato.org/pub_display.php?pub_id=4893

Beck, Roger, Colin Hoskins, and J. Martin Connolly. 1992. Rent Extraction through Political Extortion: An Empirical Examination, *Journal of Legal Studies*, 21: 217.

Beisner, John H. and Jessica Davidson Miller. 2001. They're Making a Federal Case Out of It…In State Court, *Civil Justice Report*, Center for Legal Policy at the Manhattan Institute, September 3. http://www.manhattan-institute.org/html/cjr_3.htm#10

Brown, Stephen J. and Jerold B. Warner. 1985. Using Daily Stock Returns, *Journal of Financial Economics*, 14: 3–31.

Buckberg, Elaine, Todd Foster, Ronald Miller, and Stephanie Plancich. February 2005. Recent Trends in Shareholder Class Action Litigation: Bear Market Cases Bring Big Settlements, NERA Economic Consulting. http://www.nera.com/Publication.asp?p_ID=2367

Carroll, Stephen J. and Deborah R. Hensler, Jennifer Gross, Elizabeth M. Sloss, Matthias Schonlau, Allan Abrahamse, and J. Scott Ashwood. 2005. *Asbestos Litigation Summary*. http://www.rand.org/pubs/monographs/MG162/index.html

CDC Best Practices for Comprehensive Tobacco Control Programs, August 1999. http://www.cdc.gov/tobacco/research_data/stat_nat_data/bestprac-execsummary.htm

Cherry, Sheila R. 2000. Litigation Lotto. Insight on the News Online, April 3. http://www.insightmag.com/

Common Cause. 1997. Tobacco Political Giving Hits Record $9.9 Million for '96 Elections, May 13.

Frank, Ted. 2007. The Class Action Fairness Act Two Years Later. *Liability Outlook*, AEI Online, March 27. http://www.aei.org/publications/filter.all,pubID. 25851/pub_detail.asp

Fulbright and Jaworski L.L.P. 2005. Litigation as the Great Equalizer, *Business Wire*, October 10. http://www.s-ox.com/news/detail.cfm?articleID=1234

Fund, John and Martin Wooster. 2000. *The Dangers of Regulation Through Litigation*. Washington, D. C. : American Tort Reform Foundation.

Handler, Milton. 1971. The Shift from Substantive to Procedural Innovations in Antitrust Suits—The Twenty-Third Annual Antitrust Review. *Columbia Law Review,* 71: 1.

Haymond, Jeffrey. 2001. Blowing Smoke: A Case of Rent Extraction. *Journal of Public Finance and Public Choice*, 19: 23.

Haymond, Jeffrey and James E. West. 2003. Class Action Extraction? *Public Choice*, 116: 91.

Helland, Eric and Alexander Tabarrok. 2006. *Judge and Jury*. Oakland, CA: The Independent Institute.

Hensler, Deborah R., Nicholas M. Pace, Bonita Dombey-Moore, Beth Giddens, Jennifer Gross, and Erick K. Moller. 2000. *Class Action Dilemmas: Pursuing Public Goals for Private Gain*. RAND Institute for Civil Justice.

Hooper, John P. 2005. The Class Action Fairness Act: Tort Reform Worth the Wait, *Class Actions,* Mealey's Litigation Report, 5: 2.

Interim Report of the Committee on Capital Markets Regulation. November 20, 2006. http://www.capmktsreg.org/research.html

Kiement, Alon and Zvika Neeman. 2004. Incentive Structures for Class Action Lawyers. *Journal of Law, Economics & Organization*, 20: 102–124.

LaCroix, Kevin M. 2007. A Closer Look at the 2006 Securities Lawsuits. *Insights,* January 2007. http://www.oakbridgeins.com/insights.htm

Levy, Robert A. 1999. States Share Blame for Tobacco Lawyers' Greed. *CATO Today's Commentary.*

Mathis, Deborah. 1998. Ashcroft: Taxing, Spending More Addictive in D.C. Than Nicotine, *Gannett News Service,* 13 May.

McChesney, Fred S. 1997. *Money for Nothing: Politics, Rent Extraction and Political Extortion*, Cambridge, MA: Harvard University Press.

Miller, Ronald, Todd Foster, and Elaine Buckberg. April 2006. Recent Trends in Shareholder Class Action Litigation: Beyond the Mega-Settlements, Is Stabilization Ahead?, NERA Economic Consulting. http://www.nera.com/ Publication.asp?p_ID=2777

Priest, George L. 1997. Procedural Versus Substantive Controls of Mass Tort Class Actions. *Journal of Legal Studies,* 26: 521.

RAND Research Brief, 2007, Anatomy of an Insurance Class Action. http://www. rand.org/pubs/research_briefs/RB9249/

Regulation by Litigation: The New Wave of Government-Sponsored Litigation, Manhattan Institute, 2000. http://www.manhattan-institute.org/html/ mics_1_a.htm

Ridenour, Amy Moritz. September 1997. Trial Lawyers the Biggest Winners from Tobacco Settlement, National Center for Public Policy Research Paper #171. http://www.nationalcenter.org/NPA171.html.

Simmons, Laura E. and Ellen M. Ryan. 2006. Securities Class Action Settlements: 2006 Review and Analysis, *Cornerstone Research.* http://securities.cornerstone.com/

Securities Class Action Case Filings 2006: A Year in Review, *Cornerstone Research.* http://securities.cornerstone.com/

Show Us the Money. 2001. An Update on the States' Allocation of the Tobacco Settlement Dollars, *A Report by the Campaign for Tobacco-Free Kids, American Cancer Society, American Heart Association, and American Lung Association,* January 11. http://www.tobaccofreekids.org/reports/settlements/settlement2001.pdf

Stigler, George J. 1971. The Theory of Economic Regulation. *Bell Journal of Economics and Management Science,* 2: 3.

Stone, Peter H. 2000. Jousting Over Judges. *National Journal,* 32: 2004.

Tabarrok, Alexander and Eric Helland. 1999. Court Politics: The Political Economy of Tort Awards. *Journal of Law and Economics,* XLII: 157.

Tullock, Gordon. 1967. The Welfare Costs of Tariffs, Monopoly, and Theft. *Western Economic Journal,* 5: 224.

Viscusi, W. Kip. Fall 1995. Secondhand Smoke: Facts and Fantasy. *Regulation,* 18: 3.

Willging, Thomas E. and Emery G. Lee III. 2007. *The Impact of the Class Action Fairness Act of 2005 on the Federal Courts,* Federal Judicial Center, April.

Willging, Thomas E., Laural L. Hooper, and Robert J. Niemic. 1996. *Empirical Study of Class Actions in Four Federal District Courts: Final Report to the Advisory Committee on Civil Rules.* Washington, D. C. : Federal Judicial Center.

White, Michelle J. Summer 2003. Resolving the "Elephantine Mass." *Regulation,* 26: 48.

Yates, Bob. 2006. Class Action Fairness Act; More Than a Year Later. *Chicago Lawyer,* 29: 12.

CHAPTER 11

Coate, Stephen and Stephen Morris. 1995. On the Form of Transfers to Special Interests. *Journal of Political Economy,* 103: 1210–1234.

Day, Jim. 2006. Law Schools Receive Gifts; Firms Name New Partners, *Chicago Lawyer,* March.

DeJarlais, Nathalie A. 1987. The Consumer Trust Fund: A Cy Pres Solution to Undistributed Funds in Consumer Class Actions. *Hastings Law Journal,* 38: 729–767.

Draba, Robert E. 2004. Motorsports Merchandise: A Cy Pres Distribution Not Quite "As Near As Possible." *Loyola Consumer Law Review,* 16: 121–157.

Forde, Kevin. 1996. What Can a Court Do with Leftover Class Action Funds? Almost Anything! *Judge's Journal,* 35: 19–34.

Hanssen, F. Andrew. 2002. On the Politics of Judicial Selection: Lawyers and State Campaigns for the Merit Plan. *Public Choice,* 110: 79–97.

Hayek, Freidrich A. 1991. *The Fatal Conceit: The Errors of Socialism,* ed. W. W. Bartley III. Chicago, IL: University of Chicago Press.

Hensler, Deborah R., Nicholas M. Pace, Bonnie Dombey-Moore, Elizabeth Giddens, Jennifer Gross, and Erik Moller. 2000. *Class Action Dilemmas.* Santa Monica, CA: RAND Corporation.

Howard, Trisha L. and Paul Hampel. 2003. Tobacco Firm Lawyer Derides Court's Reputation: Plaintiffs' Attorney Defends Verdict, His $1 Billion Fee, *St. Louis Post-Dispatch,* March 23.

Kearney Joseph D. and Thomas W. Merrill. 2000. The Influence of Amicus Curiae Briefs on the Supreme Court. *University of Pennsylvania Law Review*, 148: 743–801.

Krueger, George J. and Judd A. Serotta. 2005. Class Action Reform and the Problem of Civil Judicial Confiscation, *Legal Intelligencer*, March 10.

Lenzer, Robert and Matthew Miller. 2003. Buying Justice, *Forbes*, July 21.

McCall, James R., Patricia Sturdevant, Laura Kaplan, and Gaill Hillebrand. 1995. Greater Representation for California Consumers—Fluid Recovery, Consumer Trust Funds, and Representative Actions. *Hastings Law Journal*, 46: 797–851.

McKee, Mike. 2006. Calif. Justices Let Stand Microsoft Settlement and Millions in Attorneys Fees, *Recorder*, April 21.

Miller, Geoffrey P. and Lori S. Singer. 1997. Nonpecuniary Class Action Settlements. *Law and Contemporary Problems*, 60: 97.

Newberg, Herbert and Alba Conte. 2002. *Newberg on Class Actions*, 4th ed. 2: 10.17.

Rubin, Paul. 2005. Public Choice and Tort Reform. *Public Choice*, 124: 223–236.

Posner, Richard A. 1993. What Do Judges Maximize? (The Same Thing Everybody Else Does). *Supreme Court Economic Review*, 3: 1–41.

———. 2005. Judicial Behavior and Performance: An Economic Approach. *Florida State University Law Review*, 32: 1259–1279.

Schauer, Frederick. 2000. Incentives, Reputation and the Inglorious Determinants of Judicial Behavior. *University of Cincinnati Law Review*, 68: 615–636.

Schwartz, Victor E., Mark A. Behrens, and Cary Silverman. 2003. I'll Take That: Legal and Public Policy Problems Raised By Statutes that Require Punitive Damages Awards Be Shared with the State. *Missouri Law Review*, 68: 525–558.

Shepherd, Stewart R. 1972. Damage Distribution in Class Actions: The Cy Pres Remedy. *University of Chicago Law Review*, 39: 448.

Tabarrok, Alexander and Eric Helland. 1999. Court Politics: The Political Economy of Tort Awards. *Journal of Law & Economics*, 42: 157–187.

Vock, Daniel C. 2004. Tobacco Case Takes on Star-studded Life of Its Own, *Chicago Lawyer*, November.

Yahya, Moin A. 2005. Can I Sue without Being Injured?: Why the Benefit of the Bargain Theory for Product Liability Is Bad Law and Bad Economics. *Georgetown Journal of Law and Public Policy*, 3: 83.

CHAPTER 12

American Arbitration Association. American Arbitration Association web site. http://www.adr.org.

American Bar Association. 2003. ABA Presidential Commission on Access to Lawyers. July 21. Chicago, IL: American Bar Association. http://www.abanet. org/abanet/common/print/newprintview.cfm?ref=http://www.abanet.org/ legalservices/delivery/accesscommn.html.

———. 2004. Consortium on Legal Services and the Public. *Legal Needs and Civil Justice: A Survey of Americans: Major Findings from the Comprehensive Legal Needs Study.* Chicago, IL: American Bar Association. http://www.abanet.org/ legalservices/downloads/sclaid/legalneedstudy.pdf.

———. 2007a. *2007–2008 ABA Standards for Approval of Law Schools.* Chicago, IL: American Bar Association. http://www.abanet.org/legaled/standards/ 20072008StandardsWebContent/Chapter%201.pdf.

American Bar Association. 2007b. Unified Bars, Issues Update 2007. Chicago, IL: American Bar Association. http://www.abanet.org/barserv/issuesupdate/updates07/unifiedbars.pdf.

Andrews, Lori B. 1980. *Birth of a Salesman: Lawyer Advertising and Solicitation.* Chicago, IL: ABA Press.

Baker, Dean. 2006. *The Conservative Nanny State: How the Wealthy Use the Government to Stay Rich and Get Richer.* Washington, DC: Center for Economic Research and Policy. http://www.conservativenannystate.org/cnswebbook.pdf.

Ballard, Mark. 2002. The Little Ad That Changed Everything. *National Law Journal,* September 25. http://www.law.com/jsp/law/LawArticleFriendly.jsp?id=1032128590255.

Barton, Benjamin H. 2007. Do Judges Systematically Favor the Interests of the Legal Profession? *Alabama Law Review,* 59(2): 453–505 (Winter). http://www.law.ua.edu/lawreview/articles/Volume%2059/Issue%202/Barton.pdf.

Bond, Ronald S., John E. Kwoka, Jr., John J. Phelan, and Ira Taylor Whitten. 1980. *Effects of Restrictions on Advertising and Commercial Practice in the Professions: The Case of Optometry.* Staff Report, Bureau of Economics, Federal Trade Commission, Washington, DC: U.S. Government Printing Office.

Caplan, Bryan and Edward P. Stringham. 2007. Privatizing the Adjudication of Disputes, Independent Institute Working Paper Number 69, Oakland, CA: The Independent Institute. http://www.independent.org/pdf/working_papers/69_private.pdf.

Carroll, Sidney L. and Robert J. Gaston. 1981. Occupational Restrictions and the Quality of Services Received: Some Evidence. *Southern Economic Journal,* 47: 959–976.

Christensen, Barlow F. 1980. The Unauthorized Practice of Law: Do Good Fences Make Good Neighbors—Or Even Good Sense? *American Bar Foundation Research Journal,* 5(2): 159–216 (Spring).

Cox, Carolyn and Susan Foster. U.S. Federal Trade Commission, Bureau of Economics. 1990. *The Costs and Benefits of Occupational Regulation.* Washington, DC: U.S. Government Printing Office.

The Florida Bar. 2005. Unified State Bars/The Florida Bar. http://www.floridabar.org/DIVCOM/PI/BIPS2001.nsf/1119bd38ae090a748525676f0053b606/ee84c9f3e29ca3b58525669e004e0cee?OpenDocument.

Friedman, Milton. 1962, 1982, 2002. *Capitalism and Freedom.* Chicago, IL: University of Chicago.

Fuller, Lon. 1981. *The Principles of Social Order.* Durham, NC: Duke University Press.

Fund, John. 2007. License to Kill Jobs. *Wall Street Journal.* August 27. http://www.opinionjournal.com/diary/?id=110010524. (Jim Weeney comment available online at: http://www.opinionjournal.com/diary/responses.html?article_id=110010524.)

Good Housekeeping web site, About the Good Housekeeping Seal. http://www.goodhousekeeping.com/product-testing/seal-holders/about-good-housekeeping-seal.

Hadfield, Gillian K. 2008. Legal Barriers to Innovation: The Growing Economic Cost of Professional Control Over Corporate Legal Markets. *Stanford Law Review,* 60. http://works.bepress.com/ghadfield/29/.

Hadfield, Gillan K. and Eric Talley. 2006. On Public versus Private Provision of Corporate Law. *Journal of Law, Economics and Organization,* 14: 137–163. http://ssrn.com/abstract=570641.

Hood, John. 1992. Does Occupational Licensing Protect Consumers? *The Freeman: Ideas on Liberty,* 42(11) (November). http://www.thefreemanonline.org/columns/does-occupational-licensing-protect-consumers/.

Jacobs, William W., Brenda W. Doubrava, Robert P. Weaver, Douglas O. Stewart, Eric L. Prahl, William R. Porter, Nathaniel Greenspun, and R. Dennis Murphy. 1984. Improving Consumer Access to Legal Services: The Case for Removing Restrictions on Truthful Advertising, U.S. Federal Trade Commission, Cleveland Regional Office, and United States Federal Trade Commission, Bureau of Economics, Washington, DC: U.S. Government Printing Office.

Johnson, Denise R. 1998. The Legal Needs of the Poor as a Starting Point for Systemic Reform. *Yale Law and Policy Review,* 17 (1): 479, 488.

Keller, Tim. 2003. State Licensing Laws Unduly Burden New Firms. *Tucson Citizen.* December 3.

Kleiner, Morris M. 2006. *Licensing Occupations: Ensuring Quality or Restricting Competition?* Kalamazoo, MI: W.E. Upjohn Institute for Employment Research.

Lang, Larry and Ronald Marks. 1980. Consumer Response to Advertisements for Legal Services: An Empirical Analysis. *Journal of the Academy of Marketing Science,* 8: 357–385.

LECG Ltd. 2000. Restrictions on Competition in the Provision of Professional Services. A Report for the Office of Fair Trading. In Canada Office of Fair Trading. 2001. *Competition in Professions.* http://www.oft.gov.uk/shared_oft/reports/professional_bodies/oft328.pdf.

Leef, George C. 1998. *The Case for a Free Market in Legal Services.* Policy Analysis No. 322. Washington, DC: Cato Institute. October 9. http://www.cato.org/pubs/pas/pa322xa.pdf.

Madison, James. 1792. Property. *National Gazette.* March 29. Reprinted in Robert A. Rutland et al. (ed.). 1983. *The Papers of James Madison,* Vol. 14: *6 April 1791–16 March 1793,* 266–268. Charlottesville, VA: University Press of Virginia.

McHugh, Jack P. 2003. We're All Licensees Now. Mackinac Center for Public Policy. July 24. http://www.mackinac.org/article.aspx?ID=5570.

Moran, Rachel F. 2006. Of Rankings and Regulation: Are *the U.S. News & World Report* Rankings Really a Subversive Force in Legal Education? *Indiana Law Journal,* 81: 383–399. http://www.indianalawjournal.org/articles/81/81_1_Moran.pdf

Orange County Register. 2004. It's Time to Revoke the State's License. August 19.

Pagliero, Mario. 2004. What Is the Objective of Professional Licensing? Evidence from the U.S. Market for Lawyers. Ph.D. Thesis, Department of Economics, London Business School.

Rhode, Deborah L. 1996. Professionalism in Perspective: Alternative Approaches to Nonlawyer Practice. *New York University Review of Law and Social Change,* 22.

———. 2002. The Profession and the Public Interest. *Stanford Law Review,* 54: 1501–1522.

Rothbard, Murray N. 1973. *For a New Liberty: The Libertarian Manifesto.* New York: Macmillan.

Sandefur, Timothy. 2002. The Common Law Right to Earn a Living. *The Independent Review,* 7(1) (Summer 2002). http://www.independent.org/pdf/tir/tir_07_1_sandefur.pdf.

Smith, Adam. 1774. Correspondence of Adam Smith. Chapter 143.: To William Cullen in E. C. Mossner and I. S. Ross, (ed.). 1987. *The Glasgow Edition of the Works and Correspondence of Adam Smith*, vol. VI, 173–179. Indianapolis, IN: Liberty Fund. http://oll.libertyfund.org/title/203/57957.

Spooner, Lysander. 1835. To the Members of the Legislature of Massachusetts. *Worcester Republican*. August 26.

Summers, Adam B. 2004. The New Drug War. *The Freeman: Ideas on Liberty*, 54(3): 31–33 (April). http://www.fee.org/pdf/the-freeman/summers0404.pdf.

Tannehill, Morris and Linda Tannehill. 1970. *The Market for Liberty*. Lansing, MI: Privately printed.

Tenn, Steven. 2000. Occupational Licensing: An Effective Barrier to Entry? Unpublished dissertation, Chicago, IL: University of Chicago.

U.S. Department of Justice. 2006. Justice Department Asks Court to Hold American Bar Association in Civil Contempt, June 23. http://www.justice.gov/atr/public/press_releases/2006/216804.pdf.

U.S. Federal Trade Commission. 2004. Identifying and Tackling Dysfunctional Markets, Washington, DC: U.S. Government Printing Office. http://www.ftc.gov/bc/international/docs/US%20FTC%20paper%200n%20identifying%20and%20tackling%20dysfunctional%20markets.pdf.

Virginia State Bar. 1962. *Minimum Fee Schedule Report*.

Williams, Walter E. 2000. How Regulation and Taxation Stifle Entrepreneurship, Speech given at the Pioneer Institute for Public Policy Research. April 4. http://www.pioneerinstitute.org/pdf/pdialg_32.pdf.

Young, S. David. Occupational Licensing. The Library of Economics and Liberty. http://www.econlib.org/library/Enc1/OccupationalLicensing.html.

———. 1987. *The Rule of Experts: Occupational Licensing in America*. Washington, DC: Cato Institute.

Notes on Contributors

About the Editor

Edward J. López is Research Fellow at the Independent Institute, Associate Professor of Law and Economics at San Jose State University, and co-editor of the *Journal of Economics and Finance Education*. He served as President of the Association of Private Enterprise Education from 2010 to 2011. His main areas of research are in public choice and law and economics, and he has published over three dozen scholarly articles and book chapters in the areas of takings, campaign finance, entrepreneurship, congressional voting, and political institutions in journals such as the *Review of Law & Economics*, *Public Choice*, the *Southern Economic Journal*, *The Independent Review*, and others. He was previously a visiting scholar at Liberty Fund, Inc., and a staff economist on the Joint Economic Committee of Congress. He earned a B.S. in economics from Texas A&M University and Ph.D. in economics at George Mason University.

Contributors

Benjamin H. Barton is a graduate of Haverford College and the University of Michigan School of Law. He is the Director of Clinical Programs and an Associate Professor of Law at the University of Tennessee. His scholarship has appeared in top law reviews and has been discussed in the *New York Times*, *Time Magazine,* and the *Wall Street Journal*.

John Brätland has published on the subjects of property rights, privatization, eminent domain, exhaustible resources, entrepreneurship, intergenerational equity, intergenerational sustainability, industrial organization, environmental economics, and federal land policy. His articles have appeared in *The Independent Review, Quarterly Journal of Austrian Economics, Natural Resources Journal* and the *Journal of Libertarian Studies*.

As a senior economist with the U.S. Department of the Interior, John Brätland has done extensive research on the ways in which private property rights can serve as viable institutional alternatives to current governmental ownership and political management of the nation's natural resources. He is an adjunct faculty member of the Ludwig von Mises Institute.

Adriana S. Cordis is Assistant Professor of Economics at the University of South Carolina Upstate. She earned a Ph.D. in applied economics from Clemson University in May 2008. Her research interests are primarily in the areas of public choice, law, and economics. She is currently working on projects that focus on the political economy of corruption and the economics of federal disaster declarations and relief payments. Her research has been published in the *Economics of Governance Journal*. Prior to joining the University of South Carolina Upstate, she worked as a Visiting Assistant Professor of Economics at Clemson University and as an economist for Ernst & Young in New York.

Nicholas A. Curott is Mercatus Graduate Fellow and a Ph.D. student in economics at George Mason University. Prior to coming to Mason, Nicholas earned a B.A. in economics and classics from the University of Colorado at Boulder and an M.A. in economics from San Jose State University. Nicholas is assistant editor of the *Journal of Private Enterprise*. His research focuses on Austrian economics and public choice.

Joshua C. Hall is Assistant Professor of Economics and Management at Beloit College in Wisconsin. He teaches and researches in the area of applied microeconomics—including urban economics, public finance, and the economics of education. He is author or co-author of over 50 journal articles, book chapters, policy reports, and book reviews in addition to assisting with the annual *Economic Freedom of the World Report*.

Jahn K. Hakes received his Ph.D. in economics from Duke University and has most recently served as Assistant Professor at Albion College. His research interests include public policy economics, applied econometrics, environmental and energy economics, and the economics of sports.

Jeffrey Haymond is a Colonel in the United States Air Force, where he has spent much of his nonacademic career in the military space arena. A former economics instructor at the Air Force Academy, Colonel Haymond received his Ph.D. from George Mason University, and has published articles in the fields of Austrian economics and public choice. He was formerly an Air Force Fellow at The Brookings Institution, and a commander at both the squadron and group levels. Colonel Haymond is currently the Vice Commander of the Space Development Test Wing at Kirtland Air Force Base, New Mexico.

Charles N.W. Keckler is Visiting Assistant Professor of Law at Penn State Law, teaching civil procedure and evidence. Professor Keckler's research focuses on reforms to the litigation system, empirical studies of the judicial process, and how best to strengthen civil society. He also has a strong interest in how the law can encourage, and make use of, advances in science and technology. His writings include articles published in the *Hastings Law Journal* and the *Journal of Law, Economics, & Policy*.

Until 2009, Professor Keckler was a deputy assistant secretary for policy at the U.S. Department of Health and Human Services, where he worked on regulatory matters and on improving federal human services programs for disadvantaged populations. Prior to his government service, Professor Keckler taught civil procedure and comparative law at George Mason University School of Law, and he began his academic career as a lecturer at Northwestern Law School. He practiced as an appellate and trial litigator with Mayer Brown in Chicago, and is a member of the Bars of Illinois and the District of Columbia, as well as of the U.S. Courts of Appeals for the Fourth, Sixth, and Seventh Circuits. Immediately after graduating law school, he clerked for Chief Judge Danny J. Boggs on the Sixth Circuit.

Roger G. Koppl is Director of the Institute for Forensic Science Administration of Fairleigh Dickinson University, where he is also Professor of Economics and Finance. He has served on the faculty of the Copenhagen Business School, Auburn University, and Auburn University at Montgomery. He has held visiting positions at George Mason University, New York University, and the Max Planck Institute of Economics. Professor Koppl is a past president of the Society for the Development of Austrian Economics. He is the editor of *Advances in Austrian Economics* and the book review editor of the *Journal of Economic Behavior & Organization*. He is Senior Researcher at the Pennsylvania Laboratory for Experimental Evolutionary Psychology (PLEEP) and at FDU's Florham Laboratory for Experimental Social Science (FLESS).

Matt E. Ryan is Assistant Professor of Economics at Duquesne University. He received his Ph.D. in economics from West Virginia University, and has been an Associate Fellow at the Public Policy Foundation of West Virginia, the Ken & Randy Kendrick Fellow at West Virginia University, the Charles G. Koch Doctoral Fellow at West Virginia University, and Fellow at the American Institute for Economic Research. His articles have appeared in such journals as *The Independent Review, American Journal of Economics and Sociology, Journal of Private Enterprise*, and *California Labor and Employment Review*. He is co-editor of *Unleashing Capitalism: Why Prosperity Stops at the West Virginia Border, and How to Fix It*, which won the Sir Antony Fisher International Memorial Award.

Russell S. Sobel, Ph.D., is Professor of Economics and James Clark Coffman Distinguished Chair in Entrepreneurial Studies in the College of Business and Economics at West Virginia University. He has published over 150 books and articles and is co-editor of *Economics: Private and Public Choice*, a nationally best-selling textbook. Dr. Sobel was the founding director of the West Virginia University Entrepreneurship Center and served in that role until 2006. His research has been the subject of articles in the *New York Times, Wall Street Journal, Washington Post*, and *The Economist*, and he has appeared on CNBC, CSPAN, and the *CBS Evening News*. Dr. Sobel teaches regular courses in economics for U.S. Congressional Staff and West Virginia K–12 schoolteachers, and he serves as Senior Economist and Director of the Center for Economic Growth for the Public Policy Foundation of West Virginia.

Ilya Somin is Associate Professor at George Mason University School of Law. His research focuses on constitutional law, property law, and the study of popular political participation and its implications for constitutional democracy. He has served as visiting professor of law at the University of Pennsylvania Law School, the University of Hamburg, Germany, and the University of Torcuato Di Tella in Buenos Aires, Argentina. Before joining the faculty at George Mason, Professor Somin was the John M. Olin Fellow in Law at Northwestern University Law School and, he clerked for the Hon. Judge Jerry E. Smith of the U.S. Court of Appeals for the Fifth Circuit.

He currently serves as co-editor of the *Supreme Court Economic Review*, and his work has appeared in numerous scholarly journals, including the *Yale Law Journal, Stanford Law Review, Northwestern University Law Review, Georgetown Law Journal, Critical Review*, and others. He has also published articles in a variety of popular press outlets, including the *Los Angeles Times, Wall Street Journal, OpinionJournal.com, Newark Star Ledger, Orlando Sentinel, South China Morning Post, Legal Times, National Law Journal* and *Reason*. Somin recently testified on property rights issues at the Senate Supreme Court confirmation hearings for Judge Sonia Sotomayor.

Edward P. Stringham is the Shelby Cullom Davis Visiting Associate Professor at Trinity College and Associate Professor of Economics at San Jose State University. He is past president of the Association of Private Enterprise Education, editor of the *Journal of Private Enterprise*, editor of two books, and author of more than two dozen articles in refereed journals including the *Journal of Institutional and Theoretical Economics, Public Choice*, and the *Quarterly Review of Economics and Finance*.

Stringham earned his Ph.D. from George Mason University, and has won the Templeton Culture of Enterprise Best Article Award, Paper of the Year Award from the Association of Private Enterprise, Best Article Award from the Society for the Development of Austrian Economics, second place in the Independent Institute Garvey Contest, and Distinguished Young Scholar Award from the Liberalni Institut and the Prague School of Economics.

Adam B. Summers is a policy analyst at Reason Foundation. He has written extensively on privatization, government reform, occupational licensing, law and economics, public pension reform, and various other political and economic topics. His articles have been published by the *Wall Street Journal, Los Angeles Times, San Diego Union-Tribune, Orange County Register, San Francisco Chronicle, Los Angeles Daily News, Baltimore Sun*, and others. Summers earned an M.A. in economics from George Mason University and a B.A. in economics and political science from the University of California, Los Angeles.

Robert D. Tollison is Professor of Economics and BB&T Senior Fellow at Clemson University, member of the Board of Advisors of the Independent Institute, and Editor of *Public Choice*. He received his Ph.D.

in economics from the University of Virginia, and he has been Woodrow Wilson Fellow in Economics, University of Alabama; Assistant Professor of Economics, Cornell University; Senior Staff Economist, President's Council of Economic Advisers; Professor of Economics, Virginia Polytechnic Institute and State University; Acting Director of the Office of Policy Planning and Director of the Bureau of Economics, Federal Trade Commission; Abney Professor of Economics, Clemson University; Duncan Black Professor of Economics, George Mason University; Director, Center for Study of Public Choice; Visiting Professor, University of Miami Law School; Visiting Professor of Economics, Arizona State University; Visiting Professor of Policy Sciences, Florida State University; Bradley Visiting Professor of Economics, Clemson University; and Kirby Distinguished Visiting Professor, Private Enterprise Research Center, Texas A&M University. Professor Tollison has been President, Southern Economic Association; President, Public Choice Society; member of the Economic Policy Committee, U.S. Chamber of Commerce; Special Director, Japanese Public Choice Society; and Associate Economics Editor, *Public Policy*. He is the author or editor of more than 25 scholarly volumes, a contributor to one hundred books, and the author of more than 300 scholarly articles and reviews.

Aleksandar Tomic is Associate Professor of Economics at Wesleyan College. His main research focuses on rational behavior of judges and differences in criminal sentencing between elected and appointed judges. His work on racial disparities in criminal case dismissals has appeared in the *American Law and Economics Review*.

INDEX

Note: Page numbers in italics refer to illustrations.

on legal sanctions as prices on
  behavior, 2
vs. public choice, 3–6, 15n.1
rationality assumed by, 4–5, 16n.2
reform approach, overview of, 5–6
Law and Order index, 86
law school accreditation, 235, 247–250
Lawson, Robert, 81
lawyer-judge hypothesis, 169–189
  and advertising/client solicitation/
    fees, 178–182, 191nn.14–17,
    192n.23
  attorney-client privilege, 174–178,
    190–191nn.7–13
  *Brown v. Legal Foundation of
    Washington*, 182, 184–185,
    191n.19, 192nn.23–24
  empirical studies of, 169–170, 190n.2
  Florida Bar v. Went For It, Inc.,
    180–182, 191n.17, 192n.23
  IOLTA (Interest on Lawyers Trust
    Accounts) takings cases, 182–185,
    191–192nn.18–24
  and judicial independence, 171
  and judicial salaries, 170
  and judicial selection, 13, 170, 189,
    190nn.3–4
  lawyer regulation, 172–174, 190n.4
  Miranda rights, 185–188,
    192nn.25–26
  Ohralik v. Ohio State Bar Association,
    179–182, 191nn.15–16
  overview of, 12–13, 169, 190n.1
  *Phillips v. Washington Legal
    Foundation*, 183–184,
    191nn.19–20, 192n.23
  ramifications of, 188–189
  R.M.J., In re, 180
  Shapiro v. Kentucky Bar Association,
    180–181
  theoretical basis of, 169–174, 189
  *Washington Legal Foundation v.
    Texas Equal Access to Justice
    Foundation*, 183, 191n.20
Lederman, D., 81
legal thinking, 171
Leges Marchiarum, 35n.8
Levi-Strauss Co., State v., 232n.1
Levitt, Steven D., 104
Levy, David, 51, 55

Levy, Robert, 197
Lex Mercatoria (Law Merchant), 22
licensing laws. *See* occupational
  licensing
licensing lawyers, 235–254, 254n.1
  and advertising restrictions, 235,
    245–246
  asymmetric information argument
    for, 237
  and conflict of interest, 237–238
  economic liberty violated by,
    242–244, 253–254
  history of legal services regulation,
    236, 240–241
  and lack of reciprocity, 235, 247, 253
  via law school accreditation, 235,
    247–250
  and mandatory minimum fees,
    235, 245
  overview of, 14–15, 235–236, 253–254
  poor people affected by, 244–245
  via private certification, 250–253
  public vs. special interests protected
    by, 240–242
  quality assurance via, 238–240, 253
  unauthorized practice of law, 236–
    237, 239, 241–242, 245, 253–254
  See also bar associations
Liggett Group, 198
lighthouses, 34
Lincoln, Abraham, 249
Loayza, N., 81
lobbyists, number of, 214n.28
Locke, John, 148
Long, Cheryl X., 100–101n.3
López-de-Silanes, Florencio, 71–72,
  81–83, 86, 95–96, 101n.3
*Loretto v. Teleprompter Manhattan
  CATV*, 183
Louisiana partisan elections, 49n.5
*Lowery, Bd. of County Com'rs of
  Muskogee County v.*, 140n.8
Loyn, H. R., 24
Loyola University Law School, 233n.10
Lyon, Bruce, 31

Machiavelli, Niccoló, 12
Maddex, Robert L., 86
Madison, James, 242
Madison, Marbury v., 101n.4

INDEPENDENT STUDIES IN POLITICAL ECONOMY

THE INDEPENDENT INSTITUTE
100 Swan Way, Oakland, CA 94621–1428, U.S.A. • 510-632-1366 • Fax 510-568-6040 • info@independent.org • www.independent.org